ISBN: 9781407647067

Published by:
HardPress Publishing
8345 NW 66TH ST #2561
MIAMI FL 33166-2626

Email: info@hardpress.net
Web: http://www.hardpress.net

The old Santa Fe trail
The Story of a Great Highway

by

COLONEL HENRY INMAN

TABLE OF CONTENTS

PREFACE...i

INTRODUCTION.. iii

CHAPTER I. UNDER THE SPANIARDS... 1

CHAPTER II. LA LANDE AND PURSLEY.. 12

CHAPTER III. EARLY TRADERS..19

CHAPTER IV. TRAINS AND PACKERS... 30

CHAPTER V. FIGHT WITH COMANCHES... 38

CHAPTER VI. A ROMANTIC TRAGEDY..63

CHAPTER VII. MEXICO DECLARES WAR.. 68

CHAPTER VIII. THE VALLEY OF TAOS... 76

CHAPTER IX. FIRST OVERLAND MAIL..96

CHAPTER X. CHARLES BENT...109

CHAPTER XI. LA GLORIETA...125

CHAPTER XIII. INDIAN CUSTOMS AND LEGENDS................................ 161

CHAPTER XIV. TRAPPERS..173

CHAPTER XV. UNCLE JOHN SMITH...190

CHAPTER XVI. KIT CARSON...212

CHAPTER XVII. UNCLE DICK WOOTON...228

CHAPTER XVIII. MAXWELL'S RANCH.. 248

CHAPTER XIX. BENT'S FORTS.. 258

CHAPTER XX. PAWNEE ROCK..267

CHAPTER XXI. FOOLING STAGE ROBBERS....................................278

CHAPTER XXII. A DESPERATE RIDE..284

CHAPTER XXIII. HANCOCK'S EXPEDITION... 300

CHAPTER XXIV. INVASION OF THE RAILROAD....................................... 321

FOOTNOTES...329

PREFACE.

As we look into the open fire for our fancies, so we are apt to study the dim past for the wonderful and sublime, forgetful of the fact that the present is a constant romance, and that the happenings of to-day which we count of little importance are sure to startle somebody in the future, and engage the pen of the historian, philosopher, and poet.

Accustomed as we are to think of the vast steppes of Russia and Siberia as alike strange and boundless, and to deal with the unkown interior of Africa as an impenetrable mystery, we lose sight of a locality in our own country that once surpassed all these in virgin grandeur, in majestic solitude, and in all the attributes of a tremendous wilderness.

The story of the Old Santa Fe Trail, so truthfully recalled by Colonel Henry Inman, ex-officer of the old Regular Army, in these pages, is a most thrilling one. The vast area through which the famous highway ran is still imperfectly known to most people as "The West"; a designation once appropriate, but hardly applicable now; for in these days of easy communication the real trail region is not so far removed from New York as Buffalo was seventy years ago.

At the commencement of the "commerce of the prairies," in the early portion of the century, the Old Trail was the arena of almost constant sanguinary struggles between the wily nomads of the desert and the hardy white pioneers, whose eventful lives made the civilization of the vast interior region of our continent possible. Their daring compelled its development, which has resulted in the genesis of great states and large cities. Their hardships gave birth to the American homestead; their determined will was the factor of possible achievements, the most remarkable and important of modern times.

When the famous highway was established across the great plains as a line of communication to the shores of the blue Pacific, the only method of travel was by the slow freight caravan drawn by patient oxen, or the lumbering stage coach with its complement of four or six mules. There was ever to be feared an attack by those devils of the desert, the Cheyennes, Comanches, and Kiowas. Along its whole route the remains of men, animals, and the wrecks of camps and wagons, told a story of suffering, robbery, and outrage more impressive than any language. Now the tourist or business man makes the journey in palace cars, and there is nothing to remind him of the danger or desolation of Border days; on every hand are the evidences of a powerful and advanced civilization.

It is fortunate that one is left to tell some of its story who was a living actor and had personal knowledge of many of the thrilling scenes that were enacted along the line of the great route. He was familiar with all the famous men, both white and savage, whose lives have made the story of the Trail, his own sojourn on the plains and in the Rocky Mountains extending over a period of nearly forty years.

The Old Trail has more than common interest for me, and I gladly record here my indorsement of the faithful record, compiled by a brave soldier, old comrade, and friend.

W. F. Cody, "Buffalo Bill."

INTRODUCTION.

For more than three centuries, a period extending from 1541 to 1851, historians believed, and so announced to the literary world, that Francisco Vasquez de Coronado, the celebrated Spanish explorer, in his search for the Seven Cities of Cibola and the Kingdom of Quivira, was the first European to travel over the intra-continent region of North America. In the last year above referred to, however, Buckingham Smith, of Florida, an eminent Spanish scholar, and secretary of the American Legation at Madrid, discovered among the archives of State the *Narrative of Alvar Nunez Cabeca de Vaca*, where for nearly three hundred years it had lain, musty and begrimed with the dust of ages, an unread and forgotten story of suffering that has no parallel in fiction. The distinguished antiquarian unearthed the valuable manuscript from its grave of oblivion, translated it into English, and gave it to the world of letters; conferring honour upon whom honour was due, and tearing the laurels from such grand voyageurs and discoverers as De Soto, La Salle, and Coronado, upon whose heads history had erroneously placed them, through no fault, or arrogance, however, of their own.

Cabeca, beyond any question, travelled the Old Santa Fe Trail for many miles, crossed it where it intersects the Arkansas River, a little east of Fort William or Bent's Fort, and went thence on into New Mexico, following the famous highway as far, at least, as Las Vegas. Cabeca's march antedated that of Coronado by five years. To this intrepid Spanish voyageur we are indebted for the first description of the American bison, or buffalo as the animal is erroneously called. While not so quaint in its language as that of Coronado's historian, a lustrum later, the statement cannot be perverted into any other reference than to the great shaggy monsters of the plains:--

Cattle come as far as this. I have seen them three times
and eaten of their meat. I think they are about the size
of those of Spain. They have small horns like the cows
of Morocco, and the hair very long and flocky, like that
of the merino; some are light brown, others black. To my
judgment the flesh is finer and fatter than that of this
country. The Indians make blankets of the hides of those
not full grown. They range over a district of more than
four hundred leagues, and in the whole extent of plain over
which they run the people that inhabit near there descend
and live on them and scatter a vast many skins throughout
the country.

It will be remembered by the student of the early history of our country, that when Alvar Nunez Cabeca de Vaca, a follower of the unfortunate Panphilo de Narvaez, and who had been long thought dead, landed in Spain, he gave such glowing accounts of Florida[1] and the neighbouring regions that the whole kingdom was in a ferment, and many a heart panted to emigrate to a land where the fruits were perennial, and where it was thought flowed the fabled fountain of youth.

Three expeditions to that country had already been tried: one undertaken in 1512, by Juan Ponce de Leon, formerly a companion of Columbus; another in 1520, by Vasquez de Allyon; and another by Panphilo de Narvaez. All of these had signally failed, the bones of most of the leaders and their followers having been left to bleach upon the soil they had come to conquer.

The unfortunate issue of the former expeditions did not operate as a check upon the aspiring mind of De Soto, but made him the more anxious to spring as an actor into the arena which had been the scene of the discomfiture and death of the hardy chivalry of the kingdom. He sought an audience of the emperor, and the latter, after hearing De Soto's proposition that, "he could conquer the country known as Florida at his own expense," conferred upon him the title of "Governor of Cuba and Florida."

On the 6th of April, 1538, De Soto sailed from Spain with an armament of ten vessels and a splendidly equipped army of nine hundred chosen men, amidst the roar of cannons and the inspiring strains of martial music.

It is not within the province of this work to follow De Soto through all his terrible trials on the North American continent; the wonderful story may be found in every well-organized library. It is recorded, however, that some time during the year 1542, his decimated army, then under the command of Luis de Moscoso, De Soto having died the previous May, was camped on the Arkansas River, far upward towards what is now Kansas. It was this command, too, of the unfortunate but cruel De Soto, that saw the Rocky Mountains from the east. The chronicler of the disastrous journey towards the mountains says: "The entire route became a trail of fire and blood," as they had many a desperate struggle with the savages of the plains, who "were of gigantic stucture, and fought with heavy strong clubs, with the desperation of demons. Such was their tremendous strength, that one of these warriors was a match for a Spanish soldier, though mounted on a horse, armed with a sword and cased in armour!"

Moscoso was searching for Coronado, and he was one of the most humane of all the officers of De Soto's command, for he evidently bent every energy to extricate his men from the dreadful environments of their situation; despairing of reaching the Gulf by the Mississippi, he struck westward, hoping, as Cabeca de Vaca had done, to arrive in Mexico overland.

A period of six months was consumed in Moscoso's march towards the Rocky Mountains, but he failed to find Coronado, who at that time was camped near where Wichita, Kansas, is located; according to his historian, "at the junction of the St. Peter and St. Paul" (the Big and Little Arkansas?). That point was the place of separation between Coronado and a number of his followers; many returning to Mexico, while the undaunted commander, with as many as he could induce to accompany him, continued easterly, still in search of the mythical Quivira.

How far westward Moscoso travelled cannot be determined accurately, but that his route extended up the valley of the Arkansas for more than three hundred miles, into what is now Kansas, is proved by the statement of his historian, who says: "They saw great chains of mountains and forests to the west, which they understood were uninhabited."

Another strong confirmatory fact is, that, in 1884, a group of mounds was discovered in McPherson County, Kansas, which were thoroughly explored by the professors of Bethany College, Lindsborg, who found, among other interesting relics, a piece of chain-mail armour, of hard steel; undoubtedly part of the equipment of a Spanish soldier either of the command of Cabeca de Vaca, De Soto, or of Coronado. The probability is, that it was worn by one of De Soto's unfortunate men, as neither Panphilo de Narvaez, De Vaca, or Coronado experienced any difficulty with the savages of the great plains, because those leaders were humane and treated the Indians kindly, in contradistinction to De Soto, who was the most inhuman of all the early Spanish explorers. He was of the same school as Pizarro and Cortez; possessing their daring valour, their contempt of danger, and their tenacity of purpose, as well as their cruelty and avarice. De Soto made treaties with the Indians which he constantly violated, and murdered the misguided creatures without mercy. During the retreat of Moscoso's weakened command down the Arkansas River, the Hot Springs of Arkansas were discovered. His historian writes:

And when they saw the foaming fountain, they thought
it was the long-searched-for "Fountain of Youth," reported
by fame to exist somewhere in the country, but ten of the
soldiers dying from excessive drinking, they were soon
convinced of their error.

After these intrepid explorers the restless Coronado appears on the Old Trail. In the third volume of Hakluyt's *Voyages*, published in London, 1600, Coronado's historian thus describes the great plains of Kansas and Colorado, the bison, and a tornado:--

From Cicuye they went to Quivira, which after their account
is almost three hundred leagues distant, through mighty

plains, and sandy heaths so smooth and wearisome, and bare
of wood that they made heaps of ox-dung, for want of stones
and trees, that they might not lose themselves at their
return: for three horses were lost on that plain, and one
Spaniard which went from his company on hunting. . . .
All that way of plains are as full of crooked-back oxen as
the mountain Serrena in Spain is of sheep, but there is
no such people as keep those cattle. . . . They were a
great succour for the hunger and the want of bread, which
our party stood in need of. . . .

One day it rained in that plain a great shower of hail,
as big as oranges, which caused many tears, weakness
and bowes.

These oxen are of the bigness and colour of our bulls,
but their bones are not so great. They have a great bunch
upon their fore-shoulder, and more hair on their fore part
than on their hinder part, and it is like wool. They have
as it were an horse-mane upon their backbone, and much hair
and very long from their knees downward. They have great
tufts of hair hanging down on their foreheads, and it
seemeth they have beards because of the great store of hair
hanging down at their chins and throats. The males have
very long tails, and a great knob or flock at the end,
so that in some respects they resemble the lion, and in some
other the camel. They push with their horns, they run,
they overtake and kill an horse when they are in their
rage and anger. Finally it is a foul and fierce beast of
countenance and form of body. The horses fled from them,
either because of their deformed shape, or else because
they had never before seen them.

   "The number," continues the historian, "was incredible." When the soldiers,
in their excitement for the chase, began to kill them, they rushed together in such
masses that hundreds were literally crushed to death. At one place there was a
great ravine; they jumped into it in their efforts to escape from the hunters, and so
terrible was the slaughter as they tumbled over the precipice that the depression was

completely filled up, their carcasses forming a bridge, over which the remainder passed with ease.

The next recorded expedition across the plains via the Old Trail was also by the Spaniards from Santa Fe, eastwardly, in the year 1716, "for the purpose of establishing a Military Post in the Upper Mississippi Valley as a barrier to the further encroachments of the French in that direction." An account of this expedition is found in *Memoires Historiques sur La Louisiane*, published in Paris in 1858, but never translated in its entirety. The author, Lieutenant Dumont of the French army, was one of a party ascending the Arkansas River in search of a supposed mass of emeralds. The narrative relates:

There was more than half a league to traverse to gain the
other bank of the river, and our people were no sooner
arrived than they found there a party of Missouris, sent to
M. de la Harpe by M. de Bienville, then commandant general
at Louisiana, to deliver orders to the former. Consequently
they gave the signal order, and our other two canoes having
crossed the river, the savages gave to our commandant the
letters of M. de Bienville, in which he informed him that
the Spaniards had sent out a detachment from New Mexico
to go to the Missouris and to establish a post in that
country. . . . The success of this expedition was very
calamitous to the Spaniards. Their caravan was composed of
fifteen hundred people, men, women and soldiers, having
with them a Jacobin for a chaplain, and bringing also a
great number of horses and cattle, according to the custom
of that nation to forget nothing that might be necessary for
a settlement. Their design was to destroy the Missouris,
and to seize upon their country, and with this intention
they had resolved to go first to the Osages, a neighbouring
nation, enemies of the Missouris, to form an alliance with
them, and to engage them in their behalf for the execution
of their plan. Perhaps the map which guided them was not
correct, or they had not exactly followed it, for it chanced
that instead of going to the Osages whom they sought, they
fell, without knowing it, into a village of the Missouris,
where the Spanish commander, presenting himself to the great
chief and offering him the calumet, made him understand

through an interpreter, believing himself to be speaking
to the Osage chief, that they were enemies of the Missouris,
that they had come to destroy them, to make their women
and children slaves and to take possession of their country.
He begged the chief to be willing to form an alliance
with them, against a nation whom the Osages regarded as
their enemy, and to second them in this enterprise, promising
to recompense them liberally for the service rendered,
and always to be their friend in the future. Upon this
discourse the Missouri chief understood perfectly well
the mistake. He dissimulated and thanked the Spaniard for
the confidence he had in his nation; he consented to form
an alliance with them against the Missouris, and to join
them with all his forces to destroy them; but he represented
that his people were not armed, and that they dared not
expose themselves without arms in such an enterprise.
Deceived by so favourable a reception, the Spaniards fell
into the trap laid for them. They received with due
ceremony, in the little camp they had formed on their
arrival, the calumet which the great chief of the Missouris
presented to the Spanish commander. The alliance for war
was sworn to by both parties; they agreed upon a day for
the execution of the plan which they meditated, and the
Spaniards furnished the savages with all the munitions which
they thought were needed. After the ceremony both parties
gave themselves up equally to joy and good cheer. At the
end of three days two thousand savages were armed and in
the midst of dances and amusements; each party thought
nothing but the execution of its design. It was the evening
before their departure upon their concerted expedition,
and the Spaniards had retired to their camps as usual,
when the great chief of the Missouris, having assembled
his warriors, declared to them his intentions and exhorted
them to deal treacherously with these strangers who were come
to their home only with the design of destroying them.
At daybreak the savages divided into several bands, fell on
the Spaniards, who expected nothing of the kind, and in

less than a quarter of an hour all the caravan were murdered.
No one escaped from the massacre except the chaplain, whom
the barbarians saved because of his dress; at the same time
they took possession of all the merchandise and other
effects which they found in their camp. The Spaniards had
brought with them, as I have said, a certain number of horses,
and as the savages were ignorant of the use of these animals,
they took pleasure in making the Jacobin whom they had saved,
and who had become their slave, mount them. The priest gave
them this amusement almost every day for the five or six
months that he remained with them in their village, without
any of them daring to imitate him. Tired at last of his
slavery, and regarding the lack of daring in these barbarians
as a means of Providence to regain his liberty, he made
secretly all the provisions possible for him to make,
and which he believed necessary to his plan. At last,
having chosen the best horse and having mounted him,
after performing several of his exploits before the savages,
and while they were all occupied with his manoeuvres,
he spurred up and disappeared from their sight, taking the
road to Mexico, where doubtless he arrived.

Charlevoix,[2] who travelled from Quebec to New Orleans in the year 1721,
says in one of his letters to the Duchess of Lesdiguieres, dated at Kaskaskia, July 21,
1721:

About two years ago some Spaniards, coming, as they say,
from New Mexico, and intending to get into the country of
the Illinois and drive the French from thence, whom they
saw with extreme jealousy approach so near the Missouri,
came down the river and attacked two villages of the
Octoyas,[3] who are the allies of the Ayouez,[4] and from
whom it is said also that they are derived. As the savages
had no firearms and were surprised, the Spaniards made an
easy conquest and killed a great many of them. A third
village, which was not far off from the other two, being
informed of what had passed, and not doubting but these

conquerors would attack them, laid an ambush into which
the Spaniards heedlessly fell. Others say that the savages,
having heard that the enemy were almost all drunk and
fast asleep, fell upon them in the night. However it was,
it is certain the greater part of them were killed.
There were in the party two almoners; one of them was
killed directly and the other got away to the Missouris,
who took him prisoner, but he escaped them very dexterously.
He had a very fine horse and the Missouris took pleasure
in seeing him ride it, which he did very skilfully. He took
advantage of their curiosity to get out of their hands.

One day as he was prancing and exercising his horse before
them, he got a little distance from them insensibly; then
suddenly clapping spurs to his horse he was soon out of sight.

The Missouri Indians once occupied all the territory near the junction of the
Kaw and Missouri rivers, but they were constantly decimated by the continual
depredations of their warlike and feudal enemies, the Pawnees and Sioux, and at
last fell a prey to that dreadful scourge, the small-pox, which swept them off by
thousands. The remnant of the once powerful tribe then found shelter and a home
with the Otoes, finally becoming merged in that tribe.

CHAPTER I.

UNDER THE SPANIARDS.

The Santa Fe of the purely Mexican occupation, long before the days of New Mexico's acquisition by the United States, and the Santa Fe of to-day are so widely in contrast that it is difficult to find language in which to convey to the reader the story of the phenomenal change. To those who are acquainted with the charming place as it is now, with its refined and cultured society, I cannot do better, perhaps, in attempting to show what it was under the old regime, than to quote what some traveller in the early 30's wrote for a New York leading newspaper, in regard to it. As far as my own observation of the place is concerned, when I first visited it a great many years ago, the writer of the communication whose views I now present was not incorrect in his judgment. He said:--

To dignify such a collection of mud hovels with the name
of "City," would be a keen irony; not greater, however,
than is the name with which its Padres have baptized it.
To call a place with its moral character, a very Sodom
in iniquity, "Holy Faith," is scarcely a venial sin;
it deserves Purgatory at least. Its health is the best
in the country, which is the first, second and third
recommendation of New Mexico by its greatest admirers.
It is a small town of about two thousand inhabitants,
crowded up against the mountains, at the end of a little
valley through which runs a mountain stream of the same
name tributary to the Rio Grande. It has a public square
in the centre, a Palace and an Alameda; as all Spanish
Roman Catholic towns have. It is true its Plaza, or
Public Square, is unfenced and uncared for, without trees
or grass. The Palace is nothing more than the biggest
mud-house in the town, and the churches, too, are unsightly
piles of the same material, and the Alameda[5] is on top of
a sand hill. Yet they have in Santa Fe all the parts and
parcels of a regal city and a Bishopric. The Bishop has a
palace also; the only two-storied shingle-roofed house in
the place. There is one public house set apart for eating,
drinking and gambling; for be it known that gambling is here

authorized by law. Hence it is as respectable to keep a
gambling house, as it is to sell rum in New Jersey; it is
a lawful business, and being lawful, and consequently
respectable and a man's right, why should not men gamble?
And gamble they do. The Generals and the Colonels and
the Majors and the Captains gamble. The judges and the
lawyers and the doctors and the priests gamble; and there
are gentlemen gamblers by profession! You will see squads
of poor peons daily, men, women and boys, sitting on the
ground around a deck of cards in the Public Square, gambling
for the smallest stakes.

The stores of the town generally front on the Public Square.
Of these there are a dozen, more or less, of respectable
size, and most of them are kept by others than Mexicans.
The business of the place is considerable, many of the
merchants here being wholesale dealers for the vast
territory tributary. It is supposed that about $750,000
worth of goods will be brought to this place this year, and
there may be $250,000 worth imported directly from the
United States.

In the money market there is nothing less than a five-cent
piece. You cannot purchase anything for less than five cents.
In trade they reckon ten cents the eighth of a dollar.
If you purchase nominally a dollar's worth of an article,
you can pay for it in eight ten-cent pieces; and if you
give a dollar, you receive no change. In changing a dollar
for you, you would get but eight ten-cent pieces for it.

Yet, although dirty and unkempt, and swarming with hungry
dogs, it has the charm of foreign flavour, and like
San Antonio retains some portion of the grace which long
lingered about it, if indeed it ever forsakes the spot
where Spain held rule for centuries, and the soft syllables
of the Spanish language are yet heard.

Such was a description of the "drowsy old town" of Santa Fe, sixty-five years ago. Fifteen years later Major W. H. Emory, of the United States army, writes of it as follows:[6]

The population of Santa Fe is from two to four thousand,
and the inhabitants are, it is said, the poorest people
of any town in the Province. The houses are mud bricks,
in the Spanish style, generally of one story, and built
on a square. The interior of the square is an open court,
and the principal rooms open into it. They are forbidding
in appearance from the outside, but nothing can exceed
the comfort and convenience of the interior. The thick
walls make them cool in summer and warm in winter.

The better class of people are provided with excellent beds,
but the poorer class sleep on untanned skins. The women
here, as in many other parts of the world, appear to be
much before the men in refinements, intelligence, and
knowledge of the useful arts. The higher class dress like
the American women, except, instead of a bonnet, they wear
a scarf over their head, called a reboso. This they wear
asleep or awake, in the house or abroad. The dress of the
lower classes of women is a simple petticoat, with arms and
shoulders bare, except what may chance to be covered by
the reboso.

The men who have means to do so dress after our fashion;
but by far the greater number, when they dress at all,
wear leather breeches, tight around the hips and open from
the knee down; shirt and blanket take the place of our
coat and vest.

The city is dependent on the distant hills for wood, and
at all hours of the day may be seen jackasses passing laden
with wood, which is sold at two bits, twenty-five cents,
the load. These are the most diminutive animals, and
usually mounted from behind, after the fashion of leap-frog.
The jackass is the only animal that can be subsisted in

this barren neighbourhood without great expense; our horses
are all sent to a distance of twelve, fifteen, and thirty
miles for grass.

I have interpolated these two somewhat similar descriptions of Santa Fe written
in that long ago when New Mexico was almost as little known as the topography of
the planet Mars, so that the intelligent visitor of to-day may appreciate the wonderful
changes which American thrift, and that powerful civilizer, the locomotive, have
wrought in a very few years, yet it still, as one of the foregoing writers has well said,
"has the charm of foreign flavour, and the soft syllables of the Spanish language are
still heard."

The most positive exception must be taken to the statement of the first-quoted
writer in relation to the Palace, of which he says "It is nothing more than the biggest
mud-house in the town." Now this "Palacio del Gobernador," as the old building was
called by the Spanish, was erected at a very early day. It was the long-established
seat of power when Penalosa confined the chief inquisitor within its walls in 1663,
and when the Pueblo authorities took possession of it as the citadel of their central
authority, in 1681.

The old building cannot well be overlooked by the most careless visitor to the
quaint town; it is a long, low structure, taking up the greater part of one side of the
Plaza, round which runs a colonnade supported by pillars of rough pine. In this once
leaky old Palace were kept, or rather neglected, the archives of the Territory until the
American residents, appreciating the importance of preserving precious documents
containing so much of interest to the student of history and the antiquarian, enlisted
themselves enthusiastically in the good cause, and have rescued from oblivion the
annals of a relatively remote civilization, which, but for their forethought, would
have perished from the face of the earth as completely as have the written records of
that wonderful region in Central America, whose gigantic ruins alone remain to tell
us of what was a highly cultured order of architecture in past ages, and of a people
whose intelligence was comparable to the style of the dwellings in which they lived.

The old adobe Palace is in itself a volume whose pages are filled with pathos and
stirring events. It has been the scene and witness of incidents the recital of which
would to us to-day seem incredible. An old friend, once governor of New Mexico
and now dead, thus graphically spoke of the venerable building:[7]

In it lived and ruled the Spanish captain general, so remote
and inaccessible from the viceroyalty at Mexico that he was
in effect a king, nominally accountable to the viceroy,
but practically beyond his reach and control and wholly
irresponsible to the people. Equally independent for the

same reason were the Mexican governors. Here met all the
provincial, territorial, departmental, and other legislative
bodies that have ever assembled at the capital of New Mexico.
Here have been planned all the Indian wars and measures
for defence against foreign invasion, including, as the
most noteworthy, the Navajo war of 1823, the Texan invasion
of 1842, the American of 1846, and the Confederate of 1862.
Within its walls was imprisoned, in 1809, the American
explorer Zebulon M. Pike, and innumerable state prisoners
before and since; and many a sentence of death has been
pronounced therein and the accused forthwith led away and
shot at the dictum of the man at the Palace. It has been
from time immemorial the government house with all its
branches annexed. It was such on the Fourth of July, 1776,
when the American Congress at Independence Hall in
Philadelphia proclaimed liberty throughout all the land,
not then, but now embracing it. Indeed, this old edifice
has a history. And as the history of Santa Fe is the
history of New Mexico, so is the history of the Palace
the history of Santa Fe.

The Palace was the only building having glazed windows. At one end was the
government printing office, and at the other, the guard-house and prison. Fearful
stories were connected with the prison. Edwards[8] says that he found, on examining
the walls of the small rooms, locks of human hair stuffed into holes, with rude
crosses drawn over them.

Fronting the Palace, on the south side of the Plaza, stood the remains of the
Capilla de los Soldados, or Military Chapel. The real name of the church was
"Our Lady of Light." It was said to be the richest church in the Province, but had
not been in use for a number of years, and the roof had fallen in, allowing the
elements to complete the work of destruction. On each side of the altar was the
remains of fine carving, and a weather-beaten picture above gave evidence of
having been a beautiful painting. Over the door was a large oblong slab of freestone,
elaborately carved, representing "Our Lady of Light" rescuing a human being from
the jaws of Satan. A large tablet, beautifully executed in relief, stood behind the
altar, representing various saints, with an inscription stating that it was erected by
Governor Francisco Antonio del Valle and his wife in 1761.

Church services were held in the Parroquia, or Parish church, now the Cathedral, which had two towers or steeples, in which hung four bells. The music was furnished by a violin and a triangle. The wall back of the altar was covered with innumerable mirrors, paintings, and bright-coloured tapestry.

The exact date of the first settlement of Santa Fe is uncertain. One authority says:

It was a primeval stronghold before the Spanish Conquest,

and a town of some importance to the white race when

Pennsylvania was a wilderness and the first Dutch governor

of New York was slowly drilling the Knickerbocker ancestry

in their difficult evolutions around the town-pump.

It is claimed, on what is deemed very authentic data by some, that Santa Fe is really the oldest settled town in the United States. St. Augustine, Florida, was established in 1565 and was unquestionably conceded the honour of antiquity until the acquisition of New Mexico by the Guadalupe-Hidalgo treaty. Then, of course, Santa Fe steps into the arena and carries off the laurels. This claim of precedence for Santa Fe is based upon the statement (whether historically correct or not is a question) that when the Spaniards first entered the region from the southern portion of Mexico, about 1542, they found a very large Pueblo town on the present site of Santa Fe, and that its prior existence extended far back into the vanished centuries. This is contradicted by other historians, who contend that the claim of Santa Fe to be the oldest town in the United States rests entirely on imaginary annals of an Indian Pueblo before the Spanish Conquest, and that there are but slight indications that the town was built on the site of one.[9]

The reader may further satisfy himself on these mooted points by consulting the mass of historical literature on New Mexico, and the records of its primitive times are not surpassed in interest by those of any other part of the continent. It was there the Europeans first made great conquests, and some years prior to the landing of the Pilgrims, a history of New Mexico, being the journal of Geronimo de Zarate Salmaron, was published by the Church in the City of Mexico, early in 1600. Salmaron was a Franciscan monk; a most zealous and indefatigable worker. During his eight years' residence at Jemez, near Santa Fe, he claims to have baptized over eight thousand Indians, converts to the Catholic faith. His journal gives a description of the country, its mines, etc., and was made public in order that other monks reading it might emulate his pious example.

Between 1605 and 1616 was founded the Villa of Santa Fe, or San Francisco de la Santa Fe. "Villa," or village, was an honorary title, always authorized and proclaimed by the king. Bancroft says that it was first officially mentioned on the 3d of January, 1617.

The first immigration to New Mexico was under Don Juan de Onate about 1597, and in a year afterward, according to some authorities, Santa Fe was settled. The place, as claimed by some historians, was then named El Teguayo, a Spanish adaptation of the word "Tegua," the name of the Pueblo nation, which was quite numerous, and occupied Santa Fe and the contiguous country. It very soon, from its central position and charming climate, became the leading Spanish town, and the capital of the Province. The Spaniards, who came at first into the country as friends, and were apparently eager to obtain the good-will of the intelligent natives, shortly began to claim superiority, and to insist on the performance of services which were originally mere evidences of hospitality and kindness. Little by little they assumed greater power and control over the Indians, until in the course of years they had subjected a large portion of them to servitude little differing from actual slavery.

The impolitic zeal of the monks gradually invoked the spirit of hatred and resulted in a rebellion that drove the Spaniards, in 1680, from the country. The large number of priests who were left in the midst of the natives met with horrible fates:

Not one escaped martyrdom. At Zuni, three Franciscans
had been stationed, and when the news of the Spanish retreat
reached the town, the people dragged them from their cells,
stripped and stoned them, and afterwards compelled the
servant of one to finish the work by shooting them. Having
thus whetted their appetite for cruelty and vengeance,
the Indians started to carry the news of their independence
to Moqui, and signalized their arrival by the barbarous
murder of the two missionaries who were living there.
Their bodies were left unburied, as a prey for the wild
beasts. At Jemez they indulged in every refinement of
cruelty. The old priest, Jesus Morador, was seized in
his bed at night, stripped naked and mounted on a hog,
and thus paraded through the streets, while the crowd
shouted and yelled around. Not satisfied with this,
they then forced him to carry them as a beast would,
crawling on his hands and feet, until, from repeated beating
and the cruel tortures of sharp spurs, he fell dead in
their midst. A similar chapter of horrors was enacted
at Acoma, where three priests were stripped, tied together
with hair rope, and so driven through the streets, and
finally stoned to death. Not a Christian remained free
within the limits of New Mexico, and those who had been

7

dominant a few months before were now wretched and
half-starved fugitives, huddled together in the rude huts
of San Lorenzo.

As soon as the Spaniards had retreated from the country,
the Pueblo Indians gave themselves up for a time to
rejoicing, and to the destruction of everything which could
remind them of the Europeans, their religion, and their
domination. The army which had besieged Santa Fe quickly
entered that city, took possession of the Palace as the
seat of government, and commenced the work of demolition.
The churches and the monastery of the Franciscans were
burned with all their contents, amid the almost frantic
acclamations of the natives. The gorgeous vestments of
the priests had been dragged out before the conflagration,
and now were worn in derision by Indians, who rode through
the streets at full speed, shouting for joy. The official
documents and books in the Palace were brought forth,
and made fuel for a bonfire in the centre of the Plaza;
and here also they danced the cachina, with all the
accompanying religious ceremonies of the olden time.
Everything imaginable was done to show their detestation
of the Christian faith and their determination to utterly
eradicate even its memory. Those who had been baptized
were washed with amole in the Rio Chiquito, in order to be
cleansed from the infection of Christianity. All baptismal
names were discarded, marriages celebrated by Christian
priests were annulled, the very mention of the names Jesus
and Mary was made an offence, and estuffas were constructed
to take the place of ruined churches.[10]

For twelve years, although many abortive attempts were made to recapture the
country, the Pueblos were left in possession. On the 16th of October, 1693, the
victorious Spaniards at last entered Santa Fe, bearing the same banner which had
been carried by Onate when he entered the city just a century before. The conqueror
this time was Don Diego de Vargas Zapata Lujan, whom the viceroy of New Spain
had appointed governor in the spring of 1692, with the avowed purpose of having
New Mexico reconquered as speedily as possible.

Thus it will be seen that the quaint old city has been the scene of many important historical events, the mere outline of which I have recorded here, as this book is not devoted to the historical view of the subject.

In contradistinction to the quiet, sleepy old Santa Fe of half a century ago, it now presents all the vigour, intelligence, and bustling progressiveness of the average American city of to-day, yet still smacks of that ancient Spanish regime, which gives it a charm that only its blended European and Indian civilization could make possible after its amalgamation with the United States.

The tourist will no longer find a drowsy old town, and the Plaza is no longer unfenced and uncared for. A beautiful park of trees is surrounded by low palings, and inside the shady enclosure, under a group of large cottonwoods, is a cenotaph erected to the memory of the Territory's gallant soldiers who fell in the shock of battle to save New Mexico to the Union in 1862, and conspicuous among the names carved on the enduring native rock is that of Kit Carson-- prince of frontiersmen, and one of Nature's noblemen.

Around the Plaza one sees the American style of architecture and hears the hum of American civilization; but beyond, and outside this pretty park, the streets are narrow, crooked, and have an ancient appearance. There the old Santa Fe confronts the stranger; odd, foreign-looking, and flavoured with all the peculiarities which marked the era of Mexican rule. And now, where once was heard the excited shouts of the idle crowd, of "Los Americanos!" "Los Carros!" "La entrada de la Caravana!" as the great freight wagons rolled into the streets of the old town from the Missouri, over the Santa Fe Trail, the shrill whistle of the locomotive from its trail of steel awakens the echoes of the mighty hills.

As may be imagined, great excitement always prevailed whenever a caravan of goods arrived in Santa Fe. Particularly was this the case among the feminine portion of the community. The quaint old town turned out its mixed population en masse the moment the shouts went up that the train was in sight. There is nothing there to-day comparable to the anxious looks of the masses as they watched the heavily freighted wagons rolling into the town, the teamsters dust-begrimed, and the mules making the place hideous with their discordant braying as they knew that their long journey was ended and rest awaited them. The importing merchants were obliged to turn over to the custom house officials five hundred dollars for every wagon-load, great or small; and no matter what the intrinsic value of the goods might be, salt or silk, velvets or sugar, it was all the same. The nefarious duty had to be paid before a penny's worth could be transferred to their counters. Of course, with the end of Mexican rule and the acquisition of the Province by the United States, all opposition to the traffic of the Old Santa Fe Trail ended, traders were assured a profitable market and the people purchased at relatively low prices.

What a wonderful change has taken place in the traffic with New Mexico in less than three-quarters of a century! In 1825 it was all carried on with one single annual caravan of prairie-schooners, and now there are four railroads running through the Rio Grande Valley, and one daily freight train of the Atchison, Topeka, and Santa Fe into the town unloads more freight than was taken there in a whole year when the "commerce of the prairies" was at its height!

Upon the arrival of a caravan in the days of the sleepy regime under Mexican control, the people did everything in their power to make the time pass pleasantly for every one connected with it during their sojourn. Bailes, or fandangoes, as the dancing parties were called by the natives, were given nightly, and many amusing anecdotes in regard to them are related by the old-timers.

The New Mexicans, both men and women, had a great fondness for jewelry, dress, and amusements; of the latter, the fandango was the principal, which was held in the most fashionable place of resort, where every belle and beauty in the town presented herself, attired in the most costly manner, and displaying her jewelled ornaments to the best advantage. To this place of recreation and pleasure, generally a large, capacious saloon or interior court, all classes of persons were allowed to come, without charge and without invitation. The festivities usually commenced about nine o'clock in the evening, and the tolling of the church bells was the signal for the ladies to make their entrance, which they did almost simultaneously.

New Mexican ladies were famous for their gaudy dresses, but it must be confessed they did not exercise good taste. Their robes were made without bodies; a skirt only, and a long, loose, flowing scarf or reboso dexterously thrown about the head and shoulders, so as to supersede both the use of dress-bodies and bonnets.

There was very little order maintained at these fandangoes, and still less attention paid to the rules of etiquette. A kind of swinging, gallopade waltz was the favourite dance, the cotillion not being much in vogue. Read Byron's graphic description of the waltz, and then stretch your imagination to its utmost tension, and you will perhaps have some faint conception of the Mexican fandango. Such familiarity of position as was indulged in would be repugnant to the refined rules of polite society in the eastern cities; but with the New Mexicans, in those early times, nothing was considered to be a greater accomplishment than that of being able to go handsomely through all the mazes of their peculiar dance.

There was one republican feature about the New Mexican fandango; it was that all classes, rich and poor alike, met and intermingled, as did the Romans at their Saturnalia, upon terms of equality. Sumptuous repasts or collations were rarely ever prepared for those frolicsome gatherings, but there was always an abundance of confectionery, sweetmeats, and native wine. It cost very little for a man to attend one of the fandangoes in Santa Fe, but not to get away decently and sober. In that it resembled the descent of Aeneas to Pluto's realms; it was easy enough to get there, but when it came to return, "revocare gradum, superasque evadere ad auras, hic labor, hoc opus est."

CHAPTER II.

LA LANDE AND PURSLEY.

In the beginning of the trade with New Mexico, the route across the great plains was directly west from the Missouri River to the mountains, thence south to Santa Fe by the circuitous trail from Taos. When the traffic assumed an importance demanding a more easy line of way, the road was changed, running along the left bank of the Arkansas until that stream turned northwest, at which point it crossed the river, and continued southwest to the Raton Pass.

The Atchison, Topeka, and Santa Fe Railroad track substantially follows the Trail through the mountains, which here afford the wildest and most picturesquely beautiful scenery on the continent.

The Arkansas River at the fording of the Old Trail is not more than knee-deep at an ordinary stage of water, and its bottom is well paved with rounded pebbles of the primitive rock.

The overland trade between the United States and the northern provinces of Mexico seems to have had no very definite origin; having been rather the result of an accident than of any organized plan of commercial establishment.

According to the best authorities, a French creole, named La Lande, an agent of a merchant of Kaskaskia, Illinois, was the first American adventurer to enter into the uncertain channels of trade with the people of the ultramontane region of the centre of the continent. He began his adventurous journey across the vast wilderness, with no companions but the savages of the debatable land, in 1804; and following him the next year, James Pursley undertook the same pilgrimage. Neither of these pioneers in the "commerce of the prairies" returned to relate what incidents marked the passage of their marvellous expeditions. Pursley was so infatuated with the strange country he had travelled so far to reach, that he took up his abode in the quaint old town of Santa Fe where his subsequent life is lost sight of. La Lande, of a different mould, forgot to render an account of his mission to the merchant who had sent him there, and became a prosperous and wealthy man by means of money to which he had no right.

To Captain Zebulon Pike, who afterwards was made a general, is due the impetus which the trade with Santa Fe received shortly after his return to the United States. The student of American history will remember that the expedition commanded by this soldier was inaugurated in 1806; his report of the route he had taken was the incentive for commercial speculation in the direction of trade with New Mexico, but it was so handicapped by restrictions imposed by the Mexican government, that the adventurers into the precarious traffic were not only subject to a complete confiscation of their wares, but frequently imprisoned for months as spies. Under such a condition of affairs, many of the earlier expeditions, prior to 1822, resulted in disaster, and only a limited number met with an indifferent success.

It will not be inconsistent with my text if I herewith interpolate an incident connected with Pursley, the second American to cross the desert, for the purpose of trade with New Mexico, which I find in the *Magazine of American History*:

When Zebulon M. Pike was in Mexico, in 1807, he met,
at Santa Fe, a carpenter, Pursley by name, from Bardstown,
Kentucky, who was working at his trade. He had in a
previous year, while out hunting on the Plains, met with
a series of misfortunes, and found himself near the
mountains. The hostile Sioux drove the party into the
high ground in the rear of Pike's Peak. Near the headwaters
of the Platte River, Pursley found some gold, which he
carried in his shot-pouch for months. He was finally sent
by his companions to Santa Fe, to see if they could trade
with the Mexicans, but he chose to remain in Santa Fe
in preference to returning to his comrades. He told the
Mexicans about the gold he had found, and they tried hard
to persuade him to show them the place. They even offered
to take along a strong force of cavalry. But Pursley
refused, and his patriotic reason was that he thought the
land belonged to the United States. He told Captain Pike
that he feared they would not allow him to leave Santa Fe,
as they still hoped to learn from him where the gold was
to be found. These facts were published by Captain Pike
soon after his return east; but no one took the hint,
or the risk was too great, and thus more than a half
a century passed before those same rich fields of gold
were found and opened to the world. If Pursley had been
somewhat less patriotic, and had guided the Mexicans to
the treasures, the whole history and condition of the
western part of our continent might have been entirely

different from what it now is. That region would still
have been a part of Mexico, or Spain might have been
in possession of it, owning California; and, with the gold
that would have been poured into her coffers, would have
been the leading nation of European affairs to-day.
We can easily see how American and European history in
the nineteenth century might have been changed, if that
adventurer from Kentucky had not been a true lover of his
native country.

The adventures of Captain Ezekiel Williams along the Old Trail, in the early
days of the century, tell a story of wonderful courage, endurance, and persistency.
Williams was a man of great perseverance, patience, and determination of character.
He set out from St. Louis in the late spring of 1807, to trap on the Upper Missouri
and the waters of the Yellowstone, with a party of twenty men who had chosen him
as their leader. After various exciting incidents and thrilling adventures, all of the
original party, except Williams and two others, were killed by the Indians somewhere
in the vicinity of the Upper Arkansas. The three survivors, not knowing where they
were, separated, and Captain Williams determined to take to the stream by canoe,
and trap on his way toward the settlements, while his last two companions started
for the Spanish country--that is, for the region of Santa Fe. The journal of Williams,
from which I shall quote freely, is to be found in *The Lost Trappers*, a work long out
of print.[11] As the country was an unexplored region, he might be on a river that
flowed into the Pacific, or he might be drifting down a stream that was an affluent to
the Gulf of Mexico. He was inclined to believe that he was on the sources of the Red
River. He therefore resolved to launch his canoe, and go wherever the stream might
convey him, trapping on his descent, when beaver might be plenty.

The first canoe he used he made of buffalo-skins. As this kind of water
conveyance soon begins to leak and rot, he made another of cottonwood, as soon as
he came to timber sufficiently large, in which he embarked for a port, he knew not
where.

Most of his journeyings Captain Williams performed during the hours of night,
excepting when he felt it perfectly safe to travel in daylight. His usual plan was
to glide along down the stream, until he came to a place where beaver signs were
abundant. There he would push his little bark among the willows, where he remained
concealed, excepting when he was setting his traps or visiting them in the morning.
When he had taken all the beaver in one neighbourhood, he would untie his little
conveyance, and glide onward and downward to try his luck in another place.

Thus for hundreds of miles did this solitary trapper float down this unknown river, through an unknown country, here and there lashing his canoe to the willows and planting his traps in the little tributaries around. The upper part of the Arkansas, for this proved to be the river he was on,[12] is very destitute of timber, and the prairie frequently begins at the bank of the river and expands on either side as far as the eye can reach. He saw vast herds of buffalo, and as it was the rutting season, the bulls were making a wonderful ado; the prairie resounded with their low, deep grunting or bellowing, as they tore up the earth with their feet and horns, whisking their tails, and defying their rivals to battle. Large gangs of wild horses could be seen grazing on the plains and hillsides, and the neighing and squealing of stallions might be heard at all times of the night.

Captain Williams never used his rifle to procure meat, except when it was absolutely necessary, or could be done with perfect safety. On occasions when he had no beaver, upon which he generally subsisted, he ventured to kill a deer, and after refreshing his empty stomach with a portion of the flesh, he placed the carcass in one end of the canoe. It was his invariable custom to sleep in his canoe at night, moored to the shore, and once when he had laid in a supply of venison he was startled in his sleep by the tramping of something in the bushes on the bank. Tramp! tramp! tramp! went the footsteps, as they approached the canoe. He thought at first it might be an Indian that had found out his locality, but he knew that it could not be; a savage would not approach him in that careless manner. Although there was beautiful starlight, yet the trees and the dense undergrowth made it very dark on the bank of the river, close to which he lay. He always adopted the precaution of tying his canoe with a piece of rawhide about twenty feet long, which allowed it to swing from the bank at that distance; he did this so that in case of an emergency he might cut the string, and glide off without making any noise. As the sound of the footsteps grew more distinct, he presently observed a huge grizzly bear coming down to the water and swimming for the canoe. The great animal held his head up as if scenting the venison. The captain snatched his axe as the most available means to defend himself in such a scrape, and stood with it uplifted, ready to drive it into the brains of the monster. The bear reached the canoe, and immediately put his fore paws upon the hind end of it, nearly turning it over. The captain struck one of the brute's feet with the edge of the axe, which made him let go with that foot, but he held on with the other, and he received this time a terrific blow on the head, that caused him to drop away from the canoe entirely. Nothing more was seen of the bear, and the captain thought he must have sunk in the stream and drowned. He was evidently after the fresh meat, which he scented from a great distance. In the canoe the next morning there were two of the bear's claws, which had been cut off by the well-directed blow of the axe. These were carefully preserved by Williams for many years as a trophy which he was fond of exhibiting, and the history of which he always delighted to tell.

As he was descending the river with his peltries, which consisted of one hundred and twenty-five beaver-skins, besides some of the otter and other smaller animals, he overtook three Kansas Indians, who were also in a canoe going down the river, as

15

he learned from them, to some post to trade with the whites. They manifested a very friendly disposition towards the old trapper, and expressed a wish to accompany him. He also learned from them, to his great delight, that he was on the Big Arkansas, and not more than five hundred miles from the white settlements. He was well enough versed in the treachery of the Indian character to know just how much he could repose in their confidence. He was aware that they would not allow a solitary trapper to pass through their country with a valuable collection of furs, without, at least, making an effort to rob him. He knew that their plan would be to get him into a friendly intercourse, and then, at the first opportunity, strip him of everything he possessed; consequently he was determined to get rid of them as soon as possible, and to effect this, he plied his oars with all diligence. The Indians, like most North American savages, were lazy, and had no disposition to labour in that way, but took it quite leisurely, satisfied with being carried down by the current. Williams soon left them in the rear, and, as he supposed, far behind him. When night came on, however, as he had worked all day, and slept none the night before, he resolved to turn aside into a bunch of willows to take a few hours' rest. But he had not stopped more than forty minutes when he heard some Indians pull to the shore just above him on the same side of the river. He immediately loosened his canoe from its moorings, and glided silently away. He rowed hard for two or three hours, when he again pulled to the bank and tied up.

Only a short time after he had landed, he heard Indians again going on shore on the same side of the stream as himself. A second time he repeated his tactics, slipped out of his place of concealment, and stole softly away. He pulled on vigorously until some time after midnight, when he supposed he could with safety stop and snatch a little sleep. He felt apprehensive that he was in a dangerous region, and his anxiety kept him wide awake. It was very lucky that he did not close his eyes; for as he was lying in the bottom of his canoe he heard for the third time a canoe land as before. He was now perfectly satisfied that he was dogged by the Kansans whom he had passed the preceding day, and in no very good humour, therefore, he picked up his rifle, and walked up to the bank where he had heard the Indians land. As he suspected, there were the three savages. When they saw the captain, they immediately renewed their expressions of friendship, and invited him to partake of their hospitality. He stood aloof from them, and shook his head in a rage, charging them with their villanous purposes. In the short, sententious manner of the Indians, he said to them: "You now follow me three times; if you follow me again, I kill you!" and wheeling around abruptly, returned to his canoe. A third time the solitary trapper pushed his little craft from the shore and set off down stream, to get away from a region where to sleep would be hazardous. He plied his oars the remainder of the night, and solaced himself with the thought that no evil had befallen him, except the loss of a few hours' sleep.

While he was escaping from his villanous pursuers, he was running into new dangers and difficulties. The following day he overtook a large band of the same tribe, under the leadership of a chief, who were also descending the river. Into the

16

hands of these savages he fell a prisoner, and was conducted to one of their villages. The principal chief there took all of his furs, traps, and other belongings. A very short time after his capture, the Kansans went to war with the Pawnees, and carried Captain Williams with them. In a terrible battle in which the Kansans gained a most decided victory, the old trapper bore a conspicuous part, killing a great number of the enemy, and by his excellent strategy brought about the success of his captors. When they returned to the village, Williams, who had ever been treated with kindness by the inhabitants, was now thought to be a wonderful warrior, and could have been advanced to all the savage honours; he might even have been made one of their principal chiefs. The tribe gave him his liberty for the great service he had rendered it in its difficulty with an inveterate foe, but declining all proffered promotions, he decided to return to the white settlements on the Missouri, at the mouth of the Kaw, the covetous old chief retaining all his furs, and indeed everything he possessed excepting his rifle, with as many rounds of ammunition as would be necessary to secure him provisions in the shape of game on his route. The veteran trapper had learned from the Indians while with them that they expected to go to Fort Osage on the Missouri River to receive some annuities from the government, and he felt certain that his furs would be there at the same time.

After leaving the Kansans he travelled on toward the Missouri, and soon struck the beginning of the sparse settlements. Just as evening was coming on, he arrived at a cluster of three little log-cabins, and was received with genuine backwoods hospitality by the proprietor, who had married an Osage squaw. Williams was not only very hungry, but very tired; and, after enjoying an abundant supper, he became stupid and sleepy, and expressed a wish to lie down. The generous trapper accordingly conducted him to one of the cabins, in which there were two beds, standing in opposite corners of the room. He immediately threw himself upon one, and was soon in a very deep sleep. About midnight his slumbers were disturbed by a singular and very frightful kind of noise, accompanied by struggling on the other bed. What it was, Williams was entirely at a loss to understand. There were no windows in the cabin, the door was shut, and it was as dark as Egypt. A fierce contest seemed to be going on. There were deep groanings and hard breathings; and the snapping of teeth appeared almost constant. For a moment the noise would subside, then again the struggles woud be renewed accompanied as before with groaning, deep sighing, and grinding of teeth.

The captain's bed-clothes consisted of a couple of blankets and a buffalo-robe, and as the terrible struggles continued he raised himself up in the bed, and threw the robe around him for protection, his rifle having been left in the cabin where his host slept, while his knife was attached to his coat, which he had hung on the corner post of the other bedstead from which the horrid struggles emanated. In an instant the robe was pulled off, and he was left uncovered and unprotected; in another moment a violent snatch carried away the blanket upon which he was sitting, and he was nearly tumbled off the bed with it. As the next thing might be a blow in the dark, he felt that it was high time to shift his quarters; so he made a desperate leap from the bed, and alighted on the opposite side of the room, calling for his host, who immediately came to his relief by opening the door. Williams then told him that the devil--or something as bad, he believed--was in the room, and he wanted a light. The accommodating trapper hurried away, and in a moment was back with a candle, the light of which soon revealed the awful mystery. It was an Indian, who at the time was struggling in convulsions, which he was subject to. He was a superannuated chief, a relative of the wife of the hospitable trapper, and generally made his home there. Absent when Captain Williams arrived, he came into the room at a very late hour, and went to the bed he usually occupied. No one on the claim knew of his being there until he was discovered, in a dreadfully mangled condition. He was removed to other quarters, and Williams, who was not to be frightened out of a night's rest, soon sunk into sound repose.

Williams reached the agency by the time the Kansas Indians arrived there, and, as he suspected, found that the wily old chief had brought all his belongings, which he claimed, and the agent made the savages give up the stolen property before he would pay them a cent of their annuities. He took his furs down to St. Louis, sold them there at a good price, and then started back to the Rocky Mountains on another trapping tour.

CHAPTER III.

EARLY TRADERS.

In 1812 a Captain Becknell, who had been on a trading expedition to the country of the Comanches in the summer of 1811, and had done remarkably well, determined the next season to change his objective point to Santa Fe, and instead of the tedious process of bartering with the Indians, to sell out his stock to the New Mexicans. Successful in this, his first venture, he returned to the Missouri River with a well-filled purse, and intensely enthusiastic over the result of his excursion to the newly found market.

Excited listeners to his tales of enormous profits were not lacking, who, inspired by the inducement he held out to them, cheerfully invested five thousand dollars in merchandise suited to the demands of the trade, and were eager to attempt with him the passage of the great plains. In this expedition there were thirty men, and the amount of money in the undertaking was the largest that had yet been ventured. The progress of the little caravan was without extraordinary incident, until it arrived at "The Caches" on the Upper Arkansas. There Becknell, who was in reality a man of the then "Frontier," bold, plucky, and endowed with excellent sense, conceived the ridiculous idea of striking directly across the country for Santa Fe through a region absolutely unexplored; his excuse for this rash movement being that he desired to avoid the rough and circuitous mountain route he had travelled on his first trip to Taos.

His temerity in abandoning the known for the unknown was severely punished, and his brave men suffered untold misery, barely escaping with their lives from the terrible straits to which they were reduced. Not having the remotest conception of the region through which their new trail was to lead them, and naturally supposing that water would be found in streams or springs, when they left the Arkansas they neglected to supply themselves with more than enough of the precious fluid to last a couple of days. At the end of that time they learned, too late, that they were in the midst of a desert, with all the tortures of thirst threatening them.

Without a tree or a path to guide them, they took an irregular course by observations of the North Star, and the unreliable needle of an azimuth pocket-compass. There was a total absence of water, and when what they had brought with them in their canteens from the river was exhausted, thirst began its horrible office. In a short time both men and animals were in a mental condition bordering on distraction. To alleviate their acute torment, the dogs of the train were killed, and their blood, hot and sickening, eagerly swallowed; then the ears of the mules were cut off for the same purpose, but such a substitute for water only added to their sufferings. They would have perished had not a superannuated buffalo bull that had just come from the Cimarron River, where he had gone to quench his thirst, suddenly appeared, to be immediately killed and the contents of his stomach swallowed with avidity. It is recorded that one of those who partook of the nauseous liquid said afterward, "nothing had ever passed his lips which gave him such exquisite delight as his first draught of that filthy beverage."

Although they were near the Cimarron, where there was plenty of water, which but for the affair of the buffalo they never would have suspected, they decided to retrace their steps to the Arkansas.

Before they started on their retreat, however, some of the strongest of the party followed the trail of the animal that had saved their lives to the river, where, filling all the canteens with pure water, they returned to their comrades, who were, after drinking, able to march slowly toward the Arkansas.

Following that stream, they at last arrived at Taos, having experienced no further trouble, but missed the trail to Santa Fe, and had their journey greatly prolonged by the foolish endeavour of the leader to make a short cut thither.

As early as 1815, Auguste P. Chouteau and his partner, with a large number of trappers and hunters, went out to the valley of the Upper Arkansas for the purpose of trading with Indians, and trapping on the numerous streams of the contiguous region.

The island on which Chouteau established his trading-post, and which bears his name even to this day, is in the Arkansas River on the boundary line of the United States and Mexico. It was a beautiful spot, with a rich carpet of grass and delightful groves, and on the American side was a heavily timbered bottom.

While occupying the island, Chouteau and his old hunters and trappers were attacked by about three hundred Pawnees, whom they repulsed with the loss of thirty killed and wounded. These Indians afterward declared that it was the most fatal affair in which they were ever engaged. It was their first acquaintance with American guns.

The general character of the early trade with New Mexico was founded on the system of the caravan. She depended upon the remote ports of old Mexico, whence was transported, on the backs of the patient burro and mule, all that was required by the primitive tastes of the primitive people; a very tedious and slow process, as may be inferred, and the limited traffic westwardly across the great plains was confined to this fashion. At the date of the legitimate and substantial commerce with New Mexico, in 1824, wheeled vehicles were introduced, and traffic assumed an importance it could never have otherwise attained, and which now, under the vast system of railroads, has increased to dimensions little dreamed of by its originators nearly three-quarters of a century ago.

It was eight years after Pursley's pilgrimage before the trade with New Mexico attracted the attention of speculators and adventurers. Messrs. McKnight,[13] Beard, and Chambers, with about a dozen comrades, started with a supply of goods across the unknown plains, and by good luck arrived safely at Santa Fe. Once under the jurisdiction of the Mexicans, however, their trouble began. All the party were arrested as spies, their wares confiscated, and themselves incarcerated at Chihuahua, where the majority of them were kept for almost a decade. Beard and Chambers, having by some means escaped, returned to St. Louis in 1822, and, notwithstanding their dreadful experience, told of the prospects of the trade with the Mexicans in such glowing colours that they induced some individuals of small capital to fit out another expedition, with which they again set out for Santa Fe.

It was really too late in the season; they succeeded, however, in reaching the crossing of the Arkansas without any difficulty, but there a violent snowstorm overtook them and they were compelled to halt, as it was impossible to proceed in the face of the blinding blizzard. On an island[14] not far from where the town of Cimarron, on the Santa Fe Railroad, is now situated, they were obliged to remain for more than three months, during which time most of their animals died for want of food and from the severe cold. When the weather had moderated sufficiently to allow them to proceed on their journey, they had no transportation for their goods and were compelled to hide them in pits dug in the earth, after the manner of the old French voyageurs in the early settlement of the continent. This method of secreting furs and valuables of every character is called caching, from the French word "to hide." Gregg thus describes it:

The cache is made by digging a hole in the ground, somewhat in the shape of a jug, which is lined with dry sticks, grass, or anything else that will protect its contents from the dampness of the earth. In this place the goods to be concealed are carefully stowed away; and the aperture is then so effectually closed as to protect them from the rains. In caching, a great deal of skill is often required to leave no sign whereby the cunning savage may discover the place of deposit. To this end, the excavated earth is carried some distance and carefully concealed, or thrown into a stream, if one be at hand. The place selected for a cache is usually some rolling point, sufficiently elevated to be secure from inundations. If it be well set with grass, a solid piece of turf is cut out large enough for the entrance. The turf is afterward laid back, and, taking root, in a short time

no signs remain of its ever having been molested.
However, as every locality does not afford a turfy site,
the camp-fire is sometimes built upon the place, or the
animals are penned over it, which effectually destroys
all traces.

Father Hennepin[15] thus describes, in his quaint style, how he built a cache on
the bank of the Mississippi, in 1680:

We took up the green sodd, and laid it by, and digg'd a hole
in the Earth where we put our Goods, and cover'd them with
pieces of Timber and Earth, and then put in again the green
Turf; so that 'twas impossible to suspect that any Hole had
been digg'd under it, for we flung the Earth into the River.

After caching their goods, Beard and the party went on to Taos, where they
bought mules, and returning to their caches transported their contents to their market.

The word "cache" still lingers among the "old-timers" of the mountains and
plains, and has become a provincialism with their descendants; one of these will tell
you that he cached his vegetables in the side of the hill; or if he is out hunting and
desires to secrete himself from approaching game, he will say, "I am going to cache
behind that rock," etc.

The place where Beard's little expedition wintered was called "The Caches"
for years, and the name has only fallen into disuse within the last two decades. I
remember the great holes in the ground when I first crossed the plains, a third of a
century ago.

The immense profit upon merchandise transported across the dangerous Trail of
the mid-continent to the capital of New Mexico soon excited the cupidity of other
merchants east of the Missouri. When the commonest domestic cloth, manufactured
wholly from cotton, brought from two to three dollars a yard at Santa Fe, and other
articles at the same ratio to cost, no wonder the commerce with the far-off market
appeared to those who desired to send goods there a veritable Golconda.

The importance of internal trade with New Mexico, and the possibilities of its
growth, were first recognized by the United States in 1824, the originator of the
movement being Mr. Thomas Hart Benton of Missouri, who frequently, from his
place in the Senate, prophesied the coming greatness of the West. He introduced
a bill which authorized the President to appoint a commission to survey a road
from the Missouri River to the boundary line of New Mexico, and from thence on

Mexican territory with the consent of the Mexican government. The signing of this bill was one of the last acts of Mr. Monroe's official life, and it was carried into effect by his successor, Mr. John Quincy Adams, but unfortunately a mistake was made in supposing that the Osage Indians alone controlled the course of the proposed route. It was partially marked out as far as the Arkansas, by raised mounds; but travellers continued to use the old wagon trail, and as no negotiations had been entered into with the Comanches, Cheyennes, Pawnees, or Kiowas, these warlike tribes continued to harass the caravans when these arrived in the broad valley of the Arkansas.

The American fur trade was at its height at the time when the Santa Fe trade was just beginning to assume proportions worthy of notice; the difference between the two enterprises being very marked. The fur trade was in the hands of immensely wealthy companies, while that to Santa Fe was carried on by individuals with limited capital, who, purchasing goods in the Eastern markets, had them transported to the Missouri River, where, until the trade to New Mexico became a fixed business, everything was packed on mules. As soon, however, as leading merchants invested their capital, about 1824, the trade grew into vast proportions, and wagons took the place of the patient mule. Later, oxen were substituted for mules, it having been discovered that they possessed many advantages over the former, particularly in being able to draw heavier loads than an equal number of mules, especially through sandy or muddy places.

For a long time, the traders were in the habit of purchasing their mules in Santa Fe and driving them to the Missouri; but as soon as that useful animal was raised in sufficient numbers in the Southern States to supply the demand, the importation from New Mexico ceased, for the reason that the American mule was in all respects an immensely superior animal.

Once mules were an important object of the trade, and those who dealt in them and drove them across to the river on the Trail met with many mishaps; frequently whole droves, containing from three to five hundred, were stolen by the savages en route. The latter soon learned that it was a very easy thing to stampede a caravan of mules, for, once panic-stricken, it is impossible to restrain them, and the Indians having started them kept them in a state of rampant excitement by their blood-curdling yells, until they had driven them miles beyond the Trail.

A story is told of a small band of twelve men, who, while encamped on the Cimarron River, in 1826, with but four serviceable guns among them, were visited by a party of Indians, believed to be Arapahoes, who made at first strong demonstrations of friendship and good-will. Observing the defenceless condition of the traders, they went away, but soon returned about thirty strong, each provided with a lasso, and all on foot. The chief then began by informing the Americans that his men were tired of walking, and must have horses. Thinking it folly to offer any resistance, the terrified traders told them if one animal apiece would satisfy them, to go and catch them. This they soon did; but finding their request so easily complied with, the Indians held a little parley together, which resulted in a new demand for more--they must have two apiece! "Well, catch them!" was the acquiescent reply of the unfortunate band; upon which the savages mounted those they had already secured, and, swinging their lassos over their heads, plunged among the stock with a furious yell, and drove off the entire caballada of nearly five hundred head of horses, mules, and asses.

In 1829 the Indians of the plains became such a terror to the caravans crossing to Santa Fe, that the United States government, upon petition of the traders, ordered three companies of infantry and one of riflemen, under command of Major Bennet Riley, to escort the annual caravan, which that year started from the town of Franklin, Missouri, then the eastern terminus of the Santa Fe trade, as far as Chouteau's Island, on the Arkansas, which marked the boundary between the United States and Mexico. [16] The caravan started from the island across the dreary route unaccompanied by any troops, but had progressed only a few miles when it was attacked by a band of Kiowas, then one of the most cruel and bloodthirsty tribes on the plains.[17]

This escort, commanded by Major Riley, and another under Captain Wharton, composed of only sixty dragoons, five years later, were the sole protection ever given by the government until 1843, when Captain Philip St. George Cooke again accompanied two large caravans to the same point on the Arkansas as did Major Riley fourteen years before.

As the trade increased, the Comanches, Pawnees, and Arapahoes continued to commit their depredations, and it was firmly believed by many of the freighters that these Indians were incited to their devilish acts by the Mexicans, who were always jealous of "Los Americanos."

It was very rarely that a caravan, great or small, or even a detachment of troops, no matter how large, escaped the raids of these bandits of the Trail. If the list of those who were killed outright and scalped, and those more unfortunate who were taken captive only to be tortured and their bodies horribly mutilated, could be collected from the opening of the traffic with New Mexico until the years 1868-69, when General Sheridan inaugurated his memorable "winter campaign" against the allied plains tribes, and completely demoralized, cowed, and forced them on their reservations, about the time of the advent of the railroad, it would present an appalling picture; and the number of horses, mules, and oxen stampeded and stolen during the same period would amount to thousands.

As the excellent narrative of Captain Pike is not read as it should be by the average American, a brief reference to it may not be considered supererogatory. The celebrated officer, who was afterward promoted to the rank of major-general, and died in the achievement of the victory of York, Upper Canada, in 1813, was sent in

1806 on an exploring expedition up the Arkansas River, with instructions to pass the sources of Red River, for which those of the Canadian were then mistaken; he, however, even went around the head of the latter, and crossing the mountains with an almost incredible degree of peril and suffering, descended upon the Rio del Norte with his little party, then but fifteen in number.

Believing himself now on Red River, within the then assumed limits of the United States, he built a small fortification for his company, until the opening of the spring of 1807 should enable him to continue his descent to Natchitoches. As he was really within Mexican territory, and only about eighty miles from the northern settlements, his position was soon discovered, and a force sent to take him to Santa Fe, which by treachery was effected without opposition. The Spanish officer assured him that the governor, learning that he had mistaken his way, had sent animals and an escort to convey his men and baggage to a navigable point on Red River (Rio Colorado), and that His Excellency desired very much to see him at Santa Fe, which might be taken on their way.

As soon, however, as the governor had the too confiding captain in his power, he sent him with his men to the commandant general at Chihuahua, where most of his papers were seized, and he and his party were sent under an escort, via San Antonio de Bexar, to the United States.

Many citizens of the remote Eastern States, who were contemporary with Pike, declared that his expedition was in some way connected with the treasonable attempt of Aaron Burr. The idea is simply preposterous; Pike's whole line of conduct shows him to have been of the most patriotic character; never would he for a moment have countenanced a proposition from Aaron Burr!

After Captain Pike's report had been published to the world, the adventurers who were inspired by its glowing description of the country he had been so far to explore were destined to experience trials and disappointments of which they had formed no conception.

Among them was a certain Captain Sublette, a famous old trapper in the era of the great fur companies, and with him a Captain Smith, who, although veteran pioneers of the Rocky Mountains, were mere novices in the many complications of the Trail; but having been in the fastnesses of the great divide of the continent, they thought that when they got down on the plains they could go anywhere. They started with twenty wagons, and left the Missouri without a single one of the party being competent to guide the little caravan on the dangerous route.

From the Missouri the Trail was broad and plain enough for a child to follow, but when they arrived at the Cimarron crossing of the Arkansas, not a trace of former caravans was visible; nothing but the innumerable buffalo-trails leading from everywhere to the river.

When the party entered the desert, or Dry Route, as it was years afterward always, and very properly, called in certain seasons of drought, the brave but too confident men discovered that the whole region was burnt up. They wandered on for several days, the horrors of death by thirst constantly confronting them. Water must be had or they would all perish! At last Smith, in his desperation, determined to follow one of the numerous buffalo-trails, believing that it would conduct him to water of some character-- a lake or pool or even wallow. He left the train alone; asked for no one to accompany him; for he was the very impersonation of courage, one of the most fearless men that ever trapped in the mountains.

He walked on and on for miles, when, on ascending a little divide, he saw a stream in the valley beneath him. It was the Cimarron, and he hurried toward it to quench his intolerable thirst. When he arrived at its bank, to his disappointment it was nothing but a bed of sand; the sometime clear running river was perfectly dry.

Only for a moment was he staggered; he knew the character of many streams in the West; that often their waters run under the ground at a short distance from the surface, and in a moment he was on his knees digging vigorously in the soft sand. Soon the coveted fluid began to filter upwards into the little excavation he had made. He stooped to drink, and in the next second a dozen arrows from an ambushed band of Comanches entered his body. He did not die at once, however; it is related by the Indians themselves that he killed two of their number before death laid him low.

Captain Sublette and Smith's other comrades did not know what had become of him until some Mexican traders told them, having got the report from the very savages who committed the cold-blooded murder.

Gregg, in his report of this little expedition, says:

Every kind of fatality seems to have attended this small
caravan. Among other casualties, a clerk in their company,
named Minter, was killed by a band of Pawnees, before they
crossed the Arkansas. This, I believe, is the only instance
of loss of life among the traders while engaged in hunting,
although the scarcity of accidents can hardly be said to be
the result of prudence. There is not a day that hunters
do not commit some indescretion; such as straying at
a distance of five and even ten miles from the caravan,
frequently alone, and seldom in bands of more than two or

three together. In this state, they must frequently be
spied by prowling savages; so that frequency of escape,
under such circumstances, must be partly attributed to
the cowardice of the Indians; indeed, generally speaking,
the latter are very loth to charge upon even a single
armed man, unless they can take him at a decided advantage.

Not long after, this band of Captain Sublette's very
narrowly escaped total destruction. They had fallen in
with an immense horde of Blackfeet and Gros Ventres, and,
as the traders were literally but a handful among thousands
of savages, they fancied themselves for a while in imminent
peril of being virtually "eated up." But as Captain
Sublette possessed considerable experience, he was at
no loss how to deal with these treacherous savages; so that
although the latter assumed a threatening attitude,
he passed them without any serious molestation, and finally
arrived at Santa Fe in safety.

The virtual commencement of the Santa Fe trade dates from 1822, and one of
the most remarkable events in its history was the first attempt to introduce wagons
in the expeditions. This was made in 1824 by a company of traders, about eighty in
number, among whom were several gentlemen of intelligence from Missouri, who
contributed by their superior skill and undaunted energy to render the enterprise
completely successful. A portion of this company employed pack-mules; among the
rest were owned twenty-five wheeled vehicles, of which one or two were stout road-
wagons, two were carts, and the rest Dearborn carriages, the whole conveying some
twenty-five or thirty thousand dollars' worth of merchandise. Colonel Marmaduke, of
Missouri, was one of the party. This caravan arrived at Santa Fe safely, experiencing
much less difficulty than they anticipated from a first attempt with wheeled vehicles.

Gregg continues:

The early voyageurs, having but seldom experienced any
molestation from the Indians, generally crossed the plains
in detached bands, each individual rarely carrying more than
two or three hundred dollars' worth of stock. This peaceful
season, however, did not last very long; and it is greatly
to be feared that the traders were not always innocent of

having instigated the savage hostilities that ensued in after years. Many seemed to forget the wholesome precept, that they should not be savages themselves because they dealt with savages. Instead of cultivating friendly feelings with those few who remained peaceful and honest, there was an occasional one always disposed to kill, even in cold blood, every Indian that fell into their power, merely because some of the tribe had committed an outrage either against themselves or friends.

As an instance of this, he relates the following:

In 1826 two young men named McNess and Monroe, having carelessly lain down to sleep on the bank of a certain stream, since known as McNess Creek,[18] were barbarously shot, with their own guns, as it was supposed, in the very sight of the caravan. When their comrades came up, they found McNess lifeless, and the other almost expiring. In this state the latter was carried nearly forty miles to the Cimarron River, where he died, and was buried according to the custom of the prairies, a very summary proceeding, necessarily. The corpse, wrapped in a blanket, its shroud the clothes it wore, is interred in a hole varying in depth according to the nature of the soil, and upon the grave is piled stones, if any are convenient, to prevent the wolves from digging it up. Just as McNess's funeral ceremonies were about to be concluded, six or seven Indians appeared on the opposite side of the Cimarron. Some of the party proposed inviting them to a parley, while the rest, burning for revenge, evinced a desire to fire upon them at once. It is more than probable, however, that the Indians were not only innocent but ignorant of the outrage that had been committed, or they would hardly have ventured to approach the caravan. Being quick of perception, they very soon saw the belligerent attitude assumed by the company, and therefore wheeled round and attempted to escape. One shot was fired, which brought an Indian to the ground, when he was instantly riddled with balls. Almost simultaneously another discharge of several guns followed, by which all the rest were either killed or mortally wounded, except one, who escaped to bear the news to his tribe.

These wanton cruelties had a most disastrous effect upon the prospects of the trade; for the exasperated children of the desert became more and more hostile to the "pale-faces," against whom they continued to wage a cruel war for many successive years. In fact this party suffered very severely a few days afterward. They were pursued by the enraged comrades of the slain savages to the Arkansas River, where they were robbed of nearly a thousand horses and mules.

The author of this book, although having but little compassion for the Indians, must admit that, during more than a third of a century passed on the plains and in the mountains, he has never known of a war with the hostile tribes that was not caused by broken faith on the part of the United States or its agents. I will refer to two prominent instances: that of the outbreak of the Nez Perces, and that of the allied plains tribes. With the former a solemn treaty was made in 1856, guaranteeing to them occupancy of the Wallola valley forever. I. I. Stevens, who was governor of Washington Territory at the time, and ex-officio superintendent of Indian affairs in the region, met the Nez Perces, whose chief, "Wish-la-no-she," an octogenarian, when grasping the hand of the governor at the council said: "I put out my hand to the white man when Lewis and Clark crossed the continent, in 1805, and have never taken it back since." The tribe kept its word until the white men took forcible possession of the valley promised to the Indians, when the latter broke out, and a prolonged war was the consequence. In 1867 Congress appointed a commission to treat with the Cheyennes, Kiowas, and Arapahoes, appropriating four hundred thousand dollars for the expenses of the commission. It met at Medicine Lodge in August of the year mentioned, and made a solemn treaty, which the members of the commission, on the part of the United States, and the principal chiefs of the three tribes signed. Congress failed to make any appropriation to carry out the provisions of the treaty, and the Indians, after waiting a reasonable time, broke out, devastated the settlements from the Platte to the Rio Grande, destroying millions of dollars' worth of property, and sacrificing hundreds of men, women, and children. Another war was the result, which cost more millions, and under General Sheridan the hostile savages were whipped into a peace, which they have been compelled to keep.

CHAPTER IV.

TRAINS AND PACKERS.

As has been stated, until the year 1824 transportation across the plains was done by means of pack-mules, the art of properly loading which seems to be an intuitive attribute of the native Mexican. The American, of course, soon became as expert, for nothing that the genus homo is capable of doing is impossible to him; but his teacher was the dark-visaged, superstitious, and profanity-expending Mexican arriero.

A description of the equipment of a mule-train and the method of packing, together with some of the curious facts connected with its movements, may not be uninteresting, particularly as the whole thing, with rare exceptions in the regular army at remote frontier posts, has been relegated to the past, along with the caravan of the prairie and the overland coach. To this generation, barring a few officers who have served against the Indians on the plains and in the mountains, a pack-mule train would be as great a curiosity as the hairy mammoth. In the following particulars I have taken as a model the genuine Mexican pack-train or atajo, as it was called in their Spanish dialect, always used in the early days of the Santa Fe trade. The Americans made many modifications, but the basis was purely Mexican in its origin. A pack-mule was termed a mula de carga, and his equipment consisted of several parts; first, the saddle, or aparejo, a nearly square pad of leather stuffed with hay, which covered the animal's back on both sides equally. The best idea of its shape will be formed by opening a book in the middle and placing it saddle-fashion on the back of a chair. Each half then forms a flap of the contrivance. Before the aparejo was adjusted to the mule, a salea, or raw sheep-skin, made soft by rubbing, was put on the animal's back, to prevent chafing, and over it the saddle-cloth, or xerga. On top of both was placed the aparejo, which was cinched by a wide grass-bandage. This band was drawn as tightly as possible, to such an extent that the poor brute grunted and groaned under the apparently painful operation, and when fastened he seemed to be cut in two. This always appeared to be the very acme of cruelty to the uninitiated, but it is the secret of successful packing; the firmer the saddle, the more comfortably the mule can travel, with less risk of being chafed and bruised. The aparejo is furnished with a huge crupper, and this appendage is really the most cruel of all, for it is almost sure to lacerate the tail. Hardly a Mexican mule in the old days of the trade could be found which did not bear the scar of this rude supplement to the immense saddle.

The load, which is termed a carga, was generally three hundred pounds. Two arrieros, or packers, place the goods on the mule's back, one, the cargador, standing on the near side, his assistant on the other. The carga is then hoisted on top of the saddle if it is a single package; or if there are two of equal size and weight, one on each side, coupled by a rope, which balances them on the animal. Another stout rope

30

is then thrown over all, drawn as tightly as possible under the belly, and laced round the packs, securing them firmly in their place. Over the load, to protect it from rain, is thrown a square piece of matting called a petate. Sometimes, when a mule is a little refractory, he is blindfolded by a thin piece of leather, generally embroidered, termed the tapojos, and he remains perfectly quiet while the process of packing is going on. When the load is securely fastened in its place, the blinder is removed. The man on the near side, with his knee against the mule for a purchase, as soon as the rope is hauled taut, cries out "Adios," and his assistant answers "Vaya!" Then the first says again, "Anda!" upon which the mule trots off to its companions, all of which feed around until the animals of the whole train are packed. It seldom requires more than five minutes for the two men to complete the packing of the animal, and in that time is included the fastening of the aperejo. It is surprising to note the degree of skill exercised by an experienced packer, and his apparently abnormal strength in handling the immense bundles that are sometimes transported. By the aid of his knees used as a fulcrum, he lifts a package and tosses it on the mule's back without any apparent effort, the dead weight of which he could not move from the ground.

An old-time atajo or caravan of pack-mules generally numbered from fifty to two hundred, and it travelled a jornado, or day's march of about twelve or fifteen miles. This day's journey was made without any stopping at noon, because if a pack-mule is allowed to rest, he generally tries to lie down, and with his heavy load it is difficult for him to get on his feet again. Sometimes he is badly strained in so doing, perhaps ruined forever. When the train starts out on the trail, the mules are so tightly bound with the ropes which confine the load that they move with great difficulty; but the saddle soon settles itself and the ropes become loosened so that they have frequently to be tightened. On the march the arriero is kept busy nearly all the time; the packs are constantly changing their position, frequently losing their balance and falling off; sometimes saddle, pack, and all swing under the animal's belly, and he must be unloaded and repacked again.

On arriving at the camping-ground the pack-saddles with their loads are ranged in regular order, their freight being between the saddles, covered with the petates to protect it from the rain, and generally a ditch is dug around to carry off the water, if the weather is stormy. After two or three days' travel each mule knows its own pack and saddle, and comes up to it at the proper moment with an intelligence that is astonishing. If an animal should come whose pack is somewhere else, he is soundly kicked in the ribs by the rightful mule, and sent bruised and battered to his place. He rarely makes a mistake in relation to the position of his own pack the second time.

This method of transportation was so cheap, because of the low rate of wages, that wagon-freighting, even in the most level region, could not compete with it. Five dollars a month was the amount paid to the muleteers, but it was oftener five with rations, costing almost nothing, of corn and beans. Meat, if used at all, was found by the arrieros themselves.

On the trail the mule-train is under a system of discipline almost as severe as that on board of a man-of-war. Every individual employed is assigned to his place and has certain duties to perform. There is a night-herder, called the savanero, whose duty it is to keep the animals from straying too far away, as they are all turned loose to shift for themselves, depending upon the grass alone for their subsistence. Each herd has a mulera, or bell-mare, which wears a bell hanging to a strap around her neck, and is kept in view of the other animals, who will never leave her. If the mare is taken away from the herd, every mule becomes really melancholy and is at a loss what to do or where to go. The cook of the party, or madre (mother) as he is called, besides his duty in preparing the food, must lead the bell-mule ahead of the train while travelling, the pack-animals following her with a devotion that is remarkable.

Sometimes in traversing the narrow ledges cut around the sides of a precipitous trail, or crossing a narrow natural bridge spanning the frightful gorges found everywhere in the mountains, a mule will be incontinently thrown off the slippery path, and fall hundreds of feet into the yawning canyon below. Generally instant death is their portion, though I recall an instance, while on an expedition against the hostile Indians thirty years ago, where a number of mules of our pack-train, loaded with ammunition, tumbled nearly five hundred feet down an almost perpendicular chasm, and yet some of them got on their feet again, and soon rejoined their companions, without having suffered any serious injury.

The wagons so long employed in this trade, after their first introduction in 1824, were manufactured in Pittsburgh, their capacity being about a ton and a half, and they were drawn by eight mules or the same number of oxen. Later much larger wagons were employed with nearly double the capacity of the first, hauled by ten and twelve mules or oxen. These latter were soon called prairie-schooners, which name continued to linger until transportation across the plains by wagons was completely extinguished by the railroads.

Under Mexican rule excessive tariff imposts were instituted, amounting to about a hundred per cent upon goods brought from the United States, and for some years, during the administration of Governor Manuel Armijo, a purely arbitrary duty was demanded of five hundred dollars for every wagon-load of merchandise brought into the Province, whether great or small, and regardless of its intrinsic value. As gold and silver were paid for the articles brought by the traders, they were also required to pay a heavy duty on the precious metals they took out of the country. Yankee ingenuity, however, evaded much of these unjust taxes. When the caravan approached Santa Fe, the freight of three wagons was transferred to one, and the empty vehicles destroyed by fire; while to avoid paying the export duty on gold and silver, they had large false axletrees to some of the wagons, in which the money was concealed, and the examining officer of the customs, perfectly unconscious of the artifice, passed them.

The army, in its expeditions against the hostile Indian tribes, always employed wagons in transporting its provisions and munitions of war, except in the mountains, where the faithful pack-mule was substituted. The American freighters, since the occupation of New Mexico by the United States, until the transcontinental railroad usurped their vocation, used wagons only; the Mexican nomenclature was soon dropped and simple English terms adopted: caravan became train, and majordomo, the person in charge, wagon-master. The latter was supreme. Upon him rested all the responsibility, and to him the teamsters rendered absolute obedience. He was necessarily a man of quick perception, always fertile in expedients in times of emergency, and something of an engineer; for to know how properly to cross a raging stream or a marshy slough with an outfit of fifty or sixty wagons required more than ordinary intelligence. Then in the case of a stampede, great clear-headedness and coolness were needed to prevent loss of life.

Stampedes were frequently very serious affairs, particularly with a large mule-train. Notwithstanding the willingness and patient qualities of that animal, he can act as absurdly as a Texas steer, and is as easily frightened at nothing. Sometimes as insignificant a circumstance as a prairie-dog barking at the entrance to his burrow, a figure in the distance, or even the shadow of a passing cloud will start every animal in the train, and away they go, rushing into each other, and becoming entangled in such a manner that both drivers and mules have often been crushed to death. It not infrequently happened that five or six of the teams would dash off and never could be found. I remember one instance that occurred on the trail between Fort Hays and Fort Dodge, during General Sheridan's winter campaign against the allied plains tribes in 1868. Three of the wagons were dragged away by the mules, in a few moments were out of sight, and were never recovered, although diligent search was made for them for some days. Ten years afterward a farmer, who had taken up a claim in what is now Rush County, Kansas, discovered in a ravine on his place the bones of some animals, decayed parts of harness, and the remains of three army-wagons, which with other evidence proved them to be the identical ones lost from the train so many years before.

The largest six-mule wagon-train that was ever strung out on the plains transported the supplies for General Custer's command during the winter above referred to. It comprised over eight hundred army-wagons, and was four miles in length in one column, or one mile when in four lines--the usual formation when in the field.

The animals of the train were either hobbled or herded at night, according to the locality; if in an Indian country, always hobbled or, preferably, tied up to the tongue of the wagon to which they belonged. The hobble is simply a strip of rawhide, with two slides of the same material. Placed on the front legs of the mule just at the fetlock, the slides pushed close to the limb, the animal could move around freely enough to graze, but was not able to travel very fast in the event of a stampede. In the Indian country, it was usual at night, or in the daytime when halting to feed, to form a corral of the wagons, by placing them in a circle, the wheels interlocked and the tongues run under the axles, into which circle the mules, on the appearance of the savages, were driven, and which also made a sort of fortress behind which the teamsters could more effectually repel an attack.

In the earlier trading expeditions to Santa Fe, the formation and march of the caravan differed materially from that of the army-train in later years. I here quote Gregg, whose authority on the subject has never been questioned. When all was ready to move out on the broad sea of prairie, he said:

We held a council, at which the respective claims of the
different aspirants for office were considered, leaders
selected, and a system of government agreed upon--as is
the standing custom of these promiscuous caravans.
A captain was proclaimed elected, but his powers were not
defined by any constitutional provision; consequently,
they were very vague and uncertain. Orders being only
viewed as mere requests, they are often obeyed or neglected
at the caprice of the subordinates. It is necessary to
observe, however, that the captain is expected to direct
the order of travel during the day and to designate the
camping-ground at night, with many other functions of
general character, in the exercise of which the company
find it convenient to acquiesce.

After this comes the task of organizing. The proprietors
are first notified by proclamation to furnish a list of
their men and wagons. The latter are generally apportioned
into four divisions, particularly when the company is large.
To each of these divisions, a lieutenant is appointed,
whose duty it is to inspect every ravine and creek on the
route, select the best crossings, and superintend what is
called in prairie parlance the forming of each encampment.

There is nothing so much dreaded by inexperienced travellers
as the ordeal of guard duty. But no matter what the
condition or employment of the individual may be, no one
has the slightest chance of evading the common law of
the prairies. The amateur tourist and the listless loafer

are precisely in the same wholesome predicament--they must all take their regular turn at the watch. There is usually a set of genteel idlers attached to every caravan, whose wits are forever at work in devising schemes for whiling away their irksome hours at the expense of others. By embarking in these trips of pleasure, they are enabled to live without expense; for the hospitable traders seldom refuse to accommodate even a loafing companion with a berth at their mess without charge. But these lounging attaches are expected at least to do good service by way of guard duty. None are ever permitted to furnish a substitute, as is frequently done in military expeditions; for he that would undertake to stand the tour of another besides his own would scarcely be watchful enough for dangers of the prairies. Even the invalid must be able to produce unequivocal proofs of his inability, or it is a chance if the plea is admitted.

The usual number of watchers is eight, each standing a fourth of every alternate night. When the party is small, the number is generally reduced, while in the case of very small bands, they are sometimes compelled for safety's sake to keep watch on duty half the night. With large caravans the captain usually appoints eight sergeants of the guard, each of whom takes an equal portion of men under his command.

The wild and motley aspect of the caravan can be but imperfectly conceived without an idea of the costumes of its various members. The most fashionable prairie dress is the fustian frock of the city-bred merchant, furnished with a multitude of pockets capable of accommodating a variety of extra tackling. Then there is the backwoodsman with his linsey or leather hunting-shirt--the farmer with his blue jean coat--the wagoner with his flannel sleeve vest--besides an assortment of other costumes which go to fill up the picture.

In the article of firearms there is also an equally interesting medley. The frontier hunter sticks to his rifle, as nothing could induce him to carry what he terms in derision "the scatter-gun." The sportsman from the interior flourishes his double-barrelled fowling-piece with equal confidence in its superiority. A great many were furnished beside with a bountiful supply of pistols and knives of every description, so that the party made altogether a very brigand-like appearance.

"Catch up! Catch up!" is now sounded from the captain's camp and echoed from every division and scattered group along the valley. The woods and dales resound with the gleeful yells of the light-hearted wagoners who, weary of inaction and filled with joy at the prospect of getting under way, become clamorous in the extreme. Each teamster vies with his fellow who shall be soonest ready; and it is a matter of boastful pride to be the first to cry out, "All's set."

The uproarious bustle which follows, the hallooing of those in pursuit of animals, the exclamations which the unruly brutes call forth from their wrathful drivers, together with the clatter of bells, the rattle of yokes and harness, the jingle of chains, all conspire to produce an uproarious confusion. It is sometimes amusing to observe the athletic wagoner hurrying an animal to its post--to see him heave upon the halter of a stubborn mule, while the brute as obstinately sets back, determined not to move a peg till his own good pleasure thinks it proper to do so--his whole manner seeming to say, "Wait till your hurry's over." I have more than once seen a driver hitch a harnessed animal to the halter, and by that process haul his mulishness forward, while each of his four projected feet would leave a furrow behind.

"All's set!" is finally heard from some teamster--

"All's set," is directly responded from every quarter.
"Stretch out!" immediately vociferates the captain.
Then the "heps!" to the drivers, the cracking of whips,
the trampling of feet, the occasional creak of wheels,
the rumbling of the wagons, while "Fall in" is heard from
head-quarters, and the train is strung out and in a few
moments has started on its long journey.

With an army-train the discipline was as perfect as that of a garrison. The wagon-master was under the orders of the commander of the troops which escorted the caravan, the camps were formed with regard to strategic principles, sentries walked their beats and were visited by an officer of the day, as if stationed at a military post.

Unquestionably the most expert packer I have known is Chris. Gilson, of Kansas. In nearly all the expeditions on the great plains and in the mountains he has been the master-spirit of the pack-trains. General Sheridan, who knew Gilson long before the war, in Oregon and Washington, regarded the celebrated packer with more than ordinary friendship. For many years he was employed by the government at the suggestion of General Sheridan, to teach the art of packing to the officers and enlisted men at several military posts in the West. He received a large salary, and for a long period was stationed at the immense cavalry depot of Fort Riley, in Kansas. Gilson was also employed by the British army during the Zulu war in Africa, as chief packer, at a salary of twenty dollars a day. Now, however, since the railroads have penetrated the once considered impenetrable fastnesses of the mountains, packing will be relegated to the lost arts.

CHAPTER V.

FIGHT WITH COMANCHES.

Early in the spring of 1828, a company of young men residing in the vicinity of Franklin, Missouri, having heard related by a neighbour who had recently returned the wonderful story of a passage across the great plains, and the strange things to be seen in the land of the Greasers, determined to explore the region for themselves; making the trip in wagons, an innovation of a startling character, as heretofore only pack-animals had been employed in the limited trade with far-off Santa Fe. The story of their journey can best be told in the words of one of the party:[19]--

We had about one thousand miles to travel, and as there was
no wagon-road in those early days across the plains to the
mountains, we were compelled to take our chances through
the vast wilderness, seeking the best route we could.

No signs of life were visible except the innumerable buffalo
and antelope that were constantly crossing our trail.
We moved on slowly from day to day without any incident
worth recording and arrived at the Arkansas; made the
passage and entered the Great American Desert lying beyond,
as listless, lonesome, and noiseless as a sleeping sea.
Having neglected to carry any water with us, we were obliged
to go withot a drop for two days and nights after leaving
the river. At last we reached the Cimarron, a cool,
sparkling stream, ourselves and our animals on the point
of perishing. Our joy at discovering it, however, was
short-lived. We had scarcely quenched our thirst when
we saw, to our dismay, a large band of Indians camped on
its banks. Their furtive glances at us, and significant
looks at each other, aroused our worst suspicions, and
we instinctively felt we were not to get away without
serious trouble. Contrary to our expectations, however,
they did not offer to molest us, and we at once made up
our minds they preferred to wait for our return, as we
believed they had somehow learned of our intention to bring

back from New Mexico a large herd of mules and ponies.

We arrived in Santa Fe on the 20th of July, without further adventure, and after having our stock of goods passed through the custom house, were granted the privilege of selling them. The majority of the party sold out in a very short time and started on their road to the States, leaving twenty-one of us behind to return later.

On the first day of September, those of us who had remained in Santa Fe commenced our homeward journey. We started with one hundred and fifty mules and horses, four wagons, and a large amount of silver coin. Nothing of an eventful character occurred until we arrived at the Upper Cimarron Springs, where we intended to encamp for the night. But our anticipations of peaceable repose were rudely dispelled; for when we rode up on the summit of the hill, the sight that met our eyes was appalling enough to excite the gravest apprehensions. It was a large camp of Comanches, evidently there for the purpose of robbery and murder. We could neither turn back nor go on either side of them on account of the mountainous character of the country, and we realized, when too late, that we were in a trap.

There was only one road open to us; that right through the camp. Assuming the bravest look possible, and keeping our rifles in position for immediate action, we started on the perilous venture. The chief met us with a smile of welcome, and said, in Spanish: "You must stay with us to-night. Our young men will guard your stock, and we have plenty of buffalo meat."

Realizing the danger of our situation, we took advantage of every moment of time to hurry through their camp. Captain Means, Ellison, and myself were a little distance behind the wagons, on horseback; observing that the balance of our men were evading them, the blood-thirsty savages

at once threw off their masks of dissimulation and in an
instant we knew the time for a struggle had arrived.

The Indians, as we rode on, seized our bridle-reins and
began to fire upon us. Ellison and I put spurs to our
horses and got away, but Captain Means, a brave man,
was ruthlessly shot and cruelly scalped while the life-blood
was pouring from his ghastly wounds.

We succeeded in fighting them off until we had left their
camp half a mile behind, and as darkness had settled down
on us, we decided to go into camp ourselves. We tied our
gray bell-mare to a stake, and went out and jingled the
bell, whenever any of us could do so, thus keeping the
animals from stampeding. We corralled our wagons for
better protection, and the Indians kept us busy all night
resisting their furious charges. We all knew that death
at our posts would be infinitely preferable to falling
into their hands; so we resolved to sell our lives as
dearly as possible.

The next day we made but five miles; it was a continuous
fight, and a very difficult matter to prevent their
capturing us. This annoyance was kept up for four days;
they would surround us, then let up as if taking time to
renew their strength, to suddenly charge upon us again,
and they continued thus to harass us until we were almost
exhausted from loss of sleep.

After leaving the Cimarron, we once more emerged on the
open plains and flattered ourselves we were well rid of
the savages; but about twelve o'clock they came down on us
again, uttering their demoniacal yells, which frightened
our horses and mules so terribly, that we lost every hoof.
A member of our party, named Hitt, in endeavouring to
recapture some of the stolen stock, was taken by the
savages, but luckily escaped from their clutches, after
having been wounded in sixteen parts of his body;

40

he was shot, tomahawked, and speared. When the painted
demons saw that one of their number had been killed by us,
they left the field for a time, while we, taking advantage
of the temporary lull, went back to our wagons and built
breastworks of them, the harness, and saddles. From noon
until two hours in the night, when the moon went down,
the savages were apparently confident we would soon fall
a prey to them, and they made charge after charge upon
our rude fortifications.

Darkness was now upon us. There were two alternatives
before us: should we resolve to die where we were, or
attempt to escape in the black hours of the night?
It was a desperate situation. Our little band looked
the matter squarely in the face, and, after a council
of war had been held, we determined to escape, if possible.

In order to carry out our resolve, it was necessary to
abandon the wagons, together with a large amount of silver
coin, as it would be impossible to take all of the precious
stuff with us in our flight; so we packed up as much of it
as we could carry, and, bidding our hard-earned wealth
a reluctant farewell, stepped out in the darkness like
spectres and hurried away from the scene of death.

Our proper course was easterly, but we went in a northerly
direction in order to avoid the Indians. We travelled
all that night, the next day, and a portion of its night
until we reached the Arkansas River, and, having eaten
nothing during that whole time excepting a few prickly-pears,
were beginning to feel weak from the weight of our burdens
and exhaustion. At this point we decided to lighten
our loads by burying all of the money we had carried
thus far, keeping only a small sum for each man.
Proceeding to a small island in the river, our treasure,
amounting to over ten thousand silver dollars, was cached
in the ground between two cottonwood trees.

Believing now that we were out of the usual range of
the predatory Indians, we shot a buffalo and an antelope
which we cooked and ate without salt or bread; but no meal
has ever tasted better to me than that one.

We continued our journey northward for three or four days
more, when, reaching Pawnee Fork, we travelled down it for
more than a week, arriving again on the Old Santa Fe Trail.
Following the Trail three days, we arrived at Walnut Creek,
then left the river again and went eastwardly to Cow Creek.
When we reached that point, we had become so completely
exhausted and worn out from subsisting on buffalo meat
alone, that it seemed as if there was nothing left for
us to do but lie down and die. Finally it was determined
to send five of the best-preserved men on ahead to
Independence, two hundred miles, for the purpose of
procuring assistance; the other fifteen to get along
as well as they could until succour reached them.

I was one of the five selected to go on in advance, and
I shall never forget the terrible suffering we endured.
We had no blankets, and it was getting late in the fall.
Some of us were entirely barefooted, and our feet so sore
that we left stains of blood at every step. Deafness, too,
seized upon us so intensely, occasioned by our weak
condition, that we coud not hear the report of a gun fired
at a distance of only a few feet.

At one place two of our men laid down their arms, declaring
they could carry them no farther, and would die if they
did not get water. We left them and went in search of some.
After following a dry branch several miles, we found
a muddy puddle from which we succeeded in getting half
a bucket full, and, although black and thick, it was life
for us and we guarded it with jealous eyes. We returned
to our comrades about daylight, and the water so refreshed
them they were able to resume the weary march. We travelled

on until we arrived at the Big Blue River, in Missouri,
on the bank of which we discovered a cabin about fifteen
miles from Independence. The occupants of the rude shanty
were women, seemingly very poor, but they freely offered us
a pot of pumpkin they were stewing. When they first saw us,
they were terribly frightened, because we looked more like
skeletons than living beings. They jumped on the bed while
we were greedily devouring the pumpkin, but we had to
refuse some salt meat which they had also proffered,
as our teeth were too sore to eat it. In a short time
two men came to the cabin and took three of our men
home with them. We had subsisted for eleven days on
one turkey, a coon, a crow, and some elm bark, with an
occasional bunch of wild grapes, and the pictures we
presented to these good people they will never, probably,
forget; we had not tasted bread or salt for thirty-two days.

The next day our newly found friends secured horses and
guided us to Independence, all riding without saddles.
One of the party had gone on to notify the citizens of
our safety, and when we arrived general muster was going on,
the town was crowded, and when the people looked upon us
the most intense excitement prevailed. All business was
suspended; the entire population flocked around us to hear
the remarkable story of our adventures, and to render us
the assistance we so much needed. We were half-naked,
foot-sore, and haggard, presenting such a pitiable picture
that the greatest sympathy was immediately aroused in
our behalf.

We then said that behind us on the Trail somewhere, fifteen
comrades were struggling toward Independence, or were
already dead from their sufferings. In a very few minutes
seven men with fifteen horses started out to rescue them.

They were gone from Independence several days, but had the
good fortune to find all the men just in time to save them

from starvation and exhaustion. Two were discovered
a hundred miles from Independence, and the remainder
scattered along the Trail fifty miles further in their rear.
Not more than two of the unfortunate party were together.
The humane rescuers seemingly brought back nothing but
living skeletons wrapped in rags; but the good people of
the place vied with each other in their attentions, and
under their watchful care the sufferers rapidly recuperated.

One would suppose that we had had enough of the great plains
after our first trip; not so, however, for in the spring
we started again on the same journey. Major Riley, with
four companies of regular soldiers, was detailed to escort
the Santa Fe traders' caravans to the boundary line between
the United States and Mexico, and we went along to recover
the money we had buried, the command having been ordered to
remain in camp to await our return until the 20th of October.

We left Fort Leavenworth about the 10th of May, and were
soon again on the plains. Many of the troops had never
seen any buffalo before, and found great sport in wantonly
slaughtering them. At Walnut Creek we halted to secure
a cannon which had been thrown into that stream two seasons
previously, and succeeded in dragging it out. With a seine
made of brush and grape vine, we caught more fine fish than
we could possibly dispose of. One morning the camp was
thrown into the greatest state of excitement by a band of
Indians running an enormous herd of buffalo right into us.
The troops fired at them by platoons, killing hundreds
of them.

We marched in two columns, and formed a hollow square
at night when we camped, in which all slept excepting
those on guard duty. Frequently some one would discover
a rattlesnake or a horned toad in bed with him, and it
did not take him a very long time to crawl out of his
blankets!

On the 10th of July, we arrived at the dividing line
separating the two countries, and went into camp. The next
day Major Riley sent a squad of soldiers to escort myself
and another of our old party, who had helped bury the
ten thousand dollars, to find it. It was a few miles
further up the Arkansas than our camp, in the Mexican
limits, and when we reached the memorable spot on the
island,[20] we found the coin safe, but the water had
washed the earth away, and the silver was exposed to view
to excite the cupidity of any one passing that way;
there were not many travellers on that lonely route in
those days, however, and it would have been just as secure,
probably, had we simply poured it on the ground.

We put the money in sacks and deposited it with Major Riley,
and, leaving the camp, started for Santa Fe with Captain
Bent as leader of the traders. We had not proceeded far
when our advanced guard met Indians. They turned, and when
within two hundred yards of us, one man named Samuel Lamme
was killed, his body being completely riddled with arrows.
His head was cut off, and all his clothes stripped from
his body. We had a cannon, but the Mexicans who hauled it
had tied it up in such a way that it could not be utilized
in time to effect anything in the first assault; but when
at last it was turned loose upon the Indians, they fled
in dismay at the terrible noise.

The troops at the crossing of the Arkansas, hearing the
firing, came to our assistance. The next morning the
hills were covered by fully two thousand Indians, who had
evidently congregated there for the purpose of annihilating
us, and the coming of the soldiers was indeed fortunate;
for as soon as the cowardly savages discovered them
they fled. Major Riley accompanied us on our march for
a few days, and, seeing no more Indians, he returned to
his camp.

We travelled on for a week, then met a hundred Mexicans
who were out on the plains hunting buffalo. They had
killed a great many and were drying the meat. We waited
until they were ready to return and then all started for
Santa Fe together.

At Rabbit-Ear Mountain the Indians had constructed
breastworks in the brush, intending to fight it out there.
The Mexicans were in the advance and had one of their
number killed before discovering the enemy. We passed
Point of Rocks and camped on the river. One of the
Mexicans went out hunting and shot a huge panther;
next morning he asked a companion to go with him and help
skin the animal. They saw the Indians in the brush, and
the one who had killed the panther said to the other,
"Now for the mountains"; but his comrade retreated,
and was despatched by the savages almost within reach
of the column.

We now decided to change our destination, intending to go
to Taos instead of Santa Fe, but the governor of the
Province sent out troops to stop us, as Taos was not a
place of entry. The soldiers remained with us a whole week,
until we arrived at Santa Fe, where we disposed of our goods
and soon began to make preparations for our return trip.

When we were ready to start back, seven priests and a
number of wealthy families, comfortably fixed in carriages,
accompanied us. The Mexican government ordered Colonel
Viscarra of the army, with five troops of cavalry,
to guard us to the camp of Major Riley.

We experienced no trouble until we arrived at the
Cimarron River. About sunset, just as we were preparing
to camp for the night, the sentinels saw a body of a
hundred Indians approaching; they fired at them and ran
to camp. Knowing they had been discovered, the Indians
came on and made friendly overtures; but the Pueblos who

who were with the command of Colonel Viscarra wanted to
fight them at once, saying the fellows meant mischief.
We declined to camp with them unless they would agree to
give up their arms; they pretended they were willing to
do so, when one of them put his gun at the breast of our
interpreter and pulled the trigger. In an instant a bloody
scene ensued; several of Viscarra's men were killed,
together with a number of mules. Finally the Indians
were whipped and tried to get away, but we chased them
some distance and killed thirty-five. Our friendly Pueblos
were delighted, and proceeded to scalp the savages,
hanging the bloody trophies on the points of their spears.
That night they indulged in a war-dance which lasted
until nearly morning.

We were delighted to see a beautiful sunshiny day after
the horrors of the preceding night, and continued our march
without farther interruption, safely arriving at the camp
on the boundary line, where Major Riley was waiting for us,
as we supposed; but his time having expired the day before,
he had left for Fort Leavenworth. A courier was despatched
to him, however, as Colonel Viscarra desired to meet the
American commander and see his troops. The courier overtook
Major Riley a short distance away, and he halted for us
to come up. Both commands then went into camp, and spent
several days comparing the discipline of the armies of
the two nations, and having a general good time.
Colonel Viscarra greatly admired our small arms, and
took his leave in a very courteous manner.

We arrived at Fort Leavenworth late in the season, and
from there we all scattered. I received my share of the
money we had cached on the island, and bade my comrades
farewell, only a few of whom I have ever seen since.

   Mr. Hitt in his notes of this same perilous trip says:

When the grass had sufficiently started to insure the

subsistence of our teams, our wagons were loaded with
a miscellaneous assortment of merchandise and the first
trader's caravan of wagons that ever crossed the plains
left Independence. Before we had travelled three weeks
on our journey, we were one evening confronted with the
novel fact of camping in a country where not a stick of
wood could be found. The grass was too green to burn,
and we were wondering how our fire could be started
with which to boil our coffee, or cook our bread. One of
our number, however, while diligently searching for
something to utilize, suddenly discovered scattered all
around him a large quantity of buffalo-chips, and he soon
had an excellent fire under way, his coffee boiling and
his bacon sizzling over the glowing coals.

We arrived in Santa Fe without incident, and as ours
was the first train of wagons that ever traversed the
narrow streets of the quaint old town, it was, of course,
a great curiosity to the natives.

After a few days' rest, sight-seeing, and purchasing stock
to replace our own jaded animals, preparations were made
for the return trip. All the money we had received for
our goods was in gold and silver, principally the latter,
in consequence of which, each member of the company had
about as much as he could conveniently manage, and,
as events turned out, much more than he could take care of.

On the morning of the third day out, when we were not
looking for the least trouble, our entire herd was
stampeded, and we were left upon the prairie without
as much as a single mule to pursue the fast-fleeing
thieves. The Mexicans and Indians had come so suddenly
upon us, and had made such an effective dash, that we
stood like children who had broken their toys on a stone
at their feet. We were so unprepared for such a stampede
that the thieves did not approach within rifle-shot range

of the camp to accomplish their object; few of them
coming within sight, even.

After the excitement had somewhat subsided and we began
to realize what had been done, it was decided that while
some should remain to guard the camp, others must go to
Santa Fe to see if they could not recover the stock.
The party that went to Santa Fe had no difficulty in
recognizing the stolen animals; but when they claimed them,
they were laughed at by the officials of the place.
They experienced no difficulty, however, in purchasing
the same stock for a small sum, which they at once did,
and hurried back to camp. By this unpleasant episode
we learned of the stealth and treachery of the miserable
people in whose country we were. We, therefore, took every
precaution to prevent a repetition of the affair, and
kept up a vigilant guard night and day.

Matters progressed very well, and when we had travelled
some three hundred miles eastwardly, thinking we were
out of range of any predatory bands, as we had seen no
sign of any living thing, we relaxed our vigilance somewhat.
One morning, just before dawn, the whole earth seemed to
resound with the most horrible noises that ever greeted
human ears; every blade of grass appeared to re-echo
the horrid din. In a few moments every man was at his post,
rifle in hand, ready for any emergency, and almost
immediately a large band of Indians made their appearance,
riding within rifle-shot of the wagons. A continuous
battle raged for several hours, the savages discharging
a shot, then scampering off out of range as fast as
their ponies could carry them. Some, more brave than
others would venture closer to the corral, and one of these
got the contents of an old-fashioned flint-lock musket
in his bowels.

We were careful not all to fire at the same time, and

several of our party, who were watching the effects of
our shots declared they could see the dust fly out of
the robes of the Indians as the bullets struck them.
It was learned afterward that a number of the savages
were wounded, and that several had died. Many were armed
with bows and arrows only, and in order to do any execution
were obliged to come near the corral. The Indians soon
discovered they were getting the worst of the fight, and,
having run off all the stock, abandoned the conflict,
leaving us in possession of the camp, but it can hardly
be said masters of the situation.

There we were; thirty-five pioneers upon the wild prairie,
surrounded by a wily and terribly cruel foe, without
transportation of any character but our own legs, and with
five hundred miles of dangerous, trackless waste between
us and the settlements. We had an abundance of money,
but the stuff was absolutely worthless for the present,
as there was nothing we could buy with it.

After the last savage had ridden away into the sand hills
on the opposite side of the river, each one of us had a
thrilling story to relate of his individual narrow escapes.
Though none was killed, many received wounds, the scars
of which they carried through life. I was wounded six
times. Once was in the thigh by an arrow, and once while
loading my rifle I had my ramrod shot off close to the
muzzle of my piece, the ball just grazing my shoulder,
tearing away a small portion of the skin. Others had
equally curious experiences, but none were seriously injured.

After the excitement incident to the battle had subsided,
the realization of our condition fully dawned upon us.
When we were first robbed, we were only a short distance
from Santa Fe, where our money easily procured other stock;
now there were three hundred miles behind us to that place,
and the picture was anything but pleasant to contemplate.

To transport supplies for thirty-five men seemed impossible.
Our money was now a burden greater than we could bear;
what was to be done with it? We would have no use for it
on our way to the settlements, yet the idea of abandoning
it seemed hard to accept. A vigilant guard was kept up
that day and night, during which time we all remained
in camp, fearing a renewal of the attack.

The next morning, as there were no apparent signs of
the Indians, it was decided to reconnoitre the surrounding
country in the hope of recovering a portion, at least,
of our lost stock, which we thought might have become
separated from the main herd. Three men were detailed
to stay in the old camp to guard it while the remainder,
in squads, scoured the hills and ravines. Not a horse
or mule was visible anywhere; the stampede had been
complete--not even the direction the animals had taken
could be discovered.

It was late in the afternoon when I, having left my
companions to continue the search and returning to camp
alone, had gotten within a mile of it, that I thought I saw
a horse feeding upon an adjoining hill. I at once turned
my steps in that direction, and had proceeded but a short
distance when three Indians jumped from their ambush in
the grass between me and the wagons and ran after me.
The men in camp had been watching my every movement,
and as soon as they saw the savages were chasing me,
they started in pursuit, running at their greatest speed
to my rescue.

The savages soon overtook me, and the first one that
came up tackled me, but in an instant found himself flat
on the ground. Before he could get up, the second one
shared the same fate. By this time the third one arrived,
and the two I had thrown grabbed me by the legs so that
I could no longer handle myself, while the third one had

a comparatively easy task in pushing me over. Fortunately,
my head fell toward the camp and my fast-approaching
comrades. The two Indians held my legs to prevent my
rising, while the third one, who was standing over me,
drew from his belt a tomahawk, and shrugging his head
in his blanket, at the same time looking over his shoulder
at my friends, with a tremendous effort and that peculiar
grunt of all savages, plunged his hatchet, as he supposed,
into my head, but instead of scuffling to free myself
and rise to my feet, I merely turned my head to one side
and the wicked weapon was buried in the ground, just
grazing my ear.

The Indian, seeing that he had missed, raised his hatchet
and once more shrugging his head in his blanket, and
turning to look over his other shoulder, attempted to
strike again, but the blow was evaded by a sudden toss
of his intended victim's head. Not satisfied with two
abortive trials, the third attempt must be made to brain me,
and repeating the same motions, with a great "Ugh!" he
seemed to put all his strength into the blow, which, like
the others, missed, and spent its force in the earth.
By this time the rescuing party had come near enough to
prevent the savage from risking another effort, and he then
addressed the other Indians in Spanish, which I understood,
saying, "We must run or the Americans will kill us!"
and loosening his grasp, he scampered off with his
companions as fast as his legs could take him, hurried on
by several pieces of lead fired from the old flintlocks
of the traders.

By sundown every man had returned to the forlorn camp,
but not an animal had been recovered. Then, with tired
limbs and weary hearts, we took turns at guarding the
wagons through the long night. The next morning each man
shouldered his rifle, and having had his proportion of
the provisions and cooking utensils assigned him,

we broke camp, and again turned to take a last look at
the country behind us, in which we had experienced so much
misfortune, and started on foot for our long march through
the dangerous region ahead of us.

Scarcely had we gotten out of sight of our abandoned camp,
when one of the party, happening to turn his eyes in that
direction, saw a large volume of smoke rising in the
vicinity; then we knew that all of our wagons, and
everything we had been forced to leave, were burning up.
This proved that, although we had been unable to discover
any signs of Indians, they had been lurking around us
all the time, and this fact warned us to exercise the
utmost vigilance in guarding our persons.

Though our burdens were very heavy, the first few days
were passed without anything to relieve the dreadful
monotony of our wearisome march; but each succeeding
twenty-four hours our loads became visibly lighter,
as our supplies were rapidly diminishing. It had already
become apparent that even in the exercise of the greatest
frugality, our stock of provisions would not last until
we could reach the settlements, so some of the most expert
shots were selected to hunt for game; but even in this
they were not successful, the very birds seeming to have
abandoned the country in its extreme desolation.

After eight days' travel, despite our most rigid economy,
an inventory showed that there was less than one hundred
pounds of flour left. Day after day the hunters repeated
the same old story: "No game!" For two weeks the allowance
of flour to each individual was but a spoonful, stirred
in water and taken three times a day.

One afternoon, however, fortune smiled upon the weary party;
one of the hunters returned to camp with a turkey he had
killed. It was soon broiling over a fire which willing
hands had kindled, and our drooping spirits were revived

for a while. While the turkey was cooking, a crow flew
over the camp, and one of the company, seizing a gun,
despatched it, and in a few moments it, too, was sizzling
along with the other bird.

Now, in addition to the pangs of hunger, a scarcity of
water confronted us, and one day we were compelled to
resort to a buffalo-wallow and suck the moist clay where
the huge animals had been stamping in the mud. We were
much reduced in strength, yet each day added new
difficulties to our forlorn situation. Some became so weak
and exhausted that it was with the greatest effort they
could travel at all. To divide the company and leave
the more feeble behind to starve, or to be murdered by
the merciless savages, was not considered for a moment;
but one alternative remained, and that was speedily accepted.
As soon as a convenient camping-ground could be found,
a halt was made, shelter established, and things made as
comfortable as possible. Here the weakest remained to rest,
while some of the strongest scoured the surrounding country
in search of game. During this temporary halt the hunters
were more successful than before, having killed two
buffaloes, besides some smaller animals, in one morning.
Again the natural dry fuel of the prairies was called
into requisition, and juicy steak was once more broiling
over the fire.

With an abundance to eat and a few days' rest, the whole
company revived and were enabled to renew their march
homeward. We were now in the buffalo range, and every day
the hunters were fortunate enough to kill one or more of
the immense animals, thus keeping our larder in excellent
condition, and starvation averted.

Doubting whether our good fortune in relation to food
would continue for the remainder of our march, and our
money becoming very cumbersome, it was decided by a majority

that at the first good place we came to we would bury it
and risk its being stolen by our enemies. When not more
than half of our journey had been accomplished, we came
to an island in the river to which we waded, and there,
between two large trees, dug a hole and deposited our
treasure. We replaced the sod over the spot, taking the
utmost precaution to conceal every sign of having disturbed
the ground. Though no Indians had been seen for several
days, a sharp lookout was kept in all directions for fear
that some lurking savage might have been watching our
movements. This task finished, with much lighter burdens,
but more anxious than ever, we again took up our march
eastwardly, and, thus relieved, were able to carry a
greater quantity of provisions.

Having journeyed until we supposed we were within a few
miles of the settlements, some of our number, scarcely able
to travel, thought the best course to pursue would be to
divide the company; one portion to press on, the weaker
ones to proceed by easier stages, and when the advance
arrived at the settlements, they were to send back a relief
for those plodding on wearily behind them. Soon a few
who were stronger than the others reached Independence,
Missouri, and immediately sent a party with horses to
bring in their comrades; so, at last, all got safely to
their homes.

In the spring of 1829, Major Bennett Riley of the United States army was ordered
with four companies of the Sixth Regular Infantry to march out on the Trail as the
first military escort ever sent for the protection of the caravans of traders going and
returning between Western Missouri and Santa Fe. Captain Philip St. George Cooke,
of the Dragoons, accompanied the command, and kept a faithful journal of the trip,
from which, and the official report of Major Riley to the Secretary of War, I have
interpolated here copious extracts.

The journal of Captain Cooke states that the battalion marched from Fort
Leavenworth, which was then called a cantonment, and, strange to say, had been
abandoned by the Third Infantry on account of its unhealthiness. It was the 5th of
June that Riley crossed the Missouri at the cantonment, and recrossed the river again

55

at a point a little above Independence, in order to avoid the Kaw, or Kansas, which had no ferry.

After five days' marching, the command arrived at Round Grove, where the caravan had been ordered to rendezvous and wait for the escort. The number of traders aggregated about seventy-nine men, and their train consisted of thirty-eight wagons drawn by mules and horses, the former preponderating. Five days' marching, at an average of fifteen miles a day, brought them to Council Grove. Leaving the Grove, in a short time Cow Creek was reached, which at that date abounded in fish; many of which, says the journal, "weighed several pounds, and were caught as fast as the line could be handled." The captain does not describe the variety to which he refers; probably they were the buffalo--a species of sucker, to be found to-day in every considerable stream in Kansas.

Having reached the Upper Valley,[21] bordered by high sand hills, the journal continues:

From the tops of the hills, we saw far away, in almost
every direction, mile after mile of prairie, blackened
with buffalo. One morning, when our march was along the
natural meadows by the river, we passed through them for
miles; they opened in front and closed continually in
the rear, preserving a distance scarcely over three hundred
paces. On one occasion, a bull had approached within
two hundred yards without seeing us, until he ascended
the river bank; he stood a moment shaking his head, and
then made a charge at the column. Several officers
stepped out and fired at him, two or three dogs also rushed
to meet him; but right onward he came, snorting blood
from mouth and nostril at every leap, and, with the speed
of a horse and the momentum of a locomotive, dashed
between two wagons, which the frightened oxen nearly upset;
the dogs were at his heels and soon he came to bay, and,
with tail erect, kicked violently for a moment, and then
sank in death--the muscles retaining the dying rigidity
of tension.

About the middle of July, the command arrived at its destination-- Chouteau's Island, then on the boundary line between the United States and New Mexico.

Our orders were to march no further; and, as a protection
to the trade, it was like the establishment of a ferry
to the mid-channel of a river.

Up to this time, traders had always used mules or horses.
Our oxen were an experiment, and it succeeded admirably;
they even did better when water was very scarce, which is
an important consideration.

A few hours after the departure of the trading company,
as we enjoyed a quiet rest on a hot afternoon, we saw
beyond the river a number of horsemen riding furiously
toward our camp. We all flocked out of the tents to hear
the news, for they were soon recognized as traders.
They stated that the caravan had been attacked, about
six miles off in the sand hills, by an innumerable host
of Indians; that some of their companions had been killed;
and they had run, of course, for help. There was not a
moment's hesitation; the word was given, and the tents
vanished as if by magic. The oxen which were grazing
near by were speedily yoked to the wagons, and into the
river we marched. Then I deemed myself the most unlucky
of men; a day or two before, while eating my breakfast,
with my coffee in a tin cup--notorious among chemists and
campaigners for keeping it hot--it was upset into my shoe,
and on pulling off the stocking, it so happened that the
skin came with it. Being thus hors de combat, I sought to
enter the combat on a horse, which was allowed; but I was
put in command of the rear guard to bring up the baggage
train. It grew late, and the wagons crossed slowly;
for the river unluckily took that particular time to
rise fast, and, before all were over, we had to swim it,
and by moonlight. We reached the encampment at one o'clock
at night. All was quiet, and remained so until dawn,
when, at the sound of our bugles, the pickets reported
they saw a number of Indians moving off. On looking
around us, we perceived ourselves and the caravan in the

most unfavorable defenceless situation possible--in the
area of a natural amphitheatre of sand hills, about fifty
feet high, and within gun-shot all around. There was
the narrowest practicable entrance and outlet.

We ascertained that some mounted traders, in spite of all
remonstrance and command, had ridden on in advance, and
when in the narrow pass beyond this spot, had been suddenly
beset by about fifty Indians; all fled and escaped save one,
who, mounted on a mule, was abandoned by his companions,
overtaken, and slain. The Indians, perhaps, equalled the
traders in number, but notwithstanding their extraordinary
advantage of ground, dared not attack them when they
made a stand among their wagons; and the latter, all well
armed, were afraid to make a single charge, which would
have scattered their enemies like sheep.

Having buried the poor fellow's body, and killed an ox for
breakfast, we left this sand hollow, which would soon have
been roasting hot, and advancing through the defile--of
which we took care to occupy the commanding ground--
proceeded to escort the traders at least one day's march
further.

When the next morning broke clear and cloudless, the command
was confronted by one of those terrible hot winds, still
frequent on the plains. The oxen with lolling tongues
were incapable of going on; the train was halted, and the
suffering animals unyoked, but they stood motionless,
making no attempt to graze. Late that afternoon, the
caravan pushed on for about ten miles, where was the
sandy bed of a dry creek, and fortunately, not far from
the Trail, up the stream, a pool of water and an acre
or two of grass was discovered. On the surface of the
water floated thick the dead bodies of small fish, which
the intense heat of the sun that day had killed.

Arriving at this point, it was determined to march no

further into the Mexican territory. At the first light
next day we were in motion to return to the river and
the American line, and no further adventure befell us.

While permanently encamped at Chouteau's Island, which is situated in the
Arkansas River, the term of enlistment of four of the soldiers of Captain Cooke's
command expired, and they were discharged. In his journal he says:

Contrary to all advice they determined to return to
Missouri. After having marched several hundred miles
over a prairie country, being often on high hills
commanding a vast prospect, without seeing a human being
or a sign of one, and, save the trail we followed, not
the slightest indication that the country had ever been
visited by man, it was exceedingly difficult to credit
that lurking foes were around us, and spying our motions.
It was so with these men; and being armed, they set out
on the first of August on foot for the settlements.
That same night three of the four returned. They reported
that, after walking about fifteen miles, they were
surrounded by thirty mounted Indians. A wary old soldier
of their number succeeded in extricating them before any
hostile act had been committed; but one of them, highly
elated and pleased at their forbearance, insisted on
returning among them to give them tobacco and shake hands.
In this friendly act he was shot down. The Indians
stripped him in an incredibly short time, and as quickly
dispersed to avoid a shot; and the old soldier, after
cautioning the others to reserve their fire, fired among
them, and probably with some effect. Had the others done
the same, the Indians would have rushed upon them before
they could have reloaded. They managed to make good
their retreat in safety to our camp.

We were instructed to wait here for the return of the
caravan, which was expected early in October.
Our provisions consisted of salt and half rations of flour,
besides a reserve of fifteen days' full rations--as to the

rest, we were dependent upon hunting. When the buffalo
became scarce, or the grass bad, we marched to other
ground, thus roving up and down the river for eighty
miles. The first thing we did after camping was to dig
and construct, with flour barrels, a well in front of
each company; water was always found at the depth of
from two to four feet varying with the corresponding
height of the river, but clear and cool. Next we would
build sod fire-places; these, with network platforms of
buffalo hide, used for smoking and drying meat, formed a
tolerable additional defence, at least against mounted men.

Hunting was a military duty, done by detail, parties of
fifteen or twenty going out with a wagon. Completely
isolated, and beyond support or even communication,
in the midst of many thousands of Indians, the utmost
vigilance was maintained. Officer of the guard every
fourth night; I was always awake and generally in motion
the whole time of duty. Night alarms were frequent; when,
as we all slept in our clothes, we were accustomed to
assemble instantly, and with scarcely a word spoken,
take our places in the grass in front of each face of
the camp, where, however wet, we sometimes lay for hours.

While encamped a few miles below Chouteau's Island, on the
eleventh of August, an alarm was given, and we were under
arms for an hour until daylight. During the morning,
Indians were seen a mile or two off, leading their horses
through the ravines. A captain, however, with eighteen
men was sent across the river after buffalo, which we saw
half a mile distant. In his absence, a large body of
Indians came galloping down the river, as if to charge
the camp, but the cattle were secured in good time.
A company, of which I was lieutenant, was ordered to
cross the river and support the first. We waded in some
disorder through the quicksands and current, and just
as we neared a dry sandbar in the middle, a volley was

fired at us by a band of Indians, who that moment rode
to the water's edge. The balls whistled very near,
but without damage; I felt an involuntary twitch of
the neck, and wishing to return the compliment instantly,
I stooped down, and the company fired over my head,
with what execution was not perceived, as the Indians
immediately retired out of our view. This had passed
in half a minute, and we were astonished to see, a little
above, among some bushes on the same bar, the party we had
been sent to support, and we heard that they had abandoned
one of the hunters, who had been killed. We then saw,
on the bank we had just left, a formidable body of the
enemy in close order, and hoping to surprise them,
we ascended the bed of the river. In crossing the channel
we were up to the arm-pits, but when we emerged on the
bank, we found that the Indians had detected the movement,
and retreated. Casting eyes beyond the river, I saw a
number of the Indians riding on both sides of a wagon
and team which had been deserted, urging the animals
rapidly toward the hills. At this juncture the adjutant
sent an order to cross and recover the body of the slain
hunter, who was an old soldier and a favourite. He was
brought in with an arrow still transfixing his breast,
but his scalp was gone.

On the fourteenth of October, we again marched on our
return. Soon after, we saw smokes arise over the distant
hills; evidently signals, indicating to different parties
of Indians our separation and march, but whether preparatory
to an attack upon the Mexicans or ourselves, or rather
our immense drove of animals, we could only guess.

Our march was constantly attended by great collections
of buffalo, which seemed to have a general muster, perhaps
for migration. Sometimes a hundred or two--a fragment
from the multitude--would approach within two or three
hundred yards of the column, and threaten a charge which

would have proved disastrous to the mules and their drivers.

Under the friendly cover of the shades of evening, on the eighth of November, our tatterdemalion veterans marched into Fort Leavenworth, and took quiet possession of the miserable huts and sheds left by the Third Infantry in the preceding May.

CHAPTER VI.

A ROMANTIC TRAGEDY.

As early as November, 1842, a rumour was current in Santa Fe, and along the line of the Trail, that parties of Texans had left the Republic for the purpose of attacking and robbing the caravans to the United States which were owned wholly by Mexicans. In consequence of this, several Americans were accused of being spies and acting in collusion with the Texans; many were arrested and carried to Santa Fe, but nothing could be proved against them, and the rumours of the intended purposes of the Texans died out.

Very early in May, however, of the following year, 1843, a certain Colonel Snively did organize a small force, comprising about two hundred men, which he led from Northern Texas, his home, to the line of the Trail, with the intention of attacking and robbing the Mexican caravans which were expected to cross the plains that month and in June.

When he arrived at the Arkansas River, he was there reinforced by another Texan colonel, named Warfield with another small command. Gregg says:

This officer, with about twenty men, had some time
previously attacked the village of Mora, on the Mexican
frontier, killing five men, and driving off a number
of horses. They were afterward followed by a party of
Mexicans, however, who stampeded and carried away, not only
their own horses, but those of the Texans. Being left
afoot, the latter burned their saddles, and walked to
Bent's Fort, where they were disbanded; whence Warfield
passed to Snively's camp, as before mentioned.

The Texans now advanced along the Santa Fe Trail, beyond
the sand hills south of the Arkansas, when they discovered
that a party of Mexicans had passed toward the river.
They soon came upon them, and a skirmish ensuing, eighteen
Mexicans were killed, and as many wounded, five of whom
afterward died. The Texans suffered no injury, though
the Mexicans were a hundred in number. The rest were all

taken prisoners except two, who escaped and bore the news
to General Armijo, who was encamped with a large force
at Cold Spring, one hundred and forty miles beyond.

Kit Carson figured conspicuously in this fight, or, rather, immediately afterward. His recital differs somewhat from Gregg's account, but the stories substantially agree. Kit said that in April, previously to the assault upon Armijo's caravan, he had hired out as hunter to Bent's and Colonel St. Vrain's train caravan, which was then making its annual tour eastwardly. When he arrived at the crossing of Walnut Creek, [22] he found the encampment of Captain Philip St. George Cooke, of the United States army, who had been detailed with his command to escort the caravans to the New Mexican boundary. His force consisted of four troops of dragoons. The captain informed Carson that coming on behind him from the States was a caravan belonging to a very wealthy Mexican.

It was a richly loaded train, and in order to insure its better protection while passing through that portion of the country infested by the blood-thirsty Comanches and Apaches, the majordomo in charge had hired one hundred Mexicans as a guard. The teamsters and others belonging to the caravan had heard that a large body of Texans were lying in wait for them, and intended to murder and plunder them in retaliation for the way Armijo had treated some Texan prisoners he had got in his power at Santa Fe some time before. Of course, it was the duty of the United States troops to escort this caravan to the New Mexico line, but there their duty would end, as they had no authority to cross the border. The Mexicans belonging to the caravan were afraid they would be at the mercy of the Texans after they had parted company with the soldiers, and when Kit Carson met them, they, knowing the famous trapper and mountaineer well, asked him to take a letter to Armijo, who was then governor of New Mexico, and resided in Santa Fe, for which service they would give him three hundred dollars in advance. The letter contained a statement of the fears they entertained, and requested the general to send Mexican troops at once to meet them.

Carson, who was then not blessed with much money, eagerly accepted the task, and immediately started on the trail for Bent's Fort, in company with another old mountaineer and bosom friend named Owens. In a short time they arrived at the Fort, where Owens decided not to go any further, because they were informed by the men at Bent's that the Utes had broken out, and were scattered along the Trail at the most dangerous points, and he was fearful that his life would be endangered if he attempted to make Santa Fe.

Kit, however, nothing daunted, and determined to do the duty for which he had been rewarded so munificently, started out alone on his perilous trip. Mr. Bent kindly furnished him with the best and fastest horse he had in his stables, but Kit, realizing the dangers to which he would be exposed, walked, leading his animal, ready to mount him at a moment's notice; thus keeping him in a condition that would enable

Carson to fly and make his escape if the savages tried to capture him. His knowledge of the Indian character, and wonderful alertness in moments of peril, served him well; for he reached the village of the hostile Indians without their discovering his proximity. Hiding himself in a rocky, bush-covered canyon, he stayed there until night came on, when he continued his journey in the darkness.

He took the trail to Taos, where he arrived in two or three days, and presented his letter to the alcalde, to be sent on to Santa Fe by special messenger.

He was to remain at Taos until an answer from the governor arrived, and then return with it as rapidly as possible to the train. While at Taos, he was informed that Armijo had already sent out a company of one hundred soldiers to meet the caravan, and was to follow in person, with a thousand more.

This first hundred were those attacked by Colonel Snively, as related by Gregg, who says that two survived, who carried the news of the disaster to Armijo at Cold Spring; but Carson told me that only one got away, by successfully catching, during the heat of the fight, a Texan pony already saddled, that was grazing around loose. With him he made Armijo's camp and related to the Mexican general the details of the terribly unequal battle. Armijo, upon receipt of the news, "turned tail," and retreated to Santa Fe.

Before Armijo left Santa Fe with his command, he had received the letter which Carson had brought from the caravan, and immediately sent one in reply for Carson to carry back, thinking that the old mountaineer might reach the wagons before he did. Carson, with his usual promptness, started on the Trail for the caravan, and came up with it while it was escorted by the dragoons, thus saving it from the fate that the Texans intended for it, as they dared not attempt any interference in the presence of the United States troops.

The rumour current in Santa Fe in relation to a probable raid of parties of Texans along the line of the Trail, for the purpose of attacking and robbing the caravans of the wealthy Mexican traders, was received with so little credence by the prominent citizens of the country, that several native trains left for the Missouri River without their proprietors having the slightest apprehension that they would not reach their destination, and make the return trip in safety.

Among those who had no fear of marauders was Don Antonio Jose Chavez, who, in February, 1843, left Santa Fe for Independence with an outfit consisting of a number of wagons, his private coach, several servants and other retainers. Don Antonio was a very wealthy Mexican engaged in a general mercantile business on a large scale in Albuquerque, who made all his purchases of goods in St. Louis, which was then the depot of supplies for the whole mountain region. He necessarily carried with him on these journeys a large amount of money, in silver, which was the legal currency of the country, and made but one trip yearly to replenish the stock of goods required in his extensive trade in all parts of Mexico.

Upon his arrival at Westport Landing, as Kansas City was then called, he would take the steamboat for St. Louis, leaving his coach, wagons, servants, and other appointments of his caravan behind him in the village of Westport, a few miles from the Landing.

Westport was at that time, like all steamboat towns in the era of water navigation, the harbor of as great a lot of ruffians as ever escaped the gallows. There was especially a noted gang of land pirates, the members of which had long indulged in speculations regarding the probable wealth of the Mexican Don, and how much coin he generally carried with him. They knew that it must be considerable from the quantity of goods that always came by boat with him from St. Louis.

At last a devilish plot was arranged to get hold of the rich trader's money. Nine men were concerned in the robbery, nearly all of whom were residents of the vicinity of Westport; their leader was one John McDaniel, recently from Texas, from which government he claimed to hold a captain's commission, and one of their number was a doctor. It was evidently the intention of this band to join Warfield's party on the Arkansas, and engage in a general robbery of the freight caravans of the Santa Fe Trail belonging to the Mexicans; but they had determined that Chavez should be their first victim, and in order to learn when he intended to leave Santa Fe on his next trip east, they sent their spies out on the great highway.

They did not dare attempt their contemplated robbery, and murder if necessary, in the State of Missouri, for there were too many citizens of the border who would never have permitted such a thing to go unpunished; so they knew that their only chance was to effect it in the Indian country of Kansas, where there was little or no law.

Cow Creek, which debouches into the Arkansas at Hutchinson, where the Atchison, Topeka and Santa Fe Railroad crosses the historic little stream,[23] was, like Big and Little Coon creeks, a most dangerous point in the transcontinental passage of freight caravans and overland coaches, in the days of the commerce of the prairies. It was on this purling little prairie brook that McDaniel's band lay in wait for the arrival of the ill-fated Don Antonio, whose imposing equipage came along, intending to encamp on the bank, one of the usual stopping-places on the route.

The Don was taken a few miles south of the Trail, and his baggage rifled. All of his party were immediately murdered, but the wealthy owner of the caravan was spared for a few moments in order to make a confession of where his money was concealed, after which he was shot down in cold blood, and his body thrown into a ravine.

It appears, however, that the ruffians had not completed their bloody work so effectually as they thought; for one of the Mexican's teamsters escaped, and, making his way to Leavenworth, reported the crime, and was soon on his way back to the Trail, guiding a detachment of United States troops in pursuit of the murderers.

John Hobbs, scout, trapper, and veteran plainsman, happened to be hunting buffalo on Pawnee Fork, on the ground where Larned is now situated, with a party from Bent's Fort. They were just on the point of crossing the Trail at the mouth of the Pawnee when the soldiers from Fort Leavenworth came along, and from them Hobbs and his companions first learned of the murder of Chavez on Cow Creek. As the men who were out hunting were all familiar with every foot of the region they were then in, the commanding officer of the troops induced them to accompany him in his search for the murderers.

Hobbs and his men cheerfully accepted the invitation, and in about four days met the band of cut-throats on the broad Trail, they little dreaming that the government had taken a hand in the matter. The band tried to escape by flight, but Hobbs shot the doctor's horse from under him, and a soldier killed another member of the band, when the remainder surrendered.

The money, about twelve or fifteen thousand dollars,[24] was all recovered, and the murderers taken to St. Louis, where some were hung and some imprisoned, the doctor escaping the death penalty by turning state's evidence. His sentence was incarceration in the penitentiary, from which he was pardoned after remaining there two years. Hobbs met the doctor some years after in San Francisco. He was then leading an honest life, publishing a newspaper, and begged his captor not to expose him.

The money taken from the robbers was placed in charge of Colonel Owens, a friend of the Chavez family and a leading Santa Fe trader. He continued on to the river, purchased a stock of goods, and sent back the caravan to Santa Fe in charge of Doctor Conley of Boonville, Missouri.

Arriving at his destination, the widow of the deceased Chavez employed the good doctor to sell the goods and take the sole supervision of her immense business interests, and there is a touch of romance attached to the terrible Kansas tragedy, which lies in the fact that the doctor in about two years married the rich widow, and lived very happily for about a decade, dying then on one of the large estates in New Mexico, which he had acquired by his fortunate union with the amiable Mexican lady.

CHAPTER VII.

MEXICO DECLARES WAR.

Mexico declared war against the United States in April, 1846. In the following May, Congress passed an act authorizing the President to call into the field fifty thousand volunteers, designed to operate against Mexico at three distinct points, and consisting of the Southern Wing, or the Army of Occupation, the Army of the Centre, and the Army of the West, the latter to direct its march upon the city of Santa Fe. The original plan was, however, somewhat changed, and General Kearney, who commanded the Army of the West, divided his forces into three separate commands. The first he led in person to the Pacific coast. One thousand volunteers, under command of Colonel A. W. Doniphan, were to make a descent upon the State of Chihuahua, while the remainder and greater part of the forces, under Colonel Sterling Price, were to garrison Santa Fe after its capture.

There is a pretty fiction told of the breaking out of the war between Mexico and the United States. Early in the spring of 1846, before it was known or even conjectured that a state of war would be declared to exist between this government and Mexico, a caravan of twenty-nine traders, on their way from Independence to Santa Fe, beheld, just after a storm and a little before sunset, a perfectly distinct image of the Bird of Liberty, the American eagle, on the disc of the sun. When they saw it they simultaneously and almost involuntarily exclaimed that in less than twelve months the Eagle of Liberty would spread his broad plumes over the plains of the West, and that the flag of our country would wave over the cities of New Mexico and Chihuahua. The student of the classics will remember that just before the assassination of Julius Caesar, both Brutus and Cassius, while in their places in the Roman Senate, saw chariots of fire in the sky. One story is as true, probably, as the other, though separated by centuries of time.

The Army of the West, under General Stephen W. Kearney, consisted of two batteries of artillery, commanded by Major Clark; three squadrons of the First United States Dragoons, commanded by Major Sumner; the First Regiment of Missouri Cavalry, commanded by Colonel Doniphan, and two companies of infantry, commanded by Captain Aubrey. This force marched in detached columns from Fort Leavenworth, and on the 1st of August, 1846, concentrated in camp on the Santa Fe Trail, nine miles below Bent's Fort.

Accompanying the expedition was a party of the United States topographical engineers, under command of Lieutenant W. H. Emory.[25] In writing of this expedition, so far as its march relates to the Old Santa Fe Trail, I shall quote freely from Emory's report and Doniphan's historian.[26]

The practicability of marching a large army over the waste, uncultivated, uninhabited prairie regions of the West was universally regarded as problematical, but the expedition proved completely successful. Provisions were conveyed in wagons, and beef-cattle driven along for the use of the men. These animals subsisted entirely by grazing. To secure them from straying off at night, they were driven into corrals formed of the wagons, or tethered to an iron picket-pin driven into the ground about fifteen inches. At the outset of the expedition many laughable scenes took place. Our horses were generally wild, fiery, and unused to military trappings and equipments. Amidst the fluttering of banners, the sounding of bugles, the rattling of artillery, the clattering of sabres and also of cooking utensils, some of them took fright and scampered pell-mell over the wide prairie. Rider, arms and accoutrements, saddles, saddle-bags, tin cups, and coffee-pots, were frequently left far behind in the chase. No very serious or fatal accident, however, occurred from this cause, and all was right as soon as the affrighted animals were recovered.

The Army of the West was, perhaps, composed of as fine material as any other body of troops then in the field. The volunteer corps consisted almost entirely of young men of the country.

On the 9th of July, a separate detachment of the troops arrived at the Little Arkansas, where the Santa Fe Trail crosses that stream-- now in McPherson County, Kansas. The mosquitoes, gnats, and black flies swarmed in that locality and nearly drove the men and animals frantic. While resting there, a courier came from the commands of General Kearney and Colonel Doniphan, stating that their men were in a starving condition, and asking for such provisions as could be spared. Lieutenant-Colonel Ruff of Doniphan's regiment, in command of the troops now camped on the Little Arkansas, was almost destitute himself. He had sent couriers forward to Pawnee Fork to stop a train of provisions at that point and have it wait there until he came up with his force, and he now directed the courier from Kearney to proceed to the same place and halt as many wagons loaded with supplies, as would suffice to furnish the three detachments with rations. One of the couriers, in attempting to ford the fork of the Pawnee, which was bank-full, was drowned. His body was found and given a military funeral; he was the first man lost on the expedition after it had reached the great plains, one having been drowned in the Missouri, at Fort Leavenworth, before the troops left.

The author of *Doniphan's Expedition* says:

In approaching the Arkansas, a landscape of the most
imposing and picturesque nature makes its appearance.
While the green, glossy undulations of the prairie to
the right seem to spread out in infinite succession,
like waves subsiding after a storm, and covered with

69

herds of gambolling buffalo, on the left, towering to
the height of seventy-five to a hundred feet, rise the
sun-gilt summits of the sand hills, along the base of
which winds the broad, majestic river, bespeckled with
verdant islets, thickly beset with cottonwood timber,
the sand hills resembling heaps of driven snow.

I refer to this statement to show how wonderfully the settlement of the region
has changed the physical aspect of that portion bordering the Arkansas River. Now
those sand hills are covered with verdure, and this metamorphosis has taken place
within the last thirty years; for the author of this work well remembers how the great
sand dunes used to shine in the sunlight, when he first saw them a third of a century
ago. In coming from Fort Leavenworth up the Smoky Hill route to the Santa Fe Trail,
where the former joined the latter at Pawnee Rock, the contour of the Arkansas could
be easily traced by the white sand hills referred to, long before it was reached.

On the 15th of July the combined forces formed a junction at Pawnee Fork, now
within the city limits of Larned, Kansas. The river was impassable, but General
Kearney, with the characteristic energy of his family, determined not to be delayed,
and to that end caused great trees to be cut down and their trunks thrown across the
stream, over which the army passed, carrying in their arms the sick, the baggage,
tents, and other paraphernalia; the animals being forced to swim. The empty bodies
of the wagons, fastened to their running gear, were floated across by means of ropes,
and hauled up the slippery bank by the troops. This required two whole days; and
on the morning of the 17th, not an accident having occurred, the entire column was
en route again, the infantry, as is declared in the official reports, keeping pace with
the cavalry right along. Their feet, however, became terribly blistered, and, like the
Continentals at Valley Forge, their tracks were marked with blood.

In a day or two after the command had left Pawnee Fork, while camping in a
beautiful spot on the bank of the Arkansas, an officer, Major Howard, who had been
sent forward to Santa Fe some time previously by the general to learn something of
the feeling of the people in relation to submitting to the government of the United
States, returned and reported

that the common people, or plebeians, were inclined to
favour the conditions of peace proposed by General Kearney;
viz. that if they would lay down their arms and take the
oath of allegiance to the government of the United States,
they should, to all intents and purposes, become citizens
of the same republic, receiving the protection and enjoying
the liberties guaranteed to other American citizens; but

that the patricians who held the offices and ruled the
country were hostile, and were making warlike preparations.
He added, further, that two thousand three hundred men
were already armed for the defence of the capital, and
that others were assembling at Taos.

This intelligence created quite a sensation in camp, and it was believed, and
earnestly hoped, that the entrance of the troops into Santa Fe would be desperately
opposed; such is the pugnacious character of the average American the moment he
dons the uniform of a soldier.

The army arrived at the Cimarron crossing of the Arkansas on the 20th, and
during the march of nearly thirty miles from their last camp, a herd of about four
hundred buffalo suddenly emerged from the Arkansas, and broke through the long
column. In an instant the troops charged upon the surprised animals with guns,
pistols, and even drawn sabres, and many of the huge beasts were slaughtered as they
went dashing and thundering among the excited troopers and infantrymen.

On the 29th an express from Bent's Fort brought news to General Kearney from
Santa Fe that Governor Armijo had called the chief men together to deliberate on
the best means of defending the city; that hostile preparations were rapidly going
on in all parts of New Mexico; and that the American advance would be vigorously
opposed. Some Mexican prisoners were taken near Bent's Fort, with blank letters on
their persons addressed to the general; it was supposed this piece of ingenuity was
resorted to to deceive the American residents at the fort. These men were thought
to be spies sent out from Santa Fe to get an idea of the strength of the army; so they
were shown everything in and around camp, and then allowed to depart in peace for
Santa Fe, to report what they had seen.

On the same date, the Army of the West crossed the Arkansas and camped on
Mexican soil about eight miles below Bent's Fort, and now the utmost vigilance was
exercised; for the troops had not only to keep a sharp lookout for the Mexicans, but
for the wily Comanches, in whose country their camp was located. Strong picket and
camp guards were posted, and the animals turned loose to graze, guarded by a large
force. Notwithstanding the care taken to confine them within certain limits, a pack
of wolves rushed through the herd, and in an instant it was stampeded, and there
ensued a scene of the wildest confusion. More than a thousand horses were dashing
madly over the prairie, their rage and fright increased at every jump by the lariats and
picket-pins which they had pulled up, and which lashed them like so many whips.
After desperate exertions by the troops, the majority were recovered from thirty to
fifty miles distant; nearly a hundred, however, were absolutely lost and never seen
again.

At this camp the troops were visited by the war chief of the Arapahoes, who manifested great surprise at the big guns, and declared that the Mexicans would not stand a moment before such terrible instruments of death, but would escape to the mountains with the utmost despatch.

On the 1st of August a new camp near Bent's Fort was established, from whence twenty men under Lieutenant de Courcy, with orders to proceed through the mountains to the valley of Taos, to learn something of the disposition and intentions of the people, and to rejoin General Kearney on the road to Santa Fe. Lieutenant de Courcy, in his official itinerary, relates the following anecdote:

We took three pack-mules laden with provisions, and as
we did not expect to be long absent, the men took no extra
clothing. Three days after we left the column our mules
fell down, and neither gentle means nor the points of our
sabres had the least effect in inducing them to rise.
Their term of service with Uncle Sam was out. "What's to
be done?" said the sergeant. "Dismount!" said I.
"Off with your shirts and drawers, men! tie up the sleeves
and legs, and each man bag one-twentieth part of the flour!"
Having done this, the bacon was distributed to the men also,
and tied to the cruppers of their saddles. Thus loaded,
we pushed on, without the slightest fear of our provision
train being cut off.

The march upon Santa Fe was resumed on the 2d of August.
As we passed Bent's Fort the American flag was raised,
in compliment to our troops, and, like our own, streamed
most animatingly in the gale that swept from the desert,
while the tops of the houses were crowded with Mexican girls
and Indian squaws, intently beholding the American army.

On the 15th of the month, the army neared Las Vegas; when two spies who had been sent on in advance to see how matters stood returned and reported that two thousand Mexicans were camped at the pass a few miles beyond the village, where they intended to offer battle.

Upon receipt of this news, the general immediately formed a line of battle. The United States dragoons with the St. Louis mounted volunteers were stationed in front, Major Clark with the battalion of volunteer light artillery in the centre, and

Colonel Doniphan's regiment in the rear. The companies of volunteer infantry were deployed on each side of the line of march as flankers. The supply trains were next in order, with Captain Walton's mounted company as rear guard. There was also a strong advance guard. The cartridges were hastily distributed; the cannon swabbed and rigged; the port-fires burning, and every rifle loaded.

In passing through the streets of the curious-looking village of Las Vegas, the army was halted, and from the roof of a large house General Kearney administered to the chief officers of the place the oath of allegiance to the United States, using the sacred cross instead of the Bible. This act completed, on marched the exultant troops toward the canyon where it had been promised them that they should meet the enemy.

On the night of the 16th, while encamped on the Pecos River, near the village of San Jose, the pickets captured a son of the Mexican General Salezar, who was acting the role of a spy, and two other soldiers of the Mexican army. Salezar was kept a close prisoner; but the two privates were by order of General Kearney escorted through the camp and shown the cannon, after which they were allowed to depart, so that they might tell what they had seen. It was learned afterward that they represented the American army as composed of five thousand troops, and possessing so many cannons that they were not able to count them.

When Armijo was certain that the Army of the West was really approaching Santa Fe, he assembled seven thousand troops, part of them well armed, and the remainder indifferently so. The Mexican general had written a note to General Kearney the day before the capture of the spies, saying that he would meet him on the following day.

General Kearney, at this, hastened on, arriving at the mouth of the Apache canyon at noon, with his whole force ready and anxious to try the mettle of the Mexicans in battle. Emory in his *Reconnoissance* says:

The sun shone with dazzling brightness; the guidons and
colours of each squadron, regiment, and battalion were
for the first time unfurled. The drooping horses seemed
to take courage from the gay array. The trumpeters
sounded "to horse" with spirit, and the hills multiplied
and re-echoed the call. All wore the aspect of a gala day.
About the middle of the day's march the two Pueblo Indians,
previously sent to sound the chief men of that formidable
tribe, were seen in the distance, at full speed, with arms
and legs both thumping the sides of their mules at every

stride. Something was now surely in the wind. The smaller and foremost of the two dashed up to the general, his face radiant with joy, and exclaimed:

"They are in the canyon, my brave; pluck up your courage and push them out." As soon as his extravagant delight at the prospect of a fight, and the pleasure of communicating the news, had subsided, he gave a pretty accurate idea of Armijo's force and position.

Shortly afterwards a rumour reached the camp that the two thousand Mexicans assembled in the canyon to oppose us, have quarrelled among themselves; and that Armijo, taking advantage of the dissensions, has fled with his dragoons and artillery to the south. It is well known that he has been averse to a battle, but some of his people threatened his life if he refused to fight. He had been, for some days, more in fear of his own people than of the American army, having seen what they are blind to--the hopelessness of resistance.

As we approached the ancient town of Pecos, a large fat fellow, mounted on a mule, came toward us at full speed, and, extending his hand to the general, congratulated him on the arrival of himself and army. He said with a roar of laughter, "Armijo and his troops have gone to h---ll, and the canyon is all clear."

On reaching the canyon, it was found to be true that the Mexican troops had dispersed and fled to the mountains, just as the old Arapahoe chief had said they would. There, however, they commenced to fortify, by chopping away the timber so that their artillery could play to better advantage upon the American lines, and by throwing up temporary breastworks. It was ascertained afterward, on undoubted authority, that Armijo had an army of nearly seven thousand Mexicans, with six pieces of artillery, and the advantage of ground, yet he allowed General Kearney, with a force of less than two thousand, to march through the almost impregnable gorge, and on to the capital of the Province, without any attempt to oppose him.

Thus was New Mexico conquered with but little loss relatively. For the further details of the movements of the Army of the West, the reader is referred to general history, as this book, necessarily, treats only of that portion of its march and the incidents connected with it while travelling the Santa Fe Trail.

CHAPTER VIII.

THE VALLEY OF TAOS.

The principal settlement in New Mexico, immediately after it was reconquered from the Indians by the Spaniards, was, of course, Santa Fe, and ranking second to it, that of the beautiful Valle de Taos, which derived its name from the Taosa Indians, a few of whose direct descendants are still occupying a portion of the region. As the pioneers in the trade with Santa Fe made their first journeys to the capital of the Province by the circuitous route of the Taos valley, and the initial consignments of goods from the Missouri were disposed of in the little villages scattered along the road, the story of the Trail would be deficient in its integrity were the thrilling historical facts connected with the romantic region omitted.

The reader will find on all maps, from the earliest published to the latest issued by the local railroads, a town with the name of Taos, which never had an existence. Fernandez de Taos is the chief city, which has been known so long by the title of the valley that perhaps the misnomer is excusable after many years' use.

Fernandez, or Taos as it is called, was once famous for its distilleries of whiskey, made out of the native wheat, a raw, fiery spirit, always known in the days of the Santa Fe trade as "Taos lightning," which was the most profitable article of barter with the Indians, who exchanged their buffalo robes and other valuable furs for a supply of it, at a tremendous sacrifice.

According to the statement of Gregg, the first white settler of the fertile and picturesque valley was a Spaniard named Pando, who established himself there about 1745. This primitive pioneer of the northern part of the Province was constantly exposed to the raids of the powerful Comanches, but succeeded in creating a temporary friendship with the tribe by promising his daughter, then a young and beautiful infant, to the chief in marriage when she arrived at a suitable age. At the time for the ratification of her father's covenant with the Indians, however, the maiden stubbornly refused to fulfil her part. The savages, enraged at the broken faith of the Spaniard, immediately swept down upon the little settlement and murdered everybody there except the betrothed girl, whom they carried off into captivity. She was forced to live with the chief as his wife, but he soon became tired of her and traded her for another woman with the Pawnees, who, in turn, sold her to a Frenchman, a resident of St. Louis. It is said that some of the most respectable families of that city are descended from her, and fifty years ago there were many people living who remembered the old lady, and her pathetic story of trials and sufferings when with the Indians.

The most tragic event in the history of the valley was the massacre of the provisional governor of the Territory of New Mexico, with a number of other Americans, shortly after its occupation by the United States.

Upon General Kearney's taking possession of Santa Fe, acting under the authority of the President, he established a civil government and put it into operation. Charles Bent was appointed governor, and the other offices filled by Americans and Mexicans who were rigidly loyal to the political change. At this time the command of the troops devolved upon Colonel Sterling Price, Colonel Doniphan, who ranked him, having departed from Santa Fe on an expedition against the Navajoes. Notwithstanding the apparent submission of the natives of New Mexico, there were many malcontents among them and the Pueblo Indians, and early in December, some of the leaders, dissatisfied with the change in the order of things, held secret meetings and formulated plots to overthrow the existing government.

Midnight of the 24th of December was the time appointed for the commencement of their revolutionary work, which was to be simultaneous all over the country. The profoundest secrecy was to be preserved, and the most influential men, whose ambition induced them to seek preferment, were alone to be made acquainted with the plot. No woman was to be privy to it, lest it should be divulged. The sound of the church bell was to be the signal, and at midnight all were to enter the Plaza at the same moment, seize the pieces of artillery, and point them into the streets.

The time chosen for the assault was Christmas-eve, when the soldiers and garrison would be indulging in wine and feasting, and scattered about through the city at the fandangoes, not having their arms in their hands. All the Americans, without distinction, throughout the State, and such New Mexicans as had favoured the American government and accepted office by appointment of General Kearney, were to be massacred or driven from the country, and the conspirators were to seize upon and occupy the government.

The conspiracy was detected in the following manner: a mulatto girl, residing in Santa Fe, had married one of the conspirators, and had by degrees obtained a knowledge of their movements and secret meetings. To prevent the effusion of blood, which would inevitably be the result of a revolution, she communicated to Colonel Price all the facts of which she was in possession, and warned him to use the utmost vigilance. The rebellion was immediately suppressed, but the restless and unsatisfied ambition of the leaders of the conspiracy did not long permit them to remain inactive. A second and still more dangerous conspiracy was formed. The most powerful and influential men in the State favoured the design, and even the officers of State and the priests gave their aid and counsel. The people everywhere, in the towns, villages, and settlements, were exhorted to arm and equip themselves; to strike for their faith, their religion, and their altars; and drive the "heretics," the "unjust invaders of the country," from their soil, and with fire and sword pursue them to annihilation. On the 18th of January this rebellion broke out in every part of the State simultaneously.

On the 14th of January, Governor Bent, believing the conspiracy completely crushed, with an escort of five persons--among whom were the sheriff and circuit attorney--had left Santa Fe to visit his family, who resided at Fernandez.

On the 19th, he was early roused from sleep by the populace, who, with the aid of the Pueblos of Taos, were collected in front of his dwelling striving to gain admittance. While they were effecting an entrance, he, with an axe, cut through an adobe wall into another house; and the Mexican wife of the occupant, a clever though shiftless Canadian, hearing him, with all her strength rendered him assistance. He retreated to a room, but, seeing no way of escaping from the infuriated assailants, who fired upon him from a window, he spoke to his weeping wife and trembling children, and, taking paper from his pocket, endeavoured to write; but fast losing strength, he commended them to God and his brothers and fell, pierced by a ball from a Pueblo. Then rushing in and tearing off his gray-haired scalp, the Indians bore it away in triumph.

The circuit attorney, T. W. Leal, was scalped alive and dragged through the streets, his relentless persecutors pricking him with lances. After hours of suffering, they threw him aside in the inclement weather, he imploring them earnestly to kill him to end his misery. A compassionate Mexican at last closed the tragic scene by shooting him. Stephen Lee, brother to the general, was killed on his own housetop. Narcisse Beaubien, son of the presiding judge of the district, hid in an outhouse with his Indian slave, at the commencement of the massacre, under a straw-covered trough. The insurgents on the search, thinking that they had escaped, were leaving, but a woman servant of the family, going to the housetop, called to them, "Kill the young ones, and they will never be men to trouble us." They swarmed back and, by cruelly putting to death and scalping him and his slave, added two more to the list of unfortunate victims.

The Pueblos and Mexicans, after their cruelties at Fernandez de Taos, attacked and destroyed Turley's Ranch on the Arroyo Hondo[27] twelve miles from Fernandez, or Taos. Arroyo Hondo runs along the base of a ridge of a mountain of moderate elevation, which divides the valley of Taos from that of the Rio Colorado, or Red River, both flowing into the Del Norte. The trail from one place to the other passes over the mountain, which is covered with pine, cedar, and a species of dwarf oak; and numerous little streams run through the many canyons.

On the bank of one of the creeks was a mill and distillery belonging to an American named Turley, who did a thriving business. He possessed herds of goats, and hogs innumerable; his barns were filled with grain, his mill with flour, and his cellars with whiskey. He had a Mexican wife and several children, and he bore the reputation of being one of the most generous and kind-hearted of men. In times of scarcity, no one ever sought his aid to be turned away empty-handed; his granaries were always open to the hungry, and his purse to the poor.

When on their road to Turley's, the Pueblos murdered two men, named Harwood and Markhead. Markhead was one of the most successful trappers and daring men among the old mountaineers. They were on their way to Taos with their pack-animals laden with furs, when the savages, meeting them, after stripping them of their goods, and securing their arms by treachery, made them mount their mules under pretence of conducting them to Taos, where they were to be given up to the leaders of the insurrection. They had hardly proceeded a mile when a Mexican rode up behind Harwood and discharged his gun into his back; he called out to Markhead that he was murdered, and fell to the ground dead.

Markhead, seeing that his own fate was sealed, made no struggle, and was likewise shot in the back with several bullets. Both men were then stripped naked, scalped, and horribly mutilated; their bodies thrown into the brush to be devoured by the wolves.

These trappers were remarkable men; Markhead, particularly, was celebrated in the mountains for his courage, reckless daring, and many almost miraculous escapes when in the very hands of the Indians. When some years previously he had accompanied Sir William Drummond Stewart on one of his expeditions across the Rockies, it happened that a half-breed Indian employed by Sir William absconded one night with some animals, which circumstance annoyed the nobleman so much, as it disturbed all his plans, that he hastily offered, never dreaming that he would be taken up, to give five hundred dollars for the scalp of the thief. The very next evening Markhead rode into camp with the hair of the luckless horse-thief dangling at the muzzle of his rifle.

The wild crowd of rebels rode on to Turley's mill. Turley had been warned of the impending uprising, but had treated the report with indifference, until one morning a man in his employ, who had been despatched to Santa Fe with several mule-loads of whiskey a few days before, made his appearance at the gate on horseback, and hastily informing the inmates of the mill that the New Mexicans had risen and massacred Governor Bent and other Americans, galloped off. Even then Turley felt assured that he would not be molested; but at the solicitation of his men, he agreed to close the gate of the yard around which were the buildings of the mill and distillery, and make preparations for defence.

A few hours afterward a large crowd of Mexicans and Pueblo Indians made their appearance, all armed with guns and bows and arrows, and, advancing with a white flag, summoned Turley to surrender his house and the Americans in it, guaranteeing that his own life should be saved, but that every other American in the valley must be destroyed; that the governor and all the Americans at Fernandez had been killed, and that not one was to be left alive in all New Mexico.

To this summons Turley answered that he would never surrender his house nor his men, and that if they wanted it or them, they must take them.

The enemy then drew off, and, after a short consultation, commenced the attack. The first day they numbered about five hundred, but were hourly reinforced by the arrival of parties of Indians from the more distant Pueblos, and New Mexicans from Fernandez, La Canada, and other places.

The building lay at the foot of a gradual slope in the sierra, which was covered with cedar bushes. In front ran the stream of the Arroyo Hondo, about twenty yards from one side of the square, and the other side was broken ground which rose abruptly and formed the bank of the ravine. In the rear and behind the still-house was some garden ground enclosed by a small fence, into which a small wicket-gate opened from the corral.

As soon as the attack was determined upon, the assailants scattered and concealed themselves under cover of the rocks and bushes which surrounded the house. From these they kept up an incessant fire upon every exposed portion of the building where they saw preparations for defence.

The Americans, on their part, were not idle; not a man but was an old mountaineer, and each had his trusty rifle, with a good store of ammunition. Whenever one of the besiegers exposed a hand's-breadth of his person, a ball from an unerring barrel whistled. The windows had been blockaded, loopholes having been left, and through these a lively fire was maintained. Already several of the enemy had bitten the dust, and parties were seen bearing off the wounded up the banks of the Canada. Darkness came on, and during the night a continual fire was kept up on the mill, whilst its defenders, reserving their ammunition, kept their posts with stern and silent determination. The night was spent in casting balls, cutting patches, and completing the defences of the building. In the morning the fight was renewed, and it was found that the Mexicans had effected a lodgment in a part of the stables, which were separated from the other portions of the building by an open space of a few feet. The assailants, during the night, had sought to break down the wall, and thus enter the main building, but the strength of the adobe and logs of which it was composed resisted effectually all their attempts.

Those in the stable seemed anxious to regain the outside, for their position was unavailable as a means of annoyance to the besieged, and several had darted across the narrow space which divided it from the other part of the building, which slightly projected, and behind which they were out of the line of fire. As soon, however, as the attention of the defenders was called to this point, the first man who attempted to cross, who happened to be a Pueblo chief, was dropped on the instant, and fell dead in the centre of the intervening space. It appeared to be an object to recover the body, for an Indian immediately dashed out to the fallen chief, and attempted to drag him within the shelter of the wall. The rifle which covered the spot again poured forth its deadly contents, and the Indian, springing into the air, fell over the body of his chief. Another and another met with a similar fate, and at last three rushed to the spot, and, seizing the body by the legs and head, had already lifted it from the ground, when three puffs of smoke blew from the barricaded windows, followed by the sharp cracks of as many rifles, and the three daring Indians were added to the pile of corpses which now covered the body of the dead chief.

As yet the besieged had met with no casualties; but after the fall of the seven Indians, the whole body of the assailants, with a shout of rage, poured in a rattling volley, and two of the defenders fell mortally wounded. One, shot through the loins, suffered great agony, and was removed to the still-house, where he was laid on a large pile of grain, as being the softest bed that could be found.

In the middle of the day the attack was renewed more fiercely than before. The little garrison bravely stood to the defence of the mill, never throwing away a shot, but firing coolly, and only when a fair mark was presented to their unerring aim. Their ammunition, however, was fast failing, and to add to the danger of their situation, the enemy set fire to the mill, which blazed fiercely, and threatened destruction to the whole building. Twice they succeeded in overcoming the flames, and, while they were thus occupied, the Mexicans and Indians charged into the corral, which was full of hogs and sheep, and vented their cowardly rage upon the animals, spearing and shooting all that came in their way. No sooner were the flames extinguished in one place than they broke out more fiercely in another; and as a successful defence was perfectly hopeless, and the numbers of the assailants increased every moment, a council of war was held by the survivors of the little garrison, when it was determined, as soon as night approached, that every one should attempt to escape as best he could.

Just at dusk a man named John Albert and another ran to the wicket-gate which opened into a kind of enclosed space, in which were a number of armed Mexicans. They both rushed out at the same moment, discharging their rifles full in the face of the crowd. Albert, in the confusion, threw himself under the fence, whence he saw his companion shot down immediately, and heard his cries for mercy as the cowards pierced him with knives and lances. He lay without motion under the fence, and as soon as it was quite dark he crept over the logs and ran up the mountain, travelled by day and night, and, scarcely stopping or resting, reached the Greenhorn, almost dead with hunger and fatigue. Turley himself succeeded in escaping from the mill and in reaching the mountain unseen. Here he met a Mexican mounted on a horse, who had been a most intimate friend of his for many years. To this man Turley offered his watch for the use of the horse, which was ten times more than it was worth, but was refused. The inhuman wretch, however, affected pity and consideration for the fugitive, and advised him to go to a certain place, where he would bring or send him assistance; but on reaching the mill, which was a mass of fire, he immediately informed the Mexicans of Turley's place of concealment, whither a large party instantly proceeded and shot him to death.

Two others escaped and reached Santa Fe in safety. The mill and Turley's house were sacked and gutted, and all his hard-earned savings, which were concealed in gold about the house, were discovered, and, of course, seized upon by the victorious Mexicans.

The following account is taken from Governor Prince's chapter on the fight at Taos, in his excellent and authentic *History of New Mexico*:--

The startling news of the assassination of the governor was swiftly carried to Santa Fe, and reached Colonel Price the next day. Simultaneously, letters were discovered calling on the people of the Rio Abajo to secure Albuquerque and march northward to aid the other insurgents; and news speedily followed that a united Mexican and Pueblo force of large magnitude was marching down the Rio Grande valley toward the capital, flushed with the success of the revolt at Taos. Very few troops were in Santa Fe; in fact, the number remaining in the whole territory was very small, and these were scattered at Albuquerque, Las Vegas, and other distant points. At the first-named town were Major Edmonson and Captain Burgwin; the former in command of the town, and the latter with a company of the First Dragoons.

Colonel Price lost no time in taking such measures as his limited resources permitted. Edmonson was directed to come immediately to Santa Fe to take command of the capital; and Burgwin to follow Price as fast as possible to the scene of hostilities. The colonel himself collected the few troops at Santa Fe, which were all on foot, but fortunately included the little battalion which under Captain Aubrey had made such extraordinary marches on the journey across the plains as to almost outwalk the cavalry. With these was a volunteer company formed of nearly all of the American inhabitants of the city, under the command of Colonel Ceran

St. Vrain, who happened to be in Santa Fe, together with
Judge Beaubien, at the time of the rising at Taos.
With this little force, amounting in all to three hundred
and ten men, Colonel Price started to march to Taos, or at
all events to meet the army which was coming toward the
capital from the north and which grew as it marched by
constant accessions from the surrounding country.
The city of Santa Fe was left in charge of a garrison under
Lieutenant-Colonel Willock. While the force was small
and the volunteers without experience in regular warfare,
yet all were nerved to desperation by the belief, since
the Taos murders, that the only alternative was victory
or annihilation.

The expedition set out on January 23d, and the next day
the Mexican army, under command of General Montoya as
commander-in-chief, aided by Generals Tafoya and Chavez,
was found occupying the heights commanding the road near
La Canada (Santa Cruz), with detachments in some strong
adobe houses near the river banks. The advance had been
seen shortly before at the rocky pass, on the road from
Pojuaque; and near there and before reaching the river, the
San Juan Pueblo Indians, who had joined the revolutionists
reluctantly and under a kind of compulsion, surrendered and
were disarmed by removing the locks from their guns.
On arriving at the Canada, Price ordered his howitzers to
the front and opened fire; and after a sharp cannonade,
directed an assault on the nearest houses by Aubrey's
battalion. Meanwhile an attempt by a Mexican detachment
to cut off the American baggage-wagons, which had not yet
come up, was frustrated by the activity of St. Vrain's
volunteers. A charge all along the line was then ordered
and handsomely executed; the houses, which, being of adobe,
had been practically so many ready-made forts, were
successively carried, and St. Vrain started in advance to
gain the Mexican rear. Seeing this manoeuvre, and fearing
its effects, the Mexicans retreated, leaving thirty-six

dead on the field. Among those killed was General Tafoya, who bravely remained on the field after the remainder had abandoned it, and was shot.

Colonel Price pressed on up the river as fast as possible, passing San Juan, and at Los Luceros, on the 28th, his little army was rejoiced at the arrival of reinforcements, consisting of a mounted company of cavalry, Captain Burgwin's company, which had been pushed up by forced marches on foot from Albuquerque, and a six-pounder brought by Lieutenant Wilson. Thus enlarged, the American force consisted of four hundred and eighty men, and continued its advance up the valley to La Joya, which was as far as the river road at that time extended. Meanwhile the Mexicans had established themselves in a narrow pass near Embudo, where the forest was dense, and the road impracticable for wagons or cannon, the troops occupying the sides of the mountains on both sides of the canyon. Burgwin was sent with three companies to dislodge them and open a passage--no easy task. But St. Vrain's company took the west slope, and another the right, while Burgwin himself marched through the gorge between. The sharp-shooting of these troops did such terrible execution that the pass was soon cleared, though not without the display of great heroism, and some loss; and the Americans entered Embudo without further opposition. The difficulties of this campaign were greatly increased by the severity of the weather, the mountains being thickly covered with snow, and the cold so intense that a number of men were frost-bitten and disabled. The next day Burgwin reached Las Trampas, where Price arrived with the remainder of the American army on the last day of January, and all together they marched into Chamisal.

Notwithstanding the cold and snow they pressed on over the mountain, and on the 3d of February reached the town of Fernandez de Taos, only to find that the Mexican and Pueblo force had fortified itself in the celebrated Pueblo of Taos, about three miles distant. That force had diminished considerably during the retreat from La Canada, many of the Mexicans returning to their homes, and its greater part now consisting of Pueblo Indians. The American troops were worn out with fatigue and exposure, and in most urgent need of rest; but their intrepid commander, desiring to give his opponents no more time to strengthen their works, and full of zeal and energy, if not of prudence, determined to commence an immediate attack.

The two great buildings at this Pueblo, certainly the most interesting and extraordinary inhabited structures in America, are well known from descriptions and engravings. They are five stories high and irregularly pyramidal in shape, each story being smaller than the one below, in order to allow ingress to the outer rooms of each tier from the roofs. Before the advent of artillery these buildings were practically impregnable, as, when the exterior ladders were drawn up, there were no means of ingress, the side walls being solid without openings, and of immense thickness. Between these great buildings, each of which can accommodate a multitude of men, runs the clear water of the Taos Creek; and to the west of the northerly building stood the old church, with walls of adobe from three to seven and a half feet in thickness. Outside of all, and having its northwest corner just beyond the church, ran an adobe wall, built for protection against hostile Indians and which now answered for an outer earthwork. The church was turned into a fortification, and was the point where the insurgents concentrated their strength; and against this Colonel Price directed his principal attack. The six-pounder and the howitzer were brought into position without delay, under the command of Lieutenant Dyer, then a young graduate of West Point, and since then chief of ordnance of the United States army, and opened a fire on the thick adobe walls. But cannon-balls made little impression on the massive banks of earth, in which they embedded themselves

without doing damage; and after a fire of two hours,
the battery was withdrawn, and the troops allowed to return
to the town of Taos for their much-needed rest.

Early the next morning, the troops, now refreshed and ready
for the combat, advanced again to the Pueblo, but found
those within equally prepared. The story of the attack and
capture of this place is so interesting, both on account
of the meeting here of old and new systems of warfare--of
modern artillery with an aboriginal stronghold--and because
the precise localities can be distinguished by the modern
tourist from the description, that it seems best to insert
the official report as presented by Colonel Price.
Nothing could show more plainly how superior strong
earthworks are to many more ambitious structures of defence,
or more forcibly display the courage and heroism of those
who took part in the battle, or the signal bravery of the
accomplished Captain Burgwin which led to his untimely death.
Colonel Price writes:

"Posting the dragoons under Captain Burgwin about two
hundred and sixty yards from the western flank of the church,
I ordered the mounted men under Captains St. Vrain and Slack
to a position on the opposite side of the town, whence they
could discover and intercept any fugitives who might attempt
to escape toward the mountains, or in the direction of
San Fernando. The residue of the troops took ground about
three hundred yards from the north wall. Here, too,
Lieutenant Dyer established himself with the six-pounder
and two howitzers, while Lieutenant Hassendaubel, of Major
Clark's battalion, light artillery, remained with Captain
Burgwin, in command of two howitzers. By this arrangement
a cross-fire was obtained, sweeping the front and eastern
flank of the church. All these arrangements being made,
the batteries opened upon the town at nine o'clock A.M.
At eleven o'clock, finding it impossible to breach the
walls of the church with the six-pounder and howitzers,

I determined to storm the building. At a signal, Captain
Burgwin, at the head of his own company and that of Captain
McMillin, charged the western flank of the church, while
Captain Aubrey, infantry battalion, and Captain Barber and
Lieutenant Boon, Second Missouri Mounted Volunteers, charged
the northern wall. As soon as the troops above mentioned
had established themselves under the western wall of the
church, axes were used in the attempt to breach it, and a
temporary ladder having been made, the roof was fired.
About this time, Captain Burgwin, at the head of a small
party, left the cover afforded by the flank of the church,
and penetrating into the corral in front of that building,
endeavoured to force the door. In this exposed situation,
Captain Burgwin received a severe wound, which deprived me
of his valuable services, and of which he died on the
7th instant. Lieutenants McIlvaine, First United States
Dragoons, and Royall and Lackland, Second Regiment
Volunteers, accompanied Captain Burgwin into the corral,
but the attempt on the church door proved fruitless, and
they were compelled to retire behind the wall. In the
meantime, small holes had been cut in the western wall, and
shells were thrown in by hand, doing good execution.
The six-pounder was now brought around by Lieutenant Wilson,
who, at the distance of two hundred yards, poured a heavy
fire of grape into the town. The enemy, during all of
this time, kept up a destructive fire upon our troops.
About half-past three o'clock, the six-pounder was run up
within sixty yards of the church, and after ten rounds,
one of the holes which had been cut with the axes was
widened into a practicable breach. The storming party,
among whom were Lieutenant Dyer, of the ordnance, and
Lieutenant Wilson and Taylor, First Dragoons, entered and
took possession of the church without opposition.
The interior was filled with dense smoke, but for which
circumstance our storming party would have suffered great
loss. A few of the enemy were seen in the gallery,
where an open door admitted the air, but they retired

without firing a gun. The troops left to support the
battery on the north side were now ordered to charge on
that side.

"The enemy then abandoned the western part of the town.
Many took refuge in the large houses on the east, while
others endeavoured to escape toward the mountains.
These latter were pursued by the mounted men under Captains
Slack and St. Vrain, who killed fifty-one of them, only two
or three men escaping. It was now night, and our troops
were quietly quartered in the house which the enemy had
abandoned. On the next morning the enemy sued for peace,
and thinking the severe loss they had sustained would prove
a salutary lesson, I granted their supplication, on the
condition that they should deliver up to me Tomas, one of
their principal men, who had instigated and been actively
engaged in the murder of Governor Bent and others.
The number of the enemy at the battle of Pueblo de Taos
was between six and seven hundred, and of these one hundred
and fifty were killed, wounded not known. Our own loss was
seven killed and forty-five wounded; many of the wounded
have since died."

The capture of the Taos Pueblo practically ended the main
attempt to expel the Americans from the Territory.
Governor Montoya, who was a very influential man in the
conspiracy and styled himself the "Santa Ana of the North,"
was tried by court-martial, convicted, and executed on
February 7th, in the presence of the army. Fourteen others
were tried for participating in the murder of Governor Bent
and the others who were killed on the 19th of January, and
were convicted and executed. Thus, fifteen in all were
hung, being an equal number to those murdered at Taos, the
Arroyo Hondo, and Rio Colorado. Of these, eight were
Mexicans and seven were Pueblo Indians. Several more were
sentenced to be hung for treason, but the President very
properly pardoned them, on the ground that treason against

the United States was not a crime of which a Mexican
citizen could be found guilty, while his country was
actually at war with the United States.

There are several thrilling, as well as laughable, incidents connected with
the Taos massacre, and the succeeding trial of the insurrectionists; in regard to
which I shall quote freely from *Wah-to-yah*, whose author, Mr. Lewis H. Garrard,
accompanied Colonel St. Vrain across the plains in 1846, and was present at the trial
and execution of the convicted participants.

One Fitzgerald, who was a private in Captain Burgwin's company of Dragoons,
in the fight at the Pueblo de Taos, killed three Mexicans with his own hand, and
performed heroic work with the bombs that were thrown into that strong Indian
fortress. He was a man of good feeling, but his brother having been killed, or rather
murdered by Salazar, while a prisoner in the Texan expedition against Santa Fe, he
swore vengeance, and entered the service with the hope of accomplishing it. The day
following the fight at the Pueblo, he walked up to the alcalde, and deliberately shot
him down. For this act he was confined to await a trial for murder.

One raw night, complaining of cold to his guard, wood was brought, which he
piled up in the middle of the room. Then mounting that, and succeeding in breaking
through the roof, he noiselessly crept to the eaves, below which a sentinel, wrapped
in a heavy cloak, paced to and fro, to prevent his escape. He watched until the
guard's back was turned, then swung himself from the wall, and with as much ease
as possible, walked to a mess-fire, where his friends in waiting supplied him with a
pistol and clothing. When day broke, the town of Fernandez lay far beneath him in
the valley, and two days after he was safe in our camp.

Many a hand-to-hand encounter ensued during the fight at Taos, one of which
was by Colonel Ceran St. Vrain, whom I knew intimately; a grand old gentleman,
now sleeping peacefully in the quaint little graveyard at Mora, New Mexico, where
he resided for many years. The gallant colonel, while riding along, noticed an
Indian with whom he was well acquainted lying stretched out on the ground as if
dead. Confident that this particular red devil had been especially prominent in the
hellish acts of the massacre, the colonel dismounted from his pony to satisfy himself
whether the savage was really dead or only shamming. He was far from being a
corpse, for the colonel had scarcely reached the spot, when the Indian jumped to his
feet and attempted to run a long, steel-pointed lance through the officer's shoulder.
Colonel St. Vrain was a large, powerfully built man; so was the Indian, I have been
told. As each of the struggling combatants endeavoured to get the better of the other,
with the savage having a little the advantage, perhaps, it appears that "Uncle Dick"
Wooton, who was in the chase after the rebels, happened to arrive on the scene, and
hitting the Indian a terrific blow on the head with his axe, settled the question as to
his being a corpse.

Court for the trial of the insurrectionists assembled at nine o'clock. On entering the room, Judges Beaubien and Houghton were occupying their official positions. After many dry preliminaries, six prisoners were brought in--ill-favoured, half-scared, sullen fellows; and the jury of Mexicans and Americans having been empanelled, the trial commenced. It certainly did appear to be a great assumption on the part of the Americans to conquer a country, and then arraign the revolting inhabitants for treason. American judges sat on the bench. New Mexicans and Americans filled the jury-box, and American soldiery guarded the halls. It was a strange mixture of violence and justice-- a middle ground between the martial and common law.

After an absence of a few minutes, the jury returned with a verdict of "guilty in the first degree"--five for murder, one for treason. Treason, indeed! What did the poor devil know about his new allegiance? But so it was; and as the jail was overstocked with others awaiting trial, it was deemed expedient to hasten the execution, and the culprits were sentenced to be hung on the following Friday--hangman's day.

Court was daily in session; five more Indians and four Mexicans were sentenced to be hung on the 30th of April. In the court room, on the occasion of the trial of these nine prisoners, were Senora Bent the late governor's wife, and Senora Boggs, giving their evidence in regard to the massacre, of which they were eye-witnesses. Mrs. Bent was quite handsome; a few years previously she must have been a beautiful woman. The wife of the renowned Kit Carson also was in attendance. Her style of beauty was of the haughty, heart-breaking kind--such as would lead a man, with a glance of the eye, to risk his life for one smile.

The court room was a small, oblong apartment, dimly lighted by two narrow windows; a thin railing keeping the bystanders from contact with the functionaries. The prisoners faced the judges, and the three witnesses--Senoras Bent, Boggs, and Carson--were close to them on a bench by the wall. When Mrs. Bent gave her testimony, the eyes of the culprits were fixed sternly upon her; when she pointed out the Indian who had killed the governor, not a muscle of the chief's face twitched or betrayed agitation, though he was aware her evidence settled his death warrant; he sat with lips gently closed, eyes earnestly fixed on her, without a show of malice or hatred--a spectacle of Indian fortitude, and of the severe mastery to which the emotions can be subjected.

Among the jurors was a trapper named Baptiste Brown, a Frenchman, as were the majority of the trappers in the early days of the border. He was an exceptionally kind-hearted man when he first came to the mountains, and seriously inclined to regard the Indians with that mistaken sentimentality characterizing the average New England philanthropist, who has never seen the untutored savage on his native heath. His ideas, however, underwent a marked change as the years rolled on and he became more familiar with the attributes of the noble red man. He was with Kit Carson in the Blackfeet country many years before the Taos massacre, when his convictions were thus modified, and it was from the famous frontiersman himself I learned the story of Baptiste's conversion.

It was late one night in their camp on one of the many creeks in the Blackfoot region, where they had been established for several weeks, and Baptiste was on duty, guarding their meat and furs from the incursions of a too inquisitive grizzly that had been prowling around, and the impertinent investigations of the wolves. His attention was attracted to something high up in a neighbouring tree, that seemed restless, changing its position constantly like an animal of prey. The Frenchman drew a bead upon it, and there came tumbling down at his feet a dead savage, with his war-paint and other Indian paraphernalia adorning his body. Baptiste was terribly hurt over the circumstance of having killed an Indian, and it grieved him for a long time. One day, a month after the incident, he was riding alone far away from our party, and out of sound of their rifles as well, when a band of Blackfeet discovered him and started for his scalp. He had no possible chance for escape except by the endurance of his horse; so a race for life began. He experienced no trouble in keeping out of the way of their arrows--the Indians had no guns then--and hoped to make camp before they could possibly wear out his horse. Just as he was congratulating himself on his luck, right in front of him there suddenly appeared a great gorge, and not daring to stop or to turn to the right or left, the only thing to do was to make his animal jump it. It was his only chance; it was death if he missed it, and death by the most horrible torture if the Indians captured him. So he drove his heels into his horse's sides, and essayed the awful leap. His willing animal made a desperate effort to carry out the desire of his daring rider, but the dizzy chasm was too wide, and the pursuing savages saw both horse and the coveted white man dash to the bottom of the frightful canyon together. Believing that their hated enemy had eluded them forever, they rode back on their trail, disgusted and chagrined, without even taking the trouble of looking over the precipice to learn the fate of Baptiste.

The horse was instantly killed, and the Frenchman had both of his legs badly broken. Far from camp, with the Indians in close proximity, he did not dare discharge his rifle--the usual signal when a trapper is lost or in danger--or to make any demonstration, so he was compelled to lie there and suffer, hoping that his comrades, missing him, would start out to search for him. They did so, but more than twenty-four hours had elapsed before they found him, as the bottom of the canyon was the last place they thought of.

Doctors, in the wild region where their camp was located, were as impossible as angels; so his companions set his broken bones as well as they could, while Baptiste suffered excruciating torture. When they had completed their crude surgery, they improvised a litter of poles, and rigged it on a couple of pack-mules, and thus carried him around with them from camp to camp until he recovered--a period extending over three months.

This affair completely cured Baptiste of his original sentimentality in relation to the Indian, and he became one of their worst haters.

When acting as a juror in the trials of rebel Mexicans and Indians, he was asleep half the time, and never heard much of the evidence, and that portion which he did was so much Greek to him. In the last nine cases, in which the Indian who had murdered Governor Bent was tried, Baptiste, as soon as the jury room was closed, sang out: "Hang 'em, hang 'em, sacre enfans des garces, dey dam gran rascale!" "But wait," suggested one of the cooler members; "let's look at the evidence and find out whether they are really guilty." Upon this wise caution, Baptiste got greatly excited, paced the floor, and cried out: "Hang de Indian anyhow; he may not be guilty now-- mais he vare soon will be. Hang 'em all, parceque dey kill Monsieur Charles; dey take son topknot, vot you call im--scalp. Hang 'em, hang 'em-- sa-a-cre-e!"

On Friday the 9th, the day for the execution, the sky was unspotted, save by hastily fleeting clouds; and as the rising sun loomed over the Taos Mountain, the bright rays, shining on the yellow and white mud-houses, reflected cheerful hues, while the shades of the toppling peaks, receding from the plain beneath, drew within themselves. The humble valley wore an air of calm repose. The Plaza was deserted; woe-begone burros drawled forth sacrilegious brays, as the warm sunbeams roused them from hard, grassless ground, to scent their breakfast among straw and bones.

Poor Mexicans hurried to and fro, casting suspicious glances around; los Yankees at El casa Americano drank their juleps, and puffed their cigarettes in silence.

The sheriff, Metcalf, formerly a mountaineer, was in want of the wherewithal to hang the condemned criminals, so he borrowed some rawhide lariats and picket-ropes of a teamster.

"Hello, Met," said one of the party present, "these reatas are mighty stiff--won't fit; eh, old feller?"

"I've got something to make 'em fit--good 'intment--don't emit very sweet perfume; but good enough for Greasers," said the sheriff, producing a dollar's worth of Mexican soft soap. "This'll make 'em slip easy--a long ways too easy for them, I 'spect."

The prison apartment was a long chilly room, badly ventilated by one small window and the open door, through which the sun lit up the earth floor, and through which the poor prisoners wistfully gazed. Two muscular Mexicans basked in its genial warmth, a tattered serape interposing between them and the ground. The ends, once fringed but now clear of pristine ornament, were partly drawn over their breasts, disclosing in the openings of their fancifully colored shirts --now glazed with filth and faded with perspiration--the bare skin, covered with straight black hair. With hands under their heads, in the mass of stringy locks rusty-brown from neglect, they returned the looks of their executioners with an unmeaning stare, and unheedingly received the salutation of--"Como le va!"

Along the sides of the room, leaning against the walls, were crowded the poor wretches, miserable in dress, miserable in features, miserable in feelings--a more disgusting collection of ragged, greasy, unwashed prisoners were, probably, never before congregated within so small a space as the jail of Taos.

About nine o'clock, active preparations were made for the execution, and the soldiery mustered. Reverend padres in long black gowns, with meek countenances, passed the sentinels, intent on spiritual consolation, or the administration of the Blessed Sacrament.

Lieutenant-Colonel Willock, commanding the military, ordered every American under arms. The prison was at the edge of the town; no houses intervened between it and the fields to the north. One hundred and fifty yards distant, a gallows was erected.

The word was passed, at last, that the criminals were coming. Eighteen soldiers received them at the gate, with their muskets at "port arms"; the six abreast, with the sheriff on the right-- nine soldiers on each side.

The poor prisoners marched slowly, with downcast eyes, arms tied behind, and bare heads, with the exception of white cotton caps stuck on the back, to be pulled over the face as the last ceremony.

The roofs of the houses in the vicinity were covered with women and children, to witness the first execution by hanging in the valley of Taos, save that of Montojo, the insurgent leader. No men were near; a few stood afar off, moodily looking on.

On the flat jail roof was placed a mountain howitzer, loaded and ranging the gallows. Near was the complement of men to serve it, one holding in his hand a lighted match. The two hundred and thirty soldiers, less the eighteen forming the guard, were paraded in front of the jail, and in sight of the gibbet, so as to secure the prisoners awaiting trial. Lieutenant-Colonel Willock, on a handsome charger, commanded a view of the whole.

When within fifteen paces of the gallows, the side-guard, filing off to the right, formed, at regular distances from each other, three sides of a hollow square; the mountaineers composed the fourth and front side, in full view of the trembling prisoners, who marched up to the tree under which was a government wagon, with two mules attached. The driver and sheriff assisted them in, ranging them on a board, placed across the hinder end, which maintained its balance, as they were six--an even number--two on each extremity, and two in the middle. The gallows was so narrow that they touched. The ropes, by reason of their size and stiffness, despite the soaping given them, were adjusted with difficulty; but through the indefatigable efforts of the sheriff and a lieutenant who had accompanied him, all preliminaries were arranged, although the blue uniform looked sadly out of place on a hangman.

With rifles at a "shoulder," the military awaited the consummation of the tragedy. There was no crowd around to disturb; a death-like stillness prevailed. The spectators on the roofs seemed scarcely to move--their eyes were directed to the doomed wretches, with harsh halters now encircling their necks.

The sheriff and his assistant sat down; after a few moments of intense expectation, the heart-wrung victims said a few words to their people. Only one of them admitted he had committed murder and deserved death. In their brief but earnest appeals, the words "mi padre, mi madre"--"my father, my mother"--were prominent. The one sentenced for treason showed a spirit of patriotism worthy of the cause for which he died--the liberty of his country; and instead of the cringing recantation of the others, his speech was a firm asseveration of his own innocence, the unjustness of his trial, and the arbitrary conduct of his murderers. As the cap was pulled over his face, the last words he uttered between his teeth with a scowl were "Carajo, los Americanos!"

At a word from the sheriff, the mules were started, and the wagon drawn from under the tree. No fall was given, and their feet remained on the board till the ropes drew tight. The bodies swayed back and forth, and while thus swinging, the hands of two came together with a firm grasp till the muscles loosened in death.

After forty minutes' suspension, Colonel Willock ordered his command to quarters, and the howitzer to be taken from its place on the roof of the jail. The soldiers were called away; the women and population in general collecting around the rear guard which the sheriff had retained for protection while delivering the dead to their weeping relatives.

While cutting a rope from one man's neck--for it was in a hard knot-- the owner, a government teamster standing by waiting, shouted angrily, at the same time stepping forward:

"Hello there! don't cut that rope; I won't have anything to tie my mules with."

"Oh! you darned fool," interposed a mountaineer, "the dead men's ghosts will be after you if you use them lariats--wagh! They'll make meat of you sartain."

"Well, I don't care if they do. I'm in government service; and if them picket-halters was gone, slap down goes a dollar apiece. Money's scarce in these diggin's, and I'm going to save all I kin to take home to the old woman and boys."

CHAPTER IX.

FIRST OVERLAND MAIL.

On the summit of one of the highest plateaus bordering the Missouri River, surrounded by a rich expanse of foliage, lies Independence, the beautiful residence suburb of Kansas City, only ten miles distant.

Tradition tells that early in this century there were a few pioneers camping at long distances from each other in the seemingly interminable woods; in summer engaged in hunting the deer, elk, and bear, and in winter in trapping. It is a well-known fact that the Big Blue was once a favourite resort of the beaver, and that even later their presence in great numbers attracted many a veteran trapper to its waters.

Before that period the quaint old cities of far-off Mexico were forbidden to foreign traders, excepting to the favoured few who were successful in obtaining permits from the Spanish government. In 1821, however, the rebellion of Iturbide crushed the power of the mother country, and established the freedom of Mexico. The embargo upon foreign trade was at once removed, and the Santa Fe Trail, for untold ages only a simple trace across the continent, became the busy highway of a relatively great commerce.

In 1817 the navigation of the Mississippi River was begun. On the 2d of August of that year the steamer *General Pike* arrived at St. Louis. The first boat to ascend the Missouri River was the *Independence*; she passed Franklin on the 28th of May, 1819, where a dinner was given to her officers. In the same and the following month of that year, the steamers *Western Engineer Expedition* and *R. M. Johnson* came along, carrying Major Long's scientific exploring party, bound for the Yellowstone.

The Santa Fe trade having been inaugurated shortly after these important events, those engaged in it soon realized the benefits of river navigation--for it enabled them to shorten the distance which their wagons had to travel in going across the plains-- and they began to look out for a suitable place as a shipping and outfitting point higher up the river than Franklin, which had been the initial starting town.

By 1827 trading-posts had been established at Blue Mills, Fort Osage, and Independence. The first-mentioned place, which is situated about six miles below Independence, soon became the favourite landing, and the exchange from wagons to boats settled and defied all efforts to remove the headquarters of the trade from there for several years. Independence, however, being the county seat and the larger place, succeeded in its claims to be the more suitable locality, and as early as 1832 it was recognized as the American headquarters and the great outfitting point for the Santa Fe commerce, which it continued to be until 1846, when the traffic was temporarily suspended by the breaking out of the Mexican War.

Independence was not only the principal outfitting point for the Santa Fe traders, but also that of the great fur companies. That powerful association used to send out larger pack-trains than any other parties engaged in the traffic to the Rocky Mountains; they also employed wagons drawn by mules, and loaded with goods for the Indians with whom their agents bartered, which also on their return trip transported the skins and pelts of animals procured from the savages. The articles intended for the Indian trade were always purchased in St. Louis, and usually shipped to Independence, consigned to the firm of Aull and Company, who outfitted the traders with mules and provisions, and in fact anything else required by them.

Several individual traders would frequently form joint caravans, and travel in company for mutual protection from the Indians. After having reached a fifty-mile limit from the State line, each trader had control of his own men; each took care of a certain number of the pack-animals, loaded and unloaded them in camp, and had general supervision of them.

Frequently there would be three hundred mules in a single caravan, carrying three hundred pounds apiece, and very large animals more. Thousands of wagons were also sent out from Independence annually, each drawn by twelve mules or six yoke of oxen, and loaded with general merchandise.

There were no packing houses in those days nearer than St. Louis, and the bacon and beef used in the Santa Fe trade were furnished by the farmers of the surrounding country, who killed their meat, cured it, and transported it to the town where they sold it. Their wheat was also ground at the local mills, and they brought the flour to market, together with corn, dried fruit, beans, peas, and kindred provisions used on the long route across the plains.

Independence very soon became the best market west of St. Louis for cattle, mules, and wagons; the trade of which the place was the acknowledged headquarters furnishing employment to several thousand men, including the teamsters and packers on the Trail. The wages paid varied from twenty-five to fifty dollars a month and rations. The price charged for hauling freight to Santa Fe was ten dollars a hundred pounds, each wagon earning from five to six hundred dollars every trip, which was made in eighty or ninety days; some fast caravans making quicker time.

The merchants and general traders of Independence in those days reaped a grand harvest. Everything to eat was in constant demand; mules and oxen were sold in great numbers every month at excellent prices and always for cash; while any good stockman could readily make from ten to fifty dollars a day.

97

One of the largest manufacturers and most enterprising young men in Independence at that time was Hiram Young, a coloured man. Besides making hundreds of wagons, he made all the ox-yokes used in the entire traffic; fifty thousand annually during the '50's and until the breaking out of the war. The forward yokes were sold at an average of one dollar and a quarter, the wheel yokes a dollar higher.

The freight transported by the wagons was always very securely loaded; each package had its contents plainly marked on the outside. The wagons were heavily covered and tightly closed. Every man belonging to the caravan was thoroughly armed, and ever on the alert to repulse an attack by the Indians.

Sometimes at the crossing of the Arkansas the quicksands were so bad that it was necessary to get the caravan over in a hurry; then forty or fifty yoke of oxen were hitched to one wagon and it was quickly yanked through the treacherous ford. This was not always the case, however; it depended upon the stage of water and recent floods.

After the close of the war with Mexico, the freight business across the plains increased to a wonderful degree. The possession of the country by the United States gave a fresh impetus to the New Mexico trade, and the traffic then began to be divided between Westport and Kansas City. Independence lost control of the overland commerce and Kansas City commenced its rapid growth. Then came the discovery of gold in California, and this gave an increased business westward; for thousands of men and their families crossed the plains and the Rocky Mountains, seeking their fortunes in the new El Dorado. The Old Trail was the highway of an enormous pilgrimage, and both Independence and Kansas City became the initial point of a wonderful emigration.

In Independence may still be seen a few of the old landmarks when it was the headquarters of the Santa Fe trade.

An overland mail was started from the busy town as early as 1849. In an old copy of the Missouri *Commonwealth*, published there under the date of July, 1850, which I found on file in the Kansas State Historical Society, there is the following account of the first mail stage westward:--

We briefly alluded, some days since, to the Santa Fe line
of mail stages, which left this city on its first monthly
journey on the 1st instant. The stages are got up in
elegant style, and are each arranged to convey eight
passengers. The bodies are beautifully painted, and made
water-tight, with a view of using them as boats in ferrying

98

streams. The team consists of six mules to each coach. The mail is guarded by eight men, armed as follows: Each man has at his side, fastened in the stage, one of Colt's revolving rifles; in a holster below, one of Colt's long revolvers, and in his belt a small Colt's revolver, besides a hunting-knife; so that these eight men are ready, in case of attack, to discharge one hundred and thirty-six shots without having to reload. This is equal to a small army, armed as in the ancient times, and from the looks of this escort, ready as they are, either for offensive or defensive warfare with the savages, we have no fears for the safety of the mails.

The accommodating contractors have established a sort of base of refitting at Council Grove, a distance of one hundred and fifty miles from this city, and have sent out a blacksmith, and a number of men to cut and cure hay, with a quantity of animals, grain, and provisions; and we understand they intend to make a sort of traveling station there, and to commence a farm. They also, we believe, intend to make a similar settlement at Walnut Creek next season. Two of their stages will start from here the first of every month.

The old stage-coach days were times of Western romance and adventure, and the stories told of that era of the border have a singular fascination in this age of annihilation of distance.

Very few, if any, of the famous men who handled the "ribbons" in those dangerous days of the slow journey across the great plains are among the living; like the clumsy and forgotten coaches they drove, they have themselves been mouldering into dust these many years.

In many places on the line of the Trail, where the hard hills have not been subjected to the plough, the deep ruts cut by the lumbering Concord coaches may yet be distinctly traced. Particularly are they visible from the Atchison, Topeka, and Santa Fe track, as the cars thunder rapidly toward the city of Great Bend, in Kansas, three miles east of that town. Let the tourist as he crosses Walnut Creek look out of his window toward the east at an angle of about thirty-five degrees, and on the flint hills which slope gradually toward the railroad, he will observe, very distinctly, the

Old Trail, where it once drew down from the divide to make the ford at the little stream.

The monthly stages started from each end of the route at the same time; later the service was increased to once a week; after a while to three times, until in the early '60's daily stages were run from both ends of the route, and this was continued until the advent of the railroad.

Each coach carried eleven passengers, nine closely stowed inside --three on a seat--and two on the outside on the boot with the driver. The fare to Santa Fe was two hundred and fifty dollars, the allowance of baggage being limited to forty pounds; all in excess of that cost half a dollar a pound. In this now seemingly large sum was included the board of the travellers, but they were not catered to in any extravagant manner; hardtack, bacon, and coffee usually exhausted the menu, save that at times there was an abundance of antelope and buffalo.

There was always something exciting in those journeys from the Missouri to the mountains in the lumbering Concord coach. There was the constant fear of meeting the wily red man, who persistently hankered after the white man's hair. Then there was the playfulness of the sometimes drunken driver, who loved to upset his tenderfoot travellers in some arroya, long after the moon had sunk below the horizon.

It required about two weeks to make the trip from the Missouri River to Santa Fe, unless high water or a fight with the Indians made it several days longer. The animals were changed every twenty miles at first, but later, every ten, when faster time was made. What sleep was taken could only be had while sitting bolt upright, because there was no laying over; the stage continued on night and day until Santa Fe was reached.

After a few years, the company built stations at intervals varying from ten miles to fifty or more; and there the animals and drivers were changed, and meals furnished to travellers, which were always substantial, but never elegant in variety or cleanliness.

Who can ever forget those meals at the "stations," of which you were obliged to partake or go hungry: biscuit hard enough to serve as "round-shot," and a vile decoction called, through courtesy, coffee --but God help the man who disputed it!

Some stations, however, were notable exceptions, particularly in the mountains of New Mexico, where, aside from the bread--usually only tortillas, made of the blue-flint corn of the country--and coffee composed of the saints may know what, the meals were excellent. The most delicious brook trout, alternating with venison of the black-tailed deer, elk, bear, and all the other varieties of game abounding in the region cost you one dollar, but the station-keeper a mere trifle; no wonder the old residents and ranchmen on the line of the Old Trail lament the good times of the overland stage!

Thirteen years ago I revisited the once well-known Kosloskie's Ranch, a picturesque cabin at the foot of the Glorieta Mountains, about half a mile from the ruins on the Rio Pecos. The old Pole was absent, but his wife was there; and, although I had not seen her for fifteen years, she remembered me well, and at once began to deplore the changed condition of the country since the advent of the railroad, declaring it had ruined their family with many others. I could not disagree with her view of the matter, as I looked on the debris of a former relative greatness all around me. I recalled the fact that once Kosloskie's Ranch was the favourite eating station on the Trail; where you were ever sure of a substantial meal--the main feature of which was the delicious brook trout, which were caught out of the stream which ran near the door while you were washing the dust out of your eyes and ears.

The trout have vacated the Pecos; the ranch is a ruin, and stands in grim contrast with the old temple and church on the hill; and both are monuments of civilizations that will never come again.

Weeds and sunflowers mark the once broad trail to the quaint Aztec city, and silence reigns in the beautiful valley, save when broken by the passage of "The Flyer" of the Atchison, Topeka, and Santa Fe railway, as it struggles up the heavy grade of the Glorieta Mountains a mile or more distant.

Besides the driver, there was another employee--the conductor or messenger, as he was called. He had charge of the mail and express matter, collected the fares, and attended generally to the requirements of those committed to his care during the tedious journey; for he was not changed like the driver, but stayed with the coach from its starting to its destination. Sometimes fourteen individuals were accommodated in case of emergency; but it was terribly crowded and uncomfortable riding, with no chance to stretch your limbs, save for a few moments at stations where you ate and changed animals.

In starting from Independence, powerful horses were attached to the coach-- generally four in number; but at the first station they were exchanged for mules, and these animals hauled it the remainder of the way. Drivers were changed about eight times in making the trip to Santa Fe; and some of them were comical fellows, but full of nerve and endurance, for it required a man of nerve to handle eight frisky mules through the rugged passes of the mountains, when the snow was drifted in immense masses, or when descending the curved, icy declivities to the base of the range. A cool head was highly necessary; but frequently accidents occurred and sometimes were serious in their results.

A snowstorm in the mountains was a terrible thing to encounter by the coach; all that could be done was to wait until it had abated, as there was no going on in the face of the blinding sheets of intensely cold vapour which the wind hurled against the sides of the mountains. All inside of the coach had to sit still and shake with the freezing branches of the tall trees around them. A summer hailstorm was much more to be dreaded, however, for nowhere else on the earth do the hailstones shoot from the clouds of greater size or with greater velocity than in the Rocky Mountains. Such an event invariably frightened the mules and caused them to stampede; and, to escape death from the coach rolling down some frightful abyss, one had to jump out, only to be beaten to a jelly by the masses of ice unless shelter could be found under some friendly ledge of rock or the thick limbs of a tree.

Nothing is more fatiguing than travelling for the first day and night in a stage-coach; after that, however, one gets used to it and the remainder of the journey is relatively comfortable.

The only way to alleviate the monotony of riding hour after hour was to walk; occasionally this was rendered absolutely necessary by some accident, such as breaking a wheel or axle, or when an animal gave out before a station was reached. In such cases, however, no deduction was made from the fare, that having been collected in advance, so it cost you just as much whether you rode or walked. You could exercise your will in the matter, but you must not lag behind the coach; the savages were always watching for such derelicts, and your hair was the forfeit!

In the worst years, when the Indians were most decidedly on the war-trail, the government furnished an escort of soldiers from the military posts; they generally rode in a six-mule army-wagon, and were commanded by a sergeant or corporal; but in the early days, before the army had concentrated at the various forts on the great plains, the stage had to rely on the courage and fighting qualities of its occupants, and the nerve and the good judgment of the driver. If the latter understood his duty thoroughly and was familiar with the methods of the savages, he always chose the cover of darkness in which to travel in localities where the danger from Indians was greater than elsewhere; for it is a rare thing in savage warfare to attack at night. The early morning seemed to be their favourite hour, when sleep oppresses most heavily; and then it was that the utmost vigilance was demanded.

One of the most confusing things to the novice riding over the great plains is the idea of distance; mile after mile is travelled on the monotonous trail, with a range of hills or a low divide in full sight, yet hours roll by and the objects seem no nearer than when they were first observed. The reason for this seems to be that every atom of vapour is eliminated from the air, leaving such an absolute clearness of atmosphere, such an indescribable transparency of space through which distant objects are seen, that they are magnified and look nearer than they really are.

Consequently, the usual method of calculating distance and areas by the eye is ever at fault until custom and familiarity force a new standard of measure.

Mirages, too, were of frequent occurrence on the great plains; some of them wonderful examples of the refracting properties of light. They assumed all manner of fantastic, curious shapes, sometimes ludicrously distorting the landscape; objects, like a herd of buffalo for instance, though forty miles away, would seem to be high in air, often reversed, and immensely magnified in their proportions.

Violent storms were also frequent incidents of the long ride. I well remember one night, about thirty years ago, when the coach in which I and one of my clerks were riding to Fort Dodge was suddenly brought to a standstill by a terrible gale of wind and hail. The mules refused to face it, and quickly turning around nearly overturned the stage, while we, with the driver and conductor, were obliged to hold on to the wheels with all our combined strength to prevent it from blowing down into a stony ravine, on the brink of which we were brought to a halt. Fortunately, these fearful blizzards did not last very long; the wind ceased blowing so violently in a few moments, but the rain usually continued until morning.

It usually happened that you either at once took a great liking for your driver and conductor, or the reverse. Once, on a trip from Kansas City, nearly a third of a century ago, when I and another man were the only occupants of the coach, we entertained quite a friendly feeling for our driver; he was a good-natured, jolly fellow, full of anecdote and stories of the Trail, over which he had made more than a hundred sometimes adventurous journeys.

When we arrived at the station at Plum Creek, the coach was a little ahead of time, and the driver who was there to relieve ours commenced to grumble at the idea of having to start out before the regular hour. He found fault because we had come into the station so soon, and swore he could drive where our man could not "drag a halter-chain," as he claimed in his boasting. We at once took a dislike to him, and secretly wished that he would come to grief, in order to cure him of his boasting. Sure enough, before we had gone half a mile from the station he incontinently tumbled the coach over into a sandy arroya, and we were delighted at the accident. Finding ourselves free from any injury, we went to work and assisted him to right the coach-- no small task; but we took great delight in reminding him several times of his ability to drive where our old friend could not "drag a halter-chain." It was very dark; neither moon or star visible, the whole heavens covered with an inky blackness of ominous clouds; so he was not so much to be blamed after all.

The very next coach was attacked at the crossing of Cow Creek by a band of Kiowas. The savages had followed the stage all that afternoon, but remained out of sight until just at dark, when they rushed over the low divide, and mounted on their ponies commenced to circle around the coach, making the sand dunes resound with echoes of their infernal yelling, and shaking their buffalo-robes to stampede the mules, at the same time firing their guns at the men who were in the coach, all of whom made a bold stand, but were rapidly getting the worst of it, when fortunately a company of United States cavalry came over the Trail from the west, and drove the savages off. Two of the men in the coach were seriously wounded, and one of the soldiers killed; but the Indian loss was never determined, as they succeeded in carrying off both their dead and wounded.

Mr. W. H. Ryus, a friend of mine now residing in Kansas City, who was a driver and messenger thirty-five years, and had many adventures, told me the following incidents:

I have crossed the plains sixty-five times by wagon and coach. In July, 1861, I was employed by Barnum, Vickery, and Neal to drive over what was known as the Long Route, that is, from Fort Larned to Fort Lyon, two hundred and forty miles, with no station between. We drove one set of mules the whole distance, camped out, and made the journey, in good weather, in four or five days. In winter we generally encountered a great deal of snow, and very cold air on the bleak and wind-swept desert of the Upper Arkansas, but we employees got used to that; only the passengers did any kicking. We had a way of managing them, however, when they got very obstreperous; all we had to do was to yell Indians! and that quieted them quicker than forty-rod whiskey does a man.

We gathered buffalo-chips, to boil our coffee and cook our buffalo and antelope steak, smoked for a while around the smouldering fire until the animals were through grazing, and then started on our lonely way again.

Sometimes the coach would travel for a hundred miles through the buffalo herds, never for a moment getting out of sight of them; often we saw fifty thousand to a hundred thousand on a single journey out or in. The Indians used to call them their cattle, and claimed to own them. They did not, like the white man, take out only the tongue, or hump, and leave all the rest to dry upon the prairie, but ate every last morsel, even to the intestines. They said the whites were welcome to all they could eat or haul away, but they did not like to see so much meat wasted as was our custom.

The Indians on the plains were not at all hostile in 1861-62; we could drive into their villages, where there were tens of thousands of them, and they would always treat us to music or a war-dance, and set before us the choicest of their venison and buffalo. In July of the last-mentioned year, Colonel Leavenworth, Jr., was crossing the Trail in my coach. He desired to see Satanta, the great Kiowa chief. The colonel's father[28] was among the Indians a great deal while on duty as an army officer, while the young colonel was a small boy. The colonel said he didn't believe that old Satanta would know him.

Just before the arrival of the coach in the region of the Indian village, the Comanches and the Pawnees had been having a battle. The Comanches had taken some scalps, and they were camping on the bank of the Arkansas River, where Dodge City is now located. The Pawnees had killed five of their warriors, and the Comanches were engaged in an exciting war-dance; I think there were from twenty to thirty thousand Indians gathered there, men, women, and children of the several tribes--Comanches, Kiowas, Cheyennes, Arapahoes, and others.

When we came in sight of their camp, the colonel knew, by the terrible noise they were making, that a war-dance was going on; but we did not know then whether it was on account of troubles among themselves, or because of a fight with the whites, but we were determined to find out. If he could get to the old chief, all would be right. So he and I started for the place whence the noise came. We met a savage and the colonel asked him whether Satanta was there, and what was going on. When he told us that they had had a fight and it was a scalp-dance, our hair lowered; for we

knew that if it was in consequence of trouble with the
whites, we stood in some danger of losing our own scalps.

The Indian took us in, and the situation, too; and conducted
us into the presence of Satanta, who stood in the middle
of the great circle, facing the dancers. It was out on an
island in the stream; the chief stood very erect, and eyed
us closely for a few seconds, then the colonel told his
own name that the Indians had known him by when he was a boy.
Satanta gave one bound--he was at least ten feet from where
we were waiting--grasped the colonel's hand and excitedly
kissed him, then stood back for another instant, gave him
a second squeeze, offered his hand to me, which I,
of course, shook heartily, then he gazed at the man he had
known as a boy so many years ago, with a countenance
beaming with delight. I never saw any one, even among
the white race, manifest so much joy as the old chief did
over the visit of the colonel to his camp.

He immediately ordered some of his young men to go out and
herd our mules through the night, which they brought back
to us at daylight. He then had the coach hauled to the
front of his lodge, where we could see all that was going on
to the best advantage. We had six travellers with us on
this journey, and it was a great sight for the tenderfeet.

It was about ten o'clock at night when we arrived at
Satanta's lodge, and we saw thousands of squaws and bucks
dancing and mourning for their dead warriors. At midnight
the old chief said we must eat something at once. So he
ordered a fire built, cooked buffalo and venison, setting
before us the very best that he had, we furnishing canned
fruit, coffee, and sugar from our coach mess. There we sat,
and talked and ate until morning; then when we were ready
to start off, Satanta and the other chiefs of the various
tribes escorted us about eight miles on the Trail, where
we halted for breakfast, they remaining and eating with us.

Colonel Leavenworth was on his way to assume command of one of the military posts in New Mexico; the Indians begged him to come back and take his quarters at either Fort Larned or Fort Dodge. They told him they were afraid their agent was stealing their goods and selling them back to them; while if the Indians took anything from the whites, a war was started.

Colonel A. G. Boone had made a treaty with these same Indians in 1860, and it was agreed that he should be their agent. It was done, and the entire savage nations were restful and kindly disposed toward the whites during his administration; any one could then cross the plains without fear of molestation. In 1861, however, Judge Wright, of Indiana, who was a member of Congress at the time, charged Colonel Boone with disloyalty.[29] He succeeded in having him removed.

Majors Russel and Waddell, the great government freight contractors across the plains, gave Colonel Boone fourteen hundred acres of land, well improved, with some fine buildings on it, about fifteen miles east of Pueblo, Colorado. It was christened Booneville, and the colonel moved there. In the fall of 1862, fifty influential Indians of the various tribes visited Colonel Boone at his new home, and begged that he would come back to them and be their agent. He told the chiefs that the President of the United States would not let him. Then they offered to sell their horses to raise money for him to go to Washington to tell the Great Father what their agent was doing; and to have him removed, or there was going to be trouble. The Indians told Colonel Boone that many of their warriors would be on the plains that fall, and they were declaring they had as much right to take something to eat from the trains as their agent had to steal goods from them.

Early in the winter of the next year, a small caravan of eight or ten wagons travelling to the Missouri River was overhauled at Nine Mile Ridge, about fifty miles west of Fort Dodge, by a band of Indians, who asked for something to eat. The teamsters, thinking them to be hostile, believed it would be a good thing to kill one of them anyhow; so they shot an inoffensive warrior, after which the train moved on to its camp and the trouble began. Every man in the whole outfit, with the exception of one teamster, who luckily got to the Arkansas River and hid, was murdered, the animals all carried away, and the wagons and contents destroyed by fire.

This foolish act by the master of the caravan was the cause of a long war, causing hundreds of atrocious murders and the destruction of a great deal of property along the whole Western frontier.

That fall, 1863, Mr. Ryus was the messenger or conductor in charge of the coach running from Kansas City to Santa Fe. He said:

It then required a month to make the round trip, about eighteen hundred miles. On account of the Indian war we had to have an escort of soldiers to go through the most dangerous portions of the Trail; and the caravans all joined forces for mutual safety, besides having an escort.

My coach was attacked several times during that season, and we had many close calls for our scalps. Sometimes the Indians would follow us for miles, and we had to halt and fight them; but as for myself, I had no desire to kill one of the miserable, outraged creatures, who had been swindled out of their just rights.

I know of but one occasion when we were engaged in a fight with them when our escort killed any of the attacking savages; it was about two miles from Little Coon Creek Station, where they surrounded the coach and commenced hostilities. In the fight one officer and one enlisted man were wounded. The escort chased the band for several miles, killed nine of them, and got their horses.

CHAPTER X.

CHARLES BENT.

Almost immediately after the ratification of the purchase of New Mexico by the United States under the stipulations of the "Guadalupe-Hidalgo Treaty," the Utes, one of the most powerful tribes of mountain Indians, inaugurated a bloody and relentless war against the civilized inhabitants of the Territory. It was accompanied by all the horrible atrocities which mark the tactics of savage hatred toward the white race. It continued for several years with more or less severity; its record a chapter of history whose pages are deluged with blood, until finally the Indians were subdued by the power of the military.

Along the line of the Santa Fe Trail, they were frequently in conjunction with the Apaches, and their depredations and atrocities were very numerous; they attacked fearlessly freight caravans, private expeditions, and overland stage-coaches, robbing and murdering indiscriminately.

In January, 1847, the mail and passenger stage left Independence, Missouri, for Santa Fe on one of its regular trips across the plains. It had its full complement of passengers, among whom were a Mr. White and family, consisting of his wife, one child, and a coloured nurse.

Day after day the lumbering Concord coach rolled on, with nothing to disturb the monotony of the vast prairies, until it had left them far behind and crossed the Range into New Mexico. Just about dawn, as the unsuspecting travellers were entering the "canyon of the Canadian,"[30] and probably waking up from their long night's sleep, a band of Indians, with blood-curdling yells and their terrific war-whoop, rode down upon them.

In that lonely and rock-sheltered gorge a party of the hostile savages, led by "White Wolf," a chief of the Apaches, had been awaiting the arrival of the coach from the East; the very hour it was due was well known to them, and they had secreted themselves there the night before so as to be on hand should it reach their chosen ambush a little before the schedule time.

Out dashed the savages, gorgeous in their feathered war-bonnets, but looking like fiends with their paint-bedaubed faces. Stopping the frightened mules, they pulled open the doors of the coach and, mercilessly dragging its helpless and surprised inmates to the ground, immediately began their butchery. They scalped and mutilated the dead bodies of their victims in their usual sickening manner, not a single individual escaping, apparently, to tell of their fiendish acts.

If the Indians had been possessed of sufficient cunning to cover up the tracks of their horrible atrocities, as probably white robbers would have done, by dragging the coach from the road and destroying it by fire or other means, the story of the murders committed in the deep canyon might never have been known; but they left the tell-tale remains of the dismantled vehicle just where they had attacked it, and the naked corpses of its passengers where they had been ruthlessly killed.

At the next stage station the employees were anxiously waiting for the arrival of the coach, and wondering what could have caused the delay; for it was due there at noon on the day of the massacre. Hour after hour passed, and at last they began to suspect that something serious had occurred; they sat up all through the night listening for the familiar rumbling of wheels, but still no stage. At daylight next morning, determined to wait no longer, as they felt satisfied that something out of the usual course had happened, a party hurriedly mounted their horses and rode down the broad trail leading to the canyon.

Upon entering its gloomy mouth after a quick lope of an hour, they discovered the ghastly remains of twelve mutilated bodies. These were gathered up and buried in one grave, on the top of the bluff overlooking the narrow gorge.

They could not be sure of the number of passengers the coach had brought until the arrival of the next, as it would have a list of those carried by its predecessor; but it would not be due for several days. They naturally supposed, however, that the twelve dead lying on the ground were its full complement.

Not waiting for the arrival of the next stage, they despatched a messenger to the last station east that the one whose occupants had been murdered had passed, and there learned the exact number of passengers it had contained. Now they knew that Mrs. White, her child, and the coloured nurse had been carried off into a captivity worse than death; for no remains of a woman were found with the others lying in the canyon.

The terrible news of the massacre was conveyed to Taos, where were stationed several companies of the Second United States Dragoons, commanded by Major William Greer; but as the weather had grown intensely cold and stormy since the date of the massacre, it took nearly a fortnight for the terrible story to reach there. The Major acted promptly when appealed to to go after and punish the savages concerned in the outrage, but several days more were lost in getting an expedition ready for the field. It was still stormy while the command was preparing for its work; but at last, one bright morning, in a piercing cold wind, five troops of the dragoons,

110

commanded by Major Greer in person, left their comfortable quarters to attempt the rescue of Mrs. White, her child, and nurse.

Kit Carson, "Uncle Dick" Wooten, Joaquin Leroux, and Tom Tobin were the principal scouts and guides accompanying the expedition, having volunteered their services to Major Greer, which he had gladly accepted.

The massacre having occurred three weeks before the command had arrived at the canyon of the Canadian, and snow having fallen almost continuously ever since, the ground was deeply covered, making it almost impossible to find the trail of the savages leading out of the gorge. No one knew where they had established their winter camp --probably hundreds of miles distant on some tributary of the Canadian far to the south.

Carson, Wooton, and Leroux, after scanning the ground carefully at every point, though the snow was ten inches deep, in a way of which only men versed in savage lore are capable, were rewarded by discovering certain signs, unintelligible to the ordinary individual[31] --that the murderers had gone south out of the canyon immediately after completing their bloody work, and that their camp was somewhere on the river, but how far off none could tell.

The command followed up the trail discovered by the scouts for nearly four hundred miles. Early one morning when that distance had been rounded, and just as the men were about to break camp preparatory to the day's march, Carson went out on a little reconnoissance on his own account, as he had noticed a flock of ravens hovering in the air when he first got out of his blankets at dawn, which was sufficient indication to him that an Indian camp was located somewhere in the vicinity; for that ominous bird is always to be found in the region where the savages take up an abode, feeding upon the carcasses of the many varieties of game killed for food. He had not proceeded more than half a mile from the camp when he discovered two Indians slowly riding over a low "divide," driving a herd of ponies before them. The famous scout was then certain their village could not be very far away. The savages did not observe him, as he took good care they should not; so he returned quickly to where Major Greer was standing by his camp-fire and reported the presence of a village very close at hand.

The Major having sent for Tom Tobin and Uncle Dick Wooton, requested them to go and find the exact location of the savages. These scouts came back in less than half an hour, and reported a large number of teepees in a thick grove of timber a mile away.

It was at once determined to surprise the savages in their winter quarters by charging right among their lodges without allowing them time to mount their ponies, as the gallant Custer rode, at the head of his famous troopers of the Seventh Cavalry,

111

into the camp of the celebrated chief "Black Kettle" on the Washita, in the dawn of a cold November morning twenty years afterward.

The command succeeded in getting within good charging distance of the village without its occupants having any knowledge of its proximity; but at this moment Major Greer was seized with an idea that he ought to have a parley with the Indians before he commenced to fight them, and for that purpose he ordered a halt, just as the soldiers were eager for the sound of the "Charge!"

Never were a body of men more enraged. Carson gave vent to his wrath in a series of elaborately carved English oaths, for which he was noted when young; Leroux, whose naturally hot blood was roused, swore at the Major in a curious mixture of bad French and worse mountain dialect, and it appeared as if the battle would begin in the ranks of the troops instead of those of the savages; for never was a body of soldiers so disgusted at the act of any commanding officer.

This delay gave the Indians, who could be seen dodging about among their lodges and preparing for a fight that was no longer a surprise, time to hide their women and children, mount their ponies, and get down into deep ravines, where the soldiers could not follow them. While the Major was trying to convince his subordinates that his course was the proper one, the Indians opened fire without any parley, and it happened that at the first volley a bullet struck him in the breast, but a suspender buckle deflected its course and he was not seriously wounded.

The change in the countenance of their commanding officer caused by the momentary pain was just the incentive the troopers wanted, and without waiting for the sound of the trumpet, they spurred their horses, dashed in, and charged the thunderstruck savages with the shock of a tornado.

In two successful charges of the gallant and impatient troopers more than a hundred of the Indians were killed and wounded, but the time lost had permitted many to escape, and the pursuit of the stragglers would have been unavailing under the circumstances; so the command turned back and returned to Taos. In the village was found the body of Mrs. White still warm, with three arrows in her breast. Had the charge been made as originally expected by the troopers, her life would have been saved. No trace of the child or of the coloured nurse was ever discovered, and it is probable that they were both killed while en route from the canyon to the village, as being valueless to keep either as slaves or for other purposes.

The fate of the Apache chief, "White Wolf," who was the leader in the outrages in the canyon of the Canadian, was fitting for his devilish deeds. It was Lieutenant David Bell's fortune to avenge the murder of Mrs. White and her family, and in an extraordinary manner.[32] The action was really dramatic, or romantic; he was on a scout with his company, which was stationed at Fort Union, New Mexico, having about thirty men with him, and when near the canyon of the Canadian they met about the same number of Indians. A parley was in order at once, probably desired by the savages, who were confronted with an equal number of troopers. Bell had assigned the baggage-mules to the care of five or six of his command, and held a mounted interview with the chief, who was no other than the infamous White Wolf of the Jicarilla Apaches. As Bell approached, White Wolf was standing in front of his Indians, who were on foot, all well armed and in perfect line. Bell was in advance of his troopers, who were about twenty paces from the Indians, exactly equal in number and extent of line; both parties were prepared to use firearms.

The parley was almost tediously long and the impending duel was arranged, White Wolf being very bold and defiant.

At last the leaders exchanged shots, the chief sinking on one knee and aiming his gun, Bell throwing his body forward and making his horse rear. Both lines, by command, fired, following the example of their superiors, the troopers, however, spurring forward over their enemies. The warriors, or nearly all of them, threw themselves on the ground, and several vertical wounds were received by horse and rider. The dragoons turned short about, and again charged through and over their enemies, the fire being continuous. As they turned for a third charge, the surviving Indians were seen escaping to a deep ravine, which, although only one or two hundred paces off, had not previously been noticed. A number of the savages thus escaped, the troopers having to pull up at the brink, but sending a volley after the descending fugitives.

In less than fifteen minutes twenty-one of the forty-six actors in this strange combat were slain or disabled. Bell was not hit, but four or five of his men were killed or wounded. He had shot White Wolf several times, and so did others after him; but so tenacious of life was the Apache that, to finish him, a trooper got a great stone and mashed his head.

This was undoubtedly the greatest duel of modern times; certainly nothing like it ever occurred on the Santa Fe Trail before or since.

The war chief of the Kiowa nation in the early '50's was Satank, a most unmitigated villain; cruel and heartless as any savage that ever robbed a stage-coach or wrenched off the hair of a helpless woman. After serving a dozen or more years with a record for hellish atrocities equalled by few of his compeers, he was deposed for alleged cowardice, as his warriors claimed, under the following circumstances:--

The village of his tribe was established in the large bottoms, eight miles from the Great Bend of the Arkansas, and about the same distance from Fort Zarah.[33] All the bucks were absent on a hunting expedition, excepting Satank and a few superannuated warriors. The troops were out from Fort Larned on a grand scout after marauding savages, when they suddenly came across the village and completely took the Kiowas by surprise. Seeing the soldiers almost upon them, Satank and other warriors jumped on their ponies and made good their escape. Had they remained, all of them would have been killed or at least captured; consequently Satank, thinking discretion better than valour at that particular juncture, incontinently fled. His warriors in council, however, did not agree with him; they thought that it was his duty to have remained at the village in defence of the women and children, as he had been urged to refrain from going on the hunt for that very purpose.

Some time before Satank lost his office of chief, there was living on Cow Creek, in a rude adobe building, a man who was ostensibly an Indian trader, but whose traffic, in reality, consisted in selling whiskey to the Indians, and consequently the United States troops were always after him. He was obliged to cache his liquor in every conceivable manner so that the soldiers should not discover it, and, of course, he dreaded the incursions of the troops much more than he did raids of the Indian marauders that were constantly on the Trail.

Satank and this illicit trader, whose name was Peacock, were great chums. One day while they were indulging in a general good time over sundry drinks of most villanous liquor, Satank said to Peacock: "Peacock, I want you to write me a letter; a real nice one, that I can show to the wagon-bosses on the Trail, and get all the 'chuck' I want. Tell them I am Satank, the great chief of the Kiowas, and for them to treat me the best they know how."

"All right, Satank," said Peacock; "I'll do so." Peacock then sat down and wrote the following epistle:--

"The bearer of this is Satank. He is the biggest liar, beggar, and thief on the plains. What he can't beg of you, he'll steal. Kick him out of camp, for he is a lazy, good-for-nothing Indian."

Satank began at once to make use of the supposed precious document, which he really believed would assure him the dignified treatment and courtesy due to his exalted rank. He presented it to several caravans during the ensuing week, and, of course, received a very cool reception in every instance, or rather a very warm one.

One wagon-master, in fact, black-snaked him out of his camp. After these repeated insults he sought another white friend, and told of his grievances. "Look here," said Satank, "I asked Peacock to write me a good letter, and he gave me this; but I don't understand it! Every time I hand it to a wagon-boss, he gives me the devil! Read it to me and tell me just what it does say."

His friend read it over, and then translated it literally to Satank. The savage assumed a countenance of extreme disgust, and after musing for a few moments, said: "Well, I understand it all now. All right!"

The next morning at daylight, Satank called for some of his braves and with them rode out to Peacock's ranch. Arriving there, he called out to Peacock, who had not yet risen: "Peacock, get up, the soldiers are coming!" It was a warning which the illicit trader quickly obeyed, and running out of the building with his field-glass in his hand, he started for his lookout, but while he was ascending the ladder with his back to Satank the latter shot him full of holes, saying, as he did so: "There, Peacock, I guess you won't write any more letters."

His warriors then entered the building and killed every man in it, save one who had been gored by a buffalo bull the day before, and who was lying in a room all by himself. He was saved by the fact that the Indian has a holy dread of small-pox, and will never enter an apartment where sick men lie, fearing they may have the awful disease.

Satanta (White Bear) was the most efficient and dreaded chief of all who have ever been at the head of the Kiowa nation. Ever restlessly active in ordering or conducting merciless forays against an exposed frontier, he was the very incarnation of deviltry in his determined hatred of the whites, and his constant warfare against civilization.

He also possessed wonderful oratorical powers; he could hurl the most violent invectives at those whom he argued with, or he could be equally pathetic when necessary. He was justly called "The Orator of the Plains," rivalling the historical renown of Tecumseh or Pontiac.

He was a short, bullet-headed Indian, full of courage and well versed in strategy. Ordinarily, when on his visits to the various military posts he wore a major-general's full uniform, a suit of that rank having been given to him in the summer of 1866 by General Hancock. He also owned an ambulance, a team of mules, and a set of harness, the last stolen, maybe, from some caravan he had raided on the Trail. In that ambulance, with a trained Indian driver, the wily chief travelled, wrapped in a savage dignity that was truly laughable. In his village, too, he assumed a great deal of style. He was very courteous to his white guests, if at the time his tribe were at all friendly with the government; nothing was too good for them. He always laid down a carpet on the floor of his lodge in the post of honour, on which they were to sit. He had large boards, twenty inches wide and three feet long, ornamented with brass tacks driven all around the edges, which he used for tables. He also had a French horn, which he blew vigorously when meals were ready.

His friendship was only dissembling. During all the time that General Sheridan was making his preparations for his intended winter campaign against the allied plains tribes, Satanta made frequent visits to the military posts, ostensibly to show the officers that he was heartily for peace, but really to inform himself of what was going on.

At that time I was stationed at Fort Harker, on the Smoky Hill. One evening, General Sheridan, who was my guest, was sitting on the verandah of my quarters, smoking and chatting with me and some other officers who had come to pay him their respects, when one of my men rode up and quietly informed me that Satanta had just driven his ambulance into the fort, and was getting ready to camp near the mule corral. On receiving this information, I turned to the general and suggested the propriety of either killing or capturing the inveterate demon. Personally I believed it would be right to get rid of such a character, and I had men under my command who would have been delighted to execute an order to that effect.

Sheridan smiled when I told him of Satanta's presence and the excellent chance to get rid of him. But he said: "That would never do; the sentimentalists in the Eastern States would raise such a howl that the whole country would be horrified!"

Of course, in these "piping times of peace" the reader, in the quiet of his own room, will think that my suggestion was brutal, and without any palliation; my excuse, however, may be found in General Washington's own motto: Exitus acta probat. If the suggestion had been acted upon, many an innocent man and woman would have escaped torture, and many a maiden a captivity worse than death.

As a specimen of Satanta's oratory, I offer the following, to show the hypocrisy of the subtle old villain, and his power over the minds of too sensitive auditors. Once Congress sent out to the central plains a commission from Washington to inquire into the causes of the continual warfare raging with the savages on the Kansas border; to learn what the grievances of the Indians were; and to find some remedy for the wholesale slaughter of men, women, and children along the line of the Old Trail.

Satanta was sent for by the commission as the leading spirit of the formidable Kiowa nation. When he entered the building at Fort Dodge in which daily sessions were held, he was told by the president to speak his mind without any reservation; to withhold nothing, but to truthfully relate what his tribe had to complain of on the part of the whites. The old rascal grew very pathetic as he warmed up to his subject. He declared that he had no desire to kill the white settlers or emigrants crossing the plains, but that those who came and lived on the land of his tribe ruthlessly slaughtered the buffalo, allowing their carcasses to rot on the prairie; killing them merely for the amusement it afforded them, while the Indian only killed when necessity demanded. He also stated that the white hunters set out fires, destroying the grass, and causing the tribe's horses to starve to death as well as the buffalo; that they cut down and otherwise destroyed the timber on the margins of the streams, making large fires of it, while the Indian was satisfied to cook his food with a few dry and dead limbs. "Only the other day," said he, "I picked up a little switch on the Trail, and it made my heart bleed to think that so small a green branch, ruthlessly torn out of the ground and thoughtlessly destroyed by some white man, would in time have grown into a stately tree for the use and benefit of my children and grandchildren."

After the pow-wow had ended, and Satanta had got a few drinks of red liquor into him, his real, savage nature asserted itself, and he said to the interpreter at the settler's store: "Now didn't I give it to those white men who came from the Great Father? Didn't I do it in fine style? Why, I drew tears from their eyes! The switch I saw on the Trail made my heart glad instead of sad; for I new there was a tenderfoot ahead of me, because an old plainsman or hunter would never have carried anything but a good quirt or a pair of spurs. So I said to my warriors, 'Come on, boys; we've got him!' and when we came in sight, after we had followed him closely on the dead run, he threw away his rifle and held tightly on to his hat for fear he should lose it!"

Another time when Satanta had remained at Fort Dodge for a very long period and had worn out his welcome, so that no one would give him anything to drink, he went to the quarters of his old friend, Bill Bennett, the overland stage agent, and begged him to give him some liquor. Bill was mixing a bottle of medicine to drench a sick mule. The moment he set the bottle down to do something else, Satanta seized it off the ground and drank most of the liquid before quitting. Of course, it made the old savage dreadfully sick as well as angry. He then started for a certain officer's quarters and again begged for something to cure him of the effects of the former dose; the officer refused, but Satanta persisted in his importunities; he would not leave without it. After a while, the officer went to a closet and took a swallow of the most nauseating medicine, placing the bottle back on its shelf. Satanta watched his chance, and, as soon as the officer left the room, he snatched the bottle out of the closet and drank its contents without stopping to breathe. It was, of course, a worse dose than the horse-medicine. The next day, very early in the morning, he assembled a number of his warriors, crossed the Arkansas, and went south to his village. Before leaving, however, he burnt all of the government contractor's hay on the bank of the river opposite the post. He then continued on to Crooked Creek, where he murdered three wood-choppers, all of which, he said afterward, he did in revenge for the attempt to poison him at Fort Dodge.

At the Comanche agency, where several of the government agents were assembled to have a talk with chiefs of the various plains tribes, Satanta said in his address: "I would willingly take hold of that part of the white man's road which is represented by the breech-loading rifles; but I don't like the corn rations--they make my teeth hurt!"

Big Tree was another Kiowa chief. He was the ally and close friend of Satanta, and one of the most daring and active of his warriors. The sagacity and bravery of these two savages would have been a credit to that of the most famous warriors of the old French and Indian Wars. Both were at last taken, tried, and sent to the Texas penitentiary for life. Satanta was eventually pardoned; but before he was made aware of the efforts that were being taken for his release, he attempted to escape, and, in jumping from a window, fell and broke his neck. His pardon arrived the next morning. Big Tree, through the work of the sentimentalists of Washington, was set free and sent to the Kiowa Reservation--near Fort Sill in the Indian Territory.

The next most audacious and terrible scourge of the plains was "Ta-ne-on-koe" (Kicking Bird). He was a great warrior of the Kiowas, and was the chief actor in some of the bloodiest raids on the Kansas frontier in the history of its troublous times.

One of his captures was that of a Miss Morgan and Mrs. White. They were finally rescued from the savages by General Custer, under the following circumstances: Custer, who was advancing with his column of invincible cavalrymen--the famous Seventh United States-- in search of the two unfortunate women, had arrived near the head waters of one of the tributaries of the Washita, and, with only his guide and interpreter, was far in advance of the column, when, on reaching the summit of an isolated bluff, they suddenly saw a village of the Kiowas, which turned out to be that of Kicking Bird, whose handsome lodge was easily distinguishable from the rest. Without waiting for his command, the general and his guide rode boldly to the lodge of the great chief, and both dismounted, holding cocked revolvers in their hands; Custer presented his at Kicking Bird's head. In the meantime, Custer's column of troopers, whom the Kiowas had good reason to remember for their bravery in many a hard-fought battle, came in full view of the astonished village. This threw the startled savages into the utmost consternation, but the warriors were held in check by signs from Kicking Bird. As the cavalry drew nearer, General Custer demanded the immediate release of the white women. Their presence in the village was at first denied by the lying chief, and not until he had been led to the limb of a huge cottonwood tree near the lodge, with a rope around his neck, did he acknowledge that he held the women and consent to give them up.

This well-known warrior, with a foreknowledge not usually found in the savage mind, seeing the beginning of the end of Indian sovereignty on the plains, voluntarily came in and surrendered himself to the authorities, and stayed on the reservation near Fort Sill.

In June, 1867, a year before the breaking out of the great Indian war on the central plains, the whole tribe of Kiowas, led by him, assembled at Fort Larned. He was the cynosure of all eyes, as he was without question one of the noblest-looking savages ever seen on the plains. On that occasion he wore the full uniform of a major-general of the United States army. He was as correctly moulded as a statue when on horseback, and when mounted on his magnificent charger the morning he rode out with General Hancock to visit the immense Indian camp a few miles above the fort on Pawnee Fork, it would have been a difficult task to have determined which was the finer-looking man.

After Kicking Bird had abandoned his wicked career, he was regarded by every army officer with whom he had a personal acquaintance as a remarkably good Indian; for he really made the most strenuous efforts to initiate his tribe into the idea that it was best for it to follow the white man's road. He argued with them that the time was very near when there would no longer be any region where the Indians could live as they had been doing, depending on the buffalo and other game for the sustenance of their families; they must adapt themselves to the methods of their conquerors.

In July, 1869, he became greatly offended with the government for its enforced removal of his tribe from its natural and hereditary hunting-grounds into the reservation allotted to it. At that time many of his warriors, together with the Comanches, made a raid on the defenceless settlements of the northern border of Texas, in which the savages were disastrously defeated, losing a large number of their most beloved warriors. On the return of the unsuccessful expedition, a great council was held, consisting of all the chiefs and head men of the two tribes which had suffered so terribly in the awful fight, to consider the best means of avenging the loss of so many braves and friends. Kicking Bird was summoned before that council and condemned as a coward; they called him a squaw, because he had refused to go with the warriors of the combined tribes on the raid into Texas.

He told a friend of mine some time afterward that he had intended never again to go against the whites; but the emergency of the case, and his severe condemnation by the council, demanded that he should do something to re-establish himself in the good graces of his tribe. He then made one of the most destructive raids into Texas that ever occurred in the history of its border warfare, which successfully restored him to the respect of his warriors.

In that raid Kicking Bird carried off vast herds of horses and a large number of scalps. Although his tribe fairly worshipped him, he was not at all satisfied with himself. He could look into the future as well as any one, and from that time on to his tragic death he laboured most zealously and earnestly in connection with the Indian agents to bring his people to live on the reservation which the government had established for them in the Territory.

At the inauguration of the so-called "Quaker Policy" by President Grant, that sect was largely intrusted with the management of Indian affairs, particularly in the selection of agents for the various tribes. A Mr. Tatham was appointed agent for the

Kiowas in 1869. He at once gained the confidence of Kicking Bird, who became very valuable to him as an assistant in controlling the savages. It was through that chief's influence that Thomas Batty, another Quaker, was allowed to take up his residence with the tribe, the first white man ever accorded that privilege. Batty was permitted to erect three tents, which were staked together, converting them into an ample schoolhouse. In that crude, temporary structure he taught the Kiowa youth the rudiments of an education. This very successful innovation shows how earnest the former dreaded savage was in his efforts to promote the welfare of his people, by trying to induce them to "take the white man's road."

Batty succeeded admirably for a year in his office of teacher, the chief all the time nobly withstanding the taunts and jeers of his warriors and their threats of taking his life, for daring to allow a white man within the sacred precincts of their village-- a thing unparalleled in the annals of the tribe.

At last trouble came; the dissatisfied members of the tribe, the ambitious and restless young men, eager for renown, made another unsuccessful raid into Texas. The result was that they lost nearly the whole of the band, among which was the favourite son of Lone Wolf, a noted chief.[34] After the death of his son, he declared that he must and would have the scalp of a white man in revenge for the untimely taking off of the young warrior. Of course, the most available white man at this juncture was Batty, the Quaker teacher, and he was chosen by Lone Wolf as the victim of savage revenge. Here the noble instincts of Kicking Bird developed themselves. He very plainly told Lone Wolf, who was constantly threatening and thirsting for blood, that he could not kill Batty until he first killed him and all his band. But Lone Wolf had fully determined to have the hair of the innocent Quaker; so Kicking Bird, to avert any collision between the two bands of Indians, kidnapped Batty and ran him off to the agency, arriving at Fort Sill about an hour before Lone Wolf's band of avengers overtook them, and thus the Quaker teacher was saved.

One day, long after these occurrences, a friend of mine was in the sutler's store at Fort Sill. In there was a stranger talking to Mr. Fox, the agent of the Indians. Soon Kicking Bird entered the establishment, and the stranger asked Mr. Fox who that fine-looking Indian was. He was told, and then he begged the agent to say to him that he would like to have a talk with him; for he it was who led that famous raid into Texas. "I never saw better generalship in the field in all my experience. He had three horses killed under him. I was the surgeon of the rangers and was, of course, in the fight."[35]

When Kicking Bird was told that the Texas doctor desired to talk with him, he replied with great dignity that he did not want to revive those troublous times. "Tell him, though," said Kicking Bird, "that was my last raid against the whites; that I am a changed man."

120

The President of the United States sent for Kicking Bird to come to Washington, and to bring with him such other influential Indians as he thought might aid in inducing the Kiowas to cease their continual raiding on the border of Texas.

In due time Kicking Bird left for the capital, taking with him Lone Wolf, Big Bow, and Sun Boy of the Kiowas, together with several of the head men of the Comanches. When the deputation of savages arrived in Washington, it was received at the presidential mansion by the chief magistrate himself. So much more attention was given to Kicking Bird than to the others, that they became very jealous, particularly when the President announced to them the appointment of Kicking Bird as the head chief of the tribe.[36] But Lone Wolf would never recognize his authority, constantly urging the young men to raid the settlements. Lone Wolf was a genuine savage, without one redeeming trait, and his hatred of the white race was unparalleled in its intensity. He was never known to smile. No other Indian can show such a record of horrible massacres as he is responsible for. His orders were rigidly obeyed, for he brooked no disobedience on the part of his warriors.

In the summer of 1876, a party of English gentlemen left Fort Harker for a buffalo hunt. They soon exhausted all their rations and started a four-mule team back to the post for more. Some of Lone Wolf's band of cut-throats came across the unfortunate teamster, killed him, and ran off the team. After the occurrence, Kicking Bird came into the agency at Fort Sill and told Mr. Haworth, the agent, that he had given his word to the Great Father at Washington he would do all he could to bring in those Indians who had been raiding by order of Lone Wolf, particularly the two who had killed the Englishmen's driver.

He succeeded in bringing in twelve Indians in all, among them the murderers of the driver. They, with Lone Wolf and Satank, were sent to the Dry Tortugas for life. The morning they started on their journey Satank talked very feelingly to Kicking Bird, with tears in his eyes. He said that they might look for his bones along the road, for he would never go to Florida. The savages were loaded into government wagons. Satank was inside of one with a soldier on each side of him, their legs hanging outside. Somehow the crafty villain managed to slip the handcuffs off his wrists, at the same instant seizing the rifle of one of his guards, and then shoved the two men out with his feet. He tried to work the lever of the rifle, but could not move it, and one of the soldiers, coming around the wagon to where he was still trying to get the gun so as he could use it, shot him down, and then threw his body on the Trail. Thus Satank made good his vow that he would never be taken to Florida. He met his death only a mile from the post.

After the departure of the condemned savages, the feeling in the tribe against Kicking Bird increased to an alarming extent. Several times the most incensed warriors tried to kill him by shooting at him from an ambush. After he became fully aware that his life was in danger, he never left his lodge without his carbine. He was as brave as a lion, fearing none of the members of Lone Wolf's band; but he often said it was only a question of a short time when he would be gotten rid of; he did not allow the matter, however, to worry him in the least, saying that he was conscious he had done his duty by his tribe and the Great Father.

In a bend of Cash Creek, about half a mile below the mill, about half a dozen of the Kiowas had their lodges, that of their chief being among them. At ten o'clock one Monday in June, 1876, Mr. Haworth, the agent, came in haste to the shops, called the master mechanic, Mr. Wykes, out, told him to jump into the carriage quickly; that Kicking Bird was dead.

When they arrived at the home of the great chief, sure enough he was dead, and some of the women were engaged in folding his body in robes. Other squaws were cutting themselves in a terrible manner, as is their custom when a relative dies, and were also breaking everything breakable about the lodge. Kicking Bird had always been scrupulously clean and neat in the care of his home; it was adorned with the most beautifully dressed buffalo robes and the finest furs, while the floor was covered with matting.

It seems that Kicking Bird, after visiting Mr. Wykes that morning, went immediately to his lodge, and sat down to eat something, but just as he had finished a cup of coffee, he fell over, dead. He had in his service a Mexican woman, and she had been bribed to poison him.

An expensive coffin was made at the agency for his remains, fashioned out of the finest black walnut to be found in the country where that timber grows to such a luxuriant extent. It was eight feet long and four feet deep, but even then it did not hold one-half of his effects, which were, according to the savage custom, interred with his body.

The cries and lamentations of the warriors and women of his band were heartrending; such a manifestation of grief was never before witnessed at the agency. A handsome fence was erected around his grave, in the cemetery at Fort Sill, and the government ordered a beautiful marble monument to be raised over it; but I do not know whether it was ever done.

Kicking Bird was only forty years old at the time of his sudden taking off, and was very wealthy for an Indian. He knew the uses of money and was a careful saver of it. A great roll of greenbacks was placed in his coffin, and that fact having leaked out, it was rumoured that his grave was robbed; but the story may not have been true.

One of the greatest terrors of the Old Santa Fe Trail was the half-breed Indian desperado Charles Bent. His mother was a Cheyenne squaw, and his father the famous trader, Colonel Bent. He was born at the base of the Rocky Mountains, and at a very early age placed in one of the best schools that St. Louis afforded. His venerable sire, with only a limited education himself, was determined that his boy should profit by the culture and refinement of civilization, so he was not allowed to return to his mountain home at Bent's Fort, and the savage conditions under which he was born, until he had attained his majority. He then spoke no language but English. His mother died while he was absent at school, and his father continued to live at the old fort, where Charles, after he had reached the age of twenty-one, joined him.

Some Washington sentimentalist, philosophizing on the Indian character, his knowledge being based on Cooper's novels probably, has said: "Civilization has very marked effects upon an Indian. If he once learns to speak English, he will soon forget all his native cunning and pride of race." Let us see how this theory worked with Charley Bent.

As soon as the educated half-breed set his foot on his native heath he readily found enough ambitious young bucks of his own age who were willing to look on him as their leader. They loved him, too, if such a thing were possible, as Fra Diavolo was loved by his wild followers. His band was known as the "Dog-Soldiers"; a sort of a semi-military organization, consisting of the most daring, blood-thirsty young men of the tribe; and sometimes "squaw-men," that is, renegade white men married to squaws, attached themselves to his command of cut-throats.

At the head of this collection of the worst savages, hardly ever numbering over a hundred, Charles Bent robbed ranches, attacked wagon-trains, overland coaches, and army caravans. He stole and murdered indiscriminately. The history of his bloody work will never be wholly revealed, for dead men have no tongues.

He would visit all alone, in the guise of plainsman, hunter, or cattleman, the emigrant trains crossing the continent, always, however, those which had only small escorts or none at all. Feigning hunger, while his needs were being kindly furnished, he would glance around him to learn what kind of an outfit it was; its value, its destination, and how well guarded. Then he would take his leave with many thanks, rejoin his band, and with it dash down on the train and kill every human being unfortunate enough not to have escaped before he arrived.

He was indefatigable in his efforts to kill off the whole corps of army scouts. He would pass himself off as a fellow-scout, as a deserter from some military post, or as an Indian trader, for he was a wonderful actor, and would have achieved histrionic honours had he chosen the stage as a profession.

He would always time his actions so as to be found apparently asleep by a little camp-fire on the bank of Pawnee Fork, Crooked, Mulberry, or Walnut creeks, all of which streams intercepted the trails running north and south between the several military posts during the Indian war, when he would seem delighted and astonished, or else simulate suspicion. Then he would either murder the unsuspecting scout with his own hands, or deliver him to the red fiends of his band to be tormented.

The government offered a reward of five thousand dollars for Bent's capture, dead or alive. It was reported currently that he was at last killed in a battle with some deputy United States marshals, and that they received the reward; but the whole thing was manufactured out of whole cloth, and if the marshals received the money, Uncle Sam was most outrageously swindled.

The facts are that he died of malarial fever superinduced by a wound received in a fight with the Kaws, near the mouth of the Walnut and not far from Fort Zarah. His "Dog-Soldiers" were whipped by the Kaws, and his band driven off. Bent lingered for some time and died.

CHAPTER XI.

LA GLORIETA.

New Mexico, at the breaking out of the Civil War, was abandoned by the government at Washington, or at least so overlooked that the charge of neglect was merited. In the report of the committee on the Conduct of the War, under date of July 15, 1862, Brevet Lieutenant-Colonel B. S. Roberts of the regular army, major of the Third Cavalry, who was stationed in the Territory in 1861, says:

It appears to me to be the determination of General Thomas[37]
not to acknowledge the service of the officers who saved
the Territory of New Mexico; and the utter neglect of the
adjutant-general's department for the last year to
communicate in any way with the commanding officer of the
department of New Mexico, or to answer his urgent appeals
for reinforcements, for money and other supplies, in
connection with his repudiation of the services of all the
army there, convinces me that he is not gratified at their
loyalty and their success in saving that Territory to
the Union.

If space could be given to the story of the carefully prepared plans of the leaders of secession for the conquest of all the territory south of a line drawn from Maryland directly west to the Pacific coast, in which were California, Arizona, and New Mexico, it would reveal some startling facts, and prove beyond question that it was the intention of Jefferson Davis to precipitate the rebellion a decade before it actually occurred. The basis of the scheme was to inaugurate a war between Texas--which, when admitted into the Union, claimed all that part of New Mexico east of the Rio Grande--and the United States, in which conflict Mississippi and some of the other Southern States were to become participants. The plan fell flat, because, in 1851, Mr. Davis failed of a re-election to the governorship of Mississippi.

So confident were many of Mr. Davis' allies in regard to the contemplated rebellion, that they boasted to their friends of the North, upon leaving Washington, that when they met again, it would be upon a Southern battle-field.

I have alluded incidentally to what is known as the Texas Santa Fe Expedition, inaugurated by the President of what was then the republic of Texas, Mirabeau B.

Lamar. It was given out to the world that it was merely one of commercial interest--to increase the trade between the two countries; but that it was intended for the conquest of New Mexico, no one now, in the light of history, doubts. It resulted in disaster, and is a story well worthy the examination of the student of American politics.[38]

In 1861 General Twiggs commanded the military department of which Texas was an important part. It will be remembered that he surrendered to the Confederate government the troops, the munitions of war, the forts, or posts as they were properly termed, and everything pertaining to the United States army under his control. It was the intention of the Confederacy to use this region as a military base from which to continue its conquests westward, and capture the various forts in New Mexico. Particularly they had their eyes upon Fort Union, where there was an arsenal, which John B. Floyd, Secretary of War, had taken especial care to have well stocked previously to the act of secession.

But the conspirators had reckoned without their host; they imagined the native Mexicans would eagerly accept their overtures, and readily support the Southern Confederacy. Mr. Davis and his coadjutors had evidently forgotten the effect of the Texas Santa Fe Expedition, in 1841, upon the people of the Province of New Mexico; but the natives themselves had not. Besides the loyalty of the Mexicans, there was a factor which the Confederate leaders had failed to consider, which was that the majority of the American pioneers had come from loyal States.

Of course, there were many secessionists both in Colorado and New Mexico who were watching the progress of rebellion in eager anticipation; and it is claimed that in Denver a rebel flag was raised--but how true that is I do not know.

John B. Floyd, Secretary of War, was one of the leading spirits of the Confederacy. A year before the Civil War he placed in command of the department of New Mexico a North Carolinian, Colonel Loring, who was in perfect sympathy with his superior, and willing to carry out his well-defined plans. In 1861 he ordered Colonel G. B. Crittenden on an expedition against the Apaches. This officer at once tried to induce his troops to attach themselves to the rebel army in Texas, but he was met with an indignant refusal by Colonel Roberts and the regular soldiers under him. The loyal colonel told Crittenden, in the most forcible language, that he would resist any such attempt on his part, and reported the action of Colonel Crittenden to the commander of the department at Santa Fe. Of course, Colonel Loring paid no attention to the complaint of disloyalty, and then Colonel Roberts conveyed the tidings to the commanding officers of several military posts in the Territory, whom he knew were true to the Union, and only one man out of nearly two thousand regular soldiers renounced his flag. Some of the officers stationed at New Mexico were of a different mind, and one of them, Major Lynde, commanding Fort Filmore, surrendered to a detachment of Texans, who paroled the enlisted men, as they firmly refused to join the rebel forces.

Upon the desertion of Colonel Loring to the Southern Confederacy, General Edward R. S. Canby was assigned to the command of the department; next in rank was the loyal Roberts. At this perilous juncture in New Mexico, there were but a thousand regulars all told, but the Territory furnished two regiments of volunteers, commanded by officers whose names had been famous on the border for years. Among these was Colonel Ceran St. Vrain, who had been conspicuous in the suppression of the Mexican insurrection of 1847, fifteen years before. Kit Carson was lieutenant-colonel; J. F. Chaves, major; and the most prominent of the line officers Captain Albert H. Pfeiffer, with a record as an Indian fighter equal to that of Carson.

At the same time Colorado was girding on her armour for the impending conflict. The governor of the prosperous Territory was William Gilpin, an old army officer, who had spent a large part of his life on the frontier, and had accompanied Colonel Doniphan, as major of his regiment, across the plains, on the expedition to New Mexico in 1846.

Colonel Gilpin at once responded to the pleadings of New Mexico for help, by organizing two companies at first, quickly following with a full regiment. This Colorado regiment was composed of as fine material as any portion of the United States could furnish. John P. Slough, a war Democrat and a lawyer, was its colonel. He afterwards became chief justice of New Mexico, and was brutally murdered in that Territory.

John M. Chivington, a strict Methodist and a presiding elder of that church, was offered the chaplaincy, but firmly declined, and, like many others who wore the clerical garb, he quickly doffed it and put on the attire of a soldier; so he was made major, and his record as a fighter was equal to the best.

The commanding general knew well the plans of the rebels as to their intended occupation of New Mexico, and, notwithstanding the weakness of his force, determined to frustrate them if within the limits of possibility. To that end he concentrated his little army, comprising a thousand regular soldiers, the two regiments of New Mexico volunteers, two companies of Colorado troops, and a portion of the territorial militia, at Fort Craig, on the Rio Grande, to await the approach of the Confederate troops, under the command of General H. H. Sibley, an old regular army officer, a native of Louisiana, and the inventor of the comfortable tent named after him.

Sibley's brigade comprised some three thousand men, the majority of them Texans, and he expected that many more would flock to his standard as he moved northward. On the 19th of February, 1862, he crossed the Rio Grande below Fort Craig, not daring to attack Canby in his intrenched position. The Union commander, in order to keep the Texas troops from gaining the high points overlooking the fort, placed portions of the Fifth, Seventh, and Tenth Regulars, together with Carson's and Pino's volunteers, on the other side of the river. No collision occurred that day, but the next afternoon Major Duncan, with his cavalry and Captain M'Rae's light battery, having been sent across to reinforce the infantry, a heavy artillery fire was immediately opened upon them by the Texans. The men under Carson behaved splendidly, but the other volunteer regiments became a little demoralized, and the general was compelled to call back the force into the fort. Sibley's force, both men and animals, suffered much from thirst, the latter stampeding, and many, wandering into our lines, were caught by the scouts of the Union forces. The next morning early Colonel Roberts was ordered to proceed about seven miles up the river to keep the Texans away from the water at a point where it was alone accessible, on account of the steepness of the banks everywhere else.

The gallant Roberts, on arriving at the ford, planted a battery there, and at once opened fire. This was the battle of Valverde, the details of which, however, do not belong to this book, having been only incidentally referred to in order to lead the reader intelligently up to that of La Glorieta, Apache Canyon, or Pigeon's Ranch, as it is indifferently called.

Valverde was lost to the Union troops, but never did men fight more valiantly, with the exception of a few who did not act the part of the true soldier. The brave M'Rae mounted one of the guns of his battery, choosing to die rather than surrender.

General Sibley, after his doubtful victory at Valverde, continued on to Albuquerque and Santa Fe. The old city offered no resistance to his occupation; in fact, some of the most influential Mexicans were pleased, their leaning being strongly toward the Southern Confederacy; but the common people were as loyal to the Union as those of any of the Northern States, a feeling intensified by their hatred for the Texans on account of the expedition of conquest in 1841, twenty-one years before. They contributed of their means to aid the United States troops, but have never received proper credit for their action in those days of trouble in the neglected Territory.

The Confederate general was disappointed at the way in which affairs were going, for he had based great hopes upon the defection of the native residents; but he determined to march forward to Fort Union, where his friend Floyd had placed such stores as were likely to be needed in the campaign which he had designed.

From Santa Fe to Fort Union, where the arsenal was located, the road runs through the deep, rocky gorge known as Apache Canyon. It is one of the wildest spots in the mountains, the walls on each side rising from one to two thousand feet above the Trail, which is within the range of ordinary cannon from every point, and in many places of point-blank rifle-shot. Granite rocks and sands abound, and the hills are covered with long-leafed pine. It is a gateway which, in the hands of a skilful engineer and one hundred resolute men, can be made perfectly impregnable.

The Atchison, Topeka, and Santa Fe Railway passes directly through this picturesque chasm, every foot of which is classic ground, and in the season of the mountain freshets constant care is needed to keep its bridges in place.

At its eastern entrance is a large residence, known as Pigeon's Ranch, from which the battle to be described derives its name, though, as stated, it is also known as that of Apache Canyon, and La Glorieta,[39] the latter, perhaps, the most classical, from the range of mountains enclosing the rent in the mighty hills.

The following detailed account of this battle I have taken from the *History of Colorado*,[40] an admirable work:

The sympathizers with and abettors of the Southern
Confederacy inaugurated their plans by posting handbills
in all conspicuous places between Denver and the
mining-camps, designating certain localities where the
highest prices would be paid for arms of every description,
and for powder, lead, shot, and percussion caps.
Simultaneously, a small force was collected and put under
discipline to co-operate with parties expected from Arkansas
and Texas who were to take possession, first of Colorado,
and subsequently of New Mexico, anticipating the easy
capture of the Federal troops and stores located there.
Being apprised of the movement, the governor immediately
decided to enlist a full regiment of volunteers.
John P. Slough was appointed colonel, Samuel F. Tappan
lieutenant-colonel, and John J. M. Chivington major.

Without railroads or telegraphs nearer than the Missouri
River, and wholly dependent upon the overland mail coach
for communication with the States and the authorities at
Washington, news was at least a week old when received.
Thus the troops passed the time in a condition of doubt
and extreme anxiety, until the 6th of January, 1862, when

information arrived that an invading force under General H. H. Sibley, from San Antonio, Texas, was approaching the southern border of New Mexico, and had already captured Forts Fillmore and Bliss, making prisoners of their garrisons without firing a gun, and securing all their stock and supplies.

Immediately upon receipt of this intelligence, efforts were made to obtain the consent of, or orders from, General Hunter, commanding the department at Fort Leavenworth, Kansas, for the regiment to go to the relief of General Canby, then in command of the department of New Mexico. On the 20th of February, orders came from General Hunter, directing Colonel Slough and the First Regiment of Colorado Volunteers to proceed with all possible despatch to Fort Union, or Santa Fe, New Mexico, and report to General Canby for service.

Two days thereafter, the command marched out of Camp Weld two miles up the Platte River, and in due time encamped at Pueblo, on the Arkansas River. At this point further advices were received from Canby, stating that he had encountered the enemy at Valverde, ten miles north of Fort Craig, but, owing to the inefficiency of the newly raised New Mexican volunteers, was compelled to retire. The Texans under Sibley marched on up the Rio Grande, levying tribute upon the inhabitants for their support. The Colorado troops were urged to the greatest possible haste in reaching Fort Union, where they were to unite with such regular troops as could be concentrated at that post, and thus aid in saving the fort and its supplies from falling into Confederate hands. Early on the following morning the order was given to proceed to Union by forced marches, and it is doubtful if the same number of men ever marched a like distance in the same length of time.

When the summit of Raton Pass was reached, another courier

from Canby met the command, who informed Colonel Slough that the Texans had already captured Albuquerque and Santa Fe with all the troops stationed at those places, together with the supplies stored there, and that they were then marching on Fort Union.

Arriving at Red River about sundown, the regiment was drawn up in line and this information imparted to the men. The request was then made for all who were willing to undertake a forced march at night to step two paces to the front, when every man advanced to the new alignment. After a hasty supper the march was resumed, and at sunrise the next morning they reached Maxwell's Ranch on the Cimarron, having made sixty-four miles in less than twenty-four hours. At ten o'clock on the second night thereafter, the command entered Fort Union. It was there discovered that Colonel Paul, in charge of the post, had mined the fort, giving orders for the removal of the women and children, and was preparing to blow up all the supplies and march to Fort Garland or some other post to the northward, on the first approach of the Confederates.

The troops remained at Union from the 13th to the 22d of March, when by order of Colonel Slough they proceeded in the direction of Santa Fe. The command consisted of the First Colorado Volunteers; two Light Batteries, one commanded by Captain Ritter and the other by Captain Claflin; Ford's Company of Colorado Volunteers unattached; two companies of the Fifth Regular Infantry; and two companies of the Seventh United States Cavalry.

The force encamped at Bernal Springs, where Colonel Slough determined to organize a detachment to enter Santa Fe by night with the view of surprising the enemy, spiking his guns, and after doing what other damage could be accomplished without bringing on a general action, falling back on the main body. The detachment chosen comprised sixty men each

from Companies A, D, and E of the Colorado regiment, with
Company F of the same mounted, and thirty-seven men each
from the companies of Captains Ford and Howland, and of
the Seventh Cavalry, the whole commanded by Major Chivington.

At sundown on the 25th of March it reached Kosloskie's Ranch,
where Major Chivington was informed that the enemy's pickets
were in the vicinity. He went into camp at once, and about
nine o'clock of the same evening sent out Lieutenant Nelson
of the First Colorado with thirty men of Company F, who
captured the Texan pickets while they were engaged in a game
of cards at Pigeon's Ranch, and before daylight on the
morning of the 26th, reported at camp with his prisoners.
After breakfast, the major, being apprised of the enemy's
whereabouts, proceeded cautiously, keeping his advance
guard well to the front. While passing near the summit
of the hill, the officer in command of the advance met
the Confederate advance, consisting of a first lieutenant
and thirty men, captured them without firing a gun, and
returning met the main body and turned them over to the
commanding officer. The Confederate lieutenant declared
that they had received no intimation of the advance from
Fort Union, but themselves expected to be there four days
later.

Descending Apache Canyon for the distance of half a mile,
Chivington's force observed the approaching Texans, about
six hundred strong, with three pieces of artillery, who,
on discovering the Federals, halted, formed line and battery,
and opened fire.

Chivington drew up his cavalry as a reserve under cover,
deployed Company D under Captain Downing to the right,
and Companies A and E under Captains Wynkoop and Anthony
to the left, directing them to ascend the mountain-side
until they were above the elevation of the enemy's artillery
and thus flank him, at the same time directing Captain

132

Howland, he being the ranking cavalry officer, to closely
observe the enemy, and when he retreated, without further
orders to charge with the cavalry. This disposition of
the troops proved wise and successful. The Texans soon
broke battery and retreated down the canyon a mile or more,
but from some cause Captain Howland failed to charge as
ordered, which enabled the Confederates to take up a new
and strong position, where they formed battery, threw their
supports well up the sides of the mountain, and again
opened fire.

Chivington dismounted Captains Howland and Lord with their
regulars, leaving their horses in charge of every fourth
man, and ordered them to join Captain Downing on the left,
taking orders from him. Our skirmishers advanced, and,
flanking the enemy's supports, drove them pell-mell down
the mountain-side, when Captain Samuel Cook, with Company F,
First Colorado, having been signalled by the major, made
as gallant and successful a charge through the canyon,
through the ranks of the Confederates and back, as was
ever performed. Meanwhile, our infantry advanced rapidly;
when the enemy commenced his retreat a second time, they
were well ahead of him on the mountain-sides and poured
a galling fire into him, which thoroughly demoralized and
broke him up, compelling the entire body to seek shelter
among the rocks down the canyon and in some cabins that
stood by the wayside.

After an hour spent in collecting the prisoners, and
caring for the wounded, both Federal and Confederate,
the latter having left in killed, wounded, and prisoners
a number equal to our whole force in the field, the first
baptism by fire of our volunteers terminated. The victory
was decided and complete. Night intervening, and there
being no water in the canyon, the little command fell back
to Pigeon's Ranch, whence a courier was despatched to
Colonel Slough, advising him of the engagement and its

result, and requesting him to bring forward the main command as rapidly as possible, as the enemy with all his forces had moved from Santa Fe toward Fort Union.

After interring the dead and making a comfortable hospital for the wounded, on the afternoon of the 27th Chivington fell back to the Pecos River at Kosloskie's Ranch and encamped. On receiving the news from Apache Canyon, Colonel Slough put his forces in motion, and at eleven o'clock at night of the 27th joined Chivington at Kosloskie's.

At daybreak on the 28th, the assembly was sounded, and the entire command resumed its march. Five miles out from their encampment Major Chivington, in command of a detachment composed of Companies A, B, H, and E of the First Colorado, and Captain Ford's Company unattached, with Captain Lewis' Company of the Fifth Regular Infantry, was ordered to take the Galisteo road, and by a detour through the mountains to gain the enemy's rear, if possible, at the west end of Apache Canyon, while Slough advanced slowly with the main body to gain his front about the same time; thus devising an attack in front and rear.

About ten o'clock, while making his way through the scrub pine and cedar brush in the mountains, Major Chivington and his command heard cannonading to their right, and were thereby apprised that Colonel Slough and his men had met the enemy. About twelve o'clock he arrived with his men on the summit of the mountain which overlooked the enemy's supply wagons, which had been left in the charge of a strong guard with one piece of artillery mounted on an elevation commanding the camp and mouth of the canyon. With great difficulty Chivington descended the precipitous mountain, charged, took, and spiked the gun, ran together the enemy's supply wagons of commissary, quartermaster, and ordnance stores, set them on fire, blew and burnt them up, bayoneted his mules in corral, took the guard

prisoners and reascended the mountain, where about dark
he was met by Lieutenant Cobb, aide-de-camp on Colonel
Slough's staff, with the information that Slough and his
men had been defeated and had fallen back to Kosloskie's.
Upon the supposition that this information was correct,
Chivington, under the guidance of a French Catholic priest,
in the intensest darkness, with great difficulty made
his way with his command through the mountains without
a road or trail, and joined Colonel Slough about midnight.

Meanwhile, after Chivington and his detachment had left
in the morning, Colonel Slough with the main body proceeded
up the canyon, and arriving at Pigeon's Ranch, gave orders
for the troops to stack arms in the road and supply their
canteens with water, as that would be the last opportunity
before reaching the further end of Apache Canyon.
While thus supplying themselves with water and visiting
the wounded in the hospital at Pigeon's Ranch, being
entirely off their guard, they were suddenly startled by
a courier from the advance column dashing down the road
at full speed and informing them that the enemy was close
at hand. Orders were immediately given to fall in and
take arms, but before the order could be obeyed the enemy
had formed battery and commenced shelling them.
They formed as quickly as possible, the colonel ordering
Captain Downing with Company D, First Colorado Volunteers,
to advance on the left, and Captain Kerber with Company I
First Colorado, to advance on the right. In the meantime
Ritter and Claflin opened a return fire on the enemy with
their batteries. Captain Downing advanced and fought
desperately, meeting a largely superior force in point
of numbers, until he was almost overpowered and surrounded;
when, happily, Captain Wilder of Company G of the First
Colorado, with a detachment of his command, came to his
relief, and extricated him and that portion of his Company
not already slaughtered. While on the opposite side,
the right, Company I had advanced into an open space,

feeling the enemy, and ambitious of capturing his battery,
when they were surprised by a detachment which was concealed
in an arroya, and which, when Kerber and his men were
within forty feet of it, opened a galling fire upon them.
Kerber lost heavily; Lieutenant Baker, being wounded,
fell back. In the meantime the enemy masked, and made
five successive charges on our batteries, determined to
capture them as they had captured Canby's at Valverde.
At one time they were within forty yards of Slough's
batteries, their slouch hats drawn down over their faces,
and rushing on with deafening yells. It seemed inevitable
that they would make the capture, when Captain Claflin
gave the order to cease firing, and Captain Samuel Robbins
with his company, K of the First Colorado, arose from the
ground like ghosts, delivering a galling fire, charged
bayonets, and on the double-quick put the rebels to flight.

During the whole of this time the cavalry, under Captain
Howland, were held in reserve, never moving except to
fall back and keep out of danger, with the exception of
Captain Cook's men, who dismounted and fought as infantry.
From the opening of the battle to its close the odds were
against Colonel Slough and his forces; the enemy being
greatly superior in numbers, with a better armament of
artillery and equally well armed otherwise. But every inch
of ground was stubbornly contested. In no instance did
Slough's forces fall back until they were in danger of
being flanked and surrounded, and for nine hours, without
rest or refreshment, the battle raged incessantly.
At one time Claflin gave orders to double-shot his guns,
they being nothing but little brass howitzers, and he
counted, "One, two, three, four," until one of his own
carriages capsized and fell down into the gulch; from which
place Captain Samuel Robbins and his company, K, extricated
it and saved it from falling into the enemy's hands.

Having been compelled to give ground all day, Colonel Slough,

between five and six o'clock in the afternoon, issued
orders to retreat. About the same time General Sibley
received information from the rear of the destruction of
his supply trains, and ordered a flag of truce to be sent
to Colonel Slough, which did not reach him, however, until
he arrived at Kosloskie's. A truce was entered into until
nine o'clock the next morning, which was afterward extended
to twenty-four hours, and under which Sibley with his
demoralized forces fell back to Santa Fe, laying that town
under tribute to supply his forces.

The 29th was spent in burying the dead, as well as those
of the Confederates which they left on the field, and
caring for the wounded. Orders were received from General
Canby directing Colonel Slough to fall back to Fort Union,
which so incensed him that while obeying the order he
forwarded his resignation, and soon after left the command.

Thus ended the battle of La Glorieta.

CHAPTER XII.[41]

THE BUFFALO.

The ancient range of the buffalo, according to history and tradition, once
extended from the Alleghanies to the Rocky Mountains, embracing all that
magnificent portion of North America known as the Mississippi valley; from the
frozen lakes above to the "Tierras Calientes" of Mexico, far to the south.

It seems impossible, especially to those who have seen them, as numerous,
apparently, as the sands of the seashore, feeding on the illimitable natural pastures of
the great plains, that the buffalo should have become almost extinct.

When I look back only twenty-five years, and recall the fact that they roamed in
immense numbers even then, as far east as Fort Harker, in Central Kansas, a little
more than two hundred miles from the Missouri River, I ask myself, "Have they all
disappeared?"

An idea may be formed of how many buffalo were killed from 1868 to 1881,
a period of only thirteen years, during which time they were indiscriminately

slaughtered for their hides. In Kansas alone there was paid out, between the dates specified, two million five hundred thousand dollars for their bones gathered on the prairies, to be utilized by the various carbon works of the country, principally in St. Louis. It required about one hundred carcasses to make one ton of bones, the price paid averaging eight dollars a ton; so the above-quoted enormous sum represented the skeletons of over thirty-one millions of buffalo.[42] These figures may appear preposterous to readers not familiar with the great plains a third of a century ago; but to those who have seen the prairie black from horizon to horizon with the shaggy monsters, they are not so. In the autumn of 1868 I rode with Generals Sheridan, Custer, Sully, and others, for three consecutive days, through one continuous herd, which must have contained millions. In the spring of 1869 the train on the Kansas Pacific Railroad was delayed at a point between Forts Harker and Hays, from nine o'clock in the morning until five in the afternoon, in consequence of the passage of an immense herd of buffalo across the track. On each side of us, and to the west as far as we could see, our vision was only limited by the extended horizon of the flat prairie, and the whole vast area was black with the surging mass of affrighted buffaloes as they rushed onward to the south.

In 1868 the Union Pacific Railroad and its branch in Kansas was nearly completed across the plains to the foothills of the Rocky Mountains, the western limit of the buffalo range, and that year witnessed the beginning of the wholesale and wanton slaughter of the great ruminants, which ended only with their practical extinction seventeen years afterward. The causes of this hecatomb of animals on the great plains were the incursion of regular hunters into the region, for the hides of the buffalo, and the crowds of tourists who crossed the continent for the mere pleasure and novelty of the trip. The latter class heartlessly killed for the excitement of the new experience as they rode along in the cars at a low rate of speed, often never touching a particle of the flesh of their victims, or possessing themselves of a single robe. The former, numbering hundreds of old frontiersmen, all expert shots, with thousands of novices, the pioneer settlers on the public domain, just opened under the various land laws, from beyond the Platte to far south of the Arkansas, within transporting distance of two railroads, day after day for years made it a lucrative business to kill for the robes alone, a market for which had suddenly sprung up all over the country.

On either side of the track of the two lines of railroads running through Kansas and Nebraska, within a relatively short distance and for nearly their whole length, the most conspicuous objects in those days were the desiccated carcasses of the noble beasts that had been ruthlessly slaughtered by the thoughtless and excited passengers on their way across the continent. On the open prairie, too, miles away from the course of legitimate travel, in some places one could walk all day on the dead bodies of the buffaloes killed by the hide-hunters, without stepping off them to the ground.

The best robes, in their relation to thickness of fur and lustre, were those taken during the winter months, particularly February, at which period the maximum of density and beauty had been reached. Then, notwithstanding the sudden and fitful variations of temperature incident to our mid-continent climate, the old hunters were especially active, and accepted unusual risks to procure as many of the coveted skins as possible. A temporary camp would be established under the friendly shelter of some timbered stream, from which the hunters would radiate every morning, and return at night after an arduous day's work, to smoke their pipes and relate their varied adventures around the fire of blazing logs.

Sometimes when far away from camp a blizzard would come down from the north in all its fury without ten minutes' warning, and in a few seconds the air, full of blinding snow, precluded the possibility of finding their shelter, an attempt at which would only result in an aimless circular march on the prairie. On such occasions, to keep from perishing by the intense cold, they would kill a buffalo, and, taking out its viscera, creep inside the huge cavity, enough animal heat being retained until the storm had sufficiently abated for them to proceed with safety to their camp.

Early in March, 1867, a party of my friends, all old buffalo hunters, were camped in Paradise valley, then a famous rendezvous of the animals they were after. One day when out on the range stalking, and widely separated from each other, a terrible blizzard came up. Three of the hunters reached their camp without much difficulty, but he who was farthest away was fairly caught in it, and night overtaking him, he was compelled to resort to the method described in the preceding paragraph. Luckily, he soon came up with a superannuated bull that had been abandoned by the herd; so he killed him, took out his viscera and crawled inside the empty carcass, where he lay comparatively comfortable until morning broke, when the storm had passed over and the sun shone brightly. But when he attempted to get out, he found himself a prisoner, the immense ribs of the creature having frozen together, and locked him up as tightly as if he were in a cell. Fortunately, his companions, who were searching for him, and firing their rifles from time to time, heard him yell in response to the discharge of their pieces, and thus discovered and released him from the peculiar predicament into which he had fallen.

At another time, several years before the acquisition of New Mexico by the United States, two old trappers were far up on the Arkansas near the Trail, in the foot-hills hunting buffalo, and they, as is generally the case, became separated. In an hour or two one of them killed a fat young cow, and, leaving his rifle on the ground, went up and commenced to skin her. While busily engaged in his work, he suddenly heard right behind him a suppressed snort, and looking around he saw to his dismay a monstrous grizzly ambling along in that animal's characteristic gait, within a few feet of him.

In front, only a few rods away, there happened to be a clump of scrubby pines, and he incontinently made a break for them, climbing into the tallest in less time than it takes to tell of it. The bear deliberately ate a hearty meal off the juicy hams of the cow, so providentially fallen in his way, and when he had satiated himself, instead of going away, he quietly stretched himself alongside of the half-devoured carcass, and went to sleep, keeping one eye open, however, on the movements of the unlucky hunter whom he had corralled in the tree. In the early evening his partner came to the spot, and killed the impudent bear, that, being full of tender buffalo meat, was sluggish and unwary, and thus became an easy victim to the unerring rifle; when the unwilling prisoner came down from his perch in the pine, feeling sheepish enough. The last time I saw him he told me he still had the bear's hide, which he religiously preserved as a memento of his foolishness in separating himself from his rifle, a thing he has never been guilty of before or since.

Kit Carson, when with Fremont on his first exploring expedition, while hunting for the command, at some point on the Arkansas, left a buffalo which he had just killed and partly cut up, to pursue a large bull that came rushing by him alone. He chased his game for nearly a quarter of a mile, not being able, however, to gain on it rapidly, owing to the blown condition of his horse. Coming up at length to the side of the fleeing beast, Carson fired, but at the same instant his horse stepped into a prairie-dog hole, fell down and threw Kit fully fifteen feet over his head. The bullet struck the buffalo low under the shoulder, which only served to enrage him so that the next moment the infuriated animal was pursuing Kit, who, fortunately not much hurt, was able to run toward the river. It was a race for life now, Carson using his nimble legs to the utmost of their capacity, accelerated very much by the thundering, bellowing bull bringing up the rear. For several minutes it was nip and tuck which should reach the stream first, but Kit got there by a scratch a little ahead. It was a big bend of the river, and the water was deep under the bank, but it was paradise compared with the hades plunging at his back; so Kit leaped into the water, trusting to Providence that the bull would not follow. The trust was well placed, for the bull did not continue the pursuit, but stood on the bank and shook his head vehemently at the struggling hunter who had preferred deep waves to the horns of a dilemma on shore.

Kit swam around for some time, carefully guarded by the bull, until his position was observed by one of his companions, who attacked the belligerent animal successfully with a forty-four slug, and then Kit crawled out and--skinned the enemy!

He once killed five buffaloes during a single race, and used but four balls, having dismounted and cut the bullet from the wound of the fourth, and thus continued the chase. He it was, too, who established his reputation as a famous hunter by shooting a buffalo cow during an impetuous race down a steep hill, discharging his rifle just as the animal was leaping on one of the low cedars peculiar to the region. The ball struck a vital spot, and the dead cow remained in the jagged branches. The Indians who were with him on that hunt looked upon the circumstance as something beyond their comprehension, and insisted that Kit should leave the carcass in the tree as "Big Medicine." Katzatoa (Smoked Shield), a celebrated chief of the Kiowas many years ago, who was over seven feet tall, never mounted a horse when hunting the buffalo; he always ran after them on foot and killed them with his lance.

Two Lance, another famous chief, could shoot an arrow entirely through a buffalo while hunting on horseback. He accomplished this remarkable feat in the presence of the Grand Duke Alexis of Russia, who was under the care of Buffalo Bill, near Fort Hays, Kansas.

During one of Fremont's expeditions, two of his chasseurs, named Archambeaux and La Jeunesse,[43] had a curious adventure on a buffalo-hunt. One of them was mounted on a mule, the other on a horse; they came in sight of a large band of buffalo feeding upon the open prairie about a mile distant. The mule was not fleet enough, and the horse was too much fatigued with the day's journey, to justify a race, and they concluded to approach the herd on foot. Dismounting and securing the ends of their lariats in the ground, they made a slight detour, to take advantage of the wind, and crept stealthily in the direction of the game, approaching unperceived until within a few hundred yards. Some old bulls forming the outer picket guard slowly raised their heads and gazed long and dubiously at the strange objects, when, discovering that the intruders were not wolves, but two hunters, they gave a significant grunt, turned about as though on pivots, and in less than no time the whole herd--bulls, cows, and calves--were making the gravel fly over the prairie in fine style, leaving the hunters to their discomfiture. They had scarcely recovered from their surprise, when, to their great consternation, they beheld the whole company of the monsters, numbering several thousand, suddenly shape their course to where the riding animals were picketed. The charge of the stampeded buffalo was a magnificent one; for the buffalo, mistaking the horse and the mule for two of their own species, came down upon them like a tornado. A small cloud of dust arose for a moment over the spot where the hunter's animals had been left; the black mass moved on with accelerated speed, and in a few seconds the horizon shut them all from view. The horse and mule, with all their trappings, saddles, bridles, and holsters, were never seen or heard of afterward.

Buffalo Bill, in less than eighteen months, while employed as hunter of the construction company of the Kansas Pacific Railroad, in 1867-68, killed nearly five thousand buffalo, which were consumed by the twelve hundred men employed in track-laying. He tells in his autobiography of the following remarkable experience he had at one time with his favourite horse Brigham, on an impromptu buffalo hunt:--

One day we were pushed for horses to work on our scrapers, so I hitched up Brigham, to see how he would work. He was not much used to that kind of labour, and I was about giving up the idea of making a work horse of him, when one of the men called to me that there were some buffaloes coming over

the hill. As there had been no buffaloes seen anywhere
in the vicinity of the camp for several days, we had become
rather short of meat. I immediately told one of our men
to hitch his horses to a wagon and follow me, as I was going
out after the herd, and we would bring back some fresh meat
for supper. I had no saddle, as mine had been left at camp
a mile distant, so taking the harness from Brigham I mounted
him bareback, and started out after the game, being armed
with my celebrated buffalo killer Lucretia Borgia--a newly
improved breech-loading needle-gun, which I had obtained
from the government.

While I was riding toward the buffaloes, I observed five
horsemen coming out from the fort, who had evidently seen
the buffaloes from the post, and were going out for a chase.
They proved to be some newly arrived officers in that part
of the country, and when they came up closer I could see
by the shoulder-straps that the senior was a captain,
while the others were lieutenants.

"Hello! my friend," sang out the captain; "I see you are
after the same game we are."

"Yes, sir; I saw those buffaloes coming over the hill,
and as we were about out of fresh meat I thought I would
go and get some," said I.

They scanned my cheap-looking outfit pretty closely, and
as my horse was not very prepossessing in appearance, having
on only a blind bridle, and otherwise looking like a work
horse, they evidently considered me a green hand at hunting.

"Do you expect to catch those buffaloes on that Gothic
steed?" laughingly asked the captain.

"I hope so, by pushing on the reins hard enough," was
my reply.

"You'll never catch them in the world, my fine fellow,"
said the captain. "It requires a fast horse to overtake
the animals on the prairie."

"Does it?" asked I, as if I didn't know it.

"Yes; but come along with us, as we are going to kill them
more for pleasure than anything else. All we want are the
tongues and a piece of tenderloin, and you may have all
that is left," said the generous man.

"I am much obliged to you, captain, and will follow you,"
I replied.

There were eleven buffaloes in the herd, and they were not
more than a mile ahead of us. The officers dashed on as if
they had a sure thing on killing them all before I could
come up with them; but I had noticed that the herd was
making toward the creek for water, and as I knew buffalo
nature, I was perfectly aware that it would be difficult
to turn them from their direct course. Thereupon, I started
toward the creek to head them off, while the officers
came up in the rear and gave chase.

The buffaloes came rushing past me not a hundred yards
distant, with the officers about three hundred yards in
the rear. Now, thought I, is the time to "get my work in,"
as they say; and I pulled off the blind bridle from my
horse, who knew as well as I did that we were out after
buffaloes, as he was a trained hunter. The moment the
bridle was off he started at the top of his speed, running
in ahead of the officers, and with a few jumps he brought me
alongside the rear buffalo. Raising old Lucretia Borgia
to my shoulder, I fired, and killed the animal at the
first shot. My horse then carried me alongside the next
one, not ten feet away, and I dropped him at the next fire.

As soon as one of the buffalo would fall, Brigham would

take me so close to the next that I could almost touch it
with my gun. In this manner I killed the eleven buffaloes
with twelve shots; and as the last animal dropped, my horse
stopped. I jumped off to the ground, knowing that he would
not leave me--it must be remembered that I had been riding
him without bridle, reins, or saddle--and, turning around
as the party of astonished officers rode up, I said to them:--

"Now, gentlemen, allow me to present to you all the tongues
and tenderloins you wish from these buffaloes."

Captain Graham, for such I soon learned was his name,
replied: "Well, I never saw the like before. Who under
the sun are you, anyhow?"

"My name is Cody," said I.

Captain Graham, who was considerable of a horseman,
greatly admired Brigham, and said: "That horse of yours
has running points."

"Yes, sir; he has not only got the points, he is a runner
and knows how to use the points," said I.

"So I noticed," said the captain.

They all finally dismounted, and we continued chatting
for some little time upon the different subjects of horses,
buffaloes, hunting, and Indians. They felt a little sore
at not getting a single shot at the buffaloes; but the way
I had killed them, they said, amply repaid them for their
disappointment. They had read of such feats in books,
but this was the first time they had ever seen anything
of the kind with their own eyes. It was the first time,
also, that they had ever witnessed or heard of a white man
running buffaloes on horseback without a saddle or bridle.

I told them that Brigham knew nearly as much about the

144

business as I did, and if I had twenty bridles they would have been of no use to me, as he understood everything, and all that he expected of me was to do the shooting. It is a fact that Brigham would stop if a buffalo did not fall at the first fire, so as to give me a second chance; but if I did not kill the animal then, he would go on, as if to say, "You are no good, and I will not fool away my time by giving you more than two shots." Brigham was the best horse I ever saw or owned for buffalo chasing.

At one time an old, experienced buffalo hunter was following at the heels of a small herd with that reckless rush to which in the excitement of the chase men abandon themselves, when a great bull just in front of him tumbled into a ravine. The rider's horse fell also, throwing the old hunter over his head sprawling, but with strange accuracy right between the bull's horns! The first to recover from the terrible shock and to regain his legs was the horse, which ran off with wonderful alacrity several miles before he stopped. Next the bull rose, and shook himself with an astonished air, as if he would like to know "how that was done?" The hunter was on the great brute's back, who, perhaps, took the affair as a good practical joke; but he was soon pitched to the ground, as the buffalo commenced to jump "stiff-legged," and the latter, giving the hunter one lingering look, which he long remembered, with remarkable good nature ran off to join his companions. Had the bull been wounded, the rider would have been killed, as the then enraged animal would have gored and trampled him to death.

An officer of the old regular army told me many years ago that in crossing the plains a herd of buffalo were fired at by a twelve-pound howitzer, the ball of which wounded and stunned an immense bull. Nevertheless, heedless of a hundred shots that had been fired at him, and of a bulldog belonging to one of the officers, which had fastened himself to his lips, the enraged beast charged upon the whole troop of dragoons, and tossed one of the horses like a feather. Bull, horse, and rider all fell in a heap. Before the dust cleared away, the trooper, who had hung for a moment to one of the bull's horns by his waistband, crawled out safe, while the horse got a ball from a rifle through his neck while in the air and two great rips in his flank from the bull.

In 1839 Kit Carson and Hobbs were trapping with a party on the Arkansas River, not far from Bent's Fort. Among the trappers was a green Irishman, named O'Neil, who was quite anxious to become proficient in hunting, and it was not long before he received his first lesson. Every man who went out of camp after game was expected to bring in "meat" of some kind. O'Neil said that he would agree to the terms, and was ready one evening to start out on his first hunt alone. He picked up his rifle and stalked after a small herd of buffalo in plain sight on the prairie not more than five or six hundred yards from camp.

All the trappers who were not engaged in setting their traps or cooking supper were watching O'Neil. Presently they heard the report of his rifle, and shortly after he came running into camp, bareheaded, without his gun, and with a buffalo bull close upon his heels; both going at full speed, and the Irishman shouting like a madman,--

"Here we come, by jabers. Stop us! For the love of God, stop us!"

Just as they came in among the tents, with the bull not more than six feet in the rear of O'Neil, who was frightened out of his wits and puffing like a locomotive, his foot caught in a tent-rope, and over he went into a puddle of water head foremost, and in his fall capsized several camp-kettles, some of which contained the trappers' supper. But the buffalo did not escape so easily; for Hobbs and Kit Carson jumped for their rifles, and dropped the animal before he had done any further damage.

The whole outfit laughed heartily at O'Neil when he got up out of the water, for a party of old trappers would show no mercy to any of their companions who met with a mishap of that character; but as he stood there with dripping clothes and face covered with mud, his mother-wit came to his relief and he declared he had accomplished the hunter's task: "For sure," said he, "haven't I fetched the mate into camp? and there was no bargain whether it should be dead or alive!"

Upon Kit's asking O'Neil where his gun was,--

"Sure," said he, "that's more than I can tell you."

Next morning Carson and Hobbs took up O'Neil's tracks and the buffalo's, and after hunting an hour or so found the Irishman's rifle, though he had little use for it afterward, as he preferred to cook and help around camp rather than expose his precious life fighting buffaloes.

A great herd of buffaloes on the plains in the early days, when one could approach near enough without disturbing it to quietly watch its organization and the apparent discipline which its leaders seemed to exact, was a very curious sight. Among the striking features of the spectacle was the apparently uniform manner in which the immense mass of shaggy animals moved; there was constancy of action indicating a degree of intelligence to be found only in the most intelligent of the brute creation. Frequently the single herd was broken up into many smaller ones, that travelled relatively close together, each led by an independent master. Perhaps a few rods only marked the dividing-line between them, but it was always unmistakably plain, and each moved synchronously in the direction in which all were going.

The leadership of a herd was attained only by hard struggles for the place; once reached, however, the victor was immediately recognized, and kept his authority until some new aspirant overcame him, or he became superannuated and was driven out of the herd to meet his inevitable fate, a prey to those ghouls of the desert, the gray wolves.

In the event of a stampede, every animal of the separate, yet consolidated, herds rushed off together, as if they had all gone mad at once; for the buffalo, like the Texas steer, mule, or domestic horse, stampedes on the slightest provocation; frequently without any assignable cause. The simplest affair, sometimes, will start the whole herd; a prairie-dog barking at the entrance to his burrow, a shadow of one of themselves or that of a passing cloud, is sufficient to make them run for miles as if a real and dangerous enemy were at their heels.

Like an army, a herd of buffaloes put out vedettes to give the alarm in case anything beyond the ordinary occurred. These sentinels were always to be seen in groups of four, five, or even six, at some distance from the main body. When they perceived something approaching that the herd should beware of or get away from, they started on a run directly for the centre of the great mass of their peacefully grazing congeners. Meanwhile, the young bulls were on duty as sentinels on the edge of the main herd watching the vedettes; the moment the latter made for the centre, the former raised their heads, and in the peculiar manner of their species gazed all around and sniffed the air as if they could smell both the direction and source of the impending danger. Should there be something which their instinct told them to guard against, the leader took his position in front, the cows and calves crowded in the centre, while the rest of the males gathered on the flanks and in the rear, indicating a gallantry that might be emulated at times by the genus homo.

Generally buffalo went to their drinking-places but once a day, and that late in the afternoon. Then they ambled along, following each other in single file, which accounts for the many trails on the plains, always ending at some stream or lake. They frequently travelled twenty or thirty miles for water, so the trails leading to it were often worn to the depth of a foot or more.

That curious depression so frequently seen on the great plains, called a buffalo-wallow, is caused in this wise: The huge animals paw and lick the salty, alkaline earth, and when once the sod is broken the loose dirt drifts away under the constant action of the wind. Then, year after year, through more pawing, licking, rolling, and wallowing by the animals, the wind wafts more of the soil away, and soon there is a considerable hole in the prairie.

Many an old trapper and hunter's life has been saved by following a buffalo-trail when he was suffering from thirst. The buffalo-wallows retain usually a great quantity of water, and they have often saved the lives of whole companies of cavalry, both men and horses.

There was, however, a stranger and more wonderful spectacle to be seen every recurring spring during the reign of the buffalo, soon after the grass had started. There were circles trodden bare on the plains, thousands, yes, millions of them, which the early travellers, who did not divine their cause, called fairy-rings. From the first of April until the middle of May was the wet season; you could depend upon its recurrence almost as certainly as on the sun and moon rising at their proper time. This was also the calving period of the buffalo, as they, unlike our domestic cattle, only rutted during a single month; consequently, the cows all calved during a certain time; this was the wet month, and as there were a great many gray wolves that roamed singly and in immense packs over the whole prairie region, the bulls, in their regular beats, kept guard over the cows while in the act of parturition, and drove the wolves away, walking in a ring around the females at a short distance, and thus forming the curious circles.

In every herd at each recurring season there were always ambitious young bulls that came to their majority, so to speak, and these were ever ready to test their claims for the leadership, so that it may be safely stated that a month rarely passed without a bloody battle between them for the supremacy; though, strangely enough, the struggle scarcely ever resulted in the death of either combatant.

Perhaps there is no animal in which maternal love is so wonderfully developed as the buffalo cow; she is as dangerous with a calf by her side as a she-grizzly with cubs, as all old mountaineers know.

The buffalo bull that has outlived his usefulness is one of the most pitiable objects in the whole range of natural history. Old age has probably been decided in the economy of buffalo life as the unpardonable sin. Abandoned to his fate, he may be discovered, in his dreary isolation, near some stream or lake, where it does not tax him too severely to find good grass; for he is now feeble, and exertion an impossibility. In this new stage of his existence he seems to have completely lost his courage. Frightened at his own shadow, or the rustling of a leaf, he is the very incarnation of nervousness and suspicion. Gregarious in his habits from birth, solitude, foreign to his whole nature, has changed him into a new creature; and his inherent terror of the most trivial things is intensified to such a degree that if a man were compelled to undergo such constant alarm, it would probably drive him insane in less than a week. Nobody ever saw one of these miserable and helplessly forlorn creatures dying a natural death, or ever heard of such an occurrence. The cowardly coyote and the gray wolf had already marked him for their own; and they rarely missed their calculations.

Riding suddenly to the top of a divide once with a party of friends in 1866, we saw standing below us in the valley an old buffalo bull, the very picture of despair. Surrounding him were seven gray wolves in the act of challenging him to mortal combat. The poor beast, undoubtedly realizing the utter hopelessness of his situation, had determined to die game. His great shaggy head, filled with burrs, was lowered to the ground as he confronted his would-be executioners; his tongue, black and parched, lolled out of his mouth, and he gave utterance at intervals to a suppressed roar.

The wolves were sitting on their haunches in a semi-circle immediately in front of the tortured beast, and every time that the fear-stricken buffalo would give vent to his hoarsely modulated groan, the wolves howled in concert in most mournful cadence.

After contemplating his antagonists for a few moments, the bull made a dash at the nearest wolf, tumbling him howling over the silent prairie; but while this diversion was going on in front, the remainder of the pack started for his hind legs, to hamstring him. Upon this the poor brute turned to the point of attack only to receive a repetition of it in the same vulnerable place by the wolves, who had as quickly turned also and fastened themselves on his heels again. His hind quarters now streamed with blood and he began to show signs of great physical weakness. He did not dare to lie down; that would have been instantly fatal. By this time he had killed three of the wolves or so maimed them that they were entirely out of the fight.

At this juncture the suffering animal was mercifully shot, and the wolves allowed to batten on his thin and tough carcass.

Often there are serious results growing out of a stampede, either by mules or a herd of buffalo. A portion of the Fifth United States Infantry had a narrow escape from a buffalo stampede on the Old Trail, in the early summer of 1866. General George A. Sykes, who commanded the Division of Regulars in the Army of the Potomac during the Civil War, was ordered to join his regiment, stationed in New Mexico, and was conducting a body of recruits, with their complement of officers, to fill up the decimated ranks of the army stationed at the various military posts, in far-off Greaser Land.

The command numbered nearly eight hundred, including the subaltern officers. These recruits, or the majority of them at least, were recruits in name only; they had seen service in many a hard campaign of the Rebellion. Some, of course, were beardless youths just out of their teens, full of that martial ardour which induced so many young men of the nation to follow the drum on the remote plains and in the fastnesses of the Rocky Mountains, where the wily savages still held almost undisputed sway, and were a constant menace to the pioneer settlers.

One morning, when the command had just settled itself in careless repose on the short grass of the apparently interminable prairie at the first halt of the day's march, a short distance beyond Fort Larned, a strange noise, like the low muttering of thunder below the horizon, greeted the ears of the little army.

All were startled by the ominous sound, unlike anything they had heard before on their dreary tour. The general ordered his scouts out to learn the cause; could it be Indians? Every eye was strained for something out of the ordinary. Even the horses of the officers and the mules of the supply-train were infected by something that seemed impending; they grew restless, stamped the earth, and vainly essayed to stampede, but were prevented by their hobbles and picket-pins.

Presently one of the scouts returned from over the divide, and reported to the general that an immense herd of buffalo was tearing down toward the Trail, and from the great clouds of dust they raised, which obscured the horizon, there must have been ten thousand of them. The roar wafted to the command, and which seemed so mysterious, was made by their hoofs as they rattled over the dry prairie.

The sound increased in volume rapidly, and soon a black, surging mass was discovered bearing right down on the Trail. Behind it could be seen a cavalcade of about five hundred Cheyennes, Comanches, and Kiowas, who had maddened the shaggy brutes, hoping to capture the train without an attack by forcing the frightened animals to overrun the command.

Luckily, something caused the herd to open before it reached the foot of the divide, and it passed in two masses, leaving the command between, not two hundred feet from either division of the infuriated beasts.

The rage of the savages was evident when they saw that their attempt to annihilate the troops had failed, and they rode off sullenly into the sand hills, as the number of soldiers was too great for them to think of charging.

Cody tells of a buffalo stampede which he witnessed in his youth on the plains, when he was a wagon-master. The caravan was on its way with government stores for the military posts in the mountains, and the wagons were hauled by oxen.

He says:

The country was alive with buffalo, and besides killing
quite a number we had a rare day for sport. One morning
we pulled out of camp, and the train was strung out to a
considerable length along the Trail, which ran near the foot
of the sand hills, two miles from the river. Between the
road and the river we saw a large herd of buffalo grazing
quietly, they having been down to the stream to drink.
Just at this time we observed a party of returning
Californians coming from the west. They, too, noticed

150

the buffalo herd, and in another moment they were dashing down upon them, urging their horses to their greatest speed. The buffalo herd stampeded at once, and broke down the sides of the hills; so hotly were they pursued by the hunters that about five hundred of them rushed pell-mell through our caravan, frightening both men and oxen. Some of the wagons were turned clear around and many of the terrified oxen attempted to run to the hills with the heavy wagons attached to them. Others were turned around so short that they broke the tongues off. Nearly all the teams got entangled in their gearing and became wild and unruly, so that the perplexed drivers were unable to manage them.

The buffalo, the cattle, and the men were soon running in every direction, and the excitement upset everybody and everything. Many of the oxen broke their yokes and stampeded. One big buffalo bull became entangled in one of the heavy wagon-chains, and it is a fact that in his desperate efforts to free himself, he not only snapped the strong chain in two, but broke the ox-yoke to which it was attached, and the last seen of him he was running toward the hills with it hanging from his horns.

Stampedes were a great source of profit to the Indians of the plains. The Comanches were particularly expert and daring in this kind of robbery. They even trained their horses to run from one point to another in expectation of the coming of the trains. When a camp was made that was nearly in range, they turned their trained animals loose, which at once flew across the prairie, passing through the herd and penetrating the very corrals of their victims. All of the picketed horses and mules would endeavour to follow these decoys, and were invariably led right into the haunts of the Indians, who easily secured them. Young horses and mules were easily frightened; and, in the confusion which generally ensued, great injury was frequently done to the runaways themselves.

At times when the herd was very large, the horses scattered over the prairie and were irrevocably lost; and such as did not become wild fell a prey to the wolves. That fate was very frequently the lot of stampeded horses bred in the States, they not having been trained by a prairie life to take care of themselves. Instead of stopping and bravely fighting off the blood-thirsty beasts, they would run. Then the whole pack were sure to leave the bolder animals and make for the runaways, which they seldom failed to overtake and despatch.

On the Old Trail some years ago one of these stampedes occurred of a band of government horses, in which were several valuable animals. It was attended, however, with very little loss, through the courage and great exertion of the men who had them in charge; many were recovered, but none without having sustained injuries.

Hon. R. M. Wright, of Dodge City, Kansas, one of the pioneers in the days of the Santa Fe trade, and in the settlement of the State, has had many exciting experiences both with the savages of the great plains, and the buffalo. In relation to the habits of the latter, no man is better qualified to speak.

He was once owner of Fort Aubrey, a celebrated point on the Trail, but was compelled to abandon it on account of constant persecution by the Indians, or rather he was ordered to do so by the military authorities. While occupying the once famous landmark, in connection with others, had a contract to furnish hay to the government at Fort Lyon, seventy-five miles further west. His journal, which he kindly placed at my disposal, says:

While we were preparing to commence the work, a vast herd
of buffalo stampeded through our range one night, and
took off with them about half of our work cattle. The next
day a stage-driver and conductor on the Overland Route told
us they had seen a number of our oxen twenty-five miles east
of Aubrey, and this information gave me an idea in which
direction to hunt for the missing beasts. I immediately
started after them, while my partner took those that
remained and a few wagons and left with them for Fort Lyon.

Let me explain here that while the Indians were supposed to
be peaceable, small war-parties of young men, who could not
be controlled by their chiefs, were continually committing
depredations, and the main body of savages themselves were
very uneasy, and might be expected to break out any day.
In consequence of this unsettled state of affairs, there
had been a brisk movement among the United States troops
stationed at the various military posts, a large number of
whom were believed to be on the road from Denver to Fort Lyon.

152

I filled my saddle-bags with jerked buffalo, hardtack and
ground coffee, and took with me a belt of cartridges,
my rifle and six-shooter, a field-glass and my blankets,
prepared for any emergency. The first day out, I found a
few of the lost cattle, and placed them on the river-bottom,
which I continued to do as fast as I recovered them, for a
distance of about eighty-five miles down the Arkansas.
There I met a wagon-train, the drivers of which told me
that I would find several more of my oxen with a train
that had arrived at the Cimarron crossing the day before.
I came up with this train in eight or ten hours' travel
south of the river, got my cattle, and started next morning
for home.

I picked up those I had left on the Arkansas as I went
along, and after having made a very hard day's travel,
about sundown I concluded I would go into camp. I had
only fairly halted when the oxen began to drop down,
so completely tired out were they, as I believed. Just as
it was growing dark, I happened to look toward the west,
and I saw several fires on a big island, near what was
called "The Lone Tree," about a mile from where I had
determined to remain for the night.

Thinking the fires were those of the soldiers that I had
heard were on the road from Denver, and anticipating and
longing for a cup of good coffee, as I had had none for
five days, knowing, too, that the troops would be full of
news, I felt good and determined to go over to their camp.

The Arkansas was low, but the banks steep, with high,
rank grass growing to the very water's edge. I found
a buffalo-trail cut through the deep bank, narrow and
precipitous, and down this I went, arriving in a short time
within a little distance of my supposed soldiers' camp.
When I had reached the middle of another deep cut in the
bank, I looked across to the island, and, great Caesar!

saw a hundred little fires, around which an aggregation
of a thousand Indians were huddled!

I slid backwards off my horse, and by dint of great exertion,
worked him up the river-bank as quietly and quickly as
possible, then led him gently away out on the prairie.
My first impulse was not to go back to the cattle; but as
we needed them very badly, I concluded to return, put them
all on their feet, and light out mighty lively, without
making any noise. I started them, and, oh dear! I was
afraid to tread upon a weed, lest it would snap and bring
the Indians down on my trail. Until I had put several
miles between them and me, I could not rest easy for
a moment. Tired as I was, tired as were both my horse
and the cattle, I drove them twenty-five miles before
I halted. Then daylight was upon me. I was at what is
known as Chouteau's Island, a once famous place in the
days of the Old Santa Fe Trail.

Of course, I had to let the oxen and my horse rest and fill
themselves until the afternoon, and I lay down, and fell
asleep, but did not sleep long, as I thought it dangerous
to remain too near the cattle. I rose and walked up a big,
dry sand creek that opened into the river, and after I had
ascended it for a couple of miles, found the banks very
steep; in fact, they rose to a height of eighteen or twenty
feet, and were sharply cut up by narrow trails made by
the buffalo.

The whole face of the earth was covered by buffalo, and
they were slowly grazing toward the Arkansas. All at once
they became frightened at something, and stampeded pell-mell
toward the very spot on which I stood. I quickly ran into
one of the precipitous little paths and up on the prairie,
to see what had scared them. They were making the ground
fairly tremble as their mighty multitude came rushing on
at full speed, the sound of their hoofs resembling thunder,

but in a continuous peal. It appeared to me that they must
sweep everything in their path, and for my own preservation
I rushed under the creek-bank, but on they came like a
tornado, with one old bull in the lead. He held up a second
to descend the narrow trail, and when he had got about
halfway down I let him have it; I was only a few steps from
him and over he tumbled. I don't know why I killed him;
out of pure wantonness, I expect, or perhaps I thought
it would frighten the others back. Not so, however;
they only quickened their pace, and came dashing down in
great numbers. Dozens of them stumbled and fell over the
dead bull; others fell over them. The top of the bank
was fairly swarming with them; they leaped, pitched, and
rolled down. I crouched as close to the bank as possible,
but many of them just grazed my head, knocking the sand
and gravel in great streams down my neck; indeed I was
half buried before the herd had passed over. That old bull
was the last buffalo I ever shot wantonly, excepting once,
from an ambulance while riding on the Old Trail, to please
a distinguished Englishman, who had never seen one shot;
then I did it only after his most earnest persuasion.

One day a stage-driver named Frank Harris and myself started
out after buffalo; they were scarce, for a wonder, and
we were very hungry for fresh meat. The day was fine and
we rode a long way, expecting sooner or later a bunch would
jump up, but in the afternoon, having seen none, we gave
it up and started for the ranch. Of course, we didn't
care to save our ammunition, so shot it away at everything
in sight, skunks, rattlesnakes, prairie-dogs, and gophers,
until we had only a few loads left. Suddenly an old bull
jumped up that had been lying down in one of those
sugar-loaf-shaped sand hills, whose tops are hollowed out
by the action of the wind. Harris emptied his revolver
into him, and so did I; but the old fellow sullenly stood
still there on top of the sand hill, bleeding profusely
at the nose, and yet absolutely refusing to die, although

he would repeatedly stagger and nearly tumble over.

It was getting late and we couldn't wait on him, so Harris
said: "I will dismount, creep up behind him, and cut his
hamstrings with my butcher-knife." The bull having now
lain down, Harris commenced operations, but his movement
seemed to infuse new life into the old fellow; he jumped
to his feet, his head lowered in the attitude of fight,
and away he went around the outside of the top of the
sand hill! It was a perfect circus with one ring; Harris,
who was a tall, lanky fellow, took hold of the enraged
animal's tail as he rose to his feet, and in a moment his
legs were flying higher than his head, but he did not dare
let go of his hold on the bull's tail, and around and
around they went; it was his only show for life. I could
not assist him a particle, but had to sit and hold his horse,
and be judge of the fight. I really thought that old bull
would never weaken. Finally, however, the "ring" performance
began to show symptoms of fatigue; slower and slower the
actions of the bull grew, and at last Harris succeeded
in cutting his hamstrings and the poor beast went down.
Harris said afterward, when the danger was all over, that
the only thing he feared was that perhaps the bull's tail
would pull out, and if it did, he was well aware that he
was a goner. We brought his tongue, hump, and a hindquarter
to the ranch with us, and had a glorious feast and a big
laugh that night with the boys over the ridiculous adventure.

General Richard Irving Dodge, United States army, in his work on the big game
of America, says:

It is almost impossible for a civilized being to realize
the value to the plains Indian of the buffalo. It furnished
him with home, food, clothing, bedding, horse equipment--
almost everything.

From 1869 to 1873 I was stationed at various posts along
the Arkansas River. Early in spring, as soon as the dry

156

and apparently desert prairie had begun to change its coat of dingy brown to one of palest green, the horizon would begin to be dotted with buffalo, single or in groups of two or three, forerunners of the coming herd. Thick and thicker, and in large groups they come, until by the time the grass is well up, the whole vast landscape appears a mass of buffalo, some individuals feeding, others lying down, but the herd slowly moving to the northward; of their number, it was impossible to form a conjecture.

Determined as they are to pursue their journey northward, yet they are exceedingly cautious and timid about it, and on any alarm rush to the southward with all speed, until that alarm is dissipated. Especially is this the case when any unusual object appears in their rear, and so utterly regardless of consequences are they, that an old plainsman will not risk a wagon-train in such a herd, where rising ground will permit those in front to get a good view of their rear.

In May, 1871, I drove in a buggy from old Fort Zarah to Fort Larned, on the Arkansas River. The distance is thirty-four miles. At least twenty-five miles of that distance was through an immense herd. The whole country was one mass of buffalo, apparently, and it was only when actually among them, that the seemingly solid body was seen to be an agglomeration of countless herds of from fifty to two hundred animals, separated from the surrounding herds by a greater or less space, but still separated.

The road ran along the broad valley of the Arkansas. Some miles from Zarah a low line of hills rises from the plain on the right, gradually increasing in height and approaching road and river, until they culminate in Pawnee Rock.

So long as I was in the broad, level valley, the herds sullenly got out of my way, and, turning, stared stupidly

157

at me, some within thirty or forty yards. When, however,
I had reached a point where the hills were no more than
a mile from the road, the buffalo on the crests, seeing an
unusual object in their rear, turned, stared an instant,
then started at full speed toward me, stampeding and
bringing with them the numberless herds through which
they passed, and pouring down on me, no longer separated
but compacted into one immense mass of plunging animals,
mad with fright, irresistible as an avalanche.

The situation was by no means pleasant. There was but
one hope of escape. My horse was, fortunately, a quiet
old beast, that had rushed with me into many a herd, and
been in at the death of many a buffalo. Reining him up,
I waited until the front of the mass was within fifty yards,
then, with a few well-directed shots, dropped some of
the leaders, split the herd and sent it off in two streams
to my right and left. When all had passed me, they stopped,
apparently satisfied, though thousands were yet within
reach of my rifle. After my servant had cut out the
tongues of the fallen, I proceeded on my journey, only to
have a similar experience within a mile or two, and this
occurred so often that I reached Fort Larned with twenty-six
tongues, representing the greatest number of buffalo that
I can blame myself with having murdered in one day.

Some years, as in 1871, the buffalo appeared to move
northward in one immense column, oftentimes from twenty
to fifty miles in width, and of unknown depth from front
to rear. Other years the northward journey was made
in several parallel columns moving at the same rate and
with their numerous flankers covering a width of a hundred
or more miles.

When the food in one locality fails, they go to another,
and toward fall, when the grass of the high prairies
becomes parched by the heat and drought, they gradually

work their way back to the south, concentrating on the rich pastures of Texas and the Indian Territory, whence, the same instinct acting on all, they are ready to start together again on their northward march as soon as spring starts the grass.

Old plainsmen and the Indians aver that the buffalo never return south; that each year's herd was composed of animals which had never made the journey before, and would never make it again. All admit the northern migration, that being too pronounced for any one to dispute, but refuse to admit the southern migration. Thousands of young calves were caught and killed every spring that were produced during this migration, and accompanied the herd northward; but because the buffalo did not return south in one vast body as they went north, it was stoutly maintained that they did not go south at all. The plainsman could give no reasonable hypothesis of his "No-return theory" on which to base the origin of the vast herds which yearly made their march northward. The Indian was, however, equal to the occasion. Every plains Indian firmly believed that the buffalo were produced in countless numbers in a country under ground; that every spring the surplus swarmed, like bees from a hive, out of the immense cave-like opening in the region of the great Llano Estacado, or Staked Plain of Texas. In 1879 Stone Calf, a celebrated chief, assured me that he knew exactly where the caves were, though he had never seen them; that the good God had provided this means for the constant supply of food for the Indian, and however recklessly the white men might slaughter, they could never exterminate them. When last I saw him, the old man was beginning to waver in this belief, and feared that the "Bad God" had shut the entrances, and that his tribe must starve.

The old trappers and plainsmen themselves, even as early as the beginning of the Santa Fe trade, noticed the gradual disappearance of the buffalo, while they still existed in countless numbers. One veteran French Canadian, an employee of the American Fur Company, way back in the early '30's, used to mourn thus: "Mais, sacre! les Amarican, dey go to de Missouri frontier, de buffalo he ron to de montaigne; de trappaire wid his fusil, he follow to de Bayou Salade, he ron again. Dans les Montaignes Espagnol, bang! bang! toute la journee, toute la journee, go de sacre voleurs. De bison he leave, parceque les fusils scare im vara moche, ici la de sem-sacre!"

CHAPTER XIII.

INDIAN CUSTOMS AND LEGENDS.

Thirty-five miles before arriving at Bent's Fort, at which point the Old Trail crossed the Arkansas, the valley widens and the prairie falls toward the river in gentle undulations. There for many years the three friendly tribes of plains Indians-- Cheyennes, Arapahoes, and Kiowas--established their winter villages, in order to avail themselves of the supply of wood, to trade with the whites, and to feed their herds of ponies on the small limbs and bark of the cottonwood trees growing along the margin of the stream for four or five miles. It was called Big Timbers, and was one of the most eligible places to camp on the whole route after leaving Council Grove. The grass, particularly on the south side of the river, was excellent; there was an endless supply of fuel, and cool water without stint.

In the severe winters that sometimes were fruitful of blinding blizzards, sweeping from the north in an intensity of fury that was almost inconceivable, the buffalo too congregated there for shelter, and to browse on the twigs of the great trees.

The once famous grove, though denuded of much of its timber, may still be seen from the car windows as the trains hurry mountainward.

Garrard, in his *Taos Trail*, presents an interesting and amusing account of a visit to the Cheyenne village with old John Smith, in 1847, when the Santa Fe trade was at its height, and that with the various tribes of savages in its golden days.

Toward the middle of the day, the village was in a great
bustle. Every squaw, child, and man had their faces
blackened--a manifestation of joy.[44]

Pell-mell they went--men, squaws, and dogs--into the icy
river. Some hastily jerked off their leggings, and held
moccasins and dresses high out of the water. Others, too
impatient, dashed the stream from beneath their impetuous
feet, scarce taking time to draw more closely the always
worn robe. Wondering what caused all this commotion, and
looking over the river, whither the yelling, half-frantic
savages were so speedily hurrying, we saw a band of Indians
advancing toward us. As the foremost braves reined their

161

champing barbs on the river-bank, mingled whoops of triumph
and delight and the repeated discharge of guns filled
the air. In the hands of three were slender willow wands,
from the smaller points of which dangled as many scalps--
the single tuft of hair on each pronouncing them Pawnees.[45]

These were raised aloft, amid unrestrained bursts of joy
from the thrice-happy, blood-thirsty throng. Children ran
to meet their fathers, sisters their brothers, girls their
lovers, returning from the scene of victorious strife;
decrepit matrons welcomed manly sons; and aged chiefs their
boys and braves. It was a scene of affection, and a proud
day in the Cheyenne annals of prowess. That small but
gallant band were relieved of their shields and lances by
tender-hearted squaws, and accompanied to their respective
homes, to repose by the lodge-fire, consume choice meat,
and to be the heroes of the family circle.

The drum at night sent forth its monotony of hollow sound,
and my Mexican Pedro and I, directed by the booming,
entered a lodge, vacated for the purpose, full of young men
and squaws, following one another in a continuous circle,
keeping the left knee stiff and bending the right with a
half-forward, half-backward step, as if they wanted to go on
and could not, accompanying it, every time the right foot
was raised, with an energetic, broken song, which, dying
away, was again and again sounded--"hay-a, hay-a, hay-a,"
they went, laying the emphasis on the first syllable.
A drum, similar to, though larger than a tambourine, covered
with parfleche,[46] was beaten upon with a stick, producing
with the voices a sound not altogether disagreeable.

Throughout the entire night and succeeding day the voices
of the singers and heavy notes of the drum reached us,
and at night again the same dull sound lulled me to sleep.
Before daylight our lodge was filled with careless dancers,
and the drum and voices, so unpleasing to our wearied ears,

were giving us the full benefit of their compass. Smith,
whose policy it was not to be offended, bore the infliction
as best be could, and I looked on much amused. The lodge
was so full that they stood without dancing, in a circle
round the fire, and with a swaying motion of the body
kept time to their music.

During the day the young men, except the dancers, piled up
dry logs in a level open space near, for a grand demonstration.
At night, when it was fired, I folded my blanket over my
shoulders, comme les sauvages, and went out. The faces
of many girls were brilliant with vermilion; others were
blacked, their robes, leggings, and skin dresses glittering
with beads and quill-work. Rings and bracelets of shining
brass encircled their taper arms and fingers, and shells
dangled from their ears. Indeed, all the finery collectable
was piled on in barbarous profusion, though a few, in good
taste through poverty, wore a single band and but few rings,
with jetty hair parted in the middle, from the forehead
to the neck, terminating in two handsome braids.

The young men who can afford the expense trade for dollars
and silver coin of less denomination--coin as a currency
is not known among them--which they flatten thin, and fasten
to a braid of buffalo hair, attached to the crown lock,
which hangs behind, outside of the robe, and adds much to
the handsome appearance of the wearer.

The girls, numbering two hundred, fell into line together,
and the men, of whom there were two hundred and fifty,
joining, a circle was formed, which travelled around with
the same shuffling step already described. The drummers
and other musicians--twenty or twenty-five of them--marched
in a contrary direction to and from and around the fire,
inside the large ring; for at the distance kept by the
outsiders the area was one hundred and fifty feet in diameter.
The Apollonian emulators chanted the great deeds performed

by the Cheyenne warriors. As they ended, the dying strain
was caught up by the hundreds of the outside circle, who,
in fast-swelling, loud tones, poured out the burden of
their song. At this juncture the march was quickened,
the scalps of the slain were borne aloft and shaken with
wild delight, and shrill war-notes, rising above the
furious din, accelerated the pulsation and strung high
the nerves. Time-worn shields, careering in mad holders'
hands, clashed; and keen lances, once reeking in Pawnee
blood, clanged. Braves seized one another with an iron
grip, in the heat of excitement, or chimed more tenderly
in the chant, enveloped in the same robe with some maiden
as they approvingly stepped through one of their own
original polkas.

Thirty of the chiefs and principal men were ranged by the
pile of blazing logs. By their invitation, I sat down with
them and smoked death and its concomitant train of evils to
those audacious tribes who doubt the courage or supremacy
of the brave, the great and powerful, Cheyenne nation.

It is Indian etiquette that the first lodge a stranger enters on visiting a village is
his home as long as he remains the guest of the tribe. It is all the same whether he
be invited or not. Upon going in, it is customary to place all your traps in the back
part, which is the most honoured spot. The proprietor always occupies that part of
his home, but invariably gives it up to a guest. With the Cheyennes, the white man,
when the tribe was at peace with him, was ever welcome, as in the early days of
the border he generally had a supply of coffee, of which the savage is particularly
fond-- Mok-ta-bo-mah-pe, as they call it. Their salutation to the stranger coming
into the presence of the owner of a lodge is "Hook-ah-hay! Num-whit,"--"How do
you do? Stay with us." Water is then handed by a squaw, as it is supposed a traveller
is thirsty after riding; then meat, for he must be hungry, too. A pipe is offered, and
conversation follows.

The lodge of the Cheyennes is formed of seventeen poles, about three inches
thick at the end which rests on the ground, slender in shape, tapering symmetrically,
and eighteen feet or more in length. They are tied together at the small ends with
buffalo-hide, then raised until the frame resembles a cone, over which buffalo-
skins are placed, very skilfully fitted and made soft by having been dubbed by the
women--that is, scraped to the requisite thinness, and made supple by rubbing with
the brains of the animal that wore it. They are sewed together with sinews of the

buffalo, generally of the long and powerful muscle that holds up the ponderous head of the shaggy beast, a narrow strip running towards the bump. In summer the lower edges of the skin are rolled up, and the wind blowing through, it is a cool, shady retreat. In winter everything is closed, and I know of no more comfortable place than a well-made Indian lodge. The army tent known as the Sibley is modelled after it, and is the best winter shelter for troops in the field that can be made. Many times while the military post where I had been ordered was in process of building, I have chosen the Sibley tent in preference to any other domicile.

When a village is to be moved, it is an interesting sight. The young and unfledged boys drive up the herd of ponies, and then the squaws catch them. The women, too, take down the lodges, and, tying the poles in two bundles, fasten them on each side of an animal, the long ends dragging on the ground. Just behind the pony or mule, as the case may be, a basket is placed and held there by buffalo-hide thongs, and into these novel carriages the little children are put, besides such traps as are not easily packed on the animal's back.

The women do all the work both in camp and when moving. They are doomed to a hopeless bondage of slavery, the fate of their sex in every savage race; but they accept their condition stoically, and there is as much affection among them for their husbands and children as I have ever witnessed among the white race. Here are two instances of their devotion, both of which came under my personal observation, and I could give hundreds of others.

Late in the fall of 1858, I was one of a party on the trail of a band of Indians who had been committing some horrible murders in a mining-camp in the northern portion of Washington Territory. On the fourth day out, just about dusk, we struck their moccasin tracks, which we followed all night, and surprised their camp in the gray light of the early morning. In less than ten minutes the fight was over, and besides the killed we captured six prisoners. Then as the rising sun commenced to gild the peaks of the lofty range on the west, having granted our captives half an hour to take leave of their families, the ankles of each were bound; they were made to kneel on the prairie, a squad of soldiers, with loaded rifles, were drawn up eight paces in front of them, and at the instant the signal--a white handkerchief--was dropped the savages tumbled over on the sod a heap of corpses. The parting between the condemned men and their young wives and children, I shall never forget. It was the most perfect exhibition of marital and filial love that I have ever witnessed. Such harsh measures may seem cruel and heartless in the light of to-day, but there was none other than martial law then in the wilderness of the Northern Pacific coast, and the execution was a stern necessity.

The other instance was ten years later. During the Indian campaign in the winter of 1868-69 I was riding with a party of officers and enlisted men, south of the Arkansas, about fourty miles from Fort Dodge. We were watching some cavalrymen

unearth three or four dead warriors who had been killed by two scouts in a fierce
unequal fight a few weeks before, and as we rode into a small ravine among the
sand hills, we suddenly came upon a rudely constructed Cheyenne lodge. Entering,
we discovered on a rough platform, fashioned of green poles, a dead warrior in full
war-dress; his shield of buffalo-hide, pipe ornamented with eagles' feathers, and
medicine bag, were lying on the ground beside him. At his head, on her knees, with
hands clasped in the attitude of prayer, was a squaw frozen to death. Which had first
succumbed, the wounded chief, or the devoted wife in the awful cold of that winter
prairie, will never be known, but it proved her love for the man who had perhaps
beaten her a hundred times. Such tender and sympathetic affection is characteristic of
the sex everywhere, no less with the poor savage than in the dominant white race.

To return to our description of the average Indian village: Each lodge at the grand
encampment of Big Timbers in the era of traffic with the nomads of the great plains,
owned its separate herd of ponies and mules. In the exodus to some other favoured
spot, two dozen or more of these individual herds travelled close to each other but
never mixed, each drove devotedly following its bell-mare, as in a pack-train. This
useful animal is generally the most worthless and wicked beast in the entire outfit.

The animals with the lodge-pole carriages go as they please, no special care being
taken to guide them, but they too instinctively keep within sound of the leader. I will
again quote Garrard for an accurate description of the moving camp when he was
with the Cheyennes in 1847:--

The young squaws take much care of their dress and horse
equipments; they dash furiously past on wild steeds,
astrideof the high-pommelled saddles. A fancifully
coloured cover, worked with beads or porcupine quills,
making a flashy, striking appearance, extended from withers
to rump of the horse, while the riders evinced an admirable
daring, worthy of Amazons. Their dresses were made of
buckskin, high at the neck, with short sleeves, or rather
none at all, fitting loosely, and reaching obliquely to
theknee, giving a Diana look to the costume; the edges
scalloped, worked with beads, and fringed. From the knee
downward the limb was encased in a tightly fitting legging,
terminating in a neat moccasin--both handsomely wrought
with beads. On the arms were bracelets of brass, which
glittered and reflected in the radiant morning sun, adding
much to their attractions. In their pierced ears, shells
from the Pacific shore were pendent; and to complete the

166

picture of savage taste and profusion, their fine
complexions were eclipsed by a coat of flaming vermilion.

Many of the largest dogs were packed with a small quantity
of meat, or something not easily injured. They looked
queerly, trotting industriously under their burdens; and,
judging from a small stock of canine physiological
information, not a little of the wolf was in their
composition.

We crossed the river on our way to the new camp. The alarm
manifested by the children in the lodge-pole drays, as they
dipped in the water, was amusing. The little fellows,
holding their breath, not daring to cry, looked imploringly
at their inexorable mothers, and were encouraged by words
of approbation from their stern fathers.

After a ride of two hours we stopped, and the chiefs,
fastening their horses, collected in circles to smoke their
pipe and talk, letting their squaws unpack the animals,
pitch the lodges, build the fires, and arrange the robes.
When all was ready, these lords of creation dispersed to
their several homes, to wait until their patient and
enduring spouses prepared some food. I was provoked, nay,
angry, to see the lazy, overgrown men do nothing to help
their wives; and when the young women pulled off their
bracelets and finery to chop wood, the cup of my wrath was
full to overflowing, and, in a fit of honest indignation,
I pronounced them ungallant and savage in the true sense
of the word.

The treatment of Indian children, particularly boys, is something startling to the
gentle sentiments of refined white mothers. The girls receive hardly any attention
from their fathers. Implicit obedience is the watchword of the lodge with them,
and they are constantly taught to appreciate their inferiority of sex. The daughter
is a mere slave; unnoticed and neglected--a mere hewer of wood and drawer of
water. With a son, it is entirely different; the father from his birth dotes on him and
manifests his affection in the most demonstrative manner.

Garrard tells of two instances that came under his observation while staying at the chief's lodge, and at John Smith's, in the Cheyenne village, of the discipline to which the boys are subjected.

In Vi-po-nah's lodge was his grandson, a boy six or seven months old. Every morning his mother washed him in cold water, and set him out in the air to make him hardy; he would come in, perfectly nude, from his airing, about half-frozen. How he would laugh and brighten up, as he felt the warmth of the fire!

Smith's son Jack took a crying fit one cold night, much to the annoyance of four or five chiefs, who had come to our lodge to talk and smoke. In vain did the mother shake and scold him with the severest Cheyenne words, until Smith, provoked beyond endurance, took the squalling youngster in his hands; he shu-ed and shouted and swore, but Jack had gone too far to be easily pacified. He then sent for a bucket of water from the river and poured cupful after cupful on Jack, who stamped and screamed and bit in his tiny rage. Notwithstanding, the icy stream slowly descended until the bucket was emptied, another was sent for, and again and again the cup was replenished and emptied on the blubbering youth. At last, exhausted with exertion and completely cooled down, he received the remaining water in silence, and, with a few words of admonition, was delivered over to his mother, in whose arms he stifled his sobs, until his heartbreaking grief and cares were drowned in sleep. What a devilish mixture Indian and American blood is!

The Indians never chastise a boy, as they think his spirit would be broken and cowed down; instead of a warrior he would be a squaw --a harsh epithet indicative of cowardice--and they resort to any method but infliction of blows to subdue a refractory scion.

Before most of the lodges is a tripod of three sticks, about seven feet in length and an inch in diameter, fastened at the top, and the lower ends brought out, so that it stands alone. On this is hung the shield and a small square bag of parfleche, containing pipes, with an accompanying pendent roll of stems, carefully wrapped in blue or red cloth, and decorated with beads and porcupine quills. This collection is held in great veneration, for the pipe is their only religion. Through its agency they invoke the Great Spirit; through it they render homage to the winds, to the earth, and to the sky.

Every one has his peculiar notion on this subject; and, in passing the pipe, one must have it presented stem downward, another the reverse; some with the bowl resting on the ground; and as this is a matter of great solemnity, their several fancies are respected. Sometimes I required them to hand it to me, when smoking, in imitation of their custom; on this, a faint smile, half mingled with respect and pity for my folly in tampering with their sacred ceremony, would appear on their faces, and with a slow negative shake of the head, they would ejaculate, "I-sto-met-mah-son-ne-wah-hein"--"Pshaw! that's foolish; don't do so."

Religion the Cheyennes have none, if, indeed, we except the respect paid to the pipe; nor do we see any sign or vestige of spiritual worship; except one remarkable thing--in offering the pipe, before every fresh filling, to the sky, the earth, and the winds, the motion made in so doing describes the form of a cross; and, in blowing the first four whiffs, the smoke is invariably sent in the same four directions. It is undoubtedly void of meaning in reference to Christian worship, yet it is a superstition, founded on ancient tradition. This tribe once lived near the head waters of the Mississippi; and, as the early Jesuit missionaries were energetic zealots, in the diffusion of their religious sentiments, probably to make their faith more acceptable to the Indians, the Roman Catholic rites were blended with the homage shown to the pipe, which custom of offering, in the form of a cross, is still retained by them; but as every custom is handed down by tradition merely, the true source has been forgotten.

In every tribe in whose country I have been stationed, which comprises nearly all the continent excepting the extreme southwestern portion, his pipe is the Indian's constant companion through life. It is his messenger of peace; he pledges his friends through its stem and its bowl, and when he is dead, it has a place in his solitary grave, with his war-club and arrows--companions on his journey to his long-fancied beautiful hunting-grounds. The pipe of peace is a sacred thing; so held by all Indian nations, and kept in possession of chiefs, to be smoked only at times of peacemaking. When the terms of treaty have been agreed upon, this sacred emblem, the stem of which is ornamented with eagle's quills, is brought forward, and the solemn pledge to keep the peace is passed through the sacred stem by each chief and warrior drawing the smoke once through it. After the ceremony is over, the warriors of the two tribes unite in the dance, with the pipe of peace held in the left hand of the chief and in his other a rattle.

Thousands of years ago, the primitive savage of the American continent carried masses of pipe-stone from the sacred quarry in Minnesota across the vast wilderness of plains, to trade with the people of the far Southwest, over the same route that long afterward became the Santa Fe Trail; therefore, it will be consistent with the character of this work to relate the history of the quarry from which all the tribes procured their material for fashioning their pipes, and the curious legends connected with it. I have met with the red sandstone pipes on the remotest portions of the Pacific coast, and east, west, north and south, in every tribe that it has been my fortune to know.

The word "Dakotah" means allied or confederated, and is the family name now comprising some thirty bands, numbering about thirty thousand Indians. They are generally designated Sioux, but that title is seldom willingly acknowledged by them. It was first given to them by the French, though its original interpretation is by no means clear. The accepted theory, because it is the most plausible, is that it is a corruption or rather an abbreviation of "Nadouessioux," a Chippewa word for enemies.

Many of the Sioux are semi-civilized; some are "blanket-Indians," so called, but there are no longer any murderous or predatory bands, and all save a few stragglers are on the reservations. From 1812 to 1876, more than half a century, they were the scourge of the West and the Northwest, but another outbreak is highly improbable. They once occupied the vast region included between the Mississippi and the Rocky Mountains, and were always migratory in their methods of living. Over fifty years ago, when the whites first became acquainted with them, they were divided into nearly fifty bands of families, each with its separate chief, but all acknowledging a superior chief to whom they were subordinate. They were at that time the happiest and most wealthy tribe on the continent, regarded from an Indian standpoint; but then the great plains were stocked with buffalo and wild horses, and that fact alone warrants the assertion of contentment and riches. No finer-looking tribe existed; they could then muster more than ten thousand warriors, every one of whom would measure six feet, and all their movements were graceful and elastic.

According to their legends, they came from the Pacific and encountered the Algonquins about the head waters of the Mississippi, where they were held in check, a portion of them, however, pushing on through their enemies and securing a foothold on the shores of Lake Michigan. This bold band was called by the Chippewas Winnebagook (men-from-the- salt-water). In their original habitat on the great northern plains was located the celebrated "red pipe-stone quarry," a relatively limited area, owned by all tribes, but occupied permanently by none; a purely neutral ground--so designated by the Great Spirit--where no war could possibly occur, and where mortal enemies might meet to procure the material for their pipes, but the hatchet was invariably buried during that time on the consecrated spot.

The quarry has long since passed out of the control and jurisdiction of the Indians and is not included in any of their reservations, though near the Sisseton agency. It is located on the summit of the high divide between the Missouri and St. Peter's rivers in Minnesota, at a point not far from where the ninety-seventh meridian of longitude (from Greenwich) intersects the forty-fifth parallel of latitude. The divide was named by the French Coteau des Prairies, and the quarry is near its southern extremity. Not a tree or bush could be seen from the majestic mound when I last was there, some twenty years ago--nothing but the apparently interminable plains, until they were lost in the deep blue of the horizon.

The luxury of smoking appears to have been known to all the tribes on the continent in their primitive state, and they indulge in the habit to excess; any one familiar with their life can assert that the American savage smokes half of his time. Where so much attention is given to a mere pleasure, it naturally follows that he would devote his leisure and ingenuity to the construction of his pipe. The bowls of these were, from time immemorial, made of the peculiar red stone from the famous quarry referred to, which, until only a little over fifty years ago, was never visited by a white man, its sanctity forbidding any such sacrilege.

That the spot should have been visited for untold centuries by all the Indian nations, who hid their weapons as they approached it, under fear of the vengeance of the Great Spirit, will not seem strange when the religion of the race is understood. One of the principal features of the quarry is a perpendicular wall of granite about thirty feet high, facing the west, and nearly two miles long. At the base of the wall there is a level prairie, running parallel to it, half a mile wide. Under this strip of land, after digging through several slaty layers of rock, the red sandstone is found. Old graves, fortifications, and excavations abound, all confirmatory of the traditions clustering around the weird place.

Within a few rods of the base of the wall is a group of immense gneiss boulders, five in number, weighing probably many hundred tons each, and under these are two holes in which two imaginary old women reside --the guardian spirits of the quarry--who were always consulted before any pipe-stone could be dug up. The veneration for this group of boulders was something wonderful; not a spear of grass was broken or bent by his feet within sixty or seventy paces from them, where the trembling Indian halted, and throwing gifts to them in humble supplication, solicited permission to dig and take away the red stone for his pipes.

Near this spot, too, on a high mound, was the "Thunder's nest," where a very small bird sat upon her eggs during fair weather. When the skies were rent with thunder at the approach of a storm, she was hatching her brood, which caused the terrible commotion in the heavens. The bird was eternal. The "medicine men" claimed that they had often seen her, and she was about as large as a little finger. Her mate was a serpent whose fiery tongue destroyed the young ones as soon as they were born, and the awful noise accompanying the act darted through the clouds.

On the wall of rocks at the quarry are thousands of inscriptions and paintings, the totems and arms of various tribes who have visited there; but no idea can be formed of their antiquity.

Of the various traditions of the many tribes, I here present a few. The Great Spirit at a remote period called all the Indian nations together at this place, and, standing on the brink of the precipice of red-stone rock, broke from its walls a piece and fashioned a pipe by simply turning it in his hands. He then smoked over them to the north, the south, the east, and the west, and told them the stone was red, that it was their flesh, that they must use it for their pipes of peace, that it belonged to all alike, and that the war-club and scalping-knife must never be raised on its ground. At the last whiff of his pipe his head went into a great cloud, and the whole surface of the ledge for miles was melted and glazed; two great ovens were opened beneath, and two women--the guardian spirits of the place-- entered them in a blaze of fire, and they are heard there yet answering to the conjurations of the medicine men, who consult them when they visit the sacred place.

The legend of the Knis-te-neu's tribe (Crees), a very small band in the British possessions, in relation to the quarry is this: In the time of a great freshet that occurred years ago and destroyed all the nations of the earth, every tribe of Indians assembled on the top of the Coteau des Prairies to get out of the way of the rushing and seething waters. When they had arrived there from all parts of the world, the water continued to rise until it covered them completely, forming one solid mass of drowned Indians, and their flesh was converted by the Great Spirit into red pipe-stone; therefore, it was always considered neutral ground, belonging to all tribes alike, and all were to make their pipes out of it and smoke together. While they were drowning together, a young woman, Kwaptan, a virgin, caught hold of the foot of a very large bird that was flying over at the time, and was carried to the top of a hill that was not far away and above the water. There she had twins, their father being the war-eagle that had carried her off, and her children have since peopled the earth. The pipe-stone, which is the flesh of their ancestors, is smoked by them as the symbol of peace, and the eagle quills decorate the heads of their warriors.

Severed about seven or eight feet from the main wall of the quarry by some convulsion of nature ages ago, there is an immense column just equal in height to the wall, seven feet in diameter and beautifully polished on its top and sides. It is called The Medicine, or Leaping Rock, and considerable nerve is required to jump on it from the main ledge and back again. Many an Indian's heart, in the past, has sighed for the honour of the feat without daring to attempt it. A few, according to the records of the tribes, have tried it with success, and left their arrows standing up in its crevice; others have made the leap and reached its slippery surface only to slide off, and suffer instant death on the craggy rocks in the awful chasm below. Every young man of the many tribes was ambitious to perform the feat, and those who had successfully accomplished it were permitted to boast of it all their lives.

CHAPTER XIV.

TRAPPERS.

The initial opening of the trade with New Mexico from the Missouri River, as has been related, was not direct to Santa Fe. The limited number of pack-trains at first passed to the north of the Raton Range, and travelled to the Spanish settlements in the valley of Taos.

On this original Trail, where now is situated the beautiful city of Pueblo, the second place of importance in Colorado, there was a little Indian trading-post called "the Pueblo," from which the present thriving place derives its name. The Atchison, Topeka, and Santa Fe Railroad practically follows the same route that the traders did to reach Pueblo, as it also does that which the freight caravans later followed from the Missouri River direct to Santa Fe.

The old Pueblo fort, as nearly as can be determined now, was built as early as 1840, or not later than 1842, and, as one authority asserts, by George Simpson and his associates, Barclay and Doyle. Beckwourth claims to have been the original projector of the fort, and to have given the general plan and its name, in which I am inclined to believe that he is correct; perhaps Barclay, Doyle, and Simpson were connected with him, as he states that there were other trappers, though he mentions no names. It was a square fort of adobe, with circular bastions at the corners, no part of the walls being more than eight feet high. Around the inside of the plaza, or corral, were half a dozen small rooms inhabited by as many Indian traders and mountain-men.

One of the earlier Indian agents, Mr. Fitzpatrick, in writing from Bent's Fort in 1847, thus describes the old Pueblo:--

About seventy-five miles above this place, and immediately
on the Arkansas River, there is a small settlement, chiefly
composed of old trappers and hunters; the male part of it
are mostly Americans (Missourians), French Canadians, and
Mexicans. It numbers about one hundred and fifty, and of
this number about sixty men have wives, and some have two.
These wives are of various Indian tribes, as follows; viz.
Blackfeet, Assiniboines, Sioux, Arapahoes, Cheyennes,
Snakes, and Comanches. The American women are Mormons,

a party of Mormons having wintered there, and then departed
for California.

The old trappers and hunters of the Pueblo fort lived entirely upon game,
and a greater part of the year without bread. As soon as their supply of meat was
exhausted, they started to the mountains with two or three pack-animals, and brought
back in two or three days loads of venison and buffalo.

The Arkansas at the Pueblo is a clear, rapid river about a hundred yards wide.
The bottom, which is enclosed on each side by high bluffs, is about a quarter of
a mile across. In the early days of which I write, the margin of the stream was
heavily timbered with cottonwood, and the tourist to-day may see the remnant of
the primitive great woods, in the huge isolated trees scattered around the bottom in
the vicinity of the Atchison, Topeka, and Santa Fe Railroad station of the charming
mountain city.

On each side vast rolling prairies stretch away for hundreds of miles, gradually
ascending on the side towards the mountains, where the highlands are sparsely
covered with pinyon and cedar. The lofty banks through which the Arkansas
occasionally passes are of shale and sandstone, rising precipitously from the water.
Ascending the river the country is wild and broken, until it enters the mountain
region, where the scenery is incomparably grand and imposing. The surrounding
prairies are naturally arid and sterile, producing but little vegetation, and the
primitive grass, though of good quality, is thin and scarce. Now, however, under a
competent system of irrigation, the whole aspect of the landscape is changed from
what it was thirty years ago, and it has all the luxuriance of a garden.

The whole country, it is claimed, was once possessed by the Shos-shones, or
Snake Indians, of whom the Comanches of the Southern plains are a branch; and,
although many hundred miles divide their hunting-grounds, they were once, if not
the same people, tribes or bands of that great and powerful nation. They retain a
language in common, and there is also a striking analogy in many of their religious
rites and ceremonies, in their folk-lore, and in some of their everyday customs. These
facts prove, at least, that there was at one time a very close alliance which bound
the two tribes together. Half a century ago they were, in point of numbers, the two
most powerful nations in all the numerous aggregations of Indians in the West; the
Comanches ruling almost supreme on the Eastern plains, while the Shos-shones were
the dominant tribe in the country beyond the Rocky Mountains, and in the mountains
themselves. Once, many years ago, before the problem of the relative strength of
the various tribes was as well solved as now, the Shos-shones were supposed to be
the most powerful, and numerically the most populous, tribe of Indians on the North
American continent.

In the immediate vicinity of the old Pueblo fort at the time of its greatest business prosperity, game was scarce; the buffalo had for some years deserted the neighbouring prairies, but they were always to be found in the mountain-valleys, particularly in one known as "Bayou Salado," which forty-five years ago abounded in elk, bear, deer, and antelope.

The fort was situated a few hundred yards above the mouth of the "Fontaine qui Bouille" River,[47] so called from two springs of mineral water near its head, under Pike's Peak, about sixty miles above its mouth.

As is the case with all the savage races of the world, the American Indians possess hereditary legends, accounting for all the phenomena of nature, or any occurrence which is beyond their comprehension. The Shos-shones had the following story to account for the presence of these wonderful springs in the midst of their favourite hunting-ground. The two fountains, one pouring forth the sweetest water imaginable, the other a stream as bitter as gall, are intimately connected with the cause of the separation of the two tribes. Their legend thus runs: Many hundreds of winters ago, when the cottonwoods on the big river were no higher than arrows, and the prairies were crowded with game, the red men who hunted the deer in the forests and the buffalo on the plains all spoke the same language, and the pipe of peace breathed its soothing cloud whenever two parties of hunters met on the boundless prairie.

It happened one day that two hunters of different nations met on the bank of a small rivulet, to which both had resorted to quench their thirst. A small stream of water, rising from a spring on a rock within a few feet of the bank, trickled over it and fell splashing into the river. One hunter sought the spring itself; the other, tired by his exertions in the chase, threw himself at once to the ground, and plunged his face into the running stream.

The latter had been unsuccessful in the hunt, and perhaps his bad fortune, and the sight of the fat deer which the other threw from his back before he drank at the crystal spring, caused a feeling of jealousy and ill-humour to take possession of his mind. The other, on the contrary, before he satisfied his thirst, raised in the hollow of his hand a portion of the water, and, lifting it toward the sun, reversed his hand, and allowed it to fall upon the ground, as a libation to the Great Spirit, who had vouch-safed him a successful hunt and the blessing of the refreshing water with which he was about to quench his thirst.

This reminder that he had neglected the usual offering only increased the feeling of envy and annoyance which filled the unsuccessful hunter's heart. The Evil Spirit at that moment entering his body, his temper fairly flew away, and he sought some pretence to provoke a quarrel with the other Indian.

"Why does a stranger," he asked, rising from the stream, "drink at the spring-head, when one to whom the fountain belongs contents himself with the water that runs from it?"

"The Great Spirit places the cool water at the spring," answered the other hunter, "that his children may drink it pure and undefiled. The running water is for the beasts which scour the plains. Ausaqua is a chief of the Shos-shones; he drinks at the head water."

"The Shos-shones is but a tribe of the Comanches," returned the other: "Wacomish leads the whole nation. Why does a Shos-shone dare to drink above him?"

"When the Manitou made his children, whether Shos-shone or Comanche, Arapaho, Cheyenne, or Pawnee, he gave them buffalo to eat, and the pure water of the fountain to quench their thirst. He said not to one, 'Drink here,' and to another, 'Drink there'; but gave the crystal spring to all, that all might drink."

Wacomish almost burst with rage as the other spoke; but his coward heart prevented him from provoking an encounter with the calm Shos-shone. The latter, made thirsty by the words he had spoken--for the Indian is ever sparing of his tongue--again stooped down to the spring to drink, when the subtle warrior of the Comanches suddenly threw himself upon the kneeling hunter and, forcing his head into the bubbling water, held him down with all his strength until his victim no longer struggled; his stiffened limbs relaxed, and he fell forward over the spring, drowned.

Mechanically the Comanche dragged the body a few paces from the water, and, as soon as the head of the dead Indian was withdrawn, the spring was suddenly and strangely disturbed. Bubbles sprang up from the bottom, and, rising to the surface, escaped in hissing gas. A thin vapour arose, and, gradually dissolving, displayed to the eyes of the trembling murderer the figure of an aged Indian, whose long, snowy hair and venerable beard, blown aside from his breast, discovered the well-known totem of the great Wankanaga, the father of the Comanche and Shos-shone nation.

Stretching out a war-club toward the Comanche, the figure thus addressed him:--

"Accursed murderer! While the blood of the brave Shos-shone cries to the Great Spirit for vengeance, may the water of thy tribe be rank and bitter in their throats!" Thus saying, and swinging his ponderous war-club round his head, he dashed out the brains of the Comanche, who fell headlong into the spring, which from that day to this remains rank and nauseous, so that not even when half dead with thirst, can one drink from it.

The good Wankanaga, however, to perpetuate the memory of the Shos-shone warrior, who was renowned in his tribe for valour and nobleness of heart, struck with the same avenging club a hard, flat rock which overhung the rivulet, and forthwith a round clear basin opened, which instantly filled with bubbling, sparkling water, sweet and cool.

From that day the two mighty tribes of the Shos-shones and Comanches have remained severed and apart, although a long and bloody war followed the treacherous murder.

The Indians regarded these wonderful springs with awe. The Arapahoes, especially, attributed to the Spirit of the springs the power of ordaining the success or failure of their war expeditions. As their warriors passed by the mysterious pools when hunting their hereditary enemies, the Utes, they never failed to bestow their votive offerings upon the spring, in order to propitiate the Manitou of the strange fountain, and insure a fortunate issue to their path of war. As late as twenty-five years ago, the visitor to the place could always find the basin of the spring filled with beads and wampum, pieces of red cloth and knives, while the surrounding trees were hung with strips of deerskin, cloth, and moccasins. Signs were frequently observed in the vicinity of the waters unmistakably indicating that a war-dance had been executed there by the Arapahoes on their way to the Valley of Salt, occupied by the powerful Utes.

Never was there such a paradise for hunters as this lone and solitary spot in the days when the region was known only to them and the trappers of the great fur companies. The shelving prairie, at the bottom of which the springs are situated, is entirely surrounded by rugged mountains and contained two or three acres of excellent grass, affording a safe pasture for their animals, which hardly cared to wander from such feeding and the salt they loved to lick.

The trappers of the Rocky Mountains belonged to a genus that has disappeared. Forty years ago there was not a hole or corner in the vast wilderness of the far West that had not been explored by these hardy men. From the Mississippi to the mouth of the Colorado of the West, from the frozen regions of the north to the Gila in Mexico, the beaver hunter has set his traps in every creek and stream. The mountains and waters, in many instances, still retain the names assigned them by those rude hunters, who were veritable pioneers paving the way for the settlement of the stern country.

A trapper's camp in the old days was quite a picture, as were all its surroundings. He did not always take the trouble to build a shelter, unless in the winter. A couple of deerskins stretched over a willow frame was considered sufficient to protect him from the storm. Sometimes he contented himself with a mere "breakwind," the rocky wall of a canyon, or large ravine. Near at hand he set up two poles, in the crotch of which another was laid, where he kept, out of reach of the hungry wolf and coyote, his meat, consisting of every variety afforded by the region in which he had pitched his camp. Under cover of the skins of the animals he had killed hung his old-fashioned powder-horn and bullet-pouch, while his trusty rifle, carefully defended from the damp, was always within reach of his hand. Round his blazing fire at night his companions, if he had any, were other trappers on the same stream; and, while engaged in cleaning their arms, making and mending moccasins, or running bullets, they told long yarns, until the lateness of the hour warned them to crawl under their blankets.

Not far from the camp, his animals, well hobbled, fed in sight; for nothing did a hunter dread more than a visit from horse-stealing Indians, and to be afoot was the acme of misery.

Some hunters who had married squaws carried about with them regular buffalo-skin lodges, which their wives took care of, according to Indian etiquette.

The old-time trappers more nearly approximated the primitive savage, perhaps, than any other class of civilized men. Their lives being spent in the remote wilderness of the mountains, frequently with no other companion than Nature herself, their habits and character often assumed a most singular cast of simplicity, mingled with ferocity, that appeared to take its colouring from the scenes and objects which surrounded them. Having no wants save those of nature, their sole concern was to provide sufficient food to support life, and the necessary clothing to protect them from the sometimes rigorous climate.

The costume of the average trapper was a hunting-shirt of dressed buckskin, with long, fringed trousers of the same material, decorated with porcupine quills. A flexible hat and moccasins covered his extremities, and over his left shoulder and under his right arm hung his powder-horn and bullet-pouch, in which he also carried flint, steel, and other odds and ends. Round his waist he wore a belt, in which was stuck a large knife in a sheath of buffalo-hide, made fast to the belt by a chain or guard of steel. It also supported a little buckskin case, which contained a whetstone, a very necessary article; for in taking off the hides of the beaver a sharp knife was required. His pipe-holder hung around his neck, and was generally a gage d'amour, a triumph of squaw workmanship, wrought with beads and porcupine quills, often made in the shape of a heart.

Necessarily keen observers of nature, they rivalled the beasts of prey in discovering the haunts and habits of game, and in their skill and cunning in capturing it outwitted the Indian himself. Constantly exposed to perils of all kinds, they became callous to any feeling of danger, and were firm friends or bitter enemies. It was a "word and a blow," the blow often coming first. Strong, active, hardy as bears, expert in the use of their weapons, they were just what an uncivilized white man might be supposed to be under conditions where he must depend upon his instincts for the support of life.

Having determined upon the locality of his trapping-ground, the hunter started off, sometimes alone, sometimes three or four of them in company, as soon as the breaking of the ice in the streams would permit, if he was to go very far north. Arriving on the spot he has selected for his permanent camp, the first thing to be done, after he had settled himself, was to follow the windings of the creeks and rivers, keeping a sharp lookout for "signs." If he saw a prostrate cottonwood tree, he carefully examined it to learn whether it was the work of beaver, and if so whether thrown for the purpose of food, or to dam the stream. The track of the animal on the mud or sand under the banks was also examined; if the sign was fresh, he set his trap in the run of the animal, hiding it under water, and attaching it by a stout chain to a picket driven in the bank, or to a bush or tree. A float-stick was made fast to the trap by a cord a few feet long, which, if the animal carried away the trap, would float on the water and point out its position. The trap was baited with "medicine," an oily substance obtained from the beaver. A stick was dipped in this and planted over the trap, and the beaver, attracted by the smell, put his leg into the trap and was caught.

When a beaver lodge was discovered, the trap was set at the edge of the dam, at a point where the animal passed from deep to shoal water, and always under the surface. Early in the morning, the hunter mounted his mule and examined all his traps.

The beaver is exceedingly wily, and if by scent or sound or sight he had any intimation of the presence of a trapper, he put at defiance all efforts to capture him, consequently it was necessary to practise great caution when in the neighbourhood of one of their lodges. The trapper then avoided riding for fear the sound of his horse's feet might strike dismay among the furry inhabitants under the water, and, instead of walking on the ground, he waded in the stream, lest he should leave a scent behind by which he might be discovered.

In the days of the great fur companies, trappers were of two kinds-- the hired hand and the free trapper. The former was hired by the company, which supplied him with everything necessary, and paid him a certain price for his furs and peltries. The other hunted on his own hook, owned his animals and traps, went where he pleased, and sold to whom he chose.

During the hunting season, regardless of the Indians, the fearless trapper wandered far and near in search of signs. His nerves were in a state of tension, his mind always clear, and his head cool. His trained eye scrutinized every part of the country, and in an instant he could detect anything that was strange. A turned leaf, a blade of grass pressed down, the uneasiness of wild animals, the actions of the birds, were all to him paragraphs written in Nature's legible hand.

All the wits of the wily savage were called into play to gain an advantage over the plucky white man; but with the resources natural to a civilized mind, the hunter seldom failed, under equal chance, to circumvent the cunning of the red man. Sometimes, following his trail for weeks, the Indian watched him set his traps on some timbered stream, and crawling up the bed of it, so that he left no tracks, he lay in the bushes until his victim came to examine his traps. Then, when he approached within a few feet of the ambush, whiz! flew the home-drawn arrow, which never failed at such close quarters to bring the unsuspecting hunter to the ground. But for one white scalp that dangled in the smoke of an Indian's lodge, a dozen black ones, at the end of the season, ornamented the camp-fires of the rendezvous where the furs were sold.

In the camp, if he was a very successful hunter, all the appliances for preparing the skins for market were at hand; if he had a squaw for a wife, she did all the hard work, as usual. Close to the entrance of their skin lodge was the "graining-block," a log of wood with the bark stripped off and perfectly smooth, set obliquely in the ground, on which the hair was removed from the deerskins which furnished moccasins and dresses for both herself and her husband. Then there were stretching frames on which the skins were placed to undergo the process of "dubbing"; that is, the removal of all flesh and fatty particles adhering to the skin. The "dubber" was made of the stock of an elk's horn, with a piece of iron or steel inserted in the end, forming a sharp knife. The last process the deerskin underwent before it was soft and pliable enough for making into garments, was the "smoking." This was effected by digging a round hole in the ground, and lighting in it an armful of rotten wood or punk; then sticks were planted around the hole, and their tops brought together and tied. The skins were placed on this frame, and all openings by which the smoke might escape being carefully stopped, in ten or twelve hours they were thoroughly cured and ready for immediate use.

The beaver was the main object of the hunter's quest; its skins were once worth from six to eight dollars a pound; then they fell to only one dollar, which hardly paid the expenses of traps, animals, and equipment for the hunt, and was certainly no adequate remuneration for the hardships, toil, and danger undergone by the trappers.

The beaver was once found in every part of North America, from Canada to the Gulf of Mexico, but has so retired from the encroachments of civilized man, that it is only to be met with occasionally on some tributary to the remote mountain streams.

The old trappers always aimed to set their traps so that the beaver would drown when taken. This was accomplished by sinking the trap several inches under water, and driving a stake through a ring on the end of the chain into the bottom of the creek. When the beaver finds himself caught, he pitches and plunges about until his strength is exhausted, when he sinks down and is drowned, but if he succeeds in getting to the shore, he always extricates himself by gnawing off the leg that is in the jaws of the trap.

The captured animals were skinned, and the tails, which are a great dainty, carefully packed into camp. The skin was then stretched over a hoop or framework of willow twigs and allowed to dry, the flesh and fatty substance adhering being first carefully scraped off. When dry, it was folded into a square sheet, the fur turned inwards, and the bundle, containing twenty skins, tightly pressed and tied, was ready for transportation. The beaver after the hide is taken off weighs about twelve pounds, and its flesh, although a little musky, is very fine. Its tail which is flat and oval in shape, is covered with scales about the size of those of a salmon. It was a great delicacy in the estimation of the old trapper; he separated it from the body, thrust a stick in one end of it, and held it before the fire with the scales on. In a few moments large blisters rose on the surface, which were very easily removed. The tail was then perfectly white, and delicious. Next to the tail the liver was another favourite of the trapper, and when properly cooked it constituted a delightful repast.

After the season was over, or the hunter had loaded all his pack-animals, he proceeded to the "rendezvous," where the buyers were to congregate for the purchase of the fur, the locality of which had been agreed upon when the hunters started out on their expedition. One of these was at Bent's old fort and one at Pueblo; another at "Brown's Hole" on Green River, and there were many more on the great streams and in the mountains. There the agents of the fur companies and traders waited for the arrival of the trappers, with such an assortment of goods as the hardy men required, including, of course, an immense supply of whiskey. The trappers dropped in day after day, in small bands, packing their loads of beaver-skins, not infrequently to the value of a thousand dollars each, the result of one hunt.

The rendezvous was frequently a continuous scene of gambling, brawling, and fighting, so long as the improvident trapper's money lasted. Seated around the large camp-fires, cross-legged in Indian fashion, with a blanket or buffalo-robe spread before them, groups were playing cards--euchre, seven-up, and poker, the regular mountain games. The usual stakes were beaver-skins, which were current as coin. When their fur was all gone, their horses, mules, rifles, shirts, hunting packs, and trousers were staked. Daring professional gamblers made the rounds of the camps, challenging each other to play for the trapper's highest stakes--his horse, or his squaw, if he had one--and it is told of one great time that two old trappers played for one another's scalps! "There goes hoss and beaver," was a common mountain expression when any severe loss was sustained, and shortly "hoss and beaver" found their way into the pockets of the unconscionable gamblers.

Frequently a trapper would squander the entire product of his hunt, amounting to hundreds of dollars, in a couple of hours. Then, supplied with another outfit, he left the rendezvous for another expedition, which had the same result time after time, although one good hunt would have enabled him to return to the settlements and live a life of comparative ease.

It is told of one old Canadian trapper, who had received as much as fifteen thousand dollars for beaver during his life in the mountains, extending over twenty years, that each season he had resolved in his mind to go back to Canada, and with this object in view always converted his furs into cash; but a fortnight at the rendezvous always "cleaned him out," and at the end of the twenty years he had not even enough credit to get a plug of tobacco.

Trading with the Indians in the primitive days of the border was just what the word signifies in its radical interpretation--a system of barter exclusively. No money was used in the transaction, as it was long afterward before the savages began to learn something of the value of currency from their connection with the sutler's and agency stores established on reservations and at military posts on the plains and in the mountains. In the early days, if an Indian by any chance happened to get possession of a piece of money (only gold or silver was recognized as a medium of exchange in the remote West), he would immediately fashion it into some kind of an ornament with which to adorn his person. Some tribes, however, did indulge in a sort of currency, worthless except among themselves. This consisted of rare shells, such as the Oligachuck, so called, of the Pacific coast nations, used by them within my own recollection, as late as 1858.

The poor Indian, as might have been expected, was generally outrageously swindled; in fact, I am inclined to believe, always. I never was present on an occasion when he was not.

The savage's idea of values was very crude until the government, in attempting to civilize and make a gentleman of him, has transformed him into a bewildered child. Very soon after his connection with the white trader, he learned that a gun was more valuable than a knife; but of their relative cost to manufacture he had no idea. For these reasons, obviously, he was always at the mercy of the unscrupulous trader who came to his village, or met him at the rendezvous to barter for his furs. I know that the price of every article he desired was fixed by the trader, and never by the Indian, consequently he rarely got the best of the bargain.

Uncle John Smith, Kit Carson, L. B. Maxwell, Uncle Dick Wooton, and a host of other well-known Indian traders, long since dead, have often told me that the first thing they did on entering a village with a pack-load of trinkets to barter, in the earlier days before the whites had encroached to any great extent, was to arrange a schedule of prices. They would gather a large number of sticks, each one representing an article they had brought. With these crude symbols the Indian made himself familiar in a little while, and when this preliminary arrangement had been completed, the trading began. The Indian, for instance, would place a buffalo-robe on the ground; then the trader commenced to lay down a number of the sticks, representing what he was willing to give for the robe. The Indian revolved the transaction in his mind until he thought he was getting a fair equivalent according to his ideas, then the bargain was made. It was claimed by these old traders, when they related this to me, that the savage generally was not satisfied, always insisting upon having more sticks placed on the pile. I suspect, however, that the trader was ever prepared for this, and never gave more than he originally intended. The price of that initial robe having been determined on, it governed the price of all the rest for the whole trade, regardless of size or fineness, for that day. What was traded for was then placed by the Indian on one side of the lodge, and the trader put what he was to give on the other. After prices had been agreed upon, business went on very rapidly, and many thousand dollars' worth of valuable furs were soon collected by the successful trader, which he shipped to St. Louis and converted into gold.

In a few years, relatively, the Indian began to appreciate the value of our medium of exchange and the power it gave him to secure at the stores in the widely scattered hamlets and at the military posts on the plains, those things he coveted, at a fairer equivalent than in the uncertain and complicated method of direct barter. It was not very long after the advent of the overland coaches on the Santa Fe Trail, that our currency, even the greenbacks, had assumed a value to the savage, which he at least partially understood. Whenever the Indians successfully raided the stages the mail sacks were no longer torn to pieces or thrown aside as worthless, but every letter was carefully scrutinized for possible bills.

I well remember, when the small copper cent, with its spread eagle upon it, was first issued, about the year 1857, how the soldiers of a frontier garrison where I was stationed at the time palmed them off upon the simple savages as two dollar and a half gold pieces, which they resembled as long as they retained their brightness, and with which the Indians were familiar, as many were received by the troops from the paymaster every two months, the savages receiving them in turn for horses and other things purchased of them by the soldiers.

I have known of Indians who gave nuggets of gold for common calico shirts costing two dollars in that region and seventy-five cents in the States, while the lump of precious metal was worth, perhaps, five or seven dollars. As late as twenty-eight years ago, I have traded for beautifully smoke-tanned and porcupine-embroidered buffalo-robes for my own use, giving in exchange a mere loaf of bread or a cupful of brown sugar.

Very early in the history of the United States, in 1786, the government, under the authority of Congress, established a plan of trade with the Indians. It comprised supplying all their physical wants without profit; factories, or stations as they were called, were erected at points that were then on the remote frontier; where factors, clerks, and interpreters were stationed. The factors furnished goods of all kinds to the Indians, and received from them in exchange furs and peltries. There was an officer in charge of all these stations called the superintendent of Indian trade, appointed by the President. As far back as 1821, there were stations at Prairie du Chien, Fort Edward, Fort Osage, with branches at Chicago, Green Bay in Arkansas, on the Red River, and other places in the then far West. These stations were movable, and changed from time to time to suit the convenience of the Indians. In 1822 the whole system was abolished by act of Congress, and its affairs wound up, the American Fur Company, the Missouri Fur Company, and a host of others having by that time become powerful. Like the great corporations of to-day, they succeeded in supplanting the government establishments. Of course, the Indians of the remote plains, which included all the vast region west of the Missouri River, never had the benefits of the government trading establishments, but were left to the tender mercies of the old plainsmen and trappers.

Until the railroad reached the mountains, when the march of a wonderful immigration closely followed, usurping the lands claimed by the savages, and the latter were driven, perforce, upon reservations, the winter camps of the Kiowas, Arapahoes, and Cheyennes were strung along the Old Trail for miles, wherever a belt of timber on the margin of the Arkansas, or its tributaries, could be found large enough to furnish fuel for domestic purposes and cottonwood bark for the vast herds of ponies in the severe snow-storms.

At these various points the Indians congregated to trade with the whites. As stated, Bent's Fort, the Pueblo Fort, and Big Timbers were favourite resorts, and the trappers and old hunters passed a lively three or four months every year, indulging in the amusements I have referred to. They were also wonderful story-tellers, and around their camp-fires many a tale of terrible adventure with Indians and vicious animals was nightly related.

Baptiste Brown was one of the most famous trappers. Few men had seen more of wild life in the great prairie wilderness. He had hunted with nearly every tribe of Indians on the plains and in the mountains, was often at Bent's Fort, and his soul-stirring narratives made him a most welcome guest at the camp-fire.

He lived most of his time in the Wind River Mountains, in a beautiful little valley named after him "Brown's Hole." It has a place on the maps to-day, and is on what was then called Prairie River, or Sheetskadee, by the Indians; it is now known as Green River, and is the source of the great Colorado.

The valley, which is several thousand feet above the sea-level, is about fifteen miles in circumference, surrounded by lofty hills, and is aptly, though not elegantly, characterized as a "hole." The mountain-grass is of the most nutritious quality; groves of cottonwood trees and willows are scattered through the sequestered spot, and the river, which enters it from the north, is a magnificent stream; in fact, it is the very ideal of a hunter's headquarters.

The temperature is very equable, and at one time, years ago, hundreds of trappers made it their winter quarters. Indians, too, of all the northern tribes, but more especially the Arapahoes, frequented it to trade with the white men.

Baptiste Brown was a Canadian who spoke villanous French and worse English; his vocabulary being largely interspersed with "enfant de garce," "sacre," "sacre enfant," and "damn" until it was a difficult matter to tell what he was talking about.

He was married to an Arapahoe squaw, and his strange wooing and winning of the dusky maiden is a thrilling love-story.

Among the maidens who came with the Arapahoes, when that tribe made a visit to "Brown's Hole" one winter for the purpose of trading with the whites, was a young, merry, and very handsome girl, named "Unami," who after a few interviews completely captured Baptiste's heart. Nothing was more common, as I have stated, than marriages between the trappers and a beautiful redskin. Isolated absolutely from women of his own colour, the poor mountaineer forgets he is white, which, considering the embrowning influence of constant exposure and sunlight, is not so marvellous after all. For a portion of the year there is no hunting, and then idleness is the order of the day. At such times the mountaineer visits the lodges of his dark neighbours for amusement, and in the spirited dance many a heart is lost to the squaws. The young trapper, like other enamoured ones of his sex in civilization, lingers around the house of his fair sweetheart while she transforms the soft skin of the doe into moccasins, ornamenting them richly with glittering beads or the coloured quills of the porcupine, all the time lightening the long hours with the plain-songs of their tribe. It was upon an occasion of this character that Baptiste, then in the prime of his youthful manhood, first loved the dark-eyed Arapahoe.

The course open to him was to woo and win her; but alas! savage papas are just like fathers in the best civilization--the only difference between them is that the former are more open and matter-of-fact, since in savage etiquette a consideration is required in exchange for the daughter, which belongs exclusively to the parent, and must be of equal marketable value to the girl.

The usual method is to select your best horse, take him to the lodge of your inamorata's parents, tie him to a tree, and walk away. If the animal is considered a fair exchange, matters are soon settled satisfactorily; if not, other gifts must be added.

At this juncture poor Baptiste was in a bad fix; he had disposed of all his season's earnings for his winter's subsistence, much of which consisted of an ample supply of whiskey and tobacco; so he had nothing left wherewith to purchase the indispensable horse. Without the animal no wife was to be had, and he was in a terrible predicament; for the hunting season was long since over, and it wanted a whole month of the time for a new starting out.

Baptiste was a very determined man, however, and he shouldered his rifle, intent on accomplishing by a laborious prosecution of the chase the means of winning his loved one from her parents, notwithstanding that the elements and the times were against him. He worked industriously, and after many days was rewarded by a goodly supply of beavers, otters, and mink which he had trapped, besides many a deerskin whose wearer he had shot. Returning to his lodge, where he cached his peltry, he again started out for the forest with hope filling his heart. Three weeks passed in indifferent success, when one morning, having entered a deep canyon, which evidently led out to an open prairie where he thought game might be found, while busy cutting his way through a thicket of briers with his knife, he suddenly came upon a little valley, where he saw what caused him to retrace his footsteps into the thicket.

And here it is necessary to relate a custom peculiar to all Indian tribes. No young man, though his father were the greatest chief in the nation, can range himself among the warriors, be entitled to enter the marriage state, or enjoy any other rights of savage citizenship until he shall have performed some act of personal bravery and daring, or be sprinkled with the blood of his enemies. In the early springtime, therefore, all the young men who are of the proper age band themselves together and take to the forest in search --like the knight-errant of old--of adventure and danger. Having decided upon a secluded and secret spot, they collect a number of poles from twenty to thirty feet in length, and, lashing them together at the small ends, form a huge conical lodge, which they cover with grass and boughs. Inside they deposit various articles, with which to "make medicine," or as a propitiatory offering to the Great Spirit; generally a green buffalo head, kettles, scalps, blankets, and other things of value, of which the most prominent and revered is the sacred pipe. The party then enters the lodge and the first ceremony is smoking this pipe. One of the young men fills it with tobacco and herbs, places a coal on it from the fire that has been already kindled in the lodge, and, taking the stem in his mouth, inhales the smoke and expels it through his nostrils. The ground is touched with the bowl, the four points of the compass are in turn saluted, and with various ceremonies it makes the round of the lodge. After many days of feasting and dancing the party is ready for a campaign, when they abandon the lodge, and it is death for any one else to enter, or by any means to desecrate it while its projectors are absent.

It was upon one of these mystic lodges that Baptiste had accidentally stumbled, and strange thoughts flashed through his mind; for within the sacred place were articles, doubtless, of value more than sufficient to purchase the necessary horse with which he could win the fair Unami. Baptiste was sorely tempted, but there was an instinctive respect for religion in the minds of the old trappers, and Brown had too much honour to think of robbing the Indian temple, although he distinctly remembered a time when a poor white trapper, having been robbed of his poncho at the beginning of winter, made free with a blanket he had found in one of these Arapahoe sacred lodges. When he was brought before the medicine men of the tribe, charged with the sacrilege, his defence, that, having been robbed, the Great Spirit took pity on him and pointed out the blanket and ordered him to clothe himself, was considered good, on the theory that the Great Spirit had an undoubted right to give away his own property; consequently the trapper was set free.

Brown, after considering the case, was about to move away, when a hand was laid on his shoulder, and turning round there stood before him an Indian in full war-paint.

The greeting was friendly, for the young savage was the brother of Baptiste's love, to whom he had given many valuable presents during the past season.

"My white brother is very wakeful; he rises early."

Baptiste laughed, and replied: "Yes, because my lodge is empty. If I had Unami for a wife, I would not have to get out before the sun; and I would always have a soft seat for her brother; he will be a great warrior."

The young brave shook his head gravely, as be pointed to his belt, where not a scalp was to be seen, and said: "Five moons have gone to sleep and the Arapahoe hatchet has not been raised. The Blackfeet are dogs, and hide in their holes."

Without adding anything to this hint that none of the young men had been able to fulfil their vows, the disconsolate savage led the way to the camp of the other Arapahoes, his companions in the quest for scalps. Baptiste was very glad to see the face of a fellow-creature once more, and he cheerfully followed the footsteps of the young brave, which were directed away from the medicine lodge toward the rocky canyon which he had already travelled that morning, where in the very centre of the dark defile, and within twenty feet of where he had recently passed, was the camp of the disappointed band. Baptiste was cordially received, and invited to share the meal of which the party were about to partake, after which the pipe was passed around. In a little while the Indians began to talk among themselves by signs, which made Baptiste feel somewhat uncomfortable, for it was apparent that he was the object of their interest.

They had argued that Brown's skin indicated that he belonged to the great tribe of their natural enemies, and with the blood of a white on their garments, they would have fulfilled the terms of their vow to their friends and the Great Spirit.

Noticing the trend of the debate, which would lead his friend into trouble, the brother of Unami arose, and waving his hand said:--

"The Arapahoe is a warrior; his feet outstrip the fleetest horse; his arrow is as the lightning of the Great Spirit; he is very brave. But a cloud is between him and the sun; he cannot see his enemy; there is yet no scalp in his lodge. The Great Spirit is good; he sends a victim, a man whose skin is white, but his heart is very red; the pale-face is a brother, and his long knife is turned from his friends, the Arapahoes; but the Great Spirit is all-powerful. My brother"--pointing to Baptiste--"is very full of blood; he can spare a little to stain the blankets of the young men, and his heart shall still be warm; I have spoken."

As Baptiste expressed it: "Sacre enfant de garce; damn, de ting vas agin my grain, but de young Arapahoe he have saved my life."

Loud acclamation followed the speech of Unami's brother, and many of those most clamorous against the white trapper, being actuated by the earnest desire of returning home with their vow accomplished, when they would be received into the list of warriors, and have wives and other honours, were unanimous in agreeing to the proposed plan.

A flint lancet was produced, Baptiste's arm was bared, and the blood which flowed from the slight wound was carefully distributed, and scattered over the robes of the delighted Arapahoes.

The scene which followed was quite unexpected to Baptiste, who was only glad to escape the death to which the majority had doomed him. The Indians, perfectly satisfied that their vow of shedding an enemy's blood had been fulfilled, were all gratitude; and to testify that gratitude in a substantial manner each man sought his pack, and laid at the feet of the surprised Baptiste a rich present. One gave an otter skin, another that of a buffalo, and so on until his wealth in furs outstripped his most sanguine expectations from his hunt. The brother of Unami stood passively looking on until all the others had successively honoured his guest, when he advanced toward Baptiste, leading by its bridle a magnificent horse, fully caparisoned, and a large pack-mule. To refuse would have been the most flagrant breach of Indian etiquette, and beside, Brown was too alive to the advantage that would accrue to him to be other than very thankful.

The camp was then broken up, and the kind savages were soon lost to Baptiste's sight as they passed down the canyon; and he, as soon as he had gained a little strength, for he was weak from the blood he had shed in the good cause, mounted his horse, after loading the mule with his gifts, and made the best of his way to his lonely lodge, where he remained several days. He then sold his furs at a good price, as it was so early in the season, bartered for a large quantity of knives, beads, powder, and balls, and returned to the Arapahoe village, where the horse was considered a fair exchange for the pretty Unami; and from that day, for over thirty years, they lived as happy as any couple in the highest civilization.

The fate of the Pueblo, where the trappers and hunters had such good times in the halcyon days of the border, like that which befell nearly all the trading-posts and ranches on the Old Santa Fe Trail, was to be partially destroyed by the savages. During the early months of the winter of 1854, the Utes swept down through the Arkansas valley, leaving a track of blood behind them, and frightening the settlers so thoroughly that many left the country never to return. The outbreak was as sudden as it was devastating. The Pueblo was captured by the savages, and every man, woman, and child in it murdered, with the exception of one aged Mexican, and he was so badly wounded that he died in a few days.

His story was that the Utes came to the gates of the fort on Christmas morning, professing the greatest friendship, and asking permission to be allowed to come inside and hold a peace conference. All who were in the fort at the time were Mexicans, and as their cupidity led them to believe that they could do some advantageous trading with the Indians, they foolishly permitted the whole band to enter. The result was that a wholesale massacre followed. There were seventeen persons in all quartered there, only one of whom escaped death--the old man referred to--and a woman and her two children, who were carried off as captives; but even she was killed before the savages had gone a mile from the place. What became of the children was never known; they probably met the same fate.

CHAPTER XV.

UNCLE JOHN SMITH.

Many of the men of the border were blunt in manners, rude in speech, driven to the absolute liberty of the far West with better natures shattered and hopes blasted, to seek in the exciting life of the plainsman and mountaineer oblivion of some incidents of their youthful days, which were better forgotten. Yet these aliens from society, these strangers to the refinements of civilization, who would tear off a bloody scalp even with grim smiles of satisfaction, were fine fellows, full of the milk of human kindness, and would share their last slapjack with a hungry stranger.

Uncle John Smith, as he was known to every trapper, trader, and hunter from the Yellowstone to the Gila, was one of the most famous and eccentric men of the early days. In 1826, as a boy, he ran away from St. Louis with a party of Santa Fe traders, and so fascinated was he with the desultory and exciting life, that he chose to sit cross-legged, smoking the long Indian pipe, in the comfortable buffalo-skin teepee, rather than cross legs on the broad table of his master, a tailor to whom he had been apprenticed when he took French leave from St. Louis.

He spent his first winter with the Blackfeet Indians, but came very near losing his scalp in their continual quarrels, and therefore allied himself with the more peaceable Sioux. Once while on the trail of a horse-stealing band of Arapahoes near the head waters of the Arkansas, the susceptible young hunter fell in love with a very pretty Cheyenne squaw, married her, and remained true to the object of his early affection during all his long and eventful life, extending over a period of forty years. For many decades he lived with his dusky wife as the Indians did, having been adopted by the tribe. He owned a large number of horses, which constituted the wealth of the plains Indians, upon the sale of which he depended almost entirely for his subsistence. He became very powerful in the Cheyenne nation; was regarded as a chief, taking an active part in the councils, and exercising much authority. His excellent judgment as a trader with the various bands of Indians while he was employed by the great fur companies made his services invaluable in the strange business complications of the remote border. Besides understanding the Cheyenne language as well as his native tongue, he also spoke three other Indian dialects, French, and Spanish, but with many Western expressions that sometimes grated harshly upon the grammatical ear.

He became a sort of autocrat on the plains and in the mountains; and for an Indian or Mexican to attempt to effect a trade without Uncle John Smith having something to say about it, and its conditions, was hardly possible. The New Mexicans often came in small parties to his Indian village, their burros packed with dry pumpkin, corn, etc., to trade for buffalo-robes, bearskins, meat, and ponies; and

Smith, who knew his power, exacted tribute, which was always paid. At one time, however, when for some reason a party of strange Mexicans refused, Uncle John harangued the people of the village, and called the young warriors together, who emptied every sack of goods belonging to the cowering Mexicans on the ground, Smith ordering the women and children to help themselves, an order which was obeyed with alacrity. The frightened Mexicans left hurriedly for El Valle de Taos, whence they had come, crossing themselves and uttering thanks to Heaven for having retained their scalps. This and other similar cases so intimidated the poor Greasers, and impressed them so deeply with a sense of Smith's power, that, ever after, his permission to trade was craved by a special deputation of the parties, accompanied by peace-offerings of corn, pumpkin, and pinole. At one time, when Smith was journeying by himself a day's ride from the Cheyenne village, he was met by a party of forty or more corn traders, who, instead of putting such a bane to their prospects speedily out of the way, gravely asked him if they could proceed, and offered him every third robe they had to accompany them, which he did. Indeed, he became so regardless of justice, in his condescension to the natives of New Mexico, that the governor of that province offered a reward of five hundred dollars for him alive or dead, but fear of the Cheyennes was so prevalent that his capture was never even attempted.

During Sheridan's memorable winter campaign against the allied tribes in 1868-69, the old man, for he was then about sixty, was my guide and interpreter. He shared my tent and mess, a most welcome addition to the few who sat at my table, and beguiled many a weary hour at night, after our tedious marches through the apparently interminable sand dunes and barren stretches of our monotonous route, with his tales of that period, more than half a century ago, when our mid-continent region was as little known as the topography of the planet Mars.

At the close of December, 1868, a few weeks after the battle of the Washita, I was camping with my command on the bank of that historic stream in the Indian Territory, waiting with an immense wagon-train of supplies for the arrival of General Custer's command, the famous Seventh Cavalry, and also the Nineteenth Kansas, which were supposed to be lost, or wandering aimlessly somewhere in the region south of us.

I had been ordered to that point by General Sheridan, with instructions to keep fires constantly burning on three or four of the highest peaks in the vicinity of our camp, until the lost troops should be guided to the spot by our signals. These signals were veritable pillars of fire by night and pillars of cloud by day; for there was an abundance of wood and hundreds of men ready to feed the hungry flames.

It was more than two weeks before General Custer and his famished troopers began to straggle in. During that period of anxious waiting we lived almost exclusively on wild turkey, and longed for nature's meat--the buffalo; but there were none of the shaggy beasts at that time in the vicinity, so we had to content ourselves with the birds, of which we became heartily tired.

For several days after our arrival on the creek, the men had been urging Uncle John to tell them another story of his early adventures; but the old trapper was in one of his silent moods--he frequently had them--and could not be persuaded to emerge from his shell of reticence despite their most earnest entreaties. I knew it would be of no use for me to press him. I could, of course, order him to any duty, and he would promptly obey; but his tongue, like the hand of Douglas, was his own. I knew, also, that when he got ready, which would be when some incident of camp-life inspired him, he would be as garrulous as ever.

One evening just before supper, a party of enlisted men who had been up the creek to catch fish, but had failed to take anything owing to the frozen condition of the stream, returned with the skeleton of a Cheyenne Indian which they had picked up on the battle-ground of a month previously--one of Custer's victims in his engagement with Black Kettle. This was the incentive Uncle John required. As he gazed on the bleached bones of the warrior, he said: "Boys, I'm going to tell you a good long story to-night. Them Ingin's bones has put me in mind of it. After we've eat, if you fellows wants to hear it, come down to headquarters tent, and I'll give it to you."

Of course word was rapidly passed from one to another, as the whole camp was eager to hear the old trapper again. In a short time, every man not on guard or detailed to keep up the signals on the hills gathered around the dying embers of the cook's fire in front of my tent; the enlisted men and teamsters in groups by themselves, the officers a little closer in a circle, in the centre of which Uncle John sat.

The night was cold, the sky covered with great fleecy patches, through which the full moon, just fairly risen, appeared to be racing, under the effect of that optical illusion caused by the rapidly moving clouds. The coyotes had commenced their nocturnal concert in the timbered recesses of the creek not far away, and on the battle-field a short distance beyond, as they battened and fought over the dead warriors and the carcasses of twelve hundred ponies killed in that terrible slaughter by the intrepid Custer and his troopers. The signals on the hills leaped into the crisp air like the tongues of dragons in the myths of the ancients; in fact, the whole aspect of the place, as we sat around the blazing logs of our camp-fire, was weird and uncanny.

Every one was eager for the veteran guide to begin his tale; but as I knew he could not proceed without smoking, I passed him my pouch of Lone Jack--the brand par excellence in the army at that time.

Uncle John loaded his corn-cob, picked up a live coal, and, pressing it down on the tobacco with his thumb, commenced to puff vigorously. As soon as his withered old face was half hidden in a cloud of smoke, he opened his story in his stereotyped way. I relate it just as he told it, but divested of much of its dialect, so difficult to write:--

"Well, boys, it's a good many years ago, in June, 1845, if I don't disremember. I was about forty-three, and had been in the mountains and on the plains more than nineteen seasons. You see, I went out there in 1826. There warn't no roads, nuthin' but the Santa Fe Trail, in them days, and Ingins and varmints.

"There was four of us. Me, Bill Comstock, Dick Curtis, and Al Thorpe. Dick was took in by the Utes two years afterwards at the foot of the Spanish Peaks, and Al was killed by the Apaches at Pawnee Rock, in 1847.

"We'd been trapping up on Medicine Bow for more than three years together, and had a pile of beaver, otter, mink, and other varmint's skins cached in the hills, which we know'd was worth a heap of money; so we concluded to take them to the river that summer. We started from our trapping camp in April, and 'long 'bout the middle of June reached the Arkansas, near what is know'd as Point o' Rocks. You all know where them is on the Trail west of Fort Dodge, and how them rocks rises up out of the prairie sudden-like. We was a travelling 'long mighty easy, for we was all afoot, and had hoofed it the whole distance, more than six hundred miles, driving five good mules ahead of us. Our furs was packed on four of them, and the other carried our blankets, extry ammunition, frying-pan, coffee-pot, and what little grub we had, for we was obliged to depend upon buffalo, antelope, and jack-rabbits; but, boys, I tell you there was millions of 'em in them days.

"We had just got into camp at Point o' Rocks. It was 'bout four o'clock in the afternoon; none of us carried watches, we always reckoned time by the sun, and could generally guess mighty close, too. It was powerful hot, I remember. We'd hobbled our mules close to the ledge, where the grass was good, so they couldn't be stampeded, as we know'd we was in the Pawnee country, and they was the most ornery Ingins on the plains. We know'd nothing that was white ever came by that part of the Trail without having a scrimmage with the red devils.

"Well, we hadn't more than took our dinner, when them mules give a terrible snort, and tried to break and run, getting awful oneasy all to once. Them critters can tell when Ingins is around. They's better than a dozen dogs. I don't know how they can tell, but they just naturally do.

"In less than five minutes after them mules began to worry, stopped eating, and had their ears pricked up a trying to look over the ledge towards the river, we heard a sharp firing down on the Trail, which didn't appear to be more than a hundred yards

193

off. You ought to seen us grab our rifles sudden, and run out from behind them rocks, where we was a camping, so comfortable-like, and just going to light our pipes for a good smoke. It didn't take us no time to get down on to the Trail, where we seen a Mexican bull train, that we know'd must have come from Santa Fe, and which had stopped and was trying to corral. More than sixty painted Pawnees was a circling around the outfit, howling as only them can howl, and pouring a shower of arrows into the oxen. Some was shaking their buffalo-robes, trying to stampede the critters, so they could kill the men easier.

"We lit out mighty lively, soon as we seen what was going on, and reached the head of the train just as the last wagon, that was furtherest down the Trail, nigh a quarter of a mile off, was cut out by part of the band. Then we seen a man, a woman, and a little boy jump out, and run to get shet of the Ingins what had cut out the wagon from the rest of the train. One of the red devils killed the man and scalped him, while the other pulled the woman up in front of him, and rid off into the sand hills, and out of sight in a minute. Then the one what had killed her husband started for the boy, who was a running for the train as fast as his little legs could go. But we was nigh enough then; and just as the Ingin was reaching down from his pony for the kid, Al Thorpe--he was a powerful fine shot--draw'd up his gun and took the red cuss off his critter without the paint-bedaubed devil know'n' what struck him.

"The boy, seeing us, broke and run for where we was, and I reckon the rest of the Ingins seen us then for the first time, too. We was up with the train now, which was kind o' halfway corralled, and Dick Curtis picked up the child--he warn't more than seven years old-- and throw'd him gently into one of the wagons, where he'd be out of the way; for we know'd there was going to be considerable more fighting before night. We know'd, too, we Americans would have to do the heft of it, as them Mexican bull-whackers warn't much account, nohow, except to cavort around and swear in Spanish, which they hadn't done nothing else since we'd come up to the train; besides, their miserable guns warn't much better than so many bows and arrows.

"We Americans talked together for a few moments as to what was best to be did, while the Ingins all this time was keeping up a lively fire for them. We made as strong a corral of the wagons as we could, driving out what oxen the Mexicans had put in the one they had made, but you can't do much with only nine wagons, nohow. Fortunately, while we was fixing things, the red cusses suddenly retreated out of the range of our rifles, and we first thought they had cleared out for good. We soon discovered, however, they were only holding a pow-wow; for in a few minutes back they come, mounted on their ponies, with all their fixin's and fresh war-paint on.

"Then they commenced to circle around us again, coming a little nearer-- Ingin fashion--every time they rid off and back. It wasn't long before they got in easy range, when they slung themselves on the off-side of their ponies and let fly their arrows and balls from under their critters' necks. Their guns warn't much 'count, being only old English muskets what had come from the Hudson Bay Fur Company, so they didn't do no harm that round, except to scare the Mexicans, which commenced to cross themselves and pray and swear.

"We four Americans warn't idle when them Ingins come a charging up; we kept our eye skinned, and whenever we could draw a bead, one of them tumbled off his pony, you bet! When they'd come back for their dead--we'd already killed three of them--we had a big advantage, wasted no shots, and dropped four of them; one apiece, and you never heard Ingins howl so. It was getting kind o' dark by this time, and the varmints didn't seem anxious to fight any more, but went down to the river and scooted off into the sand hills on the other side. We waited more than half an hour for them, but as they didn't come back, concluded we'd better light out too. We told the Mexicans to yoke up, and as good luck would have it they found all the cattle close by, excepting them what pulled the wagon what the Ingins had cut out, and as it was way down the Trail, we had to abandon it; for it was too dark to hunt it up, as we had no time to fool away.

"We put all our outfit into the train; it wasn't loaded, but going empty to the Missouri, to fetch back a sawmill for New Mexico. Then we made a soft bed in the middle wagon out of blankets for the kid, and rolled out 'bout ten o'clock, meaning to put as many miles between us and them Ingins as the oxen could stand. We four hoofed it along for a while, then rid a piece, catching a nap now and then as best we could, for we was monstrous tired. By daylight we'd made fourteen miles, and was obliged to stop to let the cattle graze. We boiled our coffee, fried some meat, and by that time the little boy waked. He'd slept like a top all night and hadn't no supper either; so when I went to the wagon where he was to fetch him out, he just put them baby arms of his'n around my neck, and says, 'Where's mamma?'

"I tell you, boys, that nigh played me out. He had no idee, 'cause he was too young to realize what had happened; we know'd his pa was killed, but where his ma was, God only know'd!"

Here the old man stopped short in his narrative, made two or three efforts as if to swallow something that would not go down, while his eyes had a far-away look. Presently he picked up a fresh coal from the fire, placed it on his pipe, which had gone out, then puffing vigorously for a few seconds, until his head was again enveloped in smoke, he continued:--

"After I'd washed the little fellow's face and hands, I gave him a tin cup of coffee and some meat. You'd ought to seen him eat; he was hungrier than a coyote. Then while the others was a watering and picketing the mules, I sot down on the grass and took the kid into my lap to have a good look at him; for until now none of us had had a chance.

"He was the purtiest child I'd ever seen; great black eyes, and eyelashes that laid right on to his cheeks; his hair, too, was black, and as curly as a young big-horn. I asked him what his name was, and he says, 'Paul.' 'Hain't you got no other name?' says I to him again, and he answered, 'Yes, sir,' for he was awful polite; I noticed that. 'Paul Dale,' says he prompt-like, and them big eyes of his'n looked up into mine, as he says 'What be yourn?' I told him he must call me 'Uncle John,' and then he says again, as he put his arms around my neck, his little lips all a quivering, and looking so sorrowful, 'Uncle John, where's mamma; why don't she come?'

"Boys, I don't really know what I did say. A kind o' mist came before my eyes, and for a minute or two I didn't know nothing. I come to in a little while, and seeing Thorpe bringing up the mules from the river, where he'd been watering them, I says to Paul, to get his mind on to something else besides his mother, 'Don't you want to ride one of them mules when we pull out again?' The little fellow jumped off my lap, clapped his hands, forgetting his trouble all at once, child-like, and replied, 'I do, Uncle John, can I?'

"After we'd camped there 'bout three hours, the cattle full of grass and all laying down chewing their cud, we concluded to move on and make a few miles before it grow'd too hot, and to get further from the Ingins, which we expected would tackle us again, as soon as they could get back from their camp, where we felt sure they had gone for reinforcements.

"While the Mexicans was yoking up, me and Thorpe rigged an easy saddle on one of the mules, out of blankets, for the kid to ride on, and when we was all ready to pull out, I histed him on, and you never see a youngster so tickled.

"We had to travel mighty slow; couldn't make more than eighteen miles a day with oxen, and that was in two drives, one early in the morning, and one in the evening when it was cool, a laying by and grazing when it was hot. We Americans walked along the Trail, and mighty slow walking it was; 'bout two and a half miles an hour. I kept close to Paul, for I began to set a good deal of store by him; he seemed to cotton to me more than he did to the rest, wanting to stick near me most of the time as he rid on the mule. I wanted to find out something 'bout his folks, where they'd come from; so that when we got to Independence, perhaps I could turn him over to them as ought to have him; though in my own mind I was ornery enough to wish I might never find them, and he'd be obliged to stay with me. The boy was too young to tell what I wanted to find out; all I could get out of him was they'd been living in Santa Fe since he was a baby, and that his papa was a preacher. I 'spect one of them missionaries 'mong the heathenish Greasers. He said they was going back to his grandma's in the States, but he could not tell where. I couldn't get nothing out of them Mexican bull-whackers neither--what they know'd wasn't half as much as the kid--and I had to give it up.

196

"Well, we kept moving along without having any more trouble for a week; them Ingins never following us as we 'lowed they would. I really enjoyed the trip such as I never had before. Paul he was so 'fectionate and smart, that he 'peared to fill a spot in my heart what had always been hollow until then. When he'd got tired of riding the mule or in one of the wagons, he'd come and walk along the Trail with me, a picking flowers, chasing the prairie-owls and such, until his little legs 'bout played out, when I'd hist him on his mule again. When we'd go into camp, Paul, he'd run and pick up buffalo-chips for the fire, and wanted to help all he could. Then when it came time to go to sleep, the boy would always get under my blankets and cuddle up close to me. He'd be sure to say his prayers first, though; but it seemed so strange to me who hadn't heard a prayer for thirty years. I never tried to stop him, you may be certain of that. He'd ask God to bless his pa and ma, and wind up with 'Bless Uncle John too.' Then I couldn't help hugging him right up tighter; for it carried me back to Old Missouri, to the log-cabin in the woods where I was born, and used to say 'Now I lay me,' and 'Our Father' at my ma's knee, when I was a kid like him. I tell you, boys, there ain't nothing that will take the conceit out of a man here on the plains, like the company of a kid what has been brought up right.

"I reckon we'd been travelling about ten days since we left Point o' Rocks, and was on the other side of the Big Bend of the Arkansas, near the mouth of the Walnut, where Fort Zarah is now. We had went into camp at sundown, close to a big spring that's there yet. We drawed up the wagons into a corral on the edge of the river where there wasn't no grass for quite a long stretch; we done this to kind o' fortify ourselves, for we expected to have trouble with the Ingins there, if anywhere, as we warn't but seventeen miles from Pawnee Rock, the worst place on the whole Trail for them; so we picked out that bare spot where they couldn't set fire to the prairie. It was long after dark when we eat our supper; then we smoked our pipes, waiting for the oxen to fill themselves, which had been driven about a mile off where there was good grass. The Mexicans was herding them, and when they'd eat all they could hold, and was commencing to lay down, they was driven into the corral. Then all of us, except Comstock and Curtis, turned in; they was to stand guard until 'bout one o'clock, when me and Thorpe was to change places with them and stay up until morning; for, you see, we was afraid to trust them Mexicans.

"It seemed like we hadn't been asleep more than an hour when me and Thorpe was called to take our turn on guard. We got out of our blankets, I putting Paul into one of the wagons, then me and Thorpe lighted our pipes and walked around, keeping our eyes and ears open, watching the heavy fringe of timber on the creek mighty close, I tell you. Just as daylight was coming, we noticed that our mules, what was tied to a wagon in the corral, was getting uneasy, a pawing and snorting, with their long ears cocked up and looking toward the Walnut. Before I could finish saying to Thorpe, 'Them mules smells Ingins,' half a dozen or more of the darned cusses dashed out of the timber, yelling and shaking their robes, which, of course, waked up the whole camp. Me and Thorpe sent a couple of shots after them, that scattered the devils for a minute; but we hadn't hit nary one, because it was too dark yet to draw a bead on them. We was certain there was a good many more of them behind the first that had charged us; so we got all the men on the side of the corral next to the Trail. The Ingins we know'd couldn't get behind us, on account of the river, and we was bound to make them fight where we wanted them to, if they meant to fight at all.

"In less than a minute, quicker than I can tell you, sure enough, out they came again, only there was 'bout eighty of them this time. They made a dash at once, and their arrows fell like a shower of hail on the ground and against the wagon-sheets as the cusses swept by on their ponies. There wasn't anybody hurt, and our turn soon came. Just as they circled back, we poured it into them, killing six and wounding two. You see them Mexican guns had did some work that we didn't expect, and then we Americans felt better. Well, boys, them varmints made four charges like that on to us before we could get shet of them; but we killed as many as sixteen or eighteen, and they got mighty sick of it and quit; they had only knocked over one Mexican, and put an arrow into Thorpe's arm.

"I was amused at little Paul all the time the scrimmage was going on. He stood up in the wagon where I'd put him, a looking out of the hole behind where the sheet was drawed together, and every time an Ingin was tumbled off his pony, he would clap his hands and yell, 'There goes another one, Uncle John!'

"After their last charge, they rode off out of range, where they stood in little bunches talking to each other, holding some sort of a pow-wow. It riled us to see the darned cusses keep so far away from our rifles, because we wanted to lay a few more of them out, but was obliged to keep still and watch out for some new deviltry. We waited there until it was plumb night, not daring to move out yet; but we managed to boil our coffee and fry slap-jacks and meat.

"The oxen kept up a bellowing and pawing around the corral, for they was desperate hungry and thirsty, hadn't had nothing since the night before; yet we couldn't help them any, as we didn't know whether we was shet of the Ingins or not. We staid, patient-like, for two or three hours more after dark to see what the Ingins was going to do, as while we sot round our little fire of buffalo-chips, smoking our pipes, we could still hear the red devils a howling and chanting, while they picked up their dead laying along the river-bottom.

"As soon as morning broke--we'd ketched a nap now and then during the night-- we got ready for another charge of the Ingins, their favourite time being just 'bout daylight; but there warn't hide or hair of an Ingin in sight. They'd sneaked off in the darkness long before the first streak of dawn; had enough of fighting, I expect. As soon as we discovered they'd all cleared out, we told the drivers to hitch up, and while they was yoking and watering, me 'n' Curtis and Comstock buried the dead Mexican on the bank of the river, as we didn't want to leave his bones to be picked by the coyotes, which was already setting on the sand hills watching and waiting for us to break camp. By the time we'd finished our job, and piled some rocks on his grave, so as the varmints couldn't dig him up, the train was strung out on the Trail, and then we rolled out mighty lively for oxen; for the critters was hungry, and we had to travel three or four miles the other side of the Walnut, where the grass was green, before they could feed. The oxen seen it on the hills and they lit out almost at a trot. It was 'bout sun-up when we got there, when we turned the animals loose, corralled, and had breakfast.

"After we'd had our smoke, all we had to do was to put in the time until five o'clock; for we couldn't move before then, as it would be too hot by the time the oxen got filled. Paul and me went down to the creek fishing; there was tremendous cat in the Walnut them days, and by noon we'd ketched five big beauties, which we took to camp and cooked for dinner. After I'd had my smoke, Paul and me went back to the creek, where we stretched ourselves under a good-sized box-elder tree--there wasn't no shade nowhere else--and took a sleep, while Comstock and Curtis went jack-rabbit hunting across the river, as we was getting scarce of meat.

"Thorpe, who was hit in the arm with an arrow, couldn't do much but nuss his wound; so him and the Mexicans stood guard, a looking out for Ingins, as we didn't know but what the cusses might come back and make another raid on us, though we really didn't expect they would have the gall to bother us any more--least not the same outfit what had fought us the day before. That evening, 'bout six o'clock, we rolled out again and went into camp late, having made twelve miles, and didn't see a sign of Ingins.

"In ten days more we got to Independence without having no more trouble of no kind, and was surprised at our luck. At Independence we Americans left the train, sold our furs, got a big price, too-- each of us had a shot-bag full of gold and silver, more money than we know'd what to do with. Me, Curtis, and Thorpe concluded we'd buy a new outfit, consisting of another six-mule wagon, and harness, so we'd have a full team, meaning to go back to the mountains with the first big caravan what left.

"All the folks in the settlement what seen Paul took a great fancy to him. Some wanted to adopt him, and some said I'd ought to take him to St. Louis and place him in an orphan asylum; but I 'lowed if there was going to be any adopting done, I'd do it myself, 'cause the kid seemed now just as if he was my own; besides the little fellow I know'd loved me and didn't want me to leave him. I had kin-folks in Independence, an old aunt, and me and Paul staid there. She had a young gal with her, and she learned Paul out of books; so he picked up considerable, as we had to wait more than two months before Colonel St. Vrain's caravan was ready to start for New Mexico.

"I bought Paul a coal-black pony, and had a suit of fine buckskin made for him out of the pelt of a black-tail deer I'd shot the winter before on Powder River. The seams of his trousers was heavily fringed, and with his white sombrero, a riding around town on his pony, he looked like one of them Spanish Dons what the papers nowadays has pictures of; only he was smarter-looking than any Don I ever see in my life.

"It was 'bout the last of August when we pulled out from Independence. Comstock staid with us until we got ready to go, and then lit out for St. Louis, and I hain't never seen him since. The caravan had seventy-five six-mule teams in it, without counting ours, loaded with dry-goods and groceries for Mora, New Mexico, where Colonel St. Vrain, the owner, lived and had a big store. We had no trouble with the Ingins going back across the plains; we seen lots, to be sure, hanging on our trail, but they never attacked us; we was too strong for them.

"'Bout the last of September we reached Bent's Old Fort, on the Arkansas, where the Santa Fe Trail crosses the river into New Mexico, and we camped there the night we got to it.

"I know'd they had cows up to the fort; so just before we was ready for supper, I took Paul and started to see if we couldn't get some milk for our coffee. It wasn't far, and we was camped a few hundred yards from the gate, just outside the wall. Well, we went into the kitchen, Paul right alongside of me, and there I seen a white woman leaning over the adobe hearth a cooking--they had always only been squaws before. She naturally looked up to find out who was coming in, and when she seen the kid, all at once she give a scream, dropped the dish-cloth she had in her hand, made a break for Paul, throw'd her arms around him, nigh upsetting me, and says, while she was a sobbing and taking on dreadful,--

"'My boy! My boy! Then I hain't prayed and begged the good Lord all these days and nights for nothing!' Then she kind o' choked again, while Paul, he says, as he hung on to her,--

"'O mamma! O mamma! I know'd you'd come back! I know'd you'd come back!'

"Well, there, boys, I just walked out of that kitchen a heap faster than I'd come into it, and shut the door. When I got outside, for a few minutes I couldn't see nothing, I was worked up so. As soon as I come to, I went through the gate down to camp as quick as my legs would carry me, to tell Thorpe and Curtis that Paul had found his ma. They wanted to know all about it, but I couldn't tell them nothing, I was so dumfounded at the way things had turned out. We talked among ourselves a moment, then reckoned it was the best to go up to the fort together, and ask the woman how on earth she'd got shet of the Ingins what had took her off, and how it come she was cooking there. We started out and when we got into the kitchen, there was Paul and Mrs. Dale, and you never see no people so happy. They was just as wild as a stampeded steer; she seemed to have growed ten years younger than when I first went up there, and as for Paul, he was in heaven for certain.

"First we had to tell her how we'd got the kid, and how we'd learned to love him. All the time we was telling of it, and our scrimmages with the Ingins, she was a crying and hugging Paul as if her heart was broke. After we'd told all we know'd, we asked her to tell us her story, which she did, and it showed she was a woman of grit and education.

"She said the Ingins what had captured her took her up to their camp on the Saw Log, a little creek north of Fort Dodge--you all know where it is--and there she staid that night. Early in the morning they all started for the north. She watched their ponies mighty close as they rid along that day, so as to find out which was the fastest; for she had made up her mind to make her escape the first chance she got. She looked at the sun once in a while, to learn what course they was taking; so that she could go back when she got ready, strike the Sante Fe Trail, and get to some ranch, as she had seen several while passing through the foot-hills of the Raton Range when she was with the Mexican train.

"It was on the night of the fourth day after they had left Saw Log, and had rid a long distance--was more than a hundred miles on their journey--when she determined to try and light out. The whole camp was fast asleep, for the Ingins was monstrous tired. She crawled out of the lodge where she'd been put with some old squaws, and going to where the ponies had been picketed, she took a little iron-gray she'd had her eye on, jumped on his back, with only the lariat for a bridle and without any saddle, not even a blanket, took her bearings from the north star, and cautiously moved out. She started on a walk, until she'd got 'bout four miles from camp, and then struck a lope, keeping it up all night. By next morning she'd made some forty miles, and then for the first time since she'd left her lodge, pulled up and looked back, to see if any of the Ingins was following her. When she seen there wasn't a living thing in sight, she got off her pony, watered him out of a small branch, took a drink herself, but not daring to rest yet, mounted her animal again and rid on as fast as she could without wearing him out too quickly.

"Hour after hour she rid on, the pony appearing to have miraculous endurance, until sundown. By that time she'd crossed the Saline, the Smoky Hill, and got to the top of the divide between that river and the Arkansas, or not more than forty miles from the Santa Fe Trail. Then her wonderful animal seemed to weaken; she couldn't even make him trot, and she was so nearly played out herself, she could hardly set steady. What to do, she didn't know. The pony was barely able to move at a slow walk. She was afraid he would drop dead under her, and she was compelled to dismount, and in almost a minute, as soon as she laid down on the prairie, was fast asleep.

"She had no idee how long she had slept when she woke up. The sun was only 'bout two hours high. Then she know'd she had been unconscious since sundown of the day before, or nigh twenty-four hours. Rubbing her eyes, for she was kind o' bewildered, and looking around, there she saw her pony as fresh, seemingly, as when she'd started. He'd had plenty to eat, for the grass was good, but she'd had nothing. She pulled a little piece of dried buffalo-meat out of her bosom, which she'd brought along, all she could find at the lodge, and now nibbled at that, for she was mighty hungry. She was terribly sore and stiff too, but she mounted at once and pushed on, loping and walking him by spells. Just at daylight she could make out the Arkansas right in front of her in the dim gray of the early morning, not very far off. On the west, the Raton Mountains loomed up like a great pile of blue clouds, the sight of which cheered her; for she know'd she would soon reach the Trail.

"It wasn't quite noon when she struck the Santa Fe Trail. When she got there, looking to the east, she saw in the distance, not more than three miles away, a large caravan coming, and then, almost wild with delight, she dismounted, sot down on the grass, and waited for it to arrive. In less than an hour, the train come up to where she was, and as good luck would have it, it happened to be an American outfit, going to Taos with merchandise. As soon as the master of the caravan seen her setting on the prairie, he rid up ahead of the wagons, and she told him her story. He was a kind-hearted man; had the train stop right there on the bank of the river, though he wasn't half through his day's drive, so as to make her comfortable as possible, and give her something to eat; for she was 'bout played out. He bought the Ingin pony, giving her thirty dollars for it, and after she had rested for some time, the caravan moved out. She rid in one of the wagons, on a bed of blankets, and the next evening arrived at Bent's Old Fort. There she found women-folks, who cared for her and nussed her; for she was dreadfully sore and tired after her long ride. Then she was hired to cook, meaning to work until she'd earned enough to take her back to Pennsylvany, to her mother's, where she had started for when the Ingins attackted the train.

"That night, after listening to her mirac'lous escape, we made up a 'pot' for her, collecting 'bout eight hundred dollars. The master of Colonel St. Vrain's caravan, what had come out with us, told her he was going back again to the river in a couple of weeks, and he'd take her and Paul in without costing her a cent; besides, she'd be safer than with any other outfit, as his train was a big one, and he had all American teamsters.

"Next morning the caravan went on to Mora, and after we'd bid good-by to Mrs. Dale and Paul, before which I give the boy two hundred dollars for himself, me, Thorpe, and Curtis pulled out with our team north for Frenchman's Creek, and I never felt so miserable before nor since as I did parting with the kid that morning. I hain't never seen him since; but he must be nigh forty now. Mebby he went into the war and was killed; mebby he got to be a general, but I hain't forgot him."

Uncle John knocked the ashes out of his pipe, and without saying another word went into the tent. In a few moments the camp was as quiet as a country village on Sunday, excepting the occasional howling of a hungry wolf down in the timbered recesses of the Washita, or the crackling and sputtering of the signal fires on the hilltops.

In a few days afterward, we were camping on Hackberry Creek, in the Indian Territory. We had been living on wild turkey, as before for some time, and still longed for a change. At last one of my hunters succeeded in bagging a dozen or more quails. Late that evening, when my cook brought the delicious little birds, beautifully spitted and broiled on peeled willow twigs, into my tent, I passed one to Uncle John. Much to the surprise of every one, he refused. He said, "Boys, I don't eat no quail!"

We looked at him in astonishment; for he was somewhat of a gourmand, and prided himself upon the "faculty," as he termed it, of being able to eat anything, from a piece of jerked buffalo-hide to the juiciest young antelope steak.

I remonstrated with the venerable guide; said to him, "You are making a terrible mistake, Uncle John. Tomorrow I expect to leave here, and as we are going directly away from the buffalo country, we don't know when we shall strike fresh meat again. You'd better try one," and I again proffered one of the birds.

"Boys," said he again, "I don't tech quail; I hain't eat one for more than twenty years. One of the little cusses saved my life once, and I swore right thar and then that I would starve first; and I have kept my oath, though I've seen the time mighty often sence I could a killed 'em with my quirt, when all I had to chaw on for four days was the soles of a greasy pair of old moccasins.

"Well, boys, it's a good many years ago--in June, if I don't disremember, 1847. We was a coming in from way up in Cache le Poudre and from Yellowstone Lake, whar we'd been a trapping for two seasons. We was a working our way slowly back to Independence, Missouri, where we was a going to get a new outfit. Let's see, there was me, and a man by the name of Boyd, and Lew Thorp--Lew was a working for Colonel Boone at the time--and two more men, whose names I disremember now, and a nigger wench we had for a cook. We had mighty good luck, and had a big pile of skins; and the Indians never troubled us till we got down on Pawnee Bottom, this side of Pawnee Rock. We all of us had mighty good ponies, but Thorp had a team and wagon, which he was driving for Colonel Boone.

"We had went into camp on Pawnee Bottom airly in the afternoon, and I told the boys to look out for Ingins--for I knowed ef we was to have any trouble with them it would be somewhere in that vicinity. But we didn't see a darned redskin that night, nor the sign of one.

"The wolves howled considerable, and come pretty close to the fire for the bacon rinds we'd throwed away after supper.

"You see the buffalo was scurse right thar then--it was the wrong time o' year. They generally don't get down on to the Arkansas till about September, and when they're scurse the wolves and coyotes are mighty sassy, and will steal a piece of bacon rind right out of the pan, if you don't watch 'em. So we picketed our ponies a little closer before we turned in, and we all went to sleep except one, who sort o' kept watch on the stock.

"I was out o' my blankets mighty airly next morning, for I was kind o' suspicious. I could always tell when Ingins was prowling around, and I had a sort of present'ment something was going to happen --I didn't like the way the coyotes kept yelling--so I rested kind o' oneasy like, and was out among the ponies by the first streak o' daylight.

"About the time I could see things, I discovered three or four buffalo grazing off on the creek bottom, about a half-mile away, and I started for my rifle, thinking I would examine her.

"Pretty soon I seed Thorp and Boyd crawl out o' their blankets, too, and I called their attention to the buffalo, which was still feeding undisturbed.

"We'd been kind o' scurse of fresh meat for a couple of weeks--ever since we left the Platte--except a jack-rabbit or cottontail, and I knowed the boys would be wanting to get a quarter or two of a good fat cow, if we could find one in the herd, so that was the reason I pointed 'em out to 'em.

"The dew, you see, was mighty heavy, and the grass in the bottom was as wet as if it had been raining for a month, and I didn't care to go down whar the buffalo was just then--I knowed we had plenty of time, and as soon as the sun was up it would dry right off. So I got on to one of the ponies and led the others down to the spring near camp to water them while the wench was a getting breakfast, and some o' the rest o' the outfit was a fixing the saddles and greasing the wagon.

"Just as I was coming back--it had growed quite light then--I seed Boyd and Thorp start out from camp with their rifles and make for the buffalo; so I picketed the ponies, gets my rifle, and starts off too.

"By the time I'd reached the edge of the bottom, Thorp and Boyd was a crawling up on to a young bull way off to the right, and I lit out for a fat cow I seen bunched up with the rest of the herd on the left.

"The grass was mighty tall on some parts of the Arkansas bottom in them days, and I got within easy shooting range without the herd seeing me.

"The buffalo was now between me and Thorp and Boyd, and they was furtherest from camp. I could see them over the top of the grass kind o' edging up to the bull, and I kept a crawling on my hands and knees toward the cow, and when I got about a hundred and fifty yards of her, I pulled up my rifle and drawed a bead.

"Just as I was running my eyes along the bar'l, a darned little quail flew right out from under my feet and lit exactly on my front sight and of course cut off my aim--we didn't shoot reckless in those days; every shot had to tell, or a man was the laughing-stock for a month if he missed his game.

"I shook the little critter off and brought up my rifle again when, durn my skin, if the bird didn't light right on to the same place; at the same time my eyes grow'd kind o' hazy-like and in a minute I didn't know nothing.

"When I come to, the quail was gone. I heerd a couple of rifle shots, and right in front of where the bull had stood and close to Thorp and Boyd, half a dozen Ingins jumped up out o' the tall grass and, firing into the two men, killed Thorp instantly and wounded Boyd.

"He and me got to camp--keeping off the Ingins, who knowed I was loaded-- when we, with the rest of the outfit, drove the red devils away.

"They was Apaches, and the fellow that shot Thorp was a half-breed nigger and Apache. He scalped Thorp and carred off the whole upper part of his skull with it. He got Thorp's rifle and bullet-pouch too, and his knife.

"We buried Thorp in the bottom there, and some of the party cut their names on the stones that they covered his body up with, to keep the coyotes from eating up his bones.

"Boyd got on to the river with us all right, and I never heerd of him after we separated at Booneville. We pulled out soon after the Indians left, but we didn't get no buffalo-meat.

"You see, boys, if I'd a fired into that cow, the devils would a had me before I could a got a patch on my ball--didn't have no breech-loaders in them days, and it took as much judgment to know how to load a rifle properly as it did to shoot it.

"Them Ingins knowed all that--they knowed I hadn't fired, so they kept a respectable distance. I would a fired, but the quail saved my life by interfering with my sight--and that's the reason I don't eat no quail. I hain't superstitious, but I don't believe they was meant to be eat."

Uncle John stuck to his text, I believe, until he died, and you could never disabuse his mind of the idea that the quail lighting on his rifle was not a special interposition of Providence.

Only four years after he told his story, in 1872, one of the newly established settlers, living a few miles west of Larned on Pawnee Bottom, having observed in one of his fields a singular depression, resembling an old grave, determined to dig down and see if there was any special cause for the strange indentation on his land.

A couple of feet below the surface he discovered several flat pieces of stone, on one of which the words "Washington" and "J. Hildreth" were rudely cut, also a line separating them, and underneath: "December tenth" and "J. M., 1850." On another was carved the name "J. H. Shell," with other characters that could not be deciphered. On a third stone were the initials "H. R., 1847"; underneath which was plainly cut "J. R. Boyd," and still beneath "J. R. Pring." At the very bottom of the excavation were found the lower portion of the skull, one or two ribs, and one of the bones of the leg of a human being. The piece of skull was found near the centre of the grave, for such it certainly was.

At the time of the discovery I was in Larned, and I immediately consulted my book of notes and memoranda taken hurriedly at intervals on the plains and in the mountains, during more than half my lifetime, to see if I could find anything that would solve the mystery attached to the quiet prairie-grave and its contents, and I then recalled Uncle John Smith's story of the quail as related to me at my camp. I also met Colonel A. G. Boone that winter in Washington; he remembered the circumstances well. Thorp was working for him, as Smith had said, and was killed by an Apache, who, in scalping him, tore the half of his head away, and it was thus found mutilated, so many years afterward.

Uncle John was in one of his garrulous moods that night, and as we were not by any means tired of hearing the veteran trapper talk, without much urging he told us the following tale:--

"Well, boys, thirty years ago, beaver, mink, and otter was found in abundacious quantities on all the streams in the Rocky Mountains. The trade in them furs was a paying business, for the little army of us fellows called trappers. They ain't any of 'em left now, no mor'n the animals we used to hunt. We had to move about from place to place, just as if we was so many Ingins. Sometimes we'd construct little cabins in the timber, or a dugout where the game was plenty, where we'd stay maybe for a month or two, and once in a while--though not often--a whole year.

"The Ingins was our mortal enemies; they'd get a scalp from our fellows occasionally, but for every one they had of ours we had a dozen of theirs.

"In the summer of 1846, there was a little half dugout, half cabin, opposite the mouth of Frenchman's Creek, put up by Bill Thorpe, Al Boyd, and Rube Stevens. Bill and Al was men grown, and know'd more 'bout the prairies and timber than the Ingins themselves. They'd hired out to the Northwest Fur Company when they was mere kids, and kept on trapping ever since. Rube--'Little Rube' as all the old men called him--was 'bout nineteen, and plumb dumb; he could hear well enough though, for he wasn't born that way. When he was seventeen his father moved from his farm in Pennsylvany, to take up a claim in Oregon, and the whole family was compelled to cross the plains to get there; for there wasn't no other way. While they was camped in the Bitter-Root valley one evening, just 'bout sundown, a party of Blackfeet surprised the outfit, and massacred all of them but Rube. They carried him off, kept him as a slave, and, to make sure of him, cut out his tongue at the roots. But some of the women who wasn't quite so devilish as their husbands, and who took pity on him, went to work and cured him of his awful wound. He was used mighty mean by the bucks of the tribe, and made up his mind to get away from them or kill himself; for he could not live under their harsh treatment. After he'd been with them for mor'n a year, the tribe had a terrible battle with the Sioux, and in the scrimmage Rube stole a pony and lit out. He rode on night and day until he came across the cabin of the two trappers I have told you 'bout, and they, of course, took the poor boy in and cared for him.

"Rube was a splendid shot with the rifle, and he swore to himself that he would never leave the prairies and do nothing for the rest of his life but kill Ingins, who had made him a homeless orphan, and so mutilated him.

"After Rube had been with Boyd and Thorpe a year, they was all one day in the winter examining their traps which was scattered 'long the stream for miles. After re-baiting them, they concluded to hunt for meat, which was getting scarce at the cabin; they let Rube go down to the creek where it widened out lake-like, to fish through a hole in the ice, and Al and Bill took their rifles and hunted in the timber for deer. They all got separated of course, Rube being furtherest away, while Al and Bill did not wander so far from each other that they could not be heard if one wanted his companion.

"Al shot a fat black-tail deer, and just as he was going to stoop down to cut its throat, Bill yelled out to him:--

"'Drop everything Al, for God's sake, and let's make for the dugout; they're coming, a whole band of Sioux!'

"'If we can get to the cabin,' replied Al, 'we can keep off the whole nation. I wonder where Rube is? I hope he'll get here and save his scalp.'

"At this instant, poor Rube dashed up to them, an Ingin close upon his tracks; he had unfortunately forgotten to take his rifle with him when he went to the creek, and now he was at the mercy of the savage; at least both he and his pursuer so thought. But before the Ingin had fairly uttered his yell of exultation, Al who with Bill had held his rifle in readiness for an emergency, lifted the red devil off his feet, and he fell dead without ever knowing what had struck him.

"Rube, thus delivered from a sudden death, ran at the top of his speed with his two friends for the cabin, for, if they could reach it, they did not fear a hundred paint-bedaubed savages.

"Luckily they arrived in time. Where they lived was part dugout and part cabin. It was about ten feet high, and right back of it was a big ledge of rock, which made it impossible for any one to get into it from that side. The place had no door; they did not dare to put one there when it was built, for they were likely to be surprised at any moment by a prowling band, so the only entrance was a square hole in the roof, through which one at a time had to crawl to enter.

"The boys got inside all right just as the Ingins came a yelling up. Bill looked out of a hole in the wall and counted thirty of the devils, and said at once: 'Off with your coats; don't let them have anything to catch hold of but our naked bodies if they get in, and we can handle ourselves better.'

"'Thirty to three,' said Al. 'Whew! this ain't going to be any boy's play; we've got to fight for all there is in it, and the chances are mightily agin us.'

"Rube he took an axe, and stood right under the hole in the roof, so that if any of the devils got in he could brain them. In a minute five rifles cracked; for the Ingins was pretty well armed for them times, and their bullets rattled agin the logs like hail agin a tent. Some of 'em was on top the roof by this time, and soon the leader of the party, a big painted devil, thrust his ugly face into the hole; but he had hardly got a good look before Bill dropped him by a well-directed shot and he tumbled in on the floor.

"'You darned fool,' said Bill, as he saw the effect of his shot; 'did you think we was asleep?'

"There was one opening that served for air, and a savage, seeing the boys had forgotten to barricade it, tried to push himself through, an' not succeeding, tried to back out, but at that instant Bill caught him by the wrist--Bill was a powerful man-- and picking up a beaver-trap that laid on the floor, actually beat his brains out with it.

"While this circus was going on inside, three more of the Ingins got on the roof and wrenched off a couple of the logs that covered it; but in a minute they came tumbling down and lay dead on the floor.

"'That leaves only twenty-five, don't it?' inquired Al, as he mopped his face with his shirt-sleeve.

"'Howl, you red devils,' said Bill, as the Ingins commenced their awful yelling when they saw their comrades fall into the room. 'Don't you know, you blame fools, you've fell in with experienced hands at the shooting business?'

"Spat! Something hit Al, and he was the first wounded, but it was only a scratch, and he kept right on attending to business.

"'By gosh! look at Rube, will you?' said Al. The dumb boy had in his grasp the very chief of the band, who had just then discovered the hole in the roof made by the three Ingins who had passed in their checks for their impudence, and was trying his best to push himself down. Rube had made a strike at him with an axe, but the edge was turned aside, and the savage was getting the better of the boy; he had grappled Rube by the hair and one arm, and they was flying 'round like a wild cat and a hound. Bill tried three times to sink his knife into the old chief, but there was such a cavortin' in the wrastle between him and the boy, he was afraid to try any more, for fear it might hit Rube instead. Suddenly the Ingin fell to the floor as dead as a trapped beaver what's been drowned; Rube had struck his buckhorn-handled hunting-knife right into the heart of the brute.

"'Set him agin the hole in the side of the building,' said Bill; 'he ain't fit for nothing else than to stop a gap'; so Rube set him agin the hole, and pinned him there with half a dozen knives what was lying round loose.

"Just as they had fastened the dead body of the old chief to the side of the cabin, a perfect shower of bullets came rattling round like a hailstorm. 'All right, let's have your waste lead,' said Bill.

"'A few more of these dead Ingins and we can make a regular fort of this old cabin; we want two for that chunk,' said Al, as he pointed with his rifle to a large gap on the west side of the wall; but before he had fairly got the words out of his mouth, two of the attacking party jumped down into the room. Al, being a regular giant, as soon as they landed, surprised them by seizing one with each hand by the throat, and he actually held them at arm's-length till he had squeezed the very life out of them, and they both fell corpses.

"While Al was performing his two-Ingin act, a great light burst into the cabin, and by the time he had choked his enemies to death, he saw, while the Ingins outside gave a terrible yell of exultation, that they had fired the place.

"'Damn 'em,' shouted Bill, as he pitched the corpse of the chief from the gap where Rube had set him. 'Fellows, we've got to get out of here right quick; follow me, boys!'

"Holding their rifles in hand, and clutching a hunting-knife also, they stepped out into the brush surrounding the place, and started on a run for the heavy timber on the bank of the creek.

"They had reckoned onluckily; a wild war-whoop greeted the flying men as they reached the edge of the forest, and without being able to use their arms, they were taken prisoners. Bill and Al, fastened with their backs against each other, and Little Rube by himself, were bound to separate trees, but not so far apart that they could not speak to each other, and some of the Ingins began to gather sticks and pile them around the trees.

"'What are they going to do with us?' anxiously inquired Bill of Al.

"'Roast us, you bet,' replied the other. 'They'll find me tough enough, anyhow.'

"'It must be a painful death,' soliloquized Bill.

"'Well, it isn't the most pleasant one, you can gamble on that,' said Al, turning his looks toward Bill; 'but see what the devils are doing to poor Rube.'

"Bill cast his eyes in the direction of the dumb boy, who was fastened to a small pine, about a hundred feet distant. Standing directly in front of it was a gigantic Ingin, flourishing his scalping-knife within an inch of Rube's head, trying to make the boy flinch. But the young fellow merely scowled at him in a rage, his muscles never quivering for an instant.

"While the men were trying to console each other, two of the savages, who had gone away for a short time, returned, bearing the carcass of the deer that Al had killed in the morning, and commenced to cut it up. They had made several small fires, and roasting the meat before them, began to gorge themselves, Indian fashion, with the savoury morsels. The men were awfully hungry, too, but not a mouthful did they get of their own game.

"The Ingins were more'n an hour feasting, while their prisoners kept a looking for some help to get 'em out of the scrape they was in.

"'Bout a mile down the creek, me and six other trappers had a camp, and that morning, being scarce of meat, we all went a hunting. We had killed two or three elk and was 'bout going back to camp with our game, when we heard firing, and supposed it was a party of hunters, like ourselves, so we did not pay any attention to it at first; but when it kept up so long, and there was such a constant volley, I told our boys it might be a scrimmage with a party of red devils, and we concluded to go and see.

"We left our elk where they were, and started in the direction of the shooting, taking mighty good care not to be surprised ourselves. We crept carefully on, and a little before sundown seen a camp-fire burning in the timber quite a smart piece ahead of us. We stopped then, and Ike Pettet and myself crept on cautiously on our hands and knees through the brush to learn what the fire meant. In a little while we seen it was an Ingin camp, and we counted twenty-two warriors seated 'round their fires a eating as unconcernedly as if we warn't nowhere near 'em. We didn't feel like tackling so many, so just as we was 'bout to crawl away and leave 'em in ondisturbed possession of their camp, we heard some parties talking in English. Then we pricked up our ears and listened mighty interested I tell you. Looking 'round, we seen the men tied to the trees and the wood piled against 'em, and then we knowed what was up. We had to be mighty wary, for if we snapped a twig even, it was all day with us and the prisoners too; so we dragged ourselves back, and after getting out of sound of the Ingins, we just got up and lit out mighty lively for the place we'd left our companions. We met them coming slowly on 'bout two miles from the Ingin camp, and telling 'em what was up we started to help the trappers what the devils was agoing to burn. We wasn't half so long in getting at the camp as Ike and me was in going, and we soon come within good range for our rifles.

"The Ingins was still unsuspicious, and we spread ourselves in a sort of half circle so as to kind o' surround them, and at a signal I give, seven rifles cracked at once, and as many of the Injins was dropped right in their tracks; a second volley, for the red devils had not got their senses yet, tumbled seven more corpses upon the pile, and then we white men jumped in with our knives and clubbed rifles, and there was a lively scrimmage for a few minutes. The few Ingins what wasn't killed fought like devils, but as we was getting the best of 'em every second they turned tail and ran.

"We'd heard the firing of the fight at the cabin just in time; and as we cut the rawhide strings that bound the fellows to the trees, Ike, who was a right fine shot and had killed three at one time, said: 'I always like to get two or three of the red devils in a line before I pull the trigger; it saves lead.'

"Then we all went back to our camp and made a night of it, feasting on the elk we had killed, and talking over the wonderful escape of the boys and Little Rube."

211

CHAPTER XVI.

KIT CARSON.

Of the famous men whose lives are so interwoven with the history of the Old Santa Fe Trail that the story of the great highway is largely made up of their individual exploits and acts of bravery, it has been my fortune to have known nearly all intimately, during more than a third of a century passed on the great plains and in the Rocky Mountains.

First of all, Christopher, or Kit, Carson, as he is familiarly known to the world, stands at the head and front of celebrated frontiersmen, trappers, scouts, guides, and Indian fighters.

I knew him well through a series of years, to the date of his death in 1868, but I shall confine myself to the events of his remarkable career along the line of the Trail and its immediate environs. In 1826 a party of Santa Fe traders passing near his father's home in Howard County, Missouri, young Kit, who was then but seventeen years old, joined the caravan as hunter. He was already an expert with the rifle, and thus commenced his life of adventure on the great plains and in the Rocky Mountains.

His first exhibition of that nerve and coolness in the presence of danger which marked his whole life was in this initial trip across the plains. When the caravan had arrived at the Arkansas River, somewhere in the vicinity of the great bend of that stream, one of the teamsters, while carelessly pulling his rifle toward him by the barrel, discharged the weapon and received the ball in his arm, completely crushing the bones. The blood from the wound flowed so copiously that he nearly lost his life before it could be arrested. He was fixed up, however, and the caravan proceeded on its journey, the man thinking no more seriously of his injured arm. In a few days, however, the wound began to indicate that gangrene had set in, and it was determined that only by an amputation was it possible for him to live beyond a few days. Every one of the older men of the caravan positively declined to attempt the operation, as there were no instruments of any kind. At this juncture Kit, realizing the extreme necessity of prompt action, stepped forward and offered to do the job. He told the unfortunate sufferer that he had had no experience in such matters, but that as no one else would do it, he would take the chances. All the tools that Kit could find were a razor, a saw, and the king-bolt of a wagon. He cut the flesh with the razor, sawed through the bone as if it had been a piece of joist, and seared the horrible wound with the king-bolt, which he had heated to a white glow, for the purpose of stopping the flow of blood that naturally followed such rude surgery. The operation was a complete success; the man lived many years afterward, and was with his surgeon in many an expedition.

In the early days of the commerce of the prairies, Carson was the hunter at Bent's Fort for a period of eight years. There were about forty men employed at the place; and when the game was found in abundance in the mountains, it was a relatively easy task and just suited to his love of sport, but when it grew scarce, as it often did, his prowess was tasked to its utmost to keep the forty mouths from crying for food. He became such an unerring shot with the rifle during that time that he was called the "Nestor of the Rocky Mountains." His favourite game was the buffalo, although he killed countless numbers of other animals.

All of the plains tribes of Indians, as did the powerful Utes of the mountains, knew him well; for he had often visited in their camps, sat in their lodges, smoked the pipe, and played with their little boys. The latter fact may not appear of much consequence, but there are no people on earth who have a greater love for their boy children than the savages of America. The Indians all feared him, too, at the same time that they respected his excellent judgment, and frequently were governed by his wise counsel. The following story will show his power in this direction. The Sioux, one of the most numerous and warlike tribes at that time, had encroached upon the hunting-grounds of the southern Indians, and the latter had many a skirmish with them on the banks of the Arkansas along the line of the Trail. Carson, who was in the upper valley of the river, was sent for to come down and help them drive the obnoxious Sioux back to their own stamping-ground. He left Fort Bent, and went with the party of Comanche messengers to the main camp of that tribe and the Arapahoes, with whom they had united. Upon his arrival, he was told that the Sioux had a thousand warriors and many rifles, and the Comanches and Arapahoes were afraid of them on account of the great disparity of numbers, but that if he would go with them on the war-path, they felt assured they could overcome their enemies. Carson, however, instead of encouraging the Comanches and Arapahoes to fight, induced them to negotiate with the Sioux. He was sent as mediator, and so successfully accomplished his mission that the intruding tribe consented to leave the hunting-grounds of the Comanches as soon as the buffalo season was over; which they did, and there was no more trouble.

After many adventures in California with Fremont, Carson, with his inseparable friend, L. B. Maxwell, embarked in the wool-raising industry. Shortly after they had established themselves on their ranch, the Apaches made one of their frequent murdering and plundering raids through Northern New Mexico, killing defenceless women and children, running off stock of all kinds, and laying waste every little ranch they came across in their wild foray. Not very far from the city of Santa Fe, they ruthlessly butchered a Mr. White and his son, though three of their number were slain by the brave gentlemen before they were overpowered. Other of the blood-thirsty savages carried away the women and children of the desolated home and took them to their mountain retreat in the vicinity of Las Vegas. Mr. White was a highly respected merchant, and news of this outrage spreading rapidly through the settlements, it was determined that the savages should not go without punishment this time, at least. Carson's reputation as an Indian fighter was at its height, so the natives of the country sent for him, and declined to move until he came. For some unexplained reason, after he arrived at Las Vegas, he was not placed in charge of the posse, that position having already been given to a Frenchman. Carson, as was usual with him, never murmured because he was assigned to a subordinate position, but took his place, ready to do his part in whatever capacity.

The party set out for the stronghold of the savages, and rode night and day on the trail of the murderers, hoping to surprise them and recapture the women and children; but so much time had been wasted in delays, that Carson feared they would only find the mutilated bodies of the poor captives. In a few days after leaving Las Vegas, the retreat of the savages was discovered in the fastness of the mountains, where they had fortified themselves in such a manner that they could resist ten times the number of their pursuers. Carson, as soon as he saw them, without a second's hesitation, and giving a characteristic yell, dashed in, expecting, of course, that the men would follow him; but they only stood in gaping wonderment at his bravery, not daring to venture after him. He did not discover his dilemma until he had advanced so far alone that escape seemed impossible. But here his coolness, which always served him in the moment of supreme danger, saved his scalp. As the savages turned on him, he threw himself on the off side of his horse, Indian fashion, for he was as expert in a trick of that kind as the savages themselves, and rode back to the little command. He had six arrows in his horse and a bullet through his coat!

The Indians in those days were poorly armed, and did not long follow up the pursuit after Carson; for, observing the squad of mounted Mexicans, they retreated to the top of a rocky prominence, from which point they could watch every movement of the whites. Carson was raging at the apathy, not to say cowardice, of the men who had sent for him to join them, but he kept his counsel to himself; for he was anxious to save the captured women and children. He talked to the men very earnestly, however, exhorting them not to flinch in the duty they had come so far to perform, and for which he had come at their call. This had the desired effect; for he induced them to make a charge, which was gallantly performed, and in such a brave manner that the Indians fled, scarcely making an effort to defend themselves. Five of their number were killed at the furious onset of the Mexicans, but unfortunately, as he anticipated, only the murdered corpses of the women and children were the result of the victory.

President Polk appointed Carson to a second lieutenancy,[48] and his first official duty was conducting fifty soldiers under his command through the country of the Comanches, who were then at war with the whites. A fight occurred at a place known as Point of Rocks,[49] where on arriving, Carson found a company of volunteers for the Mexican War, and camped near them. About dawn the next morning, all the animals of the volunteers were captured by a band of Indians, while the herders were conducting them to the river-bottom to graze. The herders had no weapons, and luckily, in the confusion attending the bold theft, ran into Carson's camp; and as he, with his men, were ready with their rifles, they recaptured the oxen, but the horses were successfully driven off by their captors.

Several of the savages were mortally wounded by Carson's prompt charge, as signs after they had cleared out proved; but the Indian custom of tying the wounded on their ponies precluded the chance of taking any scalps. The wily Comanche, like the Arab of the desert, is generally successful in his sudden assaults, but Carson, who was never surprised, was always equal to his tactics.

One of the two soldiers whose turn it had been to stand guard that morning was discovered to have been asleep when the alarm of Indians was given, and Carson at once administered the Indian method of punishment, making the man wear the dress of a squaw for that day. Then going on, he arrived at Santa Fe, where he turned over his little command.

While there, he heard that a gang of those desperadoes so frequently the nuisance of a new country had formed a conspiracy to murder and rob two wealthy citizens whom they had volunteered to accompany over the Trail to the States. The caravan was already many miles on its way when Carson was informed of the plot. In less than an hour he had hired sixteen picked men and was on his march to intercept them. He took a short cut across the mountains, taking especial care to keep out of the way of the Indians, who were on the war-path, but as to whose movements he was always posted. In two days he came upon a camp of United States recruits, en route to the military posts in New Mexico, whose commander offered to accompany him with twenty men. Carson accepted the generous proposal, by forced marches soon overtook the caravan of traders, and at once placed one Fox, the leader of the gang, in irons, after which he informed the owners of the caravan of the escape they had made from the wretches whom they were treating so kindly. At first the gentlemen were astounded at the disclosures made to them, but soon admitted that they had noticed many things which convinced them that the plot really existed, and but for the opportune arrival of the brave frontiersman it would shortly have been carried out.

The members of the caravan who were perfectly trustworthy were then ordered to corral the rest of the conspirators, thirty-five in number, and they were driven out of camp, with the exception of Fox, the leader, whom Carson conveyed to Taos. He was imprisoned for several months, but as a crime in intent only could be proved against him, and as the adobe walls of the house where he was confined were not secure enough to retain a man who desired to release himself, he was finally liberated, and cleared out.

The traders were profuse in their thanks to Carson for his timely interference, but he refused every offer of remuneration. On their return to Santa Fe from St. Louis, however, they presented him with a magnificent pair of pistols, upon whose silver mounting was an inscription commemorating his brave deed and the gratitude of the donors.

The following summer was spent in a visit to St. Louis, and early in the fall he returned over the Trail, arriving at the Cheyenne village on the Upper Arkansas without meeting with any incident worthy of note. On reaching that point, he learned that the Indians had received a terrible affront from an officer commanding a detachment of United States troops, who had whipped one of their chiefs; and that consequently the whole tribe was enraged, and burning for revenge upon the whites. Carson was the first white man to approach the place since the insult, and so many years had elapsed since he was the hunter at Bent's Fort, and so grievously had the Indians been offended, that his name no longer guaranteed safety to the party with whom he was travelling, nor even insured respect to himself, in the state of excitement existing in the village. Carson, however, deliberately pushed himself into the presence of a war council which was just then in session to consider the question of attacking the caravan, giving orders to his men to keep close together, and guard against a surprise.

The savages, supposing that he could not understand their language, talked without restraint, and unfolded their plans to capture his party and kill them all, particularly the leader. After they had reached this decision, Carson coolly rose and addressed the council in the Cheyenne language, informing the Indians who he was, of his former associations with and kindness to their tribe, and that now he was ready to render them any assistance they might require; but as to their taking his scalp, he claimed the right to say a word.

The Indians departed, and Carson went on his way; but there were hundreds of savages in sight on the sand hills, and, though they made no attack, he was well aware that he was in their power, nor had they abandoned the idea of capturing his train. His coolness and deliberation kept his men in spirit, and yet out of the whole fifteen, which was the total number of his force, there were only two or three on whom he could place any reliance in case of an emergency.

When the train camped for the night, the wagons were corralled, and the men and mules all brought inside the circle. Grass was cut with sheath-knives and fed to the animals, instead of their being picketed out as usual, and as large a guard as possible detailed. When the camp had settled down to perfect quiet, Carson crawled outside it, taking with him a Mexican boy, and after explaining to him the danger which threatened them all, told him that it was in his power to save the lives of the company. Then he sent him on alone to Rayedo, a journey of nearly three hundred miles, to ask for an escort of United States troops to be sent out to meet the train,

216

impressing upon the brave little Mexican the importance of putting a good many miles between himself and the camp before morning. And so he started him, with a few rations of food, without letting the rest of his party know that such measures were necessary. The boy had been in Carson's service for some time, and was known to him as a faithful and active messenger, and in a wild country like New Mexico, with the outdoor life and habits of its people, such a journey was not an unusual occurrence.

Carson now returned to the camp, to watch all night himself, and at daybreak all were on the Trail again. No Indians made their appearance until nearly noon, when five warriors came galloping up toward the train. As soon as they came close enough to hear his voice, Carson ordered them to halt, and going up to them, told how he had sent a messenger to Rayedo the night before to inform the troops that their tribe were annoying him, and that if he or his men were molested, terrible punishment would be inflicted by those who would surely come to his relief. The savages replied that they would look for the moccasin tracks, which they undoubtedly found, and the whole village passed away toward the hills after a little while, evidently seeking a place of safety from an expected attack by the troops.

The young Mexican overtook the detachment of soldiers whose officer had caused all the trouble with the Indians, to whom he told his story; but failing to secure any sympathy, he continued his journey to Rayedo, and procured from the garrison of that place immediate assistance. Major Grier, commanding the post, at once despatched a troop of his regiment, which, by forced marches, met Carson twenty-five miles below Bent's Fort, and though it encountered no Indians, the rapid movement had a good effect upon the savages, impressing them with the power and promptness of the government.

Early in the spring of 1865, Carson was ordered, with three companies, to put a stop to the depredations of marauding bands of Cheyennes, Kiowas, and Comanches upon the caravans and emigrant outfits travelling the Santa Fe Trail. He left Fort Union with his command and marched over the Dry or Cimarron route to the Arkansas River, for the purpose of establishing a fortified camp at Cedar Bluffs, or Cold Spring, to afford a refuge for the freight trains on that dangerous part of the Trail. The Indians had for some time been harassing not only the caravans of the citizen traders, but also those of the government, which carried supplies to the several military posts in the Territory of New Mexico. An expedition was therefore planned by Carson to punish them, and he soon found an opportunity to strike a blow near the adobe fort on the Canadian River. His force consisted of the First Regiment of New Mexican Volunteer Cavalry and seventy-five friendly Indians, his entire command numbering fourteen commissioned officers and three hundred and ninety-six enlisted men. With these he attacked the Kiowa village, consisting of about one hundred and fifty lodges. The fight was a very severe one, and lasted from half-past eight in the morning until after sundown. The savages, with more than ordinary intrepidity and boldness, made repeated stands against the fierce onslaughts of Carson's cavalrymen, but were at last forced to give way, and were cut down as they stubbornly retreated, suffering a loss of sixty killed and wounded. In this battle only two privates and one noncommissioned officer were killed, and one non-commissioned officer and thirteen privates, four of whom were friendly Indians, wounded. The command destroyed one hundred and fifty lodges, a large amount of dried meats, berries, buffalo-robes, cooking utensils, and also a buggy and spring-wagon, the property of Sierrito,[50] the Kiowa chief.

In his official account of the fight, Carson states that he found ammunition in the village, which had been furnished, no doubt, by unscrupulous Mexican traders.

He told me that he never was deceived by Indian tactics but once in his life. He said that he was hunting with six others after buffalo, in the summer of 1835; that they had been successful, and came into their little bivouac one night very tired, intending to start for the rendezvous at Bent's Fort the next morning. They had a number of dogs, among them some excellent animals. These barked a good deal, and seemed restless, and the men heard wolves.

"I saw," said Kit, "two big wolves sneaking about, one of them quite close to us. Gordon, one of my men, wanted to fire his rifle at it, but I did not let him, for fear he would hit a dog. I admit that I had a sort of an idea that those wolves might be Indians; but when I noticed one of them turn short around, and heard the clashing of his teeth as he rushed at one of the dogs, I felt easy then, and was certain that they were wolves sure enough. But the red devil fooled me, after all, for he had two dried buffalo bones in his hands under the wolfskin, and he rattled them together every time he turned to make a dash at the dogs! Well, by and by we all dozed off, and it wasn't long before I was suddenly aroused by a noise and a big blaze. I rushed out the first thing for our mules, and held them. If the savages had been at all smart, they could have killed us in a trice, but they ran as soon as they fired at us. They killed one of my men, putting five bullets in his body and eight in his buffalo-robe. The Indians were a band of Sioux on the war-trail after a band of Snakes, and found us by sheer accident. They endeavoured to ambush us the next morning, but we got wind of their little game and killed three of them, including the chief."

Carson's nature was made up of some very noble attributes. He was brave, but not reckless like Custer; a veritable exponent of Christian altruism, and as true to his friends as the needle to the pole. Under the average stature, and rather delicate-looking in his physical proportions, he was nevertheless a quick, wiry man, with nerves of steel, and possessing an indomitable will. He was full of caution, but showed a coolness in the moment of supreme danger that was good to witness.

During a short visit at Fort Lyon, Colorado, where a favourite son of his was living, early in the morning of May 23, 1868, while mounting his horse in front of his quarters (he was still fond of riding), an artery in his neck was suddenly ruptured, from the effects of which, notwithstanding the medical assistance rendered by the fort surgeons, he died in a few moments.

His remains, after reposing for some time at Fort Lyon, were taken to Taos, so long his home in New Mexico, where an appropriate monument was erected over them. In the Plaza at Santa Fe, his name also appears cut on a cenotaph raised to commemorate the services of the soldiers of the Territory. As an Indian fighter he was matchless. The identical rifle used by him for more than thirty-five years, and which never failed him, he bequeathed, just before his death, to Montezuma Lodge, A. F. & A. M., Santa Fe, of which he was a member.

James Bridger, "Major Bridger," or "Old Jim Bridger," as we was called, another of the famous coterie of pioneer frontiersmen, was born in Washington, District of Columbia, in 1807. When very young, a mere boy in fact, he joined the great trapping expedition under the leadership of James Ashley, and with it travelled to the far West, remote from the extreme limit of border civilization, where he became the compeer and comrade of Carson, and certainly the foremost mountaineer, strictly speaking, the United States has produced.

Having left behind him all possibilities of education at such an early age, he was illiterate in his speech and as ignorant of the conventionalities of polite society as an Indian; but he possessed a heart overflowing with the milk of human kindness, was generous in the extreme, and honest and true as daylight.

He was especially distinguished for the discovery of a defile through the intricate mazes of the Rocky Mountains, which bears his name, Bridger's Pass. He rendered important services as guide and scout during the early preliminary surveys for a transcontinental railroad, and for a series of years was in the employ of the government, in the old regular army on the great plains and in the mountains, long before the breaking out of the Civil War. To Bridger also belongs the honour of having seen, first of all white men, the Great Salt Lake of Utah, in the winter of 1824-25.

After a series of adventures, hairbreadth escapes, and terrible encounters with the Indians, in 1856 he purchased a farm near Westport, Missouri; but soon left it in his hunger for the mountains, to return to it only when worn-out and blind, to be buried there without even the rudest tablet to mark the spot.

"I would rather sleep in the southern corner of a little country churchyard, than in the tomb of the Capulets." This quotation came to my mind one Sunday morning two or three years ago, as I mused over Bridger's neglected grave among the low hills beyond the quaint old town of Westport. I thought I knew, as I stood there, that he whose bones were mouldering beneath the blossoming clover at my feet, would have wished for his last couch a more perfect solitude and isolation from the wearisome world's busy sound than even the immortal Burke.

The grassy mound, over which there was no stone to record the name of its occupant, covered the remains of the last of his class, a type vanished forever, for the border is a thing of the past; and upon the gentle breeze of that delightful morning, like the droning of bees in a full flowered orchard, was wafted to my ears the hum of Kansas City's civilization, only three or four miles distant, in all of which I was sure there was nothing that would have been congenial to the old frontiersman.

At one time early in the '60's, while the engineers of the proposed Union Pacific Railway were temporarily in Denver, then an insignificant mushroom-hamlet, they became somewhat confused as to the most practicable point in the range over which to run their line. After debating the question, they determined, upon a suggestion from some of the old settlers, to send for Jim Bridger, who was then visiting in St. Louis. A pass, via the overland stage, was enclosed in a letter to him, and he was urged to start for Denver at once, though nothing of the business for which his presence was required was told him in the text.

In about two weeks the old man arrived, and the next morning, after he had rested, asked why he had been sent for from such a distance.

The engineers then began to explain their dilemma. The old mountaineer waited patiently until they had finished, when, with a look of disgust on his withered countenance, he demanded a large piece of paper, remarking at the same time,--

"I could a told you fellers all that in St. Louis, and saved you the expense of bringing me out here."

He was handed a sheet of manilla paper, used for drawing the details of bridge plans. The veteran pathfinder spread it on the ground before him, took a dead coal from the ashes of the fire, drew a rough outline map, and pointing to a certain peak just visible on the serrated horizon, said,--

"There's where you fellers can cross with your road, and nowhere else, without more diggin' an' cuttin' than you think of."

That crude map is preserved, I have been told, in the archives of the great corporation, and its line crosses the main spurs of the Rocky Mountains, just where Bridger said it could with the least work.

The resemblance of old John Smith, another of the coterie, to President Andrew Johnson was absolutely astonishing. When that chief magistrate, in his "swinging

220

around the circle," had arrived at St. Louis, and was riding through the streets of that city in an open barouche, he was pointed out to Bridger, who happened to be there. But the venerable guide and scout, with supreme disgust depicted on his countenance at the idea of any one attempting to deceive him, said to his informant,--

"H---l! Bill, you can't fool me! That's old John Smith."

At one time many years ago, during Bridger's first visit to St. Louis, then a relatively small place, a friend accidentally came across him sitting on a dry-goods box in one of the narrow streets, evidently disgusted with his situation. To the inquiry as to what he was doing there all alone, the old man replied,--

"I've been settin' in this infernal canyon ever sence mornin', waitin' for some one to come along an' invite me to take a drink. Hundreds of fellers has passed both ways, but none of 'em has opened his head. I never seen sich a onsociable crowd!"

Bridger had a fund of most remarkable stories, which he had drawn upon so often that he really believed them to be true.

General Gatlin,[51] who was graduated from West Point in the early '30's, and commanded Fort Gibson in the Cherokee Nation over sixty years ago, told me that he remembered Bridger very well; and had once asked the old guide whether he had ever been in the great canyon of the Colorado River.

"Yes, sir," replied the mountaineer, "I have, many a time. There's where the oranges and lemons bear all the time, and the only place I was ever at where the moon's always full!"

He told me and also many others, at various times, that in the winter of 1830 it began to snow in the valley of the Great Salt Lake, and continued for seventy days without cessation. The whole country was covered to a depth of seventy feet, and all the vast herds of buffalo were caught in the storm and died, but their carcasses were perfectly preserved.

"When spring came, all I had to do," declared he, "was to tumble 'em into Salt Lake, an' I had pickled buffalo enough for myself and the whole Ute Nation for years!"

He said that on account of that terrible storm, which annihilated them, there have been no buffalo in that region since.

Bridger had been the guide, interpreter, and companion of that distinguished Irish sportsman, Sir George Gore, whose strange tastes led him in 1855 to abandon life in Europe and bury himself for over two years among the savages in the wildest and most unfrequented glens of the Rocky Mountains.

The outfit and adventures of this titled Nimrod, conducted as they were on the largest scale, exceeded anything of the kind ever before seen on this continent, and the results of his wanderings will compare favourably with those of Gordon Cumming in Africa.

Some idea may be formed of the magnitude of his outfit when it is stated that his retinue consisted of about fifty individuals, including secretaries, steward, cooks, fly-makers, dog-tenders, servants, etc. He was borne over the country with a train of thirty wagons, besides numerous saddle-horses and dogs.

During his lengthened hunt he killed the enormous aggregate of forty grizzly bears and twenty-five hundred buffalo, besides numerous antelope and other small game.

Bridger said of Sir George that he was a bold, dashing, and successful hunter, and an agreeable gentleman. His habit was to lie in bed until about ten or eleven o'clock in the morning, then he took a bath, ate his breakfast, and set out, generally alone, for the day's hunt, and it was not unusual for him to remain out until ten at night, seldom returning to the tents without augmenting the catalogue of his beasts. His dinner was then served, to which he generally extended an invitation to Bridger, and after the meal was over, and a few glasses of wine had been drunk, he was in the habit of reading from some book, and eliciting from Bridger his comments thereon. His favourite author was Shakespeare, which Bridger "reckin'd was too highfalutin" for him; moreover he remarked, "thet he rather calcerlated that thar big Dutchman, Mr. Full-stuff, was a leetle too fond of lager beer," and thought it would have been better for the old man if he had "stuck to Bourbon whiskey straight."

Bridger seemed very much interested in the adventures of Baron Munchausen, but admitted after Sir George had finished reading them, that "he be dog'oned ef he swallered everything that thar Baron Munchausen said," and thought he was "a darned liar," yet he acknowledged that some of his own adventures among the Blackfeet woul be equally marvellous "if writ down in a book."

A man whose one act had made him awe-inspiring was Belzy Dodd. Uncle Dick Wooton, in relating the story, says: "I don't know what his first name was, but Belzy was what we called him. His head was as bald as a billiard ball, and he wore a wig. One day while we were all at Bent's Fort, while there were a great number of Indians about, Belzy concluded to have a bit of fun. He walked around, eying the Indians fiercely for some time, and finally, dashing in among them, he gave a series of war-whoops which discounted a Comanche yell, and pulling off his wig, threw it down at the feet of the astonished and terror-stricken red men.

222

"The savages thought the fellow had jerked off his own scalp, and not one of them wanted to stay and see what would happen next. They left the fort, running like so many scared jack-rabbits, and after that none of them could be induced to approach anywhere near Dodd."

They called him "The-white-man-who-scalps-himself," and Uncle Dick said that he believed he could have travelled across the plains alone with perfect safety.

Jim Baker was another noted mountaineer and hunter of the same era as Carson, Bridger, Wooton, Hobbs, and many others. Next to Kit Carson, Baker was General Fremont's most valued scout.

He was born in Illinois, and lived at home until he was eighteen years of age, when he enlisted in the service of the American Fur Company, went immediately to the Rocky Mountains, and remained there until his death. He married a wife according to the Indian custom, from the Snake tribe, living with her relatives many years and cultivating many of their habits, ideas, and superstitions. He firmly believed in the efficacy of the charms and incantations of the medicine men in curing diseases, divining where their enemy was to be found, forecasting the result of war expeditions, and other such ridiculous matters. Unfortunately, too, Baker would sometimes take a little more whiskey than he could conveniently carry, and often made a fool of himself, but he was a generous, noble-hearted fellow, who would risk his life for a friend at any time, or divide his last morsel of food.

Like mountaineers generally, Baker was liberal to a fault, and eminently improvident. He made a fortune by his work, but at the annual rendezvous of the traders, at Bent's Fort or the old Pueblo, would throw away the earnings of months in a few days' jollification.

He told General Marcy, who was a warm friend of his, that after one season in which he had been unusually successful in accumulating a large amount of valuable furs, from the sale of which he had realized the handsome sum of nine thousand dollars, he resolved to abandon his mountain life, return to the settlements, buy a farm, and live comfortably during the remainder of his days. He accordingly made ready to leave, and was on the eve of starting when a friend invited him to visit a monte-bank which had been organized at the rendezvous. He was easily led away, determined to take a little social amusement with his old comrade, whom he might never see again, and followed him; the result of which was that the whiskey circulated freely, and the next morning found Baker without a cent of money; he had lost everything. His entire plans were thus frustrated, and he returned to the mountains, hunting with the Indians until he died.

Jim Baker's opinions of the wild Indians of the great plains and the mountains were very decided: "That they are the most onsartinist varmints in all creation, an' I reckon thar not more'n half human; for you never seed a human, arter you'd fed an' treated him to the best fixin's in your lodge, jis turn round and steal all your horses, or ary other thing he could lay his hands on. No, not adzactly. He would feel kind o' grateful, and ask you to spread a blanket in his lodge ef you ever came his way. But the Injin don't care shucks for you, and is ready to do you a lot of mischief as soon as he quits your feed. No, Cap.," he said to Marcy when relating this, "it's not the right way to make 'em gifts to buy a peace; but ef I war gov'nor of these United States, I'll tell what I'd do. I'd invite 'em all to a big feast, and make 'em think I wanted to have a talk; and as soon as I got 'em together, I'd light in and raise the har of half of 'em, and then t'other half would be mighty glad to make terms that would stick. That's the way I'd make a treaty with the dog'oned red-bellied varmints; and as sure as you're born, Cap., that's the only way."

The general, when he first met Baker, inquired of him if he had travelled much over the settlements of the United States before he came to the mountains; to which he said: "Right smart, right smart, Cap." He then asked whether he had visited New York or New Orleans. "No, I hasn't, Cap., but I'll tell you whar I have been. I've been mighty nigh all over four counties in the State of Illinois!"

He was very fond of his squaw and children, and usually treated them kindly; only when he was in liquor did he at all maltreat them.

Once he came over into New Mexico, where General Marcy was stationed at the time, and determined that for the time being he would cast aside his leggings, moccasins, and other mountain dress, and wear a civilized wardrobe. Accordingly, he fitted himself out with one. When Marcy met him shortly after he had donned the strange clothes, he had undergone such an entire change that the general remarked he should hardly have known him. He did not take kindly to this, and said: "Consarn these store butes, Cap.; they choke my feet like h---l." It was the first time in twenty years that he had worn anything on his feet but moccasins, and they were not ready for the torture inflicted by breaking in a new pair of absurdly fitting boots. He soon threw them away, and resumed the softer foot-gear of the mountains.

Baker was a famous bear hunter, and had been at the death of many a grizzly. On one occasion he was setting his traps with a comrade on the head waters of the Arkansas, when they suddenly met two young grizzly bears about the size of full-grown dogs. Baker remarked to his friend that if they could "light in and kill the varmints" with their knives, it would be a big thing to boast of. They both accordingly laid aside their rifles and "lit in," Baker attacking one and his comrade the other. The bears immediately raised themselves on their haunches, and were ready for the encounter. Baker ran around, endeavouring to get in a blow from behind with his long knife; but the young brute he had tackled was too quick for him, and turned as he went around so as always to confront him face to face. He knew if he came within reach of his claws, that although young, he could inflict a formidable wound; moreover, he was in fear that the howls of the cubs would bring the infuriated mother to their rescue, when the hunters' chances of getting away would be slim. These thoughts floated hurriedly through his mind, and made him desirous to end the fight as soon as he could. He made many vicious lunges at the bear, but the animal invariably warded them off with his strong fore legs like a boxer. This kind of tactics, however, cost the lively beast several severe cuts on his shoulders, which made him the more furious. At length he took the offensive, and with his month frothing with rage, bounded toward Baker, who caught and wrestled with him, succeeding in giving him a death-wound under the ribs.

While all this was going on, his comrade had been furiously engaged with the other bear, and by this time had become greatly exhausted, with the odds decidedly against him. He entreated Baker to come to his assistance at once, which he did; but much to his astonishment, as soon as he entered the second contest his comrade ran off, leaving him to fight the battle alone. He was, however, again victorious, and soon had the satisfaction of seeing his two antagonists stretched out in front of him, but as he expressed it, "I made my mind up I'd never fight nary nother grizzly without a good shootin'-iron in my paws."

He established a little store at the crossing of Green River, and had for some time been doing a fair business in trafficking with the emigrants and trading with the Indians; but shortly a Frenchman came to the same locality and set up a rival establishment, which, of course, divided the limited trade, and naturally reduced the income of Baker's business.

This engendered a bitter feeling of hostility, which soon culminated in a cessation of all social intercourse between the two men. About this time General Marcy arrived there on his way to California, and he describes the situation of affairs thus:--

"I found Baker standing in his door, with a revolver loaded and cocked in each hand, very drunk and immensely excited. I dismounted and asked him the cause of all this disturbance. He answered: 'That thar yaller-bellied, toad-eatin' Parly Voo, over thar, an' me, we've been havin' a small chance of a scrimmage to-day. The sneakin' pole-cat, I'll raise his har yet, ef he don't quit these diggins'!'

"It seems that they had an altercation in the morning, which ended in a challenge, when they ran to their cabins, seized their revolvers, and from the doors, which were only about a hundred yards from each other, fired. Then they retired to their cabins, took a drink of whiskey, reloaded their revolvers, and again renewed the combat. This strange duel had been going on for several hours when I arrived, but, fortunately for them, the whiskey had such an effect on their nerves that their aim was very unsteady, and none of the shots had as yet taken effect.

"I took away Baker's revolvers, telling him how ashamed I was to find a man of his usually good sense making such a fool of himself. He gave in quietly, saying that he knew I was his friend, but did not think I would wish to have him take insults from a cowardly Frenchman.

"The following morning at daylight Jim called at my tent to bid me good-by, and seemed very sorry for what had occurred the day before. He stated that this was the first time since his return from New Mexico that he had allowed himself to drink whiskey, and when the whiskey was in him he had 'nary sense.'"

Among the many men who have distinguished themselves as mountaineers, traders, and Indian fighters along the line of the Old Trail, was one who eventually became the head chief of one of the most numerous and valorous tribes of North American savages--James P. Beckwourth. Estimates of him vary considerably. Francis Parkman, the historian, who I think never saw him and writes merely from hearsay, says: "He is a ruffian of the worst class; bloody and treacherous, without honor or honesty; such, at least, is the character he bears on the great plains. Yet in his case the standard rules of character fail; for though he will stab a man in his slumber, he will also do the most desperate and daring acts."

I never saw Beckwourth, but I have heard of him from those of my mountaineer friends who knew him intimately; I think that he died long before Parkman made his tour to the Rocky Mountains. Colonel Boone, the Bents, Carson, Maxwell, and others ascribed to him no such traits as those given by Parkman, and as to his honesty, it is an unquestioned fact that Beckwourth was the most honest trader among the Indians of all who were then engaged in the business. As Kit Carson and Colonel Boone were the only Indian agents whom I ever knew or heard of that dealt honestly with the various tribes, as they were always ready to acknowledge, and the withdrawal of the former by the government was the cause of a great war, so also Beckwourth was an honest Indian trader.

He was a born leader of men, and was known from the Yellowstone to the Rio Grande, from Santa Fe to Independence, and in St. Louis. From the latter town he ran away when a boy with a party of trappers, and himself became one of the most successful of that hardy class. The woman who bore him had played in her childhood beneath the palm trees of Africa; his father was a native of France, and went to the banks of the wild Mississippi of his own free will, but probably also from reasons of political interest to his government.

In person Beckwourth was of medium height and great muscular power, quick of apprehension, and with courage of the highest order. Probably no man ever met with more personal adventures involving danger to life, even among the mountaineers and trappers who early in the century faced the perils of the remote frontier. From his neck he always wore suspended a perforated bullet, with a large oblong bead

226

on each side of it, tied in place by a single thread of sinew. This amulet he obtained while chief of the Crows,[52] and it was his "medicine," with which he excited the superstition of his warriors.

His success as a trader among the various tribes of Indians has never been surpassed; for his close intimacy with them made him know what would best please their taste, and they bought of him when other traders stood idly at their stockades, waiting almost hopelessly for customers.

But Beckwourth himself said: "The traffic in whiskey for Indian property was one of the most infernal practices ever entered into by man. Let the most casual thinker sit down and figure up the profits on a forty-gallon cask of alcohol, and he will be thunderstruck, or rather whiskey-struck. When it was to be disposed of, four gallons of water were added to each gallon of alcohol. In two hundred gallons there are sixteen hundred pints, for each one of which the trader got a buffalo-robe worth five dollars. The Indian women toiled many long weeks to dress those sixteen hundred robes. The white traders got them for worse than nothing; for the poor Indian mother hid herself and her children until the effect of the poison passed away from the husband and father, who loved them when he had no whiskey, and abused and killed them when he had. Six thousand dollars for sixty gallons of alcohol! Is it a wonder with such profits that men got rich who were engaged in the fur trade? Or was it a miracle that the buffalo were gradually exterminated?--killed with so little remorse that the hides, among the Indians themselves, were known by the appellation of 'A pint of whiskey.'"

Beckwourth claims to have established the Pueblo where the beautiful city of Pueblo, Colorado, is now situated. He says: "On the 1st of October, 1842, on the Upper Arkansas, I erected a trading-post and opened a successful business. In a very short time I was joined by from fifteen to twenty free trappers, with their families. We all united our labour and constructed an adobe fort sixty yards square. By the following spring it had grown into quite a little settlement, and we gave it the name of Pueblo."

CHAPTER XVII.

UNCLE DICK WOOTON.

Immediately after Kit Carson, the second wreath of pioneer laurels, for bravery and prowess as an Indian fighter, and trapper, must be conceded to Richens Lacy Wooton, known first as "Dick," in his younger days on the plains, then, when age had overtaken him, as "Uncle Dick."

Born in Virginia, his father, when he was but seven years of age, removed with his family to Kentucky, where he cultivated a tobacco plantation. Like his predecessor and lifelong friend Carson, young Wooton tired of the monotony of farming, and in the summer of 1836 made a trip to the busy frontier town of Independence, Missouri, where he found a caravan belonging to Colonel St. Vrain and the Bents, already loaded, and ready to pull out for the fort built by the latter, and named for them.

Wooton had a fair business education, and was superior in this respect to his companions in the caravan to which he had attached himself. It was by those rough, but kind-hearted, men that he was called "Dick," as they could not readily master the more complicated name of "Richens."

When he started from Independence on his initial trip across the plains, he was only nineteen, but, like all Kentuckians, perfectly familiar with a rifle, and could shoot out a squirrel's eye with the certainty which long practice and hardened nerves assures.

The caravan, in which he was employed as a teamster, was composed of only seven wagons; but a larger one, in which were more than fifty, had preceded it, and as that was heavily laden, and the smaller one only lightly, it was intended to overtake the former before the dangerous portions of the Trail were reached, which it did in a few days and was assigned a place in the long line.

Every man had to take his turn in standing guard, and the first night that it fell to young Wooton was at Little Cow Creek, in the Upper Arkansas valley. Nothing had occurred thus far during the trip to imperil the safety of the caravan, nor was any attack by the savages looked for.

Wooton's post comprehended the whole length of one side of the corral, and his instructions were to shoot anything he saw moving outside of the line of mules farthest from the wagons. The young sentry was very vigilant. He did not feel at all sleepy, but eagerly watched for something that might possibly come within the prescribed distance, though not really expecting such a contingency.

About two o'clock he heard a slight noise, and saw something moving about, sixty or seventy yards from where he was lying on the ground, to which he had dropped the moment the strange sound reached his ears. Of course, his first thoughts were of Indians, and the more he peered through the darkness at the slowly moving object, the more convinced he was that it must be a blood-thirsty savage.

He rose to his feet and blazed away, the shot rousing everbody, and all came rushing with their guns to learn what the matter was.

Wooton told the wagon-master that he had seen what he supposed was an Indian trying to slip up to the mules, and that he had killed him. Some of the men crept very circumspectly to the spot where the supposed dead savage was lying, while young Wooton remained at his post eagerly waiting for their report. Presently he heard a voice cry out: "I'll be d---d ef he hain't killed 'Old Jack!'"

"Old Jack" was one of the lead mules of one of the wagons. He had torn up his picket-pin and strayed outside of the lines, with the result that the faithful brute met his death at the hands of the sentry. Wooton declared that he was not to be blamed; for the animal had disobeyed orders, while he had strictly observed them![53]

At Pawnee Fork, a few days later, the caravan had a genuine tussle with the Comanches. It was a bright moonlight night, and about two hundred of the mounted savages attacked them. It was a rare thing for Indians to begin a raid after dark, but they swept down on the unsuspecting teamsters, yelling like a host of demons. They were armed with bows and arrows generally, though a few of them had fusees. [54] They received a warm greeting, although they were not expected, the guard noticing the savages in time to prevent a stampede of the animals, which evidently was the sole purpose for which they came, as they did not attempt to break through the corral to get at the wagons. It was the mules they were after. They charged among the men, vainly endeavouring to frighten the animals and make them break loose, discharging showers of arrows as they rode by. The camp was too hot for them, however, defended as it was by old teamsters who had made the dangerous passage of the plains many times before, and were up to all the Indian tactics. They failed to get a single mule, but paid for their temerity by leaving three of their party dead, just where they had been tumbled off their horses, not even having time to carry the bodies off, as they usually do.

Wooton passed some time during the early days of his career at Bent's Fort, in 1836-37. He was a great favourite with both of the proprietors, and with them went to the several Indian villages, where he learned the art of trading with the savages.

The winters of the years mentioned were noted for the incursions of the Pawnees into the region of the fort. They always pretended friendship for the whites, when any of them were inside of its sacred precincts, but their whole manner changed when they by some stroke of fortune caught a trapper or hunter alone on the prairie or in the foot-hills; he was a dead man sure, and his scalp was soon dangling at the belt of his cowardly assassins. Hardly a day passed without witnessing some poor fellow running for the fort with a band of the red devils after him; frequently he escaped the keen edge of their scalping-knife, but every once in a while a man was killed. At one time, two herders who were with their animals within fifty yards of the fort, going out to the grazing ground, were killed and every hoof of stock run off.

A party from the fort, comprising only eight men, among whom was young Wooton, made up for lost time with the Indians, at the crossing of Pawnee Fork, the same place where he had had his first fight. The men had set out from the fort for the purpose of meeting a small caravan of wagons from the East, loaded with supplies for the Bents' trading post. It happened that a band of sixteen Pawnees were watching for the arrival of the train, too.[55] Wooton's party were well mounted, while the Pawnees were on foot, and although the savages were two to one, the advantage was decidedly in favour of the whites.

The Indians were armed with bows and arrows only, and while it was an easy matter for the whites to keep out of the way of the shower of missiles which the Indians commenced to hurl at them, the latter became an easy prey to the unerring rifles of their assailants, who killed thirteen out of the sixteen in a very short time. The remaining three took French leave of their comrades at the beginning of the conflict, and abandoning their arms rushed up to the caravan, which was just appearing over a small divide, and gave themselves up. The Indian custom was observed in their case,[56] although it was rarely that any prisoners were taken in these conflicts on the Trail. Another curious custom was also followed.[57] When the party encamped they were well fed, and the next morning supplied with rations enough to last them until they could reach one of their villages, and sent off to tell their head chief what had become of the rest of his warriors.

Wooton had an adventure once while he was stationed at Bent's Fort during a trading expedition with the Utes, on the Purgatoire, or Purgatory River,[58] about ten or twelve miles from Trinidad. He had taken with him, with others, a Shawnee Indian. Only a short time before their departure from the fort, an Indian of that tribe had been murdered by a Ute, and one day this Shawnee who was with Wooton spied a Ute, when revenge inspired him, and he forthwith killed his enemy. Knowing that as soon as the news of the shooting reached the Ute village, which was not a great distance off, the whole tribe would be down upon him, Wooton abandoned any attempt to trade with them and tried to get out of their country as quickly as he could.

As he expected, the Utes followed on his trail, and came up with his little party on a prairie where there was not the slightest chance to ambush or hide. They had to fight, because they could not help it, but resolved to sell their lives as dearly as possible, as the Utes outnumbered them twenty to one; Wooton having only eight men with him, including the Shawnee.

The pack-animals, of which they had a great many, loaded with the goods intended for the savages, were corralled in a circle, inside of which the men hurried themselves and awaited the first assault of the foe. In a few moments the Utes began to circle around the trappers and open fire. The trappers promptly responded, and they made every shot count; for all of the men, not even excepting the Shawnee, were experts with the rifle. They did not mind the arrows which the Utes showered upon them, as few, if any, reached to where they stood. The savages had a few guns, but they were of the poorest quality; besides, they did not know how to handle them then as they learned to do later, so their bullets were almost as harmless as their arrows.

The trappers made terrible havoc among the Utes' horses, killing so many of them that the savages in despair abandoned the fight and gave Wooton and his men an opportunity to get away, which they did as rapidly as possible.

The Raton Pass, through which the Old Trail ran, was a relatively fair mountain road, but originally it was almost impossible for anything in the shape of a wheeled vehicle to get over the narrow rock-ribbed barrier; saddle horses and pack-mules could, however, make the trip without much difficulty. It was the natural highway to southeastern Colorado and northeastern New Mexico, but the overland coaches could not get to Trinidad by the shortest route, and as the caravans also desired to make the same line, it occurred to Uncle Dick that he would undertake to hew out a road through the pass, which, barring grades, should be as good as the average turnpike. He could see money in it for him, as he expected to charge toll, keeping the road in repair at his own expense, and he succeeded in procuring from the legislatures of Colorado and New Mexico charters covering the rights and privileges which he demanded for his project.

In the spring of 1866, Uncle Dick took up his abode on the top of the mountains, built his home, and lived there until two years ago, when he died at a very ripe old age.

The old trapper had imposed on himself anything but an easy task in constructing his toll-road. There were great hillsides to cut out, immense ledges of rocks to blast, bridges to build by the dozen, and huge trees to fell, besides long lines of difficult grading to engineer.

Eventually Uncle Dick's road was a fact, but when it was completed, how to make it pay was a question that seriously disturbed his mind. The method he employed to solve the problem I will quote in his own words: "Such a thing as a toll-road was unknown in the country at that time. People who had come from the States understood, of course, that the object of building a turnpike was to enable the owner to collect toll from those who travelled over it, but I had to deal with a great many people who seemed to think that they should be as free to travel over my well-graded and bridged roadway as they were to follow an ordinary cow path.

"I may say that I had five classes of patrons to do business with. There was the stage company and its employees, the freighters, the military authorities, who marched troops and transported supplies over the road, the Mexicans, and the Indians.

"With the stage company, the military authorities, and the American freighters I had no trouble. With the Indians, when a band came through now and then, I didn't care to have any controversy about so small a matter as a few dollars toll! Whenever they came along, the toll-gate went up, and any other little thing I could do to hurry them on was done promptly and cheerfully. While the Indians didn't understand anything about the system of collecting tolls, they seemed to recognize the fact that I had a right to control the road, and they would generally ride up to the gate and ask permission to go through. Once in a while the chief of a band would think compensation for the privilege of going through in order, and would make me a present of a buckskin or something of that sort.

"My Mexican patrons were the hardest to get along with. Paying for the privilege of travelling over any road was something they were totally unused to, and they did not take to it kindly. They were pleased with my road and liked to travel over it, until they came to the toll-gate. This they seemed to look upon as an obstruction that no man had a right to place in the way of a free-born native of the mountain region. They appeared to regard the toll-gate as a new scheme for holding up travellers for the purpose of robbery, and many of them evidently thought me a kind of freebooter, who ought to be suppressed by law.

"Holding these views, when I asked them for a certain amount of money, before raising the toll-gate, they naturally differed with me very frequently about the propriety of complying with the request.

"In other words, there would be at such times probably an honest difference of opinion between the man who kept the toll-gate and the man who wanted to get through it. Anyhow, there was a difference, and such differences had to be adjusted. Sometimes I did it through diplomacy, and sometimes I did it with a club. It was always settled one way, however, and that was in accordance with the toll schedule, so that I could never have been charged with unjust discrimination of rates."

Soon after the road was opened a company composed of Californians and Mexicans, commanded by a Captain Haley, passed Uncle Dick's toll-gate and house, escorting a large caravan of about a hundred and fifty wagons. While they stopped there, a non-commissioned officer of the party was brutally murdered by three soldiers, and Uncle Dick came very near being a witness to the atrocious deed.

The murdered man was a Mexican, and his slayers were Mexicans too. The trouble originated at Las Vegas, where the privates had been bound and gagged, by order of the corporal, for creating a disturbance at a fandango the evening before.

The name of the corporal was Juan Torres, and he came down to Uncle Dick's one evening while the command was encamped on the top of the mountain, accompanied by the three privates, who had already plotted to kill him, though he had not the slightest suspicion of it.

Uncle Dick, in telling the story, said: "They left at an early hour, going in an opposite direction from their camp, and I closed my doors soon after, for the night. They had not been gone more than half an hour, when I heard them talking not far from my house, and a few seconds later I heard the half-suppressed cry of a man who has received his death-blow.

"I had gone to bed, and lay for a minute or two thinking whether I should get up and go to the rescue or insure my own safety by remaining where I was.

"A little reflection convinced me that the murderers were undoubtedly watching my house, to prevent any interference with the carrying out of their plot, and that if I ventured out I should only endanger my own life, while there was scarcely a possibility of my being able to save the life of the man who had been assailed.

"In the morning, when I got up, I found the dead body of the corporal stretched across Raton Creek, not more than a hundred yards from my house.

"As I surmised, he had been struck with a heavy club or stone, and it was at that time that I heard his cry. After that his brains had been beaten out, and the body left where I had found it.

"I at once notified Captain Haley of the occurrence, and identified the men who had been in company with the corporal, and who were undoubtedly his murderers.

"They were taken into custody, and made a confession, in which they stated that one of their number had stood at my door on the night of the murder to shoot me if I had ventured out to assist the corporal. Two of the scoundrels were hung afterward at Las Vegas, and the third sent to prison for life."

233

The corporal was buried near where the soldiers were encamped at the time of the tragedy, and it is his lonely grave which frequently attracts the attention of the passengers on the Atchison, Topeka, and Santa Fe trains, just before the Raton tunnel is reached, as they travel southward.

In 1866-67 the Indians broke out, infesting all the most prominent points of the Old Santa Fe Trail, and watching an opportunity to rob and murder, so that the government freight caravans and the stages had to be escorted by detachments of troops. Fort Larned was the western limit where these escorts joined the outfits going over into New Mexico.

There were other dangers attending the passage of the Trail to travellers by the stage besides the attacks of the savages. These were the so-called road agents-- masked robbers who regarded life as of little worth in the accomplishment of their nefarious purposes. Particularly were they common after the mines of New Mexico began to be operated by Americans. The object of the bandits was generally the strong box of the express company, which contained money and other valuables. They did not, of course, hesitate to take what ready cash and jewelry the passengers might happen to have upon their persons, and frequently their hauls amounted to large sums.

When the coaches began to travel over Uncle Dick's toll-road, his house was made a station, and he had many stage stories. He said:--

"Tavern-keepers in those days couldn't choose their guests, and we entertained them just as they came along. The knights of the road would come by now and then, order a meal, eat it hurriedly, pay for it, and move on to where they had arranged to hold up a stage that night. Sometimes they did not wait for it to get dark, but halted the stage, went through the treasure box in broad daylight, and then ordered the driver to move on in one direction, while they went off in another.

"One of the most daring and successful stage robberies that I remember was perpetrated by two men, when the east-bound coach was coming up on the south side of the Raton Mountains, one day about ten o'clock in the forenoon.

"On the morning of the same day, a little after sunrise, two rather genteel-looking fellows, mounted on fine horses, rode up to my house and ordered breakfast. Being informed that breakfast would be ready in a few minutes, they dismounted, hitched their horses near the door, and came into the house.

"I knew then, just as well as I do now, they were robbers, but I had no warrant for their arrest, and I should have hesitated about serving it if I had, because they looked like very unpleasant men to transact that kind of business with.

"Each of them had four pistols sticking in his belt and a repeating rifle strapped on to his saddle. When they dismounted, they left their rifles with the horses, but walked into the house and sat down at the table, without laying aside the arsenal which they carried in their belts.

"They had little to say while eating, but were courteous in their behaviour, and very polite to the waiters. When they had finished breakfast, they paid their bills, and rode leisurely up the mountain.

"It did not occur to me that they would take chances on stopping the stage in daylight, or I should have sent some one to meet the incoming coach, which I knew would be along shortly, to warn the driver and passengers to be on the lookout for robbers.

"It turned out, however, that a daylight robbery was just what they had in mind, and they made a success of it.

"About halfway down the New Mexico side of the mountain, where the canyon is very narrow, and was then heavily wooded on either side, the robbers stopped and waited for the coach. It came lumbering along by and by, neither the driver nor the passengers dreaming of a hold-up.

"The first intimation they had of such a thing was when they saw two men step into the road, one on each side of the stage, each of them holding two cocked revolvers, one of which was brought to bear on the passengers and the other on the driver, who were politely but very positively told that they must throw up their hands without any unnecessary delay, and the stage came to a standstill.

"There were four passengers in the coach, all men, but their hands went up at the same instant that the driver dropped his reins and struck an attitude that suited the robbers.

"Then, while one of the men stood guard, the other stepped up to the stage and ordered the treasure box thrown off. This demand was complied with, and the box was broken and rifled of its contents, which fortunately were not of very great value.

"The passengers were compelled to hand out their watches and other jewelry, as well as what money they had in their pockets, and then the driver was directed to move up the road. In a minute after this the robbers had disappeared with their booty, and that was the last seen of them by that particular coach-load of passengers.

"The men who planned and executed that robbery were two cool, level-headed, and daring scoundrels, known as 'Chuckle-luck' and 'Magpie.' They were killed soon

235

after this occurrence, by a member of their own band, whose name was Seward. A reward of a thousand dollars had been offered for their capture, an this tempted Seward to kill them, one night when they were asleep in camp.

"He then secured a wagon, into which he loaded the dead robbers, and hauled them to Cimarron City, where he turned them over to the authorities and received his reward."

Among the Arapahoes Wooton was called "Cut Hand," from the fact that he had lost two fingers on his left hand by an accident in his childhood. The tribe had the utmost veneration for the old trapper, and he was perfectly safe at any time in their villages or camps; it had been the request of a dying chief, who was once greatly favoured by Wooton, that his warriors should never injure him although the nation might be at war with all the rest of the whites in the world.

Uncle Dick died a few seasons ago, at the age of nearly ninety. He was blind for some time, but a surgical operation partly restored his sight, which made the old man happy, because he could look again upon the beautiful scenery surrounding his mountain home, really the grandest in the entire Raton Range. The Atchison, Topeka, and Santa Fe Railroad had one of its freight locomotives named "Uncle Dick," in honour of the veteran mountaineer, past whose house it hauled the heavy-laden trains up the steep grade crossing into the valley beyond. At the time of its baptism, now fifteen or sixteen years ago, it was the largest freight engine in the world.

Old Bill Williams was another character of the early days of the Trail, and was called so when Carson, Uncle Dick Wooton, and Maxwell were comparatively young in the mountains. He was, at the time of their advent in the remote West, one of the best known men there, and had been famous for years as a hunter and trapper. Williams was better acquainted with every pass in the Rockies than any other man of his time, and only surpassed by Jim Bridger later. He was with General Fremont on his exploring expedition across the continent; but the statement of the old trappers, and that of General Fremont, in relation to his services then, differ widely. Fremont admits Williams' knowledge of the country over which he had wandered to have been very extensive, but when put to the test on the expedition, he came very near sacrificing the lives of all. This was probably owing to Williams' failing intellect, for when he joined the great explorer he was past the meridian of life. Now the old mountaineers contend that if Fremont had profited by the old man's advice, he would never have run into the deathtrap which cost him three men, and in which he lost all his valuable papers, his instruments, and the animals which he and his party were riding. The expedition had followed the Arkansas River to its source, and the general had selected a route which he desired to pursue in crossing the mountains. It was winter, and Williams explained to him that it was perfectly impracticable to get over at that season. The general, however, ignoring the statement, listened to another of his party, a man who had no such experience but said that he could pilot the expedition. Before they had fairly started, they were caught in one of the most terrible snowstorms the region had ever witnessed, in which all their horses and mules were literally frozen to death. Then, when it was too late, they turned back, abandoning their instruments, and able only to carry along a very limited stock of food. The storm continued to rage, so that even Williams failed to prevent them from getting lost, and they wandered about aimlessly for many days before they luckily arrived at Taos, suffering seriously from exhaustion and hunger. Three of the men were frozen to death on the return trip, and the remaining fifteen were little better than dead when Uncle Dick Wooton happened to run across them and piloted them into the village. It was immediately after this disaster that the three most noted men in the mountains--Carson, Maxwell, and Dick Owens--became the guides of the pathfinder, with whom he had no trouble, and to whom he owed more of his success than history has given them credit for.

At one period of his eventful career, while he lived in Missouri, before he wandered to the mountains, Old Bill Williams was a Methodist preacher; of which fact he boasted frequently while he trapped and hunted with other pioneers. Whenever he related that portion of his early life, he declared that he "was so well known in his circuit, that the chickens recognized him as he came riding by the scattered farmhouses, and the old roosters would crow 'Here comes Parson Williams! One of us must be made ready for dinner.'"

Upon leaving the States, he travelled very extensively among the various tribes of Indians who roamed over the great plains and in the mountains. When sojourning with a certain band, he would invariably adopt their manners and customs. Whenever he grew tired of that nation, he would seek another and live as they lived. He had been so long among the savages that he looked and talked like one, and had imbibed many of their strange notions and curious superstitions.

To the missionaries he was very useful. He possessed the faculty of easily acquiring languages that other white men failed to learn, and could readily translate the Bible into several Indian dialects. His own conduct, however, was in strange contrast with the precepts of the Holy Book with which he was so familiar.

To the native Mexicans he was a holy terror and an unsolvable riddle. They thought him possessed of an evil spirit. He at one time took up his residence among them and commenced to trade. Shortly after he had established himself and gathered in a stock of goods, he became involved in a dispute with some of his customers in relation to his prices. Upon this he apparently took an intense dislike to the people whom he had begun to traffic with, and in his disgust tossed his whole mass of goods into the street, and, taking up his rifle, left at once for the mountains.

Among the many wild ideas he had imbibed from his long association with the Indians, was faith in their belief in the transmigration of souls. He used so to worry his brain for hours cogitating upon this intricate problem concerning a future state, that he actually pretended to know exactly the animal whose place he was destined to fill in the world after he had shaken off this mortal human coil.

Uncle Dick Wooton told how once, when he, Old Bill Williams, and many other trappers, were lying around the camp-fire one night, the strange fellow, in a preaching style of delivery, related to them all how he was to be changed into a buck elk and intended to make his pasture in the very region where they then were. He described certain peculiarities which would distinguish him from the common run of elk, and was very careful to caution all those present never to shoot such an animal, should they ever run across him.

Williams was regarded as a warm-hearted, brave, and generous man. He was at last killed by the Indians, while trading with them, but has left his name to many mountain peaks, rivers, and passes discovered by him.

Tom Tobin, one of the last of the famous trappers, hunters, and Indian fighters to cross the dark river, flourished in the early days, when the Rocky Mountains were a veritable terra incognita to nearly all excepting the hardy employees of the several fur companies and the limited number of United States troops stationed in their remote wilds.

Tom was an Irishman, quick-tempered, and a dead shot with either rifle, revolver, or the formidable bowie-knife. He would fight at the drop of the hat, but no man ever went away from his cabin hungry, if he had a crust to divide; or penniless, if there was anything remaining in his purse.

He, like Carson, was rather under the average stature, red-faced, and lacking much of being an Adonis, but whole-souled, and as quick in his movements as an antelope.

Tobin played an important role in avenging the death of the Americans killed in the Taos massacre, at the storming of the Indian pueblo, but his greatest achievement was the ending of the noted bandit Espinosa's life, who, at the height of his career of blood, was the terror of the whole mountain region.

At the time of the acquisition of New Mexico by the United States, Espinosa, who was a Mexican, owning vast herds of cattle and sheep, resided upon his ancestral hacienda in a sort of barbaric luxury, with a host of semi-serfs, known as Peons, to do his bidding, as did the other "Muy Ricos," the "Dons," so called, of his class of natives. These self-styled aristocrats of the wild country all boasted of their Castilian blue blood, claiming descent from the nobles of Cortez' army, but the fact is, however, with rare exceptions, that their male ancestors, the rank and file of that army, intermarried with the Aztec women, and they were really only a mixture of Indian and Spanish.

It so happened that Espinosa met an adventurous American, who, with hundreds of others, had been attached to the "Army of Occupation" in the Mexican War, or had emigrated from the States to seek their fortunes in the newly acquired and much over-rated territory.

The Mexican Don and the American became fast friends, the latter making his home with his newly found acquaintance at the beautiful ranch in the mountains, where they played the role of a modern Damon and Pythias.

Now with Don Espinosa lived his sister, a dark-eyed, bewitchingly beautiful girl about seventeen years old, with whom the susceptible American fell deeply in love, and his affection was reciprocated by the maiden, with a fervour of which only the women of the race from which she sprang are capable.

The fascinating American had brought with him from his home in one of the New England States a large amount of money, for his parents were rich, and spared no indulgence to their only son. He very soon unwisely made Espinosa his confidant, and told him of the wealth he possessed.

One night after the American had retired to his chamber, adjoining that of his host, he was surprised, shortly after he had gone to bed, by discovering a man standing over him, whose hand had already grasped the buckskin bag under his pillow which contained a considerable portion of his gold and silver. He sprang from his couch and fired his pistol at random in the darkness at the would-be robber.

Espinosa, for it was he, was wounded slightly, and, being either enraged or frightened, he stabbed with his keen-pointed stiletto, which all Mexicans then carried, the young man whom he had invited to become his guest, and the blade entered the American's heart, killing him instantly.

The report of the pistol-shot awakened the other members of the household, who came rushing into the room just as the victim was breathing his last. Among them was the sister of the murderer, who, throwing herself on the body of her dead lover, poured forth the most bitter curses upon her brother.

Espinosa, realizing the terrible position in which he had placed himself, then and there determined to become an outlaw, as he could frame no excuse for his wicked deed. He therefore hid himself at once in the mountains, carrying with him, of course, the sack containing the murdered American's money.

Some time necessarily passed before he could get together a sufficient number of cut-throats and renegades from justice to enable him wholly to defy the authorities; but at last he succeeded in rallying a strong force to his standard of blood, and became the terror of the whole region, equalling in boldness and audacity the terrible Joaquin, of California notoriety in after years.

His headquarters were in the almost impregnable fastnesses of the Sangre de Cristo Mountains, from which he made his invariably successful raids into the rich valleys below. There was nothing too bloody for him to shrink from; he robbed indiscriminately the overland coaches to Santa Fe, the freight caravans of the traders and government, the ranches of the Mexicans, or stole from the poorer classes, without any compunction. He ran off horses, cattle, sheep-- in fact, anything that he could utilize. If murder was necessary to the completion of his work, he never for a moment hesitated. Kidnapping, too, was a favourite pastime; but he rarely carried away to his rendezvous any other than the most beautiful of the New Mexican young girls, whom he held in his mountain den until they were ransomed, or subjected to a fate more terrible.

In 1864 the bandit, after nearly ten years of unparalleled outlawry, was killed by Tobin. Tom had been on his trail for some time, and at last tracked him to a temporary camp in the foot-hills, which he accidentally discovered in a grove of cottonwoods, by the smoke of the little camp-fire as it curled in light wreaths above the trees.

Tobin knew that at the time there was but one of Espinosa's followers with him, as he had watched them both for some days, waiting for an opportunity to get the drop on them. To capture the pair of outlaws alive never entered his thoughts; he was as cautious as brave, and to get them dead was much safer and easier; so he crept up to the grove on his belly, Indian fashion, and lying behind the cover of a friendly log, waited until the noted desperado stood up, when he pulled the trigger of his never-erring rifle, and Espinosa fell dead. A second shot quickly disposed of his companion, and the old trapper's mission was accomplished.

To be able to claim the reward offered by the authorities, Tom had to prove, beyond the possibility of doubt, that those whom he had killed were the dreaded bandit and one of his gang. He thought it best to cut off their heads, which he deliberately did, and packing them on his mule in a gunny-sack, he brought them into old Fort Massachusetts, afterward Fort Garland, where they were speedily recognized; but whether Tom ever received the reward, I have my doubts, as he never claimed that he did. Tobin died only a short time ago, gray, grizzled, and venerable, his memory respected by all who had ever met him.

James Hobbs, among all the men of whom I have presented a hurried sketch, had perhaps a more varied experience than any of his colleagues. During his long life on the frontier, he was in turn a prisoner among the savages, and held for years by them; an excellent soldier in the war with Mexico; an efficient officer in the revolt against Maximilian, when the attempt of Napoleon to establish an empire on this continent, with that unfortunate prince at its head, was defeated; an Indian fighter; a miner; a trapper; a trader, and a hunter.

Hobbs was born in the Shawnee nation, on the Big Blue, about twenty-three miles from Independence, Missouri. His early childhood was entrusted to one of his father's slaves. Reared on the eastern limit of the border, he very soon became familiar with the use of the rifle and shot-gun; in fact, he was the principal provider of all the meat which the family consumed.

In 1835, when only sixteen, he joined a fur-trading expedition under Charles Bent, destined for the fort on the Arkansas River built by him and his brothers.

They arrived at the crossing of the Santa Fe Trail over Pawnee Fork without special adventure, but there they had the usual tussle with the savages, and Hobbs killed his first Indian. Two of the traders were pierced with arrows, but not seriously hurt, and the Pawnees --the tribe which had attacked the outfit--were driven away discomfited, not having been successful in stampeding a single animal.

When the party reached the Caches, on the Upper Arkansas, a smoke rising on the distant horizon, beyond the sand hills south of the river, made them proceed cautiously; for to the old plainsmen, that far-off wreath indicated either the presence of the savages, or a signal to others at a greater distance of the approach of the trappers.

The next morning, nothing having occurred to delay the march, buffalo began to appear, and Hobbs killed three of them. A cow, which he had wounded, ran across the Trail in front of the train, and Hobbs dashed after her, wounding her with his pistol, and then she started to swim the river. Hobbs, mad at the jeers which greeted him from the men at his missing the animal, started for the last wagon, in which was his rifle, determined to kill the brute that had enraged him. As he was riding along rapidly, Bent cried out to him,--

"Don't try to follow that cow; she is going straight for that smoke, and it means Injuns, and no good in 'em either."

"But I'll get her," answered Hobbs, and he called to his closest comrade, John Baptiste, a boy of about his own age, to go and get his pack-mule and come along. "All right," responded John; and together the two inexperienced youngsters crossed the river against the protests of the veteran leader of the party.

After a chase of about three miles, the boys came up with the cow, but she turned and showed fight. Finally Hobbs, by riding around her, got in a good shot, which killed her. Jumping off their animals, both boys busied themselves in cutting out the choice pieces for their supper, packed them on the mule, and started back for the train. But it had suddenly become very dark, and they were in doubt as to the direction of the Trail.

Soon night came on so rapidly that neither could they see their own tracks by which they had come, nor the thin fringe of cottonwoods that lined the bank of the stream. Then they disagreed as to which was the right way. John succeeded in persuading Hobbs that he was correct, and the latter gave in, very much against his own belief on the subject.

They travelled all night, and when morning came, were bewilderingly lost. Then Hobbs resolved to retrace the tracks by which, now that the sun was up, he saw that they had been going south, right away from the Arkansas. Suddenly an immense herd of buffalo, containing at least two thousand, dashed by the boys, filling the air with the dust raised by their clattering hoofs, and right behind them rode a hundred Indians, shooting at the stampeded animals with their arrows.

"Get into that ravine!" shouted Hobbs to his companion. "Throw away that meat, and run for your life!"

It was too late; just as they arrived at the brink of the hollow, they looked back, and close behind them were a dozen Comanches.

The savages rode up, and one of the party said in very good English, "How d' do?"

"How d' do?" Hobbs replied, thinking it would be better to be as polite as the Indian, though the state of the latter's health just then was a matter of small concern.

"Texas?" inquired the Indian. The Comanches had good reasons to hate the citizens of that country, and it was a lucky thing for Hobbs that he had heard of their prejudice from the trappers, and possessed presence of mind to remember it. He replied promptly: "No, friendly; going to establish a trading-post for the Comanches."

"Friendly? Better go with us, though. Got any tobacco?"

Hobbs had some of the desired article, and he was not long in handing it over to his newly found friend.

Both of the boys were escorted to the temporary camp of the savages, but the original number of their captors was increased to over a thousand before they arrived there. They were supplied with some dried buffalo-meat, and then taken to the lodge of Old Wolf, the head chief of the tribe.

A council was called immediately to consider what disposition should be made of them, but nothing was decided upon, and the assembly of warriors adjourned until morning. Hobbs told me that it was because Old Wolf had imbibed too much brandy, a bottle of which Baptiste had brought with him from the train, and which the thirsty warrior saw suspended from his saddle-bow as they rode up to the chief's lodge; the aged rascal got beastly drunk.

About noon of the next day, after the dispersion of the council, the boys were informed that if they were not Texans, would behave themselves, and not attempt to run away, they might stay with the Indians, who would not kill them; but a string of dried scalps was pointed out, hanging on a lodge pole, of some Mexicans whom they had captured and put to herding their ponies, and who had tried to get away. They succeeded in making a few miles; the Indians chased them, after deciding in council, that, if caught, only their scalps were to be brought back. The moral of this was that the same fate awaited the boys if they followed the example of the foolish Mexicans.

Hobbs had excellent sense and judgment, and he knew that it would be the height of folly for him and Baptiste, mere boys, to try and reach either Bent's Fort or the Missouri River, not having the slightest knowledge of where they were situated.

Hobbs grew to be a great favourite with the Comanches; was given the daughter of Old Wolf in marriage, became a great chief, fought many hard battles with his savage companions, and at last, four years after, was redeemed by Colonel Bent, who paid Old Wolf a small ransom for him at the Fort, where the Indians had come to trade. Baptiste, whom the Indians never took a great fancy to, because he did not develop into a great warrior, was also ransomed by Bent, his price being only an antiquated mule.

At Bent's Fort Hobbs went out trapping under the leadership of Kit Carson, and they became lifelong friends. In a short time Hobbs earned the reputation of being an excellent mountaineer, trapper, and as an Indian fighter he was second to none, his education among the Comanches having trained him in all the strategy of the savages.

After going through the Mexican War with an excellent record, Hobbs wandered about the country, now engaged in mining in old Mexico, then fighting the Apaches under the orders of the governor of Chihuahua, and at the end of the campaign going back to the Pacific coast, where he entered into new pursuits. Sometimes he was rich, then as poor as one can imagine. He returned to old Mexico in time to become an active partisan in the revolt which overthrew the short-lived dynasty of Maximilian, and was present at the execution of that unfortunate prince. Finally he retired to the home of his childhood in the States, where he died a few months ago, full of years and honours.

William F. Cody, "Buffalo Bill," is one of the famous plainsmen, of later days, however, than Carson, Bridger, John Smith, Maxwell, and others whom I have mentioned. The mantle of Kit Carson, perhaps, fits more perfectly the shoulders of Cody than those of any other of the great frontiersman's successors, and he has had some experiences that surpassed anything which fell to their lot.

He was born in Iowa, in 1845, and when barely seven years old his father emigrated to Kansas, then far remote from civilization.

Thirty-six years ago, he was employed as guide and scout in an expedition against the Kiowas and Comanches, and his line of duty took him along the Santa Fe Trail all one summer when not out as a scout, carrying despatches between Fort Lyon and Fort Larned, the most important military posts on the great highway as well as to far-off Fort Leavenworth on the Missouri River, the headquarters of the department. Fort Larned was the general rendezvous of all the scouts on the Kansas and Colorado plains, the chief of whom was a veteran interpreter and guide, named Dick Curtis.

When Cody first reported there for his responsible duty, a large camp of the Kiowas and Comanches was established within sight of the fort, whose warriors had not as yet put on their war-paint, but were evidently restless and discontented under the restraint of their chiefs. Soon those leading men, Satanta, Lone Wolf, Satank, and others of lesser note, grew rather impudent and haughty in their deportment, and they were watched with much concern. The post was garrisoned by only two companies of infantry and one of cavalry.

General Hazen, afterward chief of the signal service in Washington, was at Fort Larned at the time, endeavouring to patch up a peace with the savages, who seemed determined to break out. Cody was special scout to the general, and one morning he was ordered to accompany him as far as Fort Zarah, on the Arkansas, near the mouth of Walnut Creek, in what is now Barton County, Kansas, the general intending to go on to Fort Harker, on the Smoky Hill. In making these trips of inspection, with incidental collateral duties, the general usually travelled in an ambulance, but on this journey he rode in a six-mule army-wagon, escorted by a detachment of a score of infantry. It was a warm August day, and an early start was made, which enabled them to reach Fort Zarah, over thirty miles distant, by noon. After dinner, the general proposed to go on to Fort Harker, forty-one miles away, without any escort, leaving orders for Cody to return to Fort Larned the next day, with the soldiers. But Cody, ever impatient of delay when there was work to do, notified the sergeant in charge of the men that he was going back that very afternoon. I tell the story of his trip as he has often told it to me, and as he has written it in his autobiography.

"I accordingly saddled up my mule and set out for Fort Larned. I proceeded on uninterruptedly until I got about halfway between the two posts, when, at Pawnee Rock, I was suddenly jumped by about forty Indians, who came dashing up to me, extending their hands and saying, 'How! How!' They were some of the Indians who had been hanging around Fort Larned in the morning. I saw they had on their war-paint, and were evidently now out on the war-path.

"My first impulse was to shake hands with them, as they seemed so desirous of it. I accordingly reached out my hand to one of them, who grasped it with a tight grip, and jerked me violently forward; then pulled my mule by the bridle, and in a moment I was completely surrounded. Before I could do anything at all, they had seized my revolvers from the holsters, and I received a blow on the head from a tomahawk which nearly rendered me senseless. My gun, which was lying across the saddle, was snatched from its place, and finally the Indian who had hold of the bridle started off toward the Arkansas River, leading the mule, which was being lashed by the other Indians, who were following. The savages were all singing, yelling, and whooping, as only Indians can do, when they are having their little game all their own way. While looking toward the river, I saw on the opposite side an immense village moving along the bank, and then I became convinced that the Indians had left the post and were now starting out on the war-path. My captors crossed the stream with me, and as we waded through the shallow water they continued to lash the mule and myself. Finally they brought me before an important-looking body of Indians, who proved to be the chiefs and principal warriors. I soon recognized old Satanta among them, as well as others whom I knew, and supposed it was all over with me.

"The Indians were jabbering away so rapidly among themselves that I could not understand what they were saying. Satanta at last asked me where I had been. As good luck would have it, a happy thought struck me. I told him I had been after a herd of cattle, or 'whoa-haws,' as they called them. It so happened that the Indians had been out of meat for several weeks, as the large herd of cattle which had been promised them had not yet arrived, although they expected them.

"The moment I mentioned that I had been searching for 'whoa-haws,' old Satanta began questioning me in a very eager manner. He asked me where the cattle were, and I replied that they were back a few miles, and that I had been sent by General Hazen to inform him that the cattle were coming, and that they were intended for his people. This seemed to please the old rascal, who also wanted to know if there were any soldiers with the herd, and my reply was that there were. Thereupon the chiefs held a consultation, and presently Satanta asked me if General Hazen had really said that they should have the cattle. I replied in the affirmative, and added that I had been directed to bring the cattle to them. I followed this up with a very dignified inquiry,

245

asking why his young men had treated me so. The old wretch intimated that it was only a 'freak of the boys'; that the young men wanted to see if I was brave; in fact, they had only meant to test me, and the whole thing was a joke.

"The veteran liar was now beating me at my own game of lying, but I was very glad, as it was in my favour. I did not let him suspect that I doubted his veracity, but I remarked that it was a rough way to treat friends. He immediately ordered his young men to give back my arms, and scolded them for what they had done. Of course, the sly old dog was now playing it very fine, as he was anxious to get possession of the cattle, with which he believed there was a 'heap' of soldiers coming. He had concluded it was not best to fight the soldiers if he could get the cattle peaceably.

"Another council was held by the chiefs, and in a few minutes old Satanta came and asked me if I would go to the river and bring the cattle down to the opposite side, so that they could get them. I replied, 'Of course; that's my instruction from General Hazen.'

"Satanta said I must not feel angry at his young men, for they had only been acting in fun. He then inquired if I wished any of his men to accompany me to the cattle herd. I replied that it would be better for me to go alone, and then the soldiers could keep right on to Fort Larned, while I could drive the herd down on the bottom. Then wheeling my mule around, I was soon recrossing the river, leaving old Satanta in the firm belief that I had told him a straight story, and that I was going for the cattle which existed only in my imagination.

"I hardly knew what to do, but thought that if I could get the river between the Indians and myself, I would have a good three-quarters of a mile the start of them, and could then make a run for Fort Larned, as my mule was a good one.

"Thus far my cattle story had panned out all right; but just as I reached the opposite bank of the river, I looked behind me and saw that ten or fifteen Indians, who had begun to suspect something crooked, were following me. The moment that my mule secured a good foothold on the bank, I urged him into a gentle lope toward the place where, according to my statement, the cattle were to be brought. Upon reaching a little ridge and riding down the other side out of view, I turned my mule and headed him westward for Fort Larned. I let him out for all that he was worth, and when I came out on a little rise of ground, I looked back and saw the Indian village in plain sight. My pursuers were now on the ridge which I had passed over, and were looking for me in every direction.

"Presently they spied me, and seeing that I was running away, they struck out in swift pursuit, and in a few minutes it became painfully evident they were gaining on me. They kept up the chase as far as Ash Creek, six miles from Fort Larned. I still led them half a mile, as their horses had not gained much during the last half of the

246

race. My mule seemed to have gotten his second wind, and as I was on the old road, I played the spurs and whip on him without much cessation; the Indians likewise urged their steeds to the utmost.

"Finally, upon reaching the dividing ridge between Ash Creek and Pawnee Fork, I saw Fort Larned only four miles away. It was now sundown, and I heard the evening gun. The troops of the small garrison little dreamed there was a man flying for his life and trying to reach the post. The Indians were once more gaining on me, and when I crossed the Pawnee Fork two miles from the post, two or three of them were only a quarter of a mile behind me. Just as I gained the opposite bank of the stream, I was overjoyed to see some soldiers in a government wagon only a short distance off. I yelled at the top of my voice, and riding up to them, told them that the Indians were after me.

"'Denver Jim,' a well-known scout, asked me how many there were, and upon my informing him that there were about a dozen, he said: 'Let's drive the wagon into the trees, and we'll lay for 'em.' The team was hurriedly driven among the trees and low box-elder bushes, and there secreted.

"We did not have to wait long for the Indians, who came dashing up, lashing their ponies, which were panting and blowing. We let two of them pass by, but we opened a lively fire on the next three or four, killing two of them at the first crack. The others following discovered that they had run into an ambush, and whirling off into the brush, they turned and ran back in the direction whence they had come. The two who had passed by heard the firing and made their escape. We scalped the two that we had killed, and appropriated their arms and equipments; then, catching their ponies, we made our way into the Post."

CHAPTER XVIII.

MAXWELL'S RANCH.

One of the most interesting and picturesque regions of all New Mexico is the immense tract of nearly two million acres known as Maxwell's Ranch, through which the Old Trail ran, and the title to which was some years since determined by the Supreme Court of the United States in favour of an alien company.[59] Dead long ago, Maxwell belonged to a generation and a class almost completely extinct, and the like of which will, in all probability, never be seen again; for there is no more frontier to develop them.

Several years prior to the acquisition of the territory by the United States, the immense tract comprised in the geographical limits of the ranch was granted to Carlos Beaubien and Guadalupe Miranda, both citizens of the province of New Mexico, and agents of the American Fur Company. Attached to the company as an employer, a trapper, and hunter, was Lucien B. Maxwell, an Illinoisan by birth, who married a daughter of Beaubien. After the death of the latter Maxwell purchased all the interest of the joint proprietor, Miranda, and that of the heirs of Beaubien, thus at once becoming the largest landowner in the United States.

At the zenith of his influence and wealth, during the War of the Rebellion, when New Mexico was isolated and almost independent of care or thought by the government at Washington, he lived in a sort of barbaric splendour, akin to that of the nobles of England at the time of the Norman conquest.

The thousands of arable acres comprised in the many fertile valleys of his immense estate were farmed in a primitive, feudal sort of way, by native Mexicans principally, under the system of peonage then existing in the Territory. He employed about five hundred men, and they were as much his thralls as were Gurth and Wamba of Cedric of Rotherwood, only they wore no engraved collars around their necks bearing their names and that of their master. Maxwell was not a hard governor, and his people really loved him, as he was ever their friend and adviser.

His house was a palace when compared with the prevailing style of architecture in that country, and cost an immense sum of money. It was large and roomy, purely American in its construction, but the manner of conducting it was strictly Mexican, varying between the customs of the higher and lower classes of that curious people.

Some of its apartments were elaborately furnished, others devoid of everything except a table for card-playing and a game's complement of chairs. The principal room, an extended rectangular affair, which might properly have been termed the Baronial Hall, was almost bare except for a few chairs, a couple of tables, and an antiquated bureau. There Maxwell received his friends, transacted business with his vassals, and held high carnival at times.

I have slept on its hardwood floor, rolled up in my blanket, with the mighty men of the Ute nation lying heads and points all around me, as close as they could possibly crowd, after a day's fatiguing hunt in the mountains. I have sat there in the long winter evenings, when the great room was lighted only by the cheerful blaze of the crackling logs roaring up the huge throats of its two fireplaces built diagonally across opposite corners, watching Maxwell, Kit Carson, and half a dozen chiefs silently interchange ideas in the wonderful sign language, until the glimmer of Aurora announced the advent of another day. But not a sound had been uttered during the protracted hours, save an occasional grunt of satisfaction on the part of the Indians, or when we white men exchanged a sentence.

Frequently Maxwell and Carson would play the game of seven-up for hours at a time, seated at one of the tables. Kit was usually the victor, for he was the greatest expert in that old and popular pastime I have ever met. Maxwell was an inveterate gambler, but not by any means in a professional sense; he indulged in the hazard of the cards simply for the amusement it afforded him in his rough life of ease, and he could very well afford the losses which the pleasure sometimes entailed. His special penchant, however, was betting on a horse race, and his own stud comprised some of the fleetest animals in the Territory. Had he lived in England he might have ruled the turf, but many jobs were put up on him by unscrupulous jockeys, by which he was outrageously defrauded of immense sums.

He was fond of cards, as I have said, both of the purely American game of poker, and also of old sledge, but rarely played except with personal friends, and never without stakes. He always exacted the last cent he had won, though the next morning, perhaps, he would present or loan his unsuccessful opponent of the night before five hundred or a thousand dollars, if he needed it; an immensely greater sum, in all probability, than had been gained in the game.

The kitchen and dining-rooms of his princely establishment were detached from the main residence. There was one of the latter for the male portion of his retinue and guests of that sex, and another for the female, as, in accordance with the severe, and to us strange, Mexican etiquette, men rarely saw a woman about the premises, though there were many. Only the quick rustle of a skirt, or a hurried view of a reboso, as its wearer flashed for an instant before some window or half-open door, told of their presence.

The greater portion of his table-service was solid silver, and at his hospitable board there were rarely any vacant chairs. Covers were laid daily for about thirty persons; for he had always many guests, invited or forced upon him in consequence of his proverbial munificence, or by the peculiar location of his manor-house which stood upon a magnificently shaded plateau at the foot of mighty mountains, a short distance from a ford on the Old Trail. As there were no bridges over the uncertain streams of the great overland route in those days, the ponderous Concord coaches, with their ever-full burden of passengers, were frequently water-bound, and Maxwell's the only asylum from the storm and flood; consequently he entertained many.

At all times, and in all seasons, the group of buildings, houses, stables, mill, store, and their surrounding grounds, were a constant resort and loafing-place of Indians. From the superannuated chiefs, who revelled lazily during the sunny hours in the shady peacefulness of the broad porches; the young men of the tribe, who gazed with covetous eyes upon the sleek-skinned, blooded colts sporting in the spacious corrals; the squaws, fascinated by the gaudy calicoes, bright ribbons, and glittering strings of beads on the counters or shelves of the large store, to the half-naked, chubby little pappooses around the kitchen doors, waiting with expectant mouths for some delicious morsel of refuse to be thrown to them--all assumed, in bearing and manner, a vested right of proprietorship in their agreeable environment.

To this motley group, always under his feet, as it were, Maxwell was ever passively gracious, although they were battening in idleness on his prodigal bounty from year to year.

His retinue of servants, necessarily large, was made up of a heterogeneous mixture of Indians, Mexicans, and half-breeds. The kitchens were presided over by dusky maidens under the tutelage of experienced old crones, and its precincts were sacred to them; but the dining-rooms were forbidden to women during the hours of meals, which were served by boys.

Maxwell was rarely, as far as my observation extended, without a large amount of money in his possession. He had no safe, however, his only place of temporary deposit for the accumulated cash being the bottom drawer of the old bureau in the large room to which I have referred, which was the most antiquated concern of common pine imaginable. There were only two other drawers in this old-fashioned piece of furniture, and neither of them possessed a lock. The third, or lower, the one that contained the money, did, but it was absolutely worthless, being one of the cheapest pattern and affording not the slightest security; besides, the drawers above it could be pulled out, exposing the treasure immediately beneath to the cupidity of any one.

I have frequently seen as much as thirty thousand dollars--gold, silver, greenbacks, and government checks--at one time in that novel depository. Occasionally these large sums remained there for several days, yet there was never any extra precaution taken to prevent its abstraction; doors were always open and the room free of access to every one, as usual.

I once suggested to Maxwell the propriety of purchasing a safe for the better security of his money, but he only smiled, while a strange, resolute look flashed from his dark eyes, as he said: "God help the man who attempted to rob me and I knew him!"

The sources of his wealth were his cattle, sheep, and the products of his area of cultivated acres--barley, oats, and corn principally-- which he disposed of to the quartermaster and commissary departments of the army, in the large military district of New Mexico. His wool-clip must have been enormous, too; but I doubt whether he could have told the number of animals that furnished it or the aggregate of his vast herds. He had a thousand horses, ten thousand cattle, and forty thousand sheep at the time I knew him well, according to the best estimates of his Mexican relatives.

He also possessed a large and perfectly appointed gristmill, which was a great source of revenue, for wheat was one of the staple crops of his many farms.

Maxwell was fond of travelling all over the Territory, his equipages comprising everything in the shape of a vehicle, through all their varieties, from the most plainly constructed buckboard to the lumbering, but comfortable and expensive, Concord coach, mounted on thorough braces instead of springs, and drawn by four or six horses. He was perfectly reckless in his driving, dashing through streams, over irrigating ditches, stones, and stumps like a veritable Jehu, regardless of consequences, but, as is usually the fortune of such precipitate horsemen, rarely coming to grief.

The headquarters of the Ute agency were established at Maxwell's Ranch in early days, and the government detailed a company of cavalry to camp there, more, however, to impress the plains tribes who roamed along the Old Trail east of the Raton Range, than for any effect on the Utes, whom Maxwell could always control, and who regarded him as a father.

On the 4th of July, 1867, Maxwell, who owned an antiquated and rusty six-pound field howitzer, suggested to the captain of the troop stationed there the propriety of celebrating the day. So the old piece was dragged from its place under a clump of elms, where it had been hidden in the grass and weeds ever since the Mexican War probably, and brought near the house. The captain and Maxwell acted the role of gunners, the former at the muzzle, the latter at the breech; the discharge was premature, blowing out the captain's eye and taking off his arm, while Maxwell escaped with a shattered thumb. As soon as the accident occurred, a sergeant was despatched to Fort Union on one of the fastest horses on the ranch, the faithful animal falling dead the moment he stopped in front of the surgeon's quarters, having made the journey of fifty-five miles in little more than four hours.

The surgeon left the post immediately, arriving at Maxwell's late that night, but in time to save the officer's life, after which he dressed Maxwell's apparently inconsiderable wound. In a few days, however, the thumb grew angry-looking; it would not yield to the doctor's careful treatment, so he reluctantly decided that amputation was necessary. After an operation was determined upon, I prevailed upon Maxwell to come to the fort and remain with me, inviting Kit Carson at the same time, that he might assist in catering to the amusement of my suffering guest. Maxwell and Carson arrived at my quarters late in the day, after a tedious ride in the big coach, and the surgeon, in order to allow a prolonged rest on account of Maxwell's feverish condition, postponed the operation until the following evening.

The next night, as soon as it grew dark--we waited for coolness, as the days were excessively hot--the necessary preliminaries were arranged, and when everything was ready the surgeon commenced. Maxwell declined the anaesthetic prepared for him, and sitting in a common office chair put out his hand, while Carson and myself stood on opposite sides, each holding an ordinary kerosene lamp. In a few seconds the operation was concluded, and after the silver-wire ligatures were twisted in their places, I offered Maxwell, who had not as yet permitted a single sigh to escape his lips, half a tumblerful of whiskey; but before I had fairly put it to his mouth, he fell over, having fainted dead away, while great beads of perspiration stood on his forehead, indicative of the pain he had suffered, as the amputation of the thumb, the surgeon told us then, was as bad as that of a leg.

He returned to his ranch as soon as the surgeon pronounced him well, and Carson to his home in Taos. I saw the latter but once more at Maxwell's; but he was en route to visit me at Fort Harker, in Kansas, when he was taken ill at Fort Lyon, where he died.

A boy's will is the wind's will,
And the thoughts of youth are long, long thoughts.

How true it now seems to me, as the recollections of my boyish days, when I read of the exploits of Kit Carson, crowd upon my memory! I firmly believed him to be at least ten feet tall, carrying a rifle so heavy that, like Bruce's sword, it required two men to lift it. I imagined he drank out of nothing smaller than a river, and picked the carcass of a whole buffalo as easily as a lady does the wing of a quail. Ten years later I made the acquaintance of the foremost frontiersman, and found him a delicate, reticent, under-sized, wiry man, as perfectly the opposite of the type my childish brain had created as it is possible to conceive.

At Fort Union our mail arrived every morning by coach over the Trail, generally pulling up at the sutler's store, whose proprietor was postmaster, about daylight. While Maxwell and Kit were my guests, I sauntered down after breakfast one morning to get my mail, and while waiting for the letters to be distributed, happened to glance at some papers lying on the counter, among which I saw a new periodical --the *Day's Doings*, I think it was--that had a full-page illustration of a scene in a forest. In the foreground stood a gigantic figure dressed in the traditional buckskin; on one arm rested an immense rifle; his other arm was around the waist of the conventional female of such sensational journals, while in front, lying prone upon the ground, were half a dozen Indians, evidently slain by the singular hero in defending the impossibly attired female. The legend related how all this had been effected by the famous Kit Carson. I purchased the paper, returned with it to my room, and after showing it to several officers who had called upon Maxwell, I handed it to Kit. He wiped his spectacles, studied the picture intently for a few seconds, turned round, and said: "Gentlemen, that thar may be true, but I hain't got no recollection of it."

I passed a delightful two weeks with Maxwell, late in the summer of 1867, at the time that the excitement over the discovery of gold on his ranch had just commenced, and adventurers were beginning to congregate in the hills and gulches from everywhere. The discovery of the precious metal on his estate was the first cause of his financial embarrassment. It was the ruin also of many other prominent men in New Mexico, who expended their entire fortune in the construction of an immense ditch, forty miles in length--from the Little Canadian or Red River--to supply the placer diggings in the Moreno valley with water, when the melted snow of Old Baldy range had exhausted itself in the late summer. The scheme was a stupendous failure; its ruins may be seen to-day in the deserted valleys, a monument to man's engineering skill, but the wreck of his hopes.

For some years previous to the discovery of gold in the mountains and gulches of Maxwell's Ranch, it was known that copper existed in the region; several shafts had been sunk and tunnels driven in various places, and gold had been found from time to time, but was kept a secret for many months. Its presence was at last revealed to Maxwell by a party of his own miners, who were boring into the heart of Old Baldy for a copper lead that had cropped out and was then lost.

Of course, to keep the knowledge of the discovery of gold from the world is an impossibility; such was the case in this instance, and soon commenced that squatter immigration out of which, after the ranch was sold and Maxwell died, grew that litigation which has resulted in favour of the company who purchased from or through the first owners after Maxwell's death.

He was a representative man of the border of the same class as his compeers--"wild-civilized men," to borrow an expressive term from John Burroughs--of strong local attachments, and overflowing with the milk of human kindness. To such as he there was an unconquerable infatuation in life on the remote plains and in the solitude of the mountains. There was never anything of the desperado in their character, while the adventurers who at times have made the far West infamous, since the advent of the railroad, were bad men originally.

Occasionally such men turn up everywhere, and become a terror to the community, but they are always wound up sooner or later; they die with their boots on; Western graveyards are full of them.

Maxwell, under contract with the Interior Department, furnished live beeves to the Ute nation, the issue of which was made weekly from his own vast herds. The cattle, as wild as those from the Texas prairies, were driven by his herders into an immense enclosed field, and there turned loose to be slaughtered by the savages.

Once when at the ranch I told Maxwell I should like to have a horse to witness the novel sight. He immediately ordered a Mexican groom to procure one; but I did not see the peculiar smile that lighted up his face, as he whispered something to the man which I did not catch. Presently the groom returned leading a magnificent gray, which I mounted, Maxwell suggesting that I should ride down to the large field and wait there until the herd arrived. I entered the great corral, patting my horse on the neck now and then, to make him familiar with my touch, and attempted to converse with some of the chiefs, who were dressed in their best, painted as if for the war-path, gaily bedecked with feathers and armed with rifles and gaudily appointed bows and arrows; but I did not succeed very well in drawing them from their normal reticence. The squaws, a hundred of them, were sitting on the ground, their knives in hand ready for the labour which is the fate of their sex in all savage tribes, while their lords' portion of the impending business was to end with the more manly efforts of the chase.

Suddenly a great cloud of dust rose on the trail from the mountains, and on came the maddened animals, fairly shaking the earth with their mighty tread. As soon as the gate was closed behind them, and uttering a characteristic yell that was blood-curdling in its ferocity, the Indians charged upon the now doubly frightened herd, and commenced to discharge their rifles, regardless of the presence of any one but themselves. My horse became paralyzed for an instant and stood poised on his hind legs, like the steed represented in that old lithographic print of Napoleon crossing the Alps; then taking the bit in his teeth, he rushed aimlessly into the midst of the flying herd, while the bullets from the guns of the excited savages rained around my head. I had always boasted of my equestrian accomplishments--I was never thrown but once in my life, and that was years afterward--but in this instance it taxed all my powers to keep my seat. In less than twenty minutes the last beef had fallen; and the warriors, inflated with the pride of their achievement, rode silently out of the field, leaving the squaws to cut up and carry away the meat to their lodges, more than three miles distant, which they soon accomplished, to the last quivering morsel.

As I rode leisurely back to the house, I saw Maxwell and Kit standing on the broad porch, their sides actually shaking with laughter at my discomfiture, they having been watching me from the very moment the herd entered the corral. It appeared that the horse Maxwell ordered the groom to bring me was a recent importation from St. Louis, had never before seen an Indian, and was as unused to the prairies and mountains as a street-car mule. Kit said that my mount reminded him of one that his antagonist in a duel rode a great many years ago when he was young. If the animal had not been such "a fourth-of-July" brute, his opponent would in all probability have finished him, as he was a splendid shot; but Kit fortunately escaped, the bullet merely grazing him under the ear, leaving a scar which he then showed me.

One night Kit Carson, Maxwell, and I were up in the Raton Mountains above the Old Trail, and having lingered too long, were caught above the clouds against our will, darkness having overtaken us before we were ready to descend into the valley. It was dangerous to undertake the trip over such a precipitous and rocky trail, so we were compelled to make the best of our situation. It was awfully cold, and as we had brought no blankets, we dared not go to sleep for fear our fire might go out, and we should freeze. We therefore determined to make a night of it by telling yarns, smoking our pipes, and walking around at times. After sitting awhile, Maxwell pointed toward the Spanish Peaks, whose snow-white tops cast a diffused light in the heavens above them, and remarked that in the deep canyon which separates them, he had had one of the "closest calls" of his life, willingly complying when I asked him to tell us the story.

"It was in 1847. I came down from Taos with a party to go to the Cimarron crossing of the Santa Fe Trail to pick up a large herd of horses for the United States Quartermaster's Department. We succeeded in gathering about a hundred and started back with them, letting them graze slowly along, as we were in no hurry. When we arrived at the foot-hills north of Bent's Fort, we came suddenly upon the trail of a large war-band of Utes, none of whom we saw, but from subsequent developments the savages must have discovered us days before we reached the mountains. I knew we were not strong enough to cope with the whole Ute nation, and concluded the best thing for us to do under the ticklish circumstances was to make a detour, and put them off our trail. So we turned abruptly down the Arkansas, intending to try and get to Taos in that direction, more than one hundred and fifty miles around. It appeared afterward that the Indians had been following us all the way. When we found this out, some of the men believed they were another party, and not the same whose trail we came upon when we turned down the river, but I always insisted they were. When we arrived within a few days' drive of Taos, we were ambushed in one of the narrow passes of the range, and had the bloodiest fight with the Utes on record. There were thirteen of us, all told, and two little children whom we were escorting to their friends at Taos, having received them at the Cimarron crossing.

"While we were quietly taking our breakfast one morning, and getting ready to pull out for the day's march, perfectly unsuspicious of the proximity of any Indians, they dashed in upon us, and in less than a minute stampeded all our stock--loose animals as well as those we were riding. While part of the savages were employed in running off the animals, fifty of their most noted warriors, splendidly mounted and horribly painted, rushed into the camp, around the fire of which the men and the little children were peacefully sitting, and, discharging their guns as they rode up, killed one man and wounded another.

"Terribly surprised as we were, it did not turn the heads of the old mountaineers, and I immediately told them to make a break for a clump of timber near by, and that we would fight them as long as one of us could stand up. There we fought and fought against fearful odds, until all were wounded except two. The little children were captured at the beginning of the trouble and carried off at once. After a while the savages got tired of the hard work, and, as is frequently the case, went away of their own free will; but they left us in a terrible plight. All were sore, stiff, and weak from their many wounds; on foot, and without any food or ammunition to procure game with, having exhausted our supply in the awfully unequal battle; besides, we were miles from home, with every prospect of starving to death.

"We could not remain where we were, so as soon as darkness came on, we started out to walk to some settlement. We dared not show ourselves by daylight, and all through the long hours when the sun was up, we were obliged to hide in the brush and ravines until night overtook us again, and we could start on our painful march.

"We had absolutely nothing to eat, and our wounds began to fester, so that we could hardly move at all. We should undoubtedly have perished, if, on the third day, a band of friendly Indians of another tribe had not gone to Taos and reported the fight to the commanding officer of the troops there. These Indians had heard of our trouble with the Utes, and knowing how strong they were, and our weakness, surmised our condition, and so hastened to convey the bad news.

"A company of dragoons was immediately sent to our rescue, under the guidance of Dick Wooton, who was and has ever been a warm personal friend of mine. They came upon us about forty miles from Taos, and never were we more surprised; we had become so starved and emaciated that we had abandoned all hope of escaping what seemed to be our inevitable fate.

"When the troops found us, we had only a few rags, our clothes having been completely stripped from our bodies while struggling through the heavy underbrush on our trail, and we were so far exhausted that we could not stand on our feet. One more day, and we would have been laid out.

"The little children were, fortunately, saved from the horror of that terrible march after the fight, as the Indians carried them to their winter camp, where, if not absolutely happy, they were under shelter and fed; escaping the starvation which would certainly have been their fate if they had remained with us. They were eventually ransomed for a cash payment by the government, and altogether had not been very harshly treated."

CHAPTER XIX.

BENT'S FORTS.

The famous Bent brothers, William, George, Robert, and Charles, were French-Canadian hunters and trappers, and had been employed almost from boyhood, in the early days of the border, by the American Fur Company in the mountains of the Northwest.

In 1826, almost immediately after the transference of the fur trade to the valley of the Arkansas, when the commerce of the prairies was fairly initiated, the three Bents and Ceran St. Vrain, also a French-Canadian and trapper, settled on the Upper Arkansas, where they erected a stockade. It was, of course, a rude affair, formed of long stakes or pickets driven into the ground, after the Mexican style known as jacal. The sides were then ceiled and roofed, and it served its purpose of a trading-post. This primitive fort was situated on the left or north bank of the river, about halfway between Pueblo and Canyon City, those beautiful mountain towns of to-day.

Two years afterward, in 1828, the proprietors of the primitive stockade in the remote wilderness found it necessary to move closer to the great hunting-grounds lower down the valley. There, about twelve miles northeast of the now thriving town of Las Animas, the Bents commenced the construction of a relatively large and more imposing-looking structure than the first. The principal material used in the new building, or rather in its walls, was adobe, or sun-dried brick, so common even to-day in New Mexican architecture. Four years elapsed before the new fort was completed, during which period its owners, like other trappers, lived in tents or teepees fashioned of buffalo-skins, after the manner of the Indians.

When at last the new station was completed, it was named Fort William, in honour of Colonel William Bent, who was the leader of the family and the most active trader among the four partners in the concern. The colonel frequently made long trips to the remote villages of the Arapahoes, Cheyennes, Kiowas, and Comanches, which were situated far to the south and east, on the Canadian River and its large tributaries. His miscellaneous assortment of merchandise he transported upon pack-mules to the Indian rendezvous, bringing back to the fort the valuable furs he had exchanged for the goods so eagerly coveted by the savages. It was while on one of his trading expeditions to the Cheyenne nation that the colonel married a young squaw of that tribe, the daughter of the principal chief.

William Bent for his day and time was an exceptionally good man. His integrity, his truthfulness on all occasions, and his remarkable courage endeared him to the red and white man alike, and Fort William prospered wonderfully under his careful and just management. Both his brothers and St. Vrain had taken up their residence in Taos, and upon the colonel devolved the entire charge of the busy establishment. It soon became the most popular rendezvous of the mountaineers and trappers, and in its immediate vicinity several tribes of Indians took up their temporary encampment.

In 1852 Fort William was destroyed under the following strange circumstances: It appears that the United States desired to purchase it. Colonel Bent had decided upon a price--sixteen thousand dollars-- but the representatives of the War Department offered only twelve thousand, which, of course, Bent refused. Negotiations were still pending, when the colonel, growing tired of the red-tape and circumlocution of the authorities, and while in a mad mood, removed all his valuables from the structure, excepting some barrels of gunpowder, and then deliberately set fire to the old landmark. When the flames reached the powder, there was an explosion which threw down portions of the walls, but did not wholly destroy them. The remains of the once noted buildings stand to-day, melancholy relics of a past epoch.

In the same year the indefatigable and indomitable colonel determined upon erecting a much more important structure. He selected a site on the same side of the Arkansas, in the locality known as Big Timbers. Regarding this new venture, Colonel or Judge Moore of Las Animas, a son-in-law of William Bent, tells in a letter to the author of the history of Colorado the following facts:--

Leaving ten men in camp to get out stone for the new post,
Colonel Bent took a part of his outfit and went to a Kiowa
village, about two hundred miles southwest, and remained
there all winter, trading with the Kiowas and Comanches.
In the spring of 1853 he returned to Big Timbers, when
the construction of the new post was begun, and the work
continued until completed in the summer of 1854; and it
was used as a trading-post until the owner leased it to
the government in the autumn of 1859. Colonel Sedgwick had
been sent out to fight the Kiowas that year, and in the fall
a large quantity of commissary stores had been sent him.
Colonel Bent then moved up the river to a point just above
the mouth of the Purgatoire, and built several rooms of
cottonwood pickets, and there spent the winter. In the
spring of 1860, Colonel Sedgwick began the construction of
officers' buildings, company quarters, corrals, and stables,
all of stone, and named the place Fort Wise, in honour of
Governor Wise of Virginia. In 1861 the name was changed to

Fort Lyon, in honour of General Lyon, who was killed at the battle of Wilson Creek, Missouri. In the spring of 1866, the Arkansas River overflowed its banks, swept up into the fort, and, undermining the walls, rendered it untenable for military purposes. The camp was moved to a point twenty miles below, and the new Fort Lyon established. The old post was repaired, and used as a stage station by Barlow, Sanderson, and Company, who ran a mail, express, and passenger line between Kansas City and Santa Fe.

The contiguous region to Fort William was in the early days a famous hunting-ground. It abounded in nearly every variety of animal indigenous to the mountains and plains, among which were the panther --the so-called California lion of to-day-- the lynx, erroneously termed wild cat, white wolf, prairie wolf, silver-gray fox, prairie fox, antelope, buffalo, gray, grizzly and cinnamon bears, together with the common brown and black species, the red deer and the black-tail, the latter the finest venison in the world. Of birds there were wild turkeys, quail, and grouse, besides an endless variety of the smaller-sized families, not regarded as belonging to the domain of game in a hunter's sense. It was a veritable paradise, too, for the trappers. Its numerous streams and creeks were famous for beaver, otter, and mink.

Scarcely an acre of the surrounding area within the radius of hundreds of miles but has been the scene of many deadly encounters with the wily red man, stories of which are still current among the few old mountaineers yet living.

The fort was six hundred and fifty miles west of Fort Leavenworth, in latitude thirty-eight degrees and two minutes north, and longitude one hundred and three degrees and three minutes west, from Greenwich. The exterior walls of the fort, whose figure was that of a parallelogram, were fifteen feet high and four feet thick. It was a hundred and thirty-five feet wide and divided into various compartments. On the northwest and southeast corners were hexagonal bastions, in which were mounted a number of cannon. The walls of the building served as the walls of the rooms, all of which faced inwards on a plaza, after the general style of Mexican architecture. The roofs of the rooms were made of poles, on which was a heavy layer of dirt, as in the houses of native Mexicans to-day. The fort possessed a billiard table, that visitors might amuse themselves, and in the office was a small telescope with a fair range of seven miles.

The occupants of the far-away establishment, in its palmy days (for years it was the only building between Council Grove and the mountains), were traders, Indians, hunters, and French trappers, who were the employees of the great fur companies. Many of the latter had Indian wives. Later, after a stage line had been put in operation across the plains to Santa Fe, the fort was relegated to a mere station for the overland route, and with the march of civilization in its course westward, the trappers, hunters, and traders vanished from the once famous rendezvous.

The walls were loopholed for musketry, and the entrance to the plaza, or corral, was guarded by large wooden gates. During the war with Mexico, the fort was headquarters for the commissary department, and many supplies were stored there, though the troops camped below on the beautiful river-bottom. In the centre of the corral, in the early days when the place was a rendezvous of the trappers, a large buffalo-robe press was erected. When the writer first saw the famous fort, now over a third of a century ago, one of the cannon, that burst in firing a salute to General Kearney, could be seen half buried in the dirt of the plaza.

By barometrical measurements taken by the engineer officers of the army at different times, the height of Bent's Fort above the ocean level is approximately eight thousand nine hundred and fifty-eight feet, and the fall of the Arkansas River from the fort to the great bend of that stream, about three hundred and eleven miles east, is seven feet and four-tenths per mile.

It was in a relatively fair state of preservation thirty-three years ago, but now not a vestige of it remains, excepting perhaps a mound of dirt, the disintegration of the mud bricks of which the historical structure was built.

The Indians whose villages were located a few miles below the fort, or at least the chief men of the various tribes, passed much of their time within the shelter of the famous structure. They were bountifully fed, and everything they needed furnished them. This was purely from policy, however; for if their wishes were not gratified, their hunters would not bring in their furs to trade. The principal chiefs never failed to be present when a meal was announced as ready, and however scarce provisions might be, the Indians must be fed.

The first farm in the fertile and now valuable lands of the valley of the Rio de las Animas[60] was opened by the Bents. The area selected for cultivation was in the beautiful bottom between the fort and the ford, a strip about a mile in length, and from one hundred and fifty to six hundred feet in width. Nothing could be grown without irrigation, and to that end an acequia, as the Mexicans call the ditch through which the water flows, was constructed, and a crop put in. Before the enterprising projectors of the scheme could reap a harvest, the hostile savages dashed in and destroyed everything.

Uncle John Smith was one of the principal traders back in the '30's, and he was very successful, perhaps because he was undoubtedly the most perfect master of the Cheyenne language at that time in the whole mountain region.

Among those who frequently came to the fort were Kit Carson, L. B. Maxwell, Uncle Dick Wooton, Baptiste Brown, Jim Bridger, Old Bill Williams, James Beckwourth, Shawnee Spiebuck, Shawnee Jake --the latter two, noted Indian trappers--besides a host of others.

The majority of the old trappers, to a stranger, until he knew their peculiar characteristics, were seemingly of an unsociable disposition. It was an erroneous idea, however, for they were the most genial companions imaginable, generous to a fault, and to fall into one of their camps was indeed a lucky thing for the lost traveller. Everything the host had was at his guest's disposal, and though coffee and sugar were the dearest of his luxuries, often purchased with a whole season's trapping, the black fluid was offered with genuine free-heartedness, and the last plug of tobacco placed at the disposition of his chance visitor, as though it could be picked up on the ground anywhere.

Goods brought by the traders to the rendezvous for sale to the trappers and hunters, although of the most inferior quality, were sold at enormously high prices.

Coffee, by the pint-cup, which was the usual measure for everything, cost from a dollar and twenty cents to three dollars; tobacco a dollar and a half a plug; alcohol from two dollars to five dollars a pint; gunpowder one dollar and sixty cents a pint-cup, and all other articles at proportionably exorbitant rates.

The annual gatherings of the trappers at the rendezvous were often the scene of bloody duels; for over their cups and cards no men were more quarrelsome than the old-time mountaineers. Rifles at twenty paces settled all difficulties, and, as may be imagined, the fall of one or the other of the combatants was certain, or, as sometimes happened, both fell at the word "Fire!"

The trapper's visits to the Mexican settlements, or to the lodges of a tribe of Indians, for the purpose of trading, often resulted in his returning to his quiet camp with a woman to grace his solitary home, the loving and lonely couple as devoted to each other in the midst of blood-thirsty enemies, howling wolves, and panthers, as if they were in some quiet country village.

The easy manners of the harum-scarum, reckless trappers at the rendezvous, and the simple, unsuspecting hearts of those nymphs of the mountains, the squaws, caused their husbands to be very jealous of the attentions bestowed upon them by strangers. Often serious difficulties arose, in the course of which the poor wife received a severe whipping with the knot of a lariat, or no very light lodge-poling at the hands of her imperious sovereign. Sometimes the affair ended in a more tragical way than a mere beating, not infrequently the gallant paying the penalty of his interference with his life.

Garrard, a traveller on the great plains and in the Rocky Mountains half a century ago, from whose excellent diary I have frequently quoted, passed many days and nights at Bent's Fort fifty years ago, and his quaint description of life there in that remote period of the extreme frontier is very amusing. Its truth has often been confirmed by Uncle John Smith, who was my guide and interpreter in the Indian expedition of 1868-69, only two decades after Garrard's experience.

Rosalie, a half-breed French and Indian squaw, wife of the carpenter, and Charlotte, the culinary divinity, were, as a Missouri teamster remarked, "the only female women here." They were nightly led to the floor to trip the light fantastic toe, and swung rudely or gently in the mazes of the contra-dance, but such a medley of steps is seldom seen out of the mountains--the halting, irregular march of the war-dance, the slipping gallopade, the boisterous pitching of the Missouri backwoodsman, and the more nice gyrations of the Frenchman; for all, irrespective of rank, age, or colour, went pell-mell into the excitement, in a manner that would have rendered a leveller of aristocracies and select companies frantic with delight. And the airs assumed by the fair ones, more particularly Charlotte, who took pattern from life in the States, were amusing. She acted her part to perfection; she was the centre of attraction, the belle of the evening. She treated the suitors for the pleasure of the next set with becoming ease and suavity of manner; she knew her worth, and managed accordingly. When the favoured gallant stood by her side waiting for the rudely scraped tune from a screeching fiddle, satisfaction, joy, and triumph over his rivals were pictured on his radiant face.

James Hobbs, of whom I have already spoken, once gave me a graphic description of the annual feast of the Comanches, Cheyennes, and Arapahoes, which always took place at Big Timbers, near Fort William.

Hobbs was married to the daughter of Old Wolf, the chief of the Comanches, a really beautiful Indian girl, with whom he lived faithfully many years. In the early summer of 1835, he went with his father-in-law and the rest of the tribe to the great feast of that season. He stated that on that occasion there were forty thousand Indians assembled, and consequently large hunting parties were sent out daily to procure food for such a vast host. The entertainment was kept up for fifteen days, enlivened by horse races, foot races, and playing ball. In these races the tribes would bet their horses on the result, the Comanches generally winning, for they are the best riders in the world. By the time the feast was ended, the Arapahoes and Cheyennes usually found themselves afoot, but Old Wolf, who was a generous fellow, always gave them back enough animals to get home with.

The game of ball was played with crooked sticks, and is very much like the American boys' "shinny." The participants are dressed in a simple breech-cloth and moccasins. It is played with great enthusiasm and affords much amusement.

At these annual feasts a council of the great chiefs of the three tribes is always held, and at the one during the season referred to, Hobbs said the Cheyenne chiefs wanted Old Wolf to visit Bent's Fort, where he had never been. Upon the arrival of the delegation there, it was heartily welcomed by all the famous men who happened to be at the place, among whom were Kit Carson, Old John Smith, and several noted trappers. Whiskey occupied a prominent place in the rejoicing, and "I found it hard work," said Hobbs, "to stand the many toasts drank to my good health." The whole party, including Old Wolf and his companion the Cheyenne chief, got very much elated, and every person in the fort smelt whiskey, if they did not get their feet tangled with it.

About midnight a messenger came inside, reporting that a thousand Comanche warriors were gathering around the fort. They demanded their leaders, fearing treachery, and desired to know why their chief had not returned. Hobbs went out and explained that he was safe; but they insisted on seeing him, so he and Hobbs showed themselves to the assembled Indians, and Old Wolf made a speech, telling them that he and the Cheyenne chief were among good friends to the Indians, and presents would be given to them the next morning. The warriors were pacified with these assurances, though they did not leave the vicinity of the fort.

It was at this time that Hobbs was ransomed by Colonel Bent, who gave Old Wolf, for him, six yards of red flannel, a pound of tobacco, and an ounce of beads.

The chief was taken in charge by a lieutenant, who showed him all over the fort, letting him see the rifle port-holes, and explaining how the place could stand a siege against a thousand Indians. Finally, he was taken out on the parapet, where there was a six-pounder at each angle. The old savage inquired how they could shoot such a thing, and at Hobbs' request, a blank cartridge was put in the piece and fired. Old Wolf sprang back in amazement, and the Indians on the outside, under the walls, knowing nothing of what was going on, ran away as fast as their legs could carry them, convinced that their chief must be dead now and their own safety dependent upon flight. Old Wolf and Hobbs sprang upon the wall and signalled and shouted to them, and they returned, asking in great astonishment what kind of a monstrous gun it was.

About noon trading commenced. The Indians wished to come into the fort, but Bent would not let any enter but the chiefs. At the back door the colonel displayed his goods, and the Indians brought forward their ponies, buffalo-robes, deer and other skins, which they traded for tobacco, beads, calico, flannel, knives, spoons, whistles, jews'-harps, etc.

Whiskey was sold to them the first day, but as it caused several fights among them before night, Bent stopped its sale, at Hobbs' suggestion and with Old Wolf's consent. Indians, when they get drunk, do not waste time by fighting with fists, like white men, but use knives and tomahawks; so that a general scrimmage is a serious affair. Two or three deaths resulted the first day, and there would have been many more if the sale of whiskey had not been stopped.

The trading continued for eight days, and Colonel Bent reaped a rich harvest of what he could turn into gold at St. Louis. Old Wolf slept in the fort each night except one during that time, and every time his warriors aroused him about twelve o'clock and compelled him to show himself on the walls to satisfy them of his safety.

About a hundred trappers were in the employ of Bent and his partners. Sometimes one-half of the company were off on a hunt, leaving but a small force at the fort for its protection, but with the small battery there its defence was considered sufficient.

One day a trapping party, consisting of Kit Carson, "Peg-leg" Smith, and James Hobbs, together with some Shawnee Indians, all under the lead of Carson, started out from Bent's Fort for the Picketwire to trap beaver.

Grizzlies were very abundant in that region then, and one of the party, named McIntire, having killed an elk the evening before, said to Hobbs that they might stand a good chance to find a grizzly by the elk he had shot but had not brought in. Hobbs said that he was willing to go with him, but as McIntire was a very green man in the mountains, Hobbs had some doubts of depending on him in case of an attack by a grizzly bear.

The two men left for the ravine in which McIntire had killed the elk very early in the morning, taking with them tomahawks, hunting-knives, rifles, and a good dog. On arriving at the ravine, Hobbs told McIntire to cross over to the other side and climb the hill, but on no account to go down into the ravine, as a grizzly is more dangerous when he has a man on the downhill side. Hobbs then went to where he thought the elk might be if he had died by the bank of the stream; but as soon as he came near the water, he saw that a large grizzly had got there before him, having scented the animal, and was already making his breakfast.

The bear was in thick, scrubby oak brush, and Hobbs, making his dog lie down, crawled behind a rock to get a favourable shot at the beast. He drew a bead on him and fired, but the bear only snarled at the wound made by the ball and started tearing through the brush, biting furiously at it as he went. Hobbs reloaded his rifle carefully, and as quickly as he could, in order to get a second shot; but, to his amazement, he saw the bear rushing down the ravine chasing McIntire, who was only about ten feet in advance of the enraged beast, running for his life, and making as much noise as a mad bull. He was terribly scared, and Hobbs hastened to his rescue, first sending his dog ahead.

Just as the dog reached the bear, McIntire darted behind a tree and flung his hat in the bear's face, at the same time sticking his rifle toward him. The old grizzly seized the muzzle of the gun in his teeth, and, as it was loaded and cocked, it either went off accidentally or otherwise and blew the bear's head open, just as the dog had fastened on his hindquarters. Hobbs ran to the assistance of his comrade with all haste, but he was out of danger and had sat down a few rods away, with his face as white as a sheet, a badly frightened man.

After that fearful scare, McIntire would cook or do anything, but said he never intended to make a business of bear-hunting; he had only wished for one adventure, and this one had satisfied him.

CHAPTER XX.

PAWNEE ROCK.

That portion of the great central plains which radiates from Pawnee Rock, including the Big Bend of the Arkansas, thirteen miles distant, where that river makes a sudden sweep to the southeast, and the beautiful valley of the Walnut, in all its vast area of more than a million square acres, was from time immemorial a sort of debatable land, occupied by none of the Indian tribes, but claimed by all to hunt in; for it was a famous pasturage of the buffalo.

None of the various bands had the temerity to attempt its permanent occupancy; for whenever hostile tribes met there, which was of frequent occurrence, in their annual hunt for their winter's supply of meat, a bloody battle was certain to ensue. The region referred to has been the scene of more sanguinary conflicts between the different Indians of the plains, perhaps, than any other portion of the continent. Particularly was it the arena of war to the death, when the Pawnees met their hereditary enemies, the Cheyennes.

Pawnee Rock was a spot well calculated by nature to form, as it has done, an important rendezvous and ambuscade for the prowling savages of the prairies, and often afforded them, especially the once powerful and murderous Pawnees whose name it perpetuates, a pleasant little retreat or eyrie from which to watch the passing Santa Fe traders, and dash down upon them like hawks, to carry off their plunder and their scalps.

Through this once dangerous region, close to the silent Arkansas, and running under the very shadow of the rock, the Old Trail wound its course. Now, at this point, it is the actual road-bed of the Atchison, Topeka, and Santa Fe Railroad, so strangely are the past and present transcontinental highways connected here.

Who, among bearded and grizzled old fellows like myself, has forgotten that most sensational of all the miserably executed illustrations in the geographies of fifty years ago, "The Santa Fe Traders attacked by Indians"? The picture located the scene of the fight at Pawnee Rock, which formed a sort of nondescript shadow in the background of a crudely drawn representation of the dangers of the Trail.

If this once giant sentinel[61] of the plains might speak, what a story it could tell of the events that have happened on the beautiful prairie stretching out for miles at its feet!

In the early fall, when the rock was wrapped in the soft amber haze which is a distinguishing characteristic of the incomparable Indian summer on the plains; or in the spring, when the mirage weaves its mysterious shapes, it loomed up in the landscape as if it were a huge mountain, and to the inexperienced eye appeared as if it were the abrupt ending of a well-defined range. But when the frost came, and the mists were dispelled; when the thin fringe of timber on the Walnut, a few miles distant, had doffed its emerald mantle, and the grass had grown yellow and rusty, then in the golden sunlight of winter, the rock sank down to its normal proportions, and cut the clear blue of the sky with sharply marked lines.

In the days when the Santa Fe trade was at its height, the Pawnees were the most formidable tribe on the eastern central plains, and the freighters and trappers rarely escaped a skirmish with them either at the crossing of the Walnut, Pawnee Rock, the Fork of the Pawnee, or at Little and Big Coon creeks. To-day what is left of the historic hill looks down only upon peaceful homes and fruitful fields, whereas for hundreds of years it witnessed nothing but battle and death, and almost every yard of brown sod at its base covered a skeleton. In place of the horrid yell of the infuriated savage, as he wrenched off the reeking scalp of his victim, the whistle of the locomotive and the pleasant whirr of the reaping-machine is heard; where the death-cry of the painted warrior rang mournfully over the silent prairie, the waving grain is singing in beautiful rhythm as it bows to the summer breeze.

Pawnee Rock received its name in a baptism of blood, but there are many versions as to the time and sponsors. It was there that Kit Carson killed his first Indian, and from that fight, as he told me himself, the broken mass of red sandstone was given its distinctive title.

It was late in the spring of 1826; Kit was then a mere boy, only seventeen years old, and as green as any boy of his age who had never been forty miles from the place where he was born. Colonel Ceran St. Vrain, then a prominent agent of one of the great fur companies, was fitting out an expedition destined for the far-off Rocky Mountains, the members of which, all trappers, were to obtain the skins of the buffalo, beaver, otter, mink, and other valuable fur-bearing animals that then roamed in immense numbers on the vast plains or in the hills, and were also to trade with the various tribes of Indians on the borders of Mexico.

Carson joined this expedition, which was composed of twenty-six mule wagons, some loose stock, and forty-two men. The boy was hired to help drive the extra animals, hunt game, stand guard, and to make himself generally useful, which, of course, included fighting Indians if any were met with on the long route.

The expedition left Fort Osage one bright morning in May in excellent spirits, and in a few hours turned abruptly to the west on the broad Trail to the mountains. The great plains in those early days were solitary and desolate beyond the power of description; the Arkansas River sluggishly followed the tortuous windings of its treeless banks with a placidness that was awful in its very silence; and whoso traced the wanderings of that stream with no companion but his own thoughts, realized in all its intensity the depth of solitude from which Robinson Crusoe suffered on his lonely island. Illimitable as the ocean, the weary waste stretched away until lost in the purple of the horizon, and the mirage created weird pictures in the landscape, distorted distances and objects which continually annoyed and deceived. Despite its loneliness, however, there was then, and ever has been for many men, an infatuation for those majestic prairies that once experienced is never lost, and it came to the boyish heart of Kit, who left them but with life, and full of years.

There was not much variation in the eternal sameness of things during the first two weeks, as the little train moved day after day through the wilderness of grass, its ever-rattling wheels only intensifying the surrounding monotony. Occasionally, however, a herd of buffalo was discovered in the distance, their brown, shaggy sides contrasting with the never-ending sea of verdure around them. Then young Kit, and two or three others of the party who were detailed to supply the teamsters and trappers with meat, would ride out after them on the best of the extra horses which were always kept saddled and tied together behind the last wagon for services of this kind. Kit, who was already an excellent horseman and a splendid shot with the rifle, would soon overtake them, and topple one after another of their huge fat carcasses over on the prairie until half a dozen or more were lying dead. The tender humps, tongues, and other choice portions were then cut out and put in a wagon which had by that time reached them from the train, and the expedition rolled on.

So they marched for about three weeks, when they arrived at the crossing of the Walnut, where they saw the first signs of Indians. They had halted for that day; the mules were unharnessed, the camp-fires lighted, and the men just about to indulge in their refreshing coffee, when suddenly half a dozen Pawnees, mounted on their ponies, hideously painted and uttering the most demoniacal yells, rushed out of the tall grass on the river-bottom, where they had been ambushed, and swinging their buffalo-robes, attempted to stampede the herd picketed near the camp. The whole party were on their feet in an instant with rifles in hand, and all the savages got for their trouble were a few well-deserved shots as they hurriedly scampered back to the river and over into the sand hills on the other side, soon to be out of sight.

The expedition travelled sixteen miles next day, and camped at Pawnee Rock, where, after the experience of the evening before, every precaution was taken to prevent a surprise by the savages. The wagons were formed into a corral, so that the animals could be secured in the event of a prolonged fight; the guards were drilled by the colonel, and every man slept with his rifle for a bed-fellow, for the old trappers knew that the Indians would never remain satisfied with their defeat on the Walnut, but would seize the first favourable opportunity to renew their attack.

At dark the sentinels were placed in position, and to young Kit fell the important post immediately in front of the south face of the Rock, nearly two hundred yards from the corral; the others being at prominent points on top, and on the open prairie on either side. All who were not on duty had long since been snoring heavily, rolled up in their blankets and buffalo-robes, when at about half-past eleven, one of the guard gave the alarm, "Indians!" and ran the mules that were nearest him into the corral. In a moment the whole company turned out at the report of a rifle ringing on the clear night air, coming from the direction of the rock. The men had gathered at the opening to the corral, waiting for developments, when Kit came running in, and as soon as he was near enough, the colonel asked him whether he had seen any Indians. "Yes," Kit replied, "I killed one of the red devils; I saw him fall!"

The alarm proved to be false; there was no further disturbance that night, so the party returned to their beds, and the sentinels to their several posts, Kit of course to his place in front of the Rock.

Early the next morning, before breakfast even, all were so anxious to see Kit's dead Indian, that they went out en masse to where he was still stationed, and instead of finding a painted Pawnee, as was expected, they found the boy's riding mule dead, shot right through the head.

Kit felt terribly mortified over his ridiculous blunder, and it was a long time before he heard the last of his midnight adventure and his raid on his own mule. But he always liked to tell the "balance of the story," as he termed it, and this is his version: "I had not slept any the night before, for I stayed awake watching to get a shot at the Pawnees that tried to stampede our animals, expecting they would return; and I hadn't caught a wink all day, as I was out buffalo hunting, so I was awfully tired and sleepy when we arrived at Pawnee Rock that evening, and when I was posted at my place at night, I must have gone to sleep leaning against the rocks; at any rate, I was wide enough awake when the cry of Indians was given by one of the guard. I had picketed my mule about twenty steps from where I stood, and I presume he had been lying down; all I remember is that the first thing I saw after the alarm was something rising up out of the grass, which I thought was an Indian. I pulled the trigger; it was a centre shot, and I don't believe the mule ever kicked after he was hit!"

The next morning about daylight, a band of Pawnees attacked the train in earnest, and kept the little command busy all that day, the next night, and until the following midnight, nearly three whole days, the mules all the time being shut in the corral without food or water. At midnight of the second day the colonel ordered the men to hitch up and attempt to drive on to the crossing of Pawnee Fork, thirteen miles distant.[62] They succeeded in getting there, fighting their way without the loss of any of their men or animals. The Trail crossed the creek in the shape of a horseshoe, or rather, in consequence of the double bend of the stream as it empties into the

Arkansas, the road crossed it twice. In making this passage, dangerous on account of its crookedness, Kit said many of the wagons were badly mashed up; for the mules were so thirsty that their drivers could not control them. The train was hardly strung out on the opposite bank when the Indians poured in a volley of bullets and a shower of arrows from both sides of the Trail; but before they could load and fire again, a terrific charge was on them, led by Colonel St. Vrain and Carson. It required only a few moments more to clean out the persistent savages, and the train went on. During the whole fight the little party lost four men killed and seven wounded, and eleven mules killed (not counting Kit's), and twenty badly wounded.

A great many years ago, very early in the days of the trade with New Mexico, seven Americans were surprised by a large band of Pawnees in the vicinity of the Rock and were compelled to retreat to it for safety. There, without water, and with but a small quantity of provisions, they were besieged by their blood-thirsty foes for two days, when a party of traders coming on the Trail relieved them from their perilous situation and the presence of their enemy. There were several graves on its summit when I first saw Pawnee Rock; but whether they contained the bones of savages or those of white men, I do not know.

Carson related to me another terrible fight that took place at the rock, when he first became a trapper. He was not a participant, but knew the parties well. About twenty-nine years ago, Kit, Jack Henderson, who was agent for the Ute Indians, Lucien B. Maxwell, General Carleton and myself were camped halfway up the rugged sides of Old Baldy, in the Raton Range. The night was intensely cold, although in midsummer, and we were huddled around a little fire of pine knots, more than seven thousand feet above the level of the sea, close to the snow limit.

Kit, or "the General," as every one called him, was in a good humour for talking, and we naturally took advantage of this to draw him out; for usually he was the most reticent of men in relating his own exploits. A casual remark made by Maxwell opened Carson's mouth, and he said he remembered one of the "worst difficults" a man ever got into.[63] So he made a fresh corn-shuck cigarette, and related the following; but the names of the old trappers who were the principals in the fight I have unfortunately forgotten.

Two men had been trapping in the Powder River country during one winter with unusually good luck, and they got an early start with their furs, which they were going to take to Weston, on the Missouri, one of the principal trading points in those days. They walked the whole distance, driving their pack-mules before them, and experienced no trouble until they struck the Arkansas valley at Pawnee Rock. There they were intercepted by a war-party of about sixty Pawnees. Both of the trappers were notoriously brave and both dead shots. Before they arrived at the rock, to which they were finally driven, they killed two of the Indians, and had not themselves received a scratch. They had plenty of powder, a pouch full of balls each, and two good rifles. They also had a couple of jack-rabbits for food in case of a siege, and the perpendicular walls of the front of the rock made them a natural fortification, an almost impregnable one against Indians.

They succeeded in securely picketing their animals at the side of the rock, where they could protect them by their unerring rifles from being stampeded. After the Pawnees had "treed" the two trappers on the rock, they picked up their dead, and packed them off to their camp at the mouth of a little ravine a short distance away. In a few moments back they all came, mounted on fast ponies, with their war-paint and other fixings on, ready to renew the fight. They commenced to circle around the place, coming closer, Indian fashion, every time, until they got within easy rifle-range, when they slung themselves on the opposite sides of their horses, and in that position opened fire. Their arrows fell like a hailstorm, but as good luck would have it, none of them struck, and the balls from their rifles were wild, as the Indians in those days were not very good shots; the rifle was a new weapon to them. The trappers at first were afraid the savages would surely try to kill the mules, but soon reflected that the Indians believed they had the "dead-wood" on them, and the mules would come handy after they had been scalped; so they felt satisfied their animals were safe for a while anyhow. The men were taking in all the chances, however; both kept their eyes skinned, and whenever one of them saw a stray leg or head, he drew a bead on it and when he pulled the trigger, its owner tumbled over with a yell of rage from his companions.

Whenever the savages attempted to carry off their dead,[64] the two trappers took advantage of the opportunity, and poured in their shots every time with telling effect.

By this time night had fallen, and the Indians did not seem anxious to renew the fight after dark; but they kept their mounted patrols on every side of the rock, at a respectable distance from such dead shots, watching to prevent the escape of the besieged. As they were hungry, one of the men went down under cover of the darkness to get a few buffalo-chips with which to cook their rabbit, and to change the animals to where they could get fresh grass. He returned safely to the summit of the rock, where a little fire was made and their supper prepared. They had to go without water all the time, and so did the mules; the men did not mind the want of it themselves, but they could not help pitying their poor animals that had had none since they left camp early that morning. It was no use to worry, though; the nearest water was at the river, and it would have been certain death to have attempted to go there unless the savages cleared out, and from all appearances they had no idea of doing that.

What gave the trappers more cause for alarm than anything else, was the fear that the Indians would fire the prairie in the morning, and endeavour to smoke them out or burn them up. The grass was in just the condition to make a lively blaze, and they might escape the flames, and then they might not. It can well be imagined how eagerly they watched for the dawn of another day, perhaps the last for them.

The first gray streaks of light had hardly peeped above the horizon, when, with an infernal yell, the Indians broke for the rock, and the trappers were certain that some new project had entered their heads. The wind was springing up pretty freshly, and nature seemed to conspire with the red devils, if they really meant to burn the trappers out; and from the movements of the savages, that was what they expected. The Indians kept at a respectful distance from the range of the trappers' rifles, who chafed because they could not stop some of the infernal yelling with a few well-directed bullets, but they had to choke their rage, and watch events closely. During a temporary lull in hostilities, one of the trappers took occasion to crawl down to where the mules were, and shift them to the west side of the rock, where the wall was the highest; so that the flame and smoke might possibly pass by them without so much danger as where they were picketed before. He had just succeeded in doing this, and, tearing up the long grass for several yards around the animals, was in the act of going back, when his partner yelled out to him: "Look out! D---n 'em, they've fired the prairie!" He was back on the top of the rock in another moment, and took in at a glance what was coming.

The spectacle for a short interval was indescribably grand; the sun was shining with all the power of its rays on the huge clouds of smoke as they rolled down from the north, tinting them a glorious crimson. The two trappers had barely time to get under the shelter of a large projecting point of the rocky wall, when the wind and smoke swept down to the ground, and instantly they were enveloped in the darkness of midnight. They could not discern a single object; neither Indians, horses, the prairie, nor the sun; and what a terrible wind!

The trappers stood breathless, clinging to the projections of rock, and did not realize the fire was so near them until they were struck in the face by pieces of burning buffalo-chips that were carried toward them with the rapidity of the awful wind. They were now badly scared, for it seemed as if they were to be suffocated. They were saved, however, almost miraculously; the sheet of flame passed them twenty yards away, as the wind fortunately shifted at the moment the fire reached the foot of the rock. The darkness was so intense that they did not discover the flame; they only knew that they were saved as the clear sky greeted them from behind the dense smoke-cloud.

Two of the Indians and their horses were caught in their own trap, and perished miserably. They had attempted to reach the east side of the rock, so as to steal around to the other side where the mules were, and either cut them loose or crawl up on the trappers while bewildered in the smoke and kill them, if they were not already dead. But they had proceeded only a few rods on their little expedition, when the terrible

273

darkness of the smoke-cloud overtook them and soon the flames, from which there was no possible escape.

All the game on the prairie which the fire swept over was killed too. Only a few buffalo were visible in that region before the fire, but even they were killed. The path of the flames, as was discovered by the caravans that passed over the Trail a few days afterward, was marked with the crisp and blackened carcasses of wolves, coyotes, turkeys, grouse, and every variety of small birds indigenous to the region. Indeed, it seemed as if no living thing it had met escaped its fury. The fire assumed such gigantic proportions, and moved with such rapidity before the wind, that even the Arkansas River did not check its path for a moment; it was carried as readily across as if the stream had not been in its way.

The first thought of the trappers on the rock was for their poor mules. One crawled to where they were, and found them badly singed, but not seriously injured. The men began to brighten up again when they knew that their means of transportation were relatively all right, and themselves also, and they took fresh courage, beginning to believe they should get out of their bad scrape after all.

In the meantime the Indians, with the exception of three or four left to guard the rock, so as to prevent the trappers from getting away, had gone back to their camp in the ravine, and were evidently concocting some new scheme for the discomfort of the besieged trappers. The latter waited patiently two or three hours for the development of events, snatching a little sleep by turns, which they needed much; for both were worn out by their constant watching. At last when the sun was about three hours high, the Indians commenced their infernal howling again, and then the trappers knew they had decided upon something; so they were on the alert in a moment to discover what it was, and euchre them if possible.

The devils this time had tied all their ponies together, covered them with branches of trees that they had gone up on the Walnut for, packed some lodge-skins on these, and then, driving the living breastworks before them, moved toward the rock. They proceeded cautiously but surely, and matters began to look very serious for the trappers. As the strange cavalcade approached, a trapper raised his rifle, and a masked pony tumbled over on the scorched sod dead. As one of the Indians ran to cut him loose, the other trapper took him off his feet by a well-directed shot; he never uttered a groan. The besieged now saw their only salvation was to kill the ponies and so demoralize the Indians that they would have to abandon such tactics, and quicker than I can tell it, they had stretched four more out on the prairie, and made it so hot for the savages that they ran out of range and began to hold a council of war.

Finding that their plan would not work--for as the last pony was shot, the rest stampeded and were running wild over the prairie--the Indians soon went back to their camp again, and the trappers now had a few spare moments in which to take an account of stock. They discovered, much to their chagrin, that they had used up all their ammunition except three or four loads, and despair hovered over them once more.

The Indians did not reappear that evening, and the cause was apparent; for in the distance could be seen a long line of wagons, one of the large American caravans en route to Santa Fe. The savages had seen it before the trappers, and had cleared out. When the train arrived opposite the rock, the relieved men came down from their little fortress, joined the caravan, and camped with the Americans that night on the Walnut. While they were resting around their camp-fire, smoking and telling of their terrible experience on the top of the rock, the Indians could be heard chanting the death-song while they were burying their warriors under the blackened sod of the prairie.

I witnessed a spirited encounter between a small band of Cheyennes and Pawnees in the fall of 1867. It occurred on the open prairie north of the mouth of the Walnut, and not a great distance from Pawnee Rock. Both tribes were hunting buffalo, and when they, by accident, discovered the presence of each other, with a yell that fairly shook the sand dunes on the Arkansas, they rushed at once into the shock of battle.

That night, in a timbered bend of the Walnut, the victors had a grand dance, in which scalps, ears, and fingers of their enemies, suspended by strings to long poles, were important accessories to their weird orgies around their huge camp-fires.[65]

One of the most horrible massacres in the history of the Trail occurred at Little Cow Creek in the summer of 1864. In July of that year a government caravan, loaded with military stores for Fort Union in New Mexico, left Fort Leavenworth for the long and dangerous journey of more than seven hundred miles over the great plains, which that season were infested by Indians to a degree almost without precedent in the annals of freight traffic.

The train was owned by a Mr. H. C. Barret, a contractor with the quartermaster's department; but he declined to take the chances of the trip unless the government would lease the outfit in its entirety, or give him an indemnifying bond as assurance against any loss. The chief quartermaster executed the bond as demanded, and Barret hired his teamsters for the hazardous journey; but he found it a difficult matter to induce men to go out that season.

Among those whom he persuaded to enter his employ was a mere boy, named McGee, who came wandering into Leavenworth a few weeks before the train was ready to leave, seeking work of any description. His parents had died on their way to Kansas, and on his arrival at Westport Landing, the emigrant outfit that had extended to him shelter and protection in his utter loneliness was disbanded; so the youthful orphan was thrown on his own resources. At that time the Indians of the great plains, especially along the line of the Santa Fe Trail, were very hostile, and continually harassing the freight caravans and stage-coaches of the overland route. Companies of men were enlisting and being mustered into the United States service to go out after the savages, and young Robert McGee volunteered with hundreds of others for the dangerous duty. The government needed men badly, but McGee's youth militated against him, and he was below the required stature; so he was rejected by the mustering officer.

Mr. Barret, in hunting for teamsters to drive his caravan, came across McGee, who, supposing that he was hiring as a government employee, accepted Mr. Barret's offer.

By the last day of June the caravan was all ready, and on the morning of the next day, July 1, the wagons rolled out of the fort, escorted by a company of United States troops, from the volunteers referred to.

The caravan wound its weary way over the lonesome Trail with nothing to relieve the monotony save a few skirmishes with the Indians; but no casualties occurred in these insignificant battles, the savages being afraid to venture too near on account of the presence of the military escort.

On the 18th of July, the caravan arrived in the vicinity of Fort Larned. There it was supposed that the proximity of that military post would be a sufficient guarantee from any attack of the savages; so the men of the train became careless, and as the day was excessively hot, they went into camp early in the afternoon, the escort remaining in bivouac about a mile in the rear of the train.

About five o'clock, a hundred and fifty painted savages, under the command of Little Turtle of the Brule Sioux, swooped down on the unsuspecting caravan while the men were enjoying their evening meal. Not a moment was given them to rally to the defence of their lives, and of all belonging to the outfit, with the exception of one boy, not a soul came out alive.

The teamsters were every one of them shot dead and their bodies horribly mutilated. After their successful raid, the savages destroyed everything they found in the wagons, tearing the covers into shreds, throwing the flour on the trail, and winding up by burning everything that was combustible.

On the same day the commanding officer of Fort Larned had learned from some of his scouts that the Brule Sioux were on the war-path, and the chief of the scouts with a handful of soldiers was sent out to reconnoitre. They soon struck the trail of Little Turtle and followed it to the scene of the massacre on Cow Creek, arriving there only two hours after the savages had finished their devilish work. Dead men were lying about in the short buffalo-grass which had been stained and matted by their flowing blood, and the agonized posture of their bodies told far more forcibly than any language the tortures which had come before a welcome death. All had been scalped; all had been mutilated in that nameless manner which seems to delight the brutal instincts of the North American savage.

Moving slowly from one to the other of the lifeless forms which still showed the agony of their death-throes, the chief of the scouts came across the bodies of two boys, both of whom had been scalped and shockingly wounded, besides being mutilated, yet, strange to say, both of them were alive. As tenderly as the men could lift them, they were conveyed at once back to Fort Larned and given in charge of the post surgeon. One of the boys died in a few hours after his arrival in the hospital, but the other, Robert McGee, slowly regained his strength, and came out of the ordeal in fairly good health.

The story of the massacre was related by young McGee, after he was able to talk, while in the hospital at the fort; for he had not lost consciousness during the suffering to which he was subjected by the savages.

He was compelled to witness the tortures inflicted on his wounded and captive companions, after which he was dragged into the presence of the chief, Little Turtle, who determined that he would kill the boy with his own hands. He shot him in the back with his own revolver, having first knocked him down with a lance handle. He then drove two arrows through the unfortunate boy's body, fastening him to the ground, and stooping over his prostrate form ran his knife around his head, lifting sixty-four square inches of his scalp, trimming it off just behind his ears.

Believing him dead by that time, Little Turtle abandoned his victim; but the other savages, as they went by his supposed corpse, could not resist their infernal delight in blood, so they thrust their knives into him, and bored great holes in his body with their lances.

After the savages had done all that their devilish ingenuity could contrive, they exultingly rode away, yelling as they bore off the reeking scalps of their victims, and drove away the hundreds of mules they had captured.

When the tragedy was ended, the soldiers, who had from their vantage-ground witnessed the whole diabolical transaction, came up to the bloody camp by order of their commander, to learn whether the teamsters had driven away their assailants, and saw too late what their cowardice had allowed to take place. The officer in command of the escort was dismissed the service, as he could not give any satisfactory reason for not going to the rescue of the caravan he had been ordered to guard.

CHAPTER XXI.

FOOLING STAGE ROBBERS.

The Wagon Mound, so called from its resemblance to a covered army-wagon, is a rocky mesa forty miles from Point of Rocks, westwardly. The stretch of the Trail from the latter to the mound has been the scene of some desperate encounters, only exceeded in number and sanguinary results by those which have occurred in the region of Pawnee Rock, the crossing of the Walnut, Pawnee Fork, and Cow Creek.

One of the most remarkable stories of this Wagon Mound country dealt with the nerve and bravery exhibited by John L. Hatcher in defence of his life, and those of the men in his caravan, about 1858.

Hatcher was a noted trader and merchant of New Mexico. He was also celebrated as an Indian fighter, and his name was a terror to the savages who infested the settlements of New Mexico and raided the Trail.

He left Taos, where he then resided, in the summer, with his caravan loaded with furs and pelts destined for Westport Landing; to be forwarded from there to St. Louis, the only market for furs in the far West. His train was a small one, comprising about fifteen wagons and handled by about as many men, including himself. At the date of his adventure the Indians were believed to be at peace with everybody; a false idea, as Hatcher well knew, for there never was such a condition of affairs as absolute immunity from their attacks. While it might be true that the old men refrained for a time from starting out on the war-path, there were ever the vastly greater number of restless young warriors who had not yet earned their eagle feathers, who could not be controlled by their chiefs, and who were always engaged in marauding, either among the border settlements or along the line of the Trail.

When Hatcher was approaching the immediate vicinity of Wagon Mound,[66] with his train strung out in single column, to his great astonishment there suddenly charged on him from over the hill about three hundred savages, all feather-bedecked and painted in the highest style of Indian art. As they rode toward the caravan, they gave the sign of peace, which Hatcher accepted for the time as true, although he knew them well. However, he invited the head men to some refreshment, as was usual on such occasions in those days, throwing a blanket on the ground, on which sugar in abundance was served out. The sweet-toothed warriors helped themselves liberally, and affected much delight at the way they were being treated; but Hatcher, with his knowledge of the savage character, was firm in the belief that they came for no other purpose than to rob the caravan and kill him and his men.

They were Comanches, and one of the most noted chiefs of the tribe was in command of the band, with some inferior chiefs under him. I think it was Old Wolf, a very old man then, whose raids into Texas had made his name a terror to the Mexicans living on the border.

While the chiefs were eating their saccharine lunch, Hatcher was losing no time in forming his wagons into a corral, but he told his friends afterward that he had no idea that either he or any of his men would escape; only fifteen or sixteen men against over three hundred merciless savages, and those the worst on the continent, and a small corral--the chances were totally hopeless! Nothing but a desperate action could avail, and maybe not even that.[67] Hatcher, after the other head men had finished eating, asked the old chief to send his young warriors away over the hill. They were all sitting close to one of the wagons, Old Wolf, in fact, leaning against the wheel resting on his blanket, with Hatcher next him on his right. Hatcher was so earnest in his appeal to have the young men sent away, that both the venerable villain and his other chiefs rose and were standing. Without a moment's notice or the slightest warning, Hatcher reached with his left hand and grabbed Old Wolf by his scalp-lock, and with his right drew his butcher-knife from its scabbard and thrust it at the throat of the chief. All this was done in an instant, as quick as lightning; no one had time to move. The situation was remarkable. The little, wiry man, surrounded by eight or nine of the most renowned warriors of the dreaded Comanches, stood firm; everybody was breathless; not a word did the savages say. Hatcher then said again to Old Wolf, in the most determined manner: "Send your young men over the hill at once, or I'll kill you right where you are!" holding on to the hair of the savage with his left hand and keeping the knife at his throat.

The other Indians did not dare to make a move; they knew what kind of a man Hatcher was; they knew he would do as he had said, and that if they attempted a rescue he would kill their favourite chief in a second.

Old Wolf shook his head defiantly in the negative. Hatcher repeated his order, getting madder all the time: "Send your young men over the hill; I tell you!" Old Wolf was still stubborn; he shook his head again. Hatcher gave him another chance: "Send your young men over the hill, I tell you, or I'll scalp you alive as you are!" Again the chief shook his head. Then Hatcher, still holding on the hair of his stubborn victim, commenced to make an incision in the head of Old Wolf, for the determined man was bound to carry out his threat; but he began very slowly.

As the chief felt the blood trickle down his forehead, he weakened. He ordered his next in command to send the young men over the hill and out of sight. The order was repeated immediately to the warriors, who were astonished spectators of the strange scene, and they quickly mounted their horses and rode away over the hill as fast as they could thump their animals' sides with their legs, leaving only five or six chiefs with Old Wolf and Hatcher.

Hatcher held on like grim death to the old chief's head, and immediately ordered his men to throw the robes out of the wagons as quickly as they could, and get inside themselves. This was promptly obeyed, and when they were all under the cover of the wagon sheets, Hatcher let go of his victim's hair, and, with a last kick, told him and his friends that they could leave. They went off, and did not return.

Some laughable incidents have enlivened the generally sanguinary history of the Old Santa Fe Trail, but they were very serious at the time to those who were the actors, and their ludicrousness came after all was over.

In the late summer of 1866, a thieving band of Apaches came into the vicinity of Fort Union, New Mexico, and after carefully reconnoitring the whole region and getting at the manner in which the stock belonging to the fort was herded, they secreted themselves in the Turkey Mountains overlooking the entire reservation, and lay in wait for several days, watching for a favourable moment to make a raid into the valley and drive off the herd.

Selecting an occasion when the guard was weak and not very alert, they in broad daylight crawled under the cover of a hill, and, mounting their horses, dashed out with the most unearthly yells and down among the animals that were quietly grazing close to the fort, which terrified these so greatly that they broke away from the herders, and started at their best gait toward the mountains, closely followed by the savages.

The astonished soldiers used every effort to avert the evident loss of their charge, and many shots were exchanged in the running fight that ensued; but the Indians were too strong for them, and they were forced to abandon the chase.

Among the herders was a bugler boy, who was remarkable for his bravery in the skirmish and for his untiring endeavours to turn the animals back toward the fort, but all without avail; on they went, with the savages, close to their heels, giving vent to the most vociferous shouts of exultation, and directing the most obscene and insulting gesticulations to the soldiers that were after them.

While this exciting contest for the mastery was going on, an old Apache chief dashed in the rear of the bold bugler boy, and could, without doubt, easily have killed the little fellow; but instead of doing this, from some idea of a good joke, or for some other incomprehensible reason, his natural blood-thirsty instinct was changed, and he merely knocked the bugler's hat from his head with the flat of his hand, and at the same time encouragingly stroked his hair, as much as to say: "You are a brave boy," and then rode off without doing him any harm.

Thirty years ago last August, I was riding from Fort Larned to Fort Union, New Mexico, in the overland coach. I had one of my clerks with me; we were the only passengers, and arrived at Fort Dodge, which was the commencement of the "long route," at midnight. There we changed drivers, and at the break of day were some twenty-four miles on our lonely journey. The coach was rattling along at a breakneck gait, and I saw that something was evidently wrong. Looking out of one of the doors, I noticed that our Jehu was in a beastly state of intoxication. It was a most dangerous portion of the Trail; the Indians were not in the best of humours, and an attack was not at all improbable before we arrived at the next station, Fort Lyon.

I said to my clerk that something must be done; so I ordered the driver to halt, which he did willingly, got out, and found that, notwithstanding his drunken mood, he was very affable and disposed to be full of fun. I suggested that he get inside the coach and lie down to sleep off his potations, to which he readily assented, while I and my clerk, after snugly fixing him on the cushions, got on the boot, I taking the lines, he seizing an old trace-chain, with which he pounded the mules along; for we felt ourselves in a ticklish predicament should we come across any of the brigands of the plains, on that lonely route, with the animals to look out for, and only two of us to do the fighting.

Suddenly we saw sitting on the bank of the Arkansas River, about a dozen rods from the Trail, an antiquated-looking savage with his war-bonnet on, and armed with a long lance and his bow and arrows. We did not care a cent for him, but I thought he might be one of the tribe's runners, lying in wait to discover the condition of the coach--whether it had an escort, and how many were riding in it, and that then he would go and tell how ridiculously small the outfit was, and swoop down on us with a band of his colleagues, that were hidden somewhere in the sand hills south of the river. He rose as we came near, and made the sign, after he had given vent to a series of "How's!" that he wanted to talk; but we were not anxious for any general conversation with his savage majesty just then, so my clerk applied the trace-chain more vigorously to the tired mules, in order to get as many miles between him and the coach as we could before he could get over into the sand hills and back.

It was, fortunately, a false alarm; the old warrior perhaps had no intentions of disturbing us. We arrived at Fort Lyon in good season, with our valorous driver absolutely sobered, requesting me to say nothing about his accident, which, of course, I did not.

As has been stated, the caravans bound for Santa Fe and the various forts along the line of the Old Trail did not leave the eastern end of the route until the grass on the plains, on which the animals depended solely for subsistence the whole way, grew sufficiently to sustain them, which was usually about the middle of May. But a great many years ago, one of the high officials of the quartermaster's department at Washington, who had never been for a moment on duty on the frontier in his life, found a good deal of fault with what he thought the dilatoriness of the officer in charge at Fort Leavenworth, who controlled the question of transportation for the several forts scattered all over the West, for not getting the freight caravans started earlier, which the functionary at the capital said must and should be done. He insisted that they must leave the Missouri River by the middle of April, a month earlier than usual, and came out himself to superintend the matter. He made the contracts accordingly, easily finding contractors that suited him. He then wrote to headquarters in a triumphant manner that he had revolutionized the whole system of army transportation of supplies to the military posts. Delighted with his success, he rode out about the second week of May to Salt Creek, only three miles from the fort, and, very much to his astonishment, found his teams, which he had believed to be on the way to Santa Fe a month ago, snugly encamped. They had "started," just as was agreed.

There are, or rather were, hundreds of stories current thirty-five years ago of stage-coach adventures on the Trail; a volume could be filled with them, but I must confine myself to a few.

John Chisholm was a famous ranchman a long while ago, who had so many cattle that it was said he did not know their number himself. At one time he had a large contract to furnish beef to an Indian agency in Arizona; he had just delivered an immense herd there, and very wisely, after receiving his cash for them, sent most of it on to Santa Fe in advance of his own journey. When he arrived there, he started for the Missouri River with a thousand dollars and sufficient small change to meet his current expenses on the road.

The very first night out from Santa Fe, the coach was halted by a band of men who had been watching Chisholm's movements from the time he left the agency in Arizona. The instant the stage came to a standstill, Chisholm divined what it meant, and had time to thrust a roll of money down one of the legs of his trousers before the door was thrown back and he was ordered to fork over what he had.

He invited the robbers to search him, and to take what they might find, but said he was not in a financial condition at that juncture to turn over much. The thieves found his watch, took that, and then began to search him. As luck would have it, they entirely missed the roll that was down his leg, and discovered but a two-dollar bill in his vest. When he told them it was all he had to buy grub on the road, one of the robbers handed him a silver dollar, remarking as he did so: "That a man who was mean enough to travel with only two dollars ought to starve, but he would give him the dollar just to let him know that he was dealing with gentlemen!"

One of the essentials to the comfort of the average soldier is tobacco. He must have it; he would sooner forego any component part of his ration than give it up.

In November, 1865, a detachment of Company L, of the Eleventh Kansas Volunteers, and of the Second Colorado were ordered from Fort Larned to Fort Lyon

282

on a scouting expedition along the line of the Trail, the savages having been very active in their raids on the freight caravans.

In a short time their tobacco began to run low, and as there was no settlement of any kind between the two military posts, there was no chance to replenish their stock. One night, while encamped on the Arkansas, the only piece that was left in the whole command, about half a plug, was unfortunately lost, and there was dismay in the camp when the fact was announced. Hours were spent in searching for the missing treasure. The next morning the march was delayed for some time, while further diligent search was instituted by all hands, but without result, and the command set out on its weary tramp, as disconsolate as may well be imagined by those who are victims to the habit of chewing the weed.

Arriving at Fort Lyon, to their greater discomfort it was learned that the sutler at that post was entirely out of the coveted article, and the troops began their return journey more disconsolate than ever. Dry leaves, grass, and even small bits of twigs, were chewed as a substitute, until, reaching the spot where they had lost the part of a plug, they determined to remain there that night and begin a more vigorous hunt for the missing piece. Just before dark their efforts were rewarded; one of the men found it, and such a scramble occurred for even the smallest nibble at it! Enormous prices were given for a single chew. It opened at one dollar for a mere sliver, rose to five, and closed at ten dollars when the last morsel was left.

CHAPTER XXII.

A DESPERATE RIDE.

In the Rocky Mountains and on the great plains along the line of the Old Trail are many rude and widely separated graves. The sequestered little valleys, the lonely gulches, and the broad prairies through which the highway to New Mexico wound its course, hide the bones of hundreds of whom the world will never have any more knowledge. The number of these solitary, and almost obliterated mounds is small when compared with the vast multitude in the cemeteries of our towns, though if the host of those whose bones are mouldering under the short buffalo-grass and tall blue-stem of the prairies between the Missouri and the mountains were tabulated, the list would be appalling. Their aggregate will never be known; for the once remote region of the mid-continent, like the ocean, rarely gave up its victims. Lives went out there as goes an expiring candle, suddenly, swiftly, and silently; no record was kept of time or place. All those who thus died are graveless and monumentless, the great circle of the heavens is the dome of their sepulchre, and the recurring blossoms of springtime their only epitaph.

Sometimes the traveller over the Old Trail will suddenly, in the most unexpected places, come across a little mound, perhaps covered with stones, under which lie the mouldering bones of some unfortunate adventurer. Above, now on a rude board, then on a detached rock, or maybe on the wall of a beetling canyon, he may frequently read, in crude pencilling or rougher carving, the legend of the dead man's ending.

The line of the Atchison, Topeka, and Santa Fe Railroad, which practically runs over the Old Trail for nearly its whole length to the mountains, is a fertile field of isolated graves. The savage and soldier, the teamster and scout, the solitary trapper or hunter, and many others who have gone down to their death fighting with the relentless nomad of the plains, or have been otherwise ruthlessly cut off, mark with their last resting-places that well-worn pathway across the continent.

The tourist, looking from his car-window as he is whirled with the speed of a tornado toward the snow-capped peaks of the "Great Divide," may see as he approaches Walnut Creek, three miles east of the town of Great Bend in Kansas, on the beautiful ranch of Hon. D. Heizer, not far from the stream, and close to the house, a series of graves, numbering, perhaps, a score. These have been most religiously cared for by the patriotic proprietor of the place during all the long years since 1864, as he believes them to be the last resting-place of soldiers who were once a portion of the garrison of Fort Zarah, the ruins of which (now a mere hole in the earth) are but a few hundred yards away, on the opposite side of the railroad track, plainly visible from the train.

The Walnut debouches into the Arkansas a short distance from where the railroad crosses the creek, and at this point, too, the trail from Fort Leavenworth merges into the Old Santa Fe. The broad pathway is very easily recognized here; for it runs over a hard, flinty, low divide, that has never been disturbed by the plough, and the traveller has only to cast his eyes in a northeasterly direction in order to see it plainly.

The creek is fairly well timbered to-day, as it has been ever since the first caravan crossed the clear water of the little stream. It was always a favourite place of ambush by the Indians, and many a conflict has occurred in the beautiful bottom bounded by a margin of trees on two sides, between the traders, trappers, troops, and the Indians, and also between the several tribes that were hereditary enemies, particularly the Pawnees and the Cheyennes. It is only about sixteen miles east of Pawnee Rock, and included in that region of debatable ground where no band of Indians dared establish a permanent village; for it was claimed by all the tribes, but really owned by none.

In 1864 the commerce of the great plains had reached enormous proportions, and immense caravans rolled day after day toward the blue hills which guard the portals of New Mexico, and the precious freight constantly tempted the wily savages to plunder.

To protect the caravans on their monotonous route through the "Desert," as this portion of the plains was then termed, troops were stationed, a mere handful relatively, at intervals on the Trail, to escort the freighters and mail coaches over the most exposed and dangerous portions of the way.

On the bank of the Walnut, at this time, were stationed three hundred unassigned recruits of the Third Wisconsin Cavalry, under the command of Captain Conkey. This point was rightly regarded as one of the most important on the whole overland route; for near it passed the favourite highway of the Indians on their yearly migrations north and south, in the wake of the strange elliptical march of the buffalo far beyond the Platte, and back to the sunny knolls of the Canadian.

This primitive cantonment which grew rapidly in strategical importance, was two years later made quite formidable defensively, and named Fort Zarah, in memory of the youngest son of Major General Curtis, who was killed by guerillas somewhere south of Fort Scott, Kansas, while escorting General James G. Blunt, of frontier fame during the Civil War.

Captain Henry Booth, during the year above mentioned, was chief of cavalry and inspecting officer of the military district of the Upper Arkansas, the western geographical limits of which extended to the foot-hills of the mountains.

One day he received an order from the head-quarters of the department to make a special inspection of all the outposts on the Santa Fe Trail. He was stationed at

Fort Riley at the time, and the evening the order arrived, active preparations were immediately commenced for his extended and hazardous trip across the plains. Lieutenant Hallowell, of the Ninth Wisconsin Battery, was to accompany him, and both officers went at once to their quarters, took down from the walls, where they had been hanging idly for weeks, their rifles and pistols, and carefully examined and brushed them up for possible service in the dreary Arkansas bottom. Camp-kettles, until late in the night, sizzled and sputtered over crackling log-fires; for their proposed ride beyond the settlements demanded cooked rations for many a weary day. All the preliminaries arranged, the question of the means of transportation was determined, and, curiously enough, it saved the lives of the two officers in the terrible gauntlet they were destined to run.

Hallowell was a famous whip, and prided himself upon the exceptionally fine turnout which he daily drove among the picturesque hills around the fort.

"Booth," said he in the evening, "let's not take a great lumbering ambulance on this trip; if you will get a good way-up team of mules from the quartermaster, we'll use my light rig, and we'll do our own driving."

To this proposition Booth readily assented, procured the mules, and, as it turned out, they were a "good way-up team."

Hallowell had a set of bows fitted to his light wagon, over which was thrown an army-wagon-sheet, drawn up behind with a cord, similar to those of the ordinary emigrant outfit to be seen daily on the roads of the Western prairies. A round hole was necessarily left in the rear end, serving the purpose of a lookout.

Two grip-sacks, containing their dress uniforms, a box of crackers and cheese, meat and sardines, together with a bottle of anti-snake bite, made up the principal freight for the long journey, and in the clear cold of the early morning they rolled out of the gates of the fort, escorted by Company L, of the Eleventh Kansas, commanded by Lieutenant Van Antwerp.

The company of one hundred mounted men acting as escort was too formidable a number for the Indians, and not a sign of one was seen as the dangerous flats of Plum Creek and the rolling country beyond were successively passed, and early in the afternoon the cantonment on Walnut Creek was reached. At this important outpost Captain Conkey's command was living in a rude but comfortable sort of a way, in the simplest of dugouts, constructed along the right bank of the stream; the officers, a little more in accordance with military dignity, in tents a few rods in rear of the line of huts.

A stockade stable had been built, with a capacity for two hundred and fifty horses, and sufficient hay had been put up by the men in the fall to carry the animals through the winter.

Captain Conkey was a brusque but kind-hearted man, and with him were stationed other officers, one of whom was a son of Admiral Goldsborough. The morning after the arrival of the inspecting officers a rigid examination of all the appointments and belongings of the place was made, and, as an immense amount of property had accumulated for condemnation, when evening came the books and papers were still untouched; so that branch of the inspection had to be postponed until the next morning.

After dark, while sitting around the camp-fire, discussing the war, telling stories, etc., Captain Conkey said to Booth: "Captain, it won't require more than half an hour in the morning to inspect the papers and finish up what you have to do; why don't you start your escort out very early, so it won't be obliged to trot after the ambulance, or you to poke along with it? You can then move out briskly and make time."

Booth, acting upon what he thought at the time an excellent suggestion, in a few moments went over the creek to Lieutenant Van Antwerp's camp, to tell him that he need not wait for the wagon in the morning, but to start out early, at half-past six, in advance.

According to instructions, the escort marched out of camp at daylight next morning, while Booth and Hallowell remained to finish their inspection. It was soon discovered, however, that either Captain Conkey had underrated the amount of work to be done, or misjudged the inspecting officers' ability to complete it in a certain time; so almost three hours elapsed after the cavalry had departed before the task ended.

At last everything was closed up, much to Hallowell's satisfaction, who had been chafing under the vexatious delay ever since the escort left. When all was in readiness, the little wagon drawn up in front of the commanding officer's quarters, and farewells said, Hallowell suggested to Booth the propriety of taking a few of the troops stationed there to go with them until they overtook their own escort, which must now be several miles on the Trail to Fort Larned. Booth asked Captain Conkey what he thought of Hallowell's suggestion. Captain Conkey replied: "Oh! there's not the slightest danger; there hasn't been an Indian seen around here for over ten days."

If either Booth or Hallowell had been as well acquainted with the methods and character of the plains Indians then as they afterward became, they would have insisted upon an escort; but both were satisfied that Captain Conkey knew what he was talking about, so they concluded to push on.

Jumping into their wagon, Lieutenant Hallowell took the reins and away they went rattling over the old log bridge that used to span the Walnut at the crossing of the Old Santa Fe Trail, as light of heart as if riding to a dance.

The morning was bright and clear with a stiff breeze blowing from the northwest, and the Trail was frozen hard in places, which made it very rough, as it had been cut up by the travel of the heavily laden caravans when it was wet. Booth sat on the left side of Hallowell with the whip in his hand, now and then striking the mules, to keep up their speed. Hallowell started up a tune--he was a good singer--and Booth joined in as they rolled along, as oblivious of any danger as though they were in their quarters at Fort Riley.

After they had proceeded some distance, Hallowell remarked to Booth: "The buffalo are grazing a long way from the road to-day; a circumstance that I think bodes no good." He had been on the plains the summer before, and was better acquainted with the Indians and their peculiarities than Captain Booth; but the latter replied that he thought it was because their escort had gone on ahead, and had probably frightened them off.

The next mile or two was passed, and still they saw no buffalo between the Trail and the Arkansas, though nothing more was said by either regarding the suspicious circumstance, and they rode rapidly on.

When they had gone about five or six miles from the Walnut, Booth, happening to glance toward the river, saw something that looked strangely like a flock of turkeys. He watched them intently for a moment, when the objects rose up and he discovered they were horsemen. He grasped Hallowell by the arm, directing his attention to them, and said, "What are they?" Hallowell gave a hasty look toward the point indicated, and replied, "Indians! by George!" and immediately turning the mules around on the Trail, started them back toward the cantonment on the Walnut at a full gallop.[68]

"Hold on!" said Booth to Hallowell when he understood the latter's movement; "maybe it's part of our escort."

"No! no!" replied Hallowell. "I know they are Indians; I've seen too many of them to be mistaken."

"Well," rejoined Booth, "I'm going to know for certain"; so, stepping out on the foot-board, and with one hand holding on to the front bow, he looked back over the top of the wagon-sheet. They were Indians, sure enough; they had fully emerged from the ravine in which they had hidden, and while he was looking at them they were slipping off their buffalo robes from their shoulders, taking arrows out of their quivers, drawing up their spears, and making ready generally for a red-hot time.

While Booth was intently regarding the movements of the savages, Hallowell inquired of him: "They're Indians, aren't they, Booth?"

"Yes," was Booth's answer, "and they're coming down on us like a whirlwind."

"Then I shall never see poor Lizzie again!" said Hallowell. He had been married only a few weeks before starting out on this trip, and his young wife's name came to his lips.

"Never mind Lizzie," responded Booth; "let's get out of here!" He was as badly frightened as Hallowell, but had no bride at Riley, and, as he tells it, "was selfishly thinking of himself only, and escape."

In answer to Booth's remark, Hallowell, in a firm, clear voice, said: "All right! You do the shooting, and I'll do the driving," and suiting the action to the words, he snatched the whip out of Booth's hand, slipped from the seat to the front of the wagon, and commenced lashing the mules furiously.

Booth then crawled back, pulled out one of his revolvers, crept, or rather fell, over the "lazy-back" of the seat, and reaching the hole made by puckering the wagon-sheet, looked out of it, and counted the Indians; thirty-four feather-bedecked, paint-bedaubed savages, as vicious a set as ever scalped a white man, swooping down on them like a hawk upon a chicken.

Hallowell, between his yells at the mules, cried out, "How far are they off now, Booth?" for of course he could see nothing of what was going on in his rear.

Booth replied as well as he could judge of the distance, while Hallowell renewed his yelling at the animals and redoubled his efforts with the lash.

Noiselessly the Indians gained on the little wagon, for they had not as yet uttered a whoop, and the determined driver, anxious to know how far the red devils were from him, again asked Booth. The latter told him how near they were, guessing at the distance, from which Hallowell gathered inspiration for fresh cries and still more vigorous blows with his whip.

Booth, all this time, was sitting on the box containing the crackers and sardines, watching the rapid approach of the cut-throats, and seeing with fear and trembling the ease with which they gained upon the little mules.

Once more Hallowell made his stereotyped inquiry of Booth; but before the latter could reply, two shots were fired from the rifles of the Indians, accompanied by a yell that was demoniacal enough to cause the blood to curdle in one's veins.

Hallowell yelled at the mules, and Booth yelled too; for what reason he could not tell, unless to keep company with his comrade, who plied the whip more mercilessly than ever upon the poor animals' backs, and the wagon flew over the rough road, nearly upsetting at every jump.

In another moment the bullets from two of the Indians' rifles passed between Booth and Hallowell, doing no damage, and almost instantly the savages charged upon them, at the same time dividing into two parties, one going on one side and one on the other, both delivering a volley of arrows into the wagon as they rode by.

Just as the savages rushed past the wagon, Hallowell cried out to Booth, "Cap, I'm hit!" and turning around to look, Booth saw an arrow sticking in Hallowell's head above his right ear. His arm was still plying the whip, which was going on unceasingly as the sails of a windmill, and his howling at the mules only stopped long enough to answer, "Not much!" in response to Booth's inquiry of "Does it hurt?" as he grabbed the arrow and pulled it out of his head.

The Indians had by this time passed on, and then, circling back, prepared for another charge. Down they came, again dividing as before into two bands, and delivering another shower of arrows. Hallowell ceased his yelling long enough to cry out, "I'm hit once more, Cap!" Looking at the plucky driver, Booth saw this time an arrow sticking over his left ear, and hanging down his back. He snatched it out, inquiring if it hurt, but received the same answer: "No, not much."

Both men were now yelling at the top of their voices; and the mules were jerking the wagon along the rough trail at a fearful rate, frightened nearly out of their wits at the sight of the Indians and the terrible shouting and whipping of the driver.

Booth crawled to the back end of the wagon again, looked out of the hole in the cover, and saw the Indians moving across the Trail, preparing for another charge. One old fellow, mounted on a black pony, was jogging along in the centre of the road behind them, but near enough and evidently determined to send an arrow through the puckered hole of the sheet. In a moment the savage stopped his pony and let fly. Booth dodged sideways--the arrow sped on its course, and whizzing through the opening, struck the black-walnut "lazy-back" of the seat, the head sticking out on the other side, and the sudden check causing the feathered end to vibrate rapidly with a vro-o-o-ing sound. With a quick blow Booth struck it, and broke the shaft from the head, leaving the latter embedded in the wood.

As quickly as possible, Booth rushed to the hole and fired his revolver at the old devil, but failed to hit him. While he was trying to get in another shot, an arrow came flying through from the left side of the Trail, and striking him on the inside of the elbow, or "crazy-bone," so completely benumbed his hand that he could not hold on to the pistol, and it dropped into the road with one load still in its chamber. Just then

290

the mules gave an extraordinary jump to one side, which jerked the wagon nearly from under him, and he fell sprawling on the end-gate, evenly balanced, with his hands on the outside, attempting to clutch at something to save himself! Seeing his predicament, the Indians thought they had him sure, so they gave a yell of exultation, supposing he must tumble out, but he didn't; he fortunately succeeded in grabbing one of the wagon-bows with his right hand and pulled himself in; but it was a close call.

While all this was going on, Hallowell had not been neglected by the Indians; about a dozen of them had devoted their time to him, but he never flinched. Just as Booth had regained his equilibrium and drawn his second revolver from its holster, Hallowell yelled to him: "Right off to your right, Cap, quick!"

Booth tumbled over the back of the seat, and, clutching at a wagon-bow to steady himself, he saw, "off to the right," an Indian who was in the act of letting an arrow drive at Hallowell; it struck the side of the box, and at the same instant Booth fired, scaring the red devil badly.

Back over the seat again he rushed to guard the rear, only to find a young buck riding close to the side of the wagon, his pony running in the deep path made by the ox-drivers in walking alongside of their teams. Putting his left arm around one of the wagon-bows to prevent his being jerked out, Booth quietly stuck his revolver through the hole in the sheet; but before he could pull the trigger, the Indian flopped over on the off side of his pony, and nothing could be seen of him excepting one arm around his animal's neck and from the knee to the toes of one leg. Booth did not wait for him to ride up; he could almost hit the pony's head with his hand, so close was he to the wagon. Booth struck at the beast several times, but the Indian kept him right up in his place by whipping him on the opposite of his neck. Presently the plucky savage's arm began to move. Booth watched him intently, and saw that he had fixed an arrow in his bow under the pony's shoulder; just as he was on the point of letting go the bowstring, with the head of the arrow not three feet from Booth's breast as he leaned out of the hole, the latter struck frantically at the weapon, dodged back into the wagon, and up came the Indian. Whenever Booth looked out, down went the Indian on the other side of his pony, to rise again in a moment, and Booth, afraid to risk himself with his head and breast exposed at this game of hide and seek, drew suddenly back as the Indian went down the third time, and in a second came up; but this was once too often. Booth had not dodged completely into the wagon, nor dropped his revolver, and as the Indian rose he fired.

The savage was naked to the waist; the ball struck him in the left nipple, the blood spirted out of the wound, his bow and arrows and lariat, with himself, rolled off the pony, falling heavily on the ground, and with one convulsive contraction of his legs and an "Ugh!" he was as dead as a stone.

"I've killed one of 'em!" called out Booth to Hallowell, as he saw his victim tumble from his pony.

"Bully for you, Cap!" came Hallowell's response as he continued his shouting, and the blows of that tireless whip fell incessantly on the backs of the poor mules.

After he had killed the warrior, Booth kept his seat on the cracker box, watching to see what the Indians were going to do next, when he was suddenly interrupted by Hallowell's crying out to him: "Off to the right again, Cap, quick!" and, whirling around instantly, he saw an Indian within three feet of the wagon, with his bow and arrow almost ready to shoot; there was no time to get over the seat, and as he could not fire so close to Hallowell, he cried to the latter: "Hit him with the whip! Hit him with the whip!" The lieutenant diverted one of the blows intended for the mules, and struck the savage fairly across the face. The whip had a knot in the end of it to prevent its unravelling, and this knot must have hit the Indian squarely in the eye; for he dropped his bow, put both hands up to his face, rubbed his eyes, and digging his heels into his pony's sides was soon out of range of a revolver; but, nevertheless, he was given a parting shot as a sort of salute.

A terrific yell from the rear at this moment caused both Booth and Hallowell to look around, and the latter to inquire: "What's the matter now, Booth?" "They are coming down on us like lightning," said he; and, sure enough, those who had been prancing around their dead comrade were tearing along the Trail toward the wagon with a more hideous noise than when they began.

Hallowell yelled louder than ever and lashed the mules more furiously still, but the Indians gained upon them as easily as a blooded racer on a common farm plug. Separating as before, and passing on each side of the wagon, they delivered another volley of bullets and arrows as they rushed on.

When this charge was made, Booth drew away from the hole in the rear and turned toward the Indians, but forgot that as he was sitting, with his back pressed against the sheet, his body was plainly outlined on the canvas.

When the Indians dashed by Hallowell cried out, "I'm hit again, Cap!" and Booth, in turning around to go to his relief, felt something pulling at him; and glancing over his left shoulder he discovered an arrow sticking into him and out through the wagon-sheet. With a jerk of his body, he tore himself loose, and going to Hallowell, asked him where he was hit. "In the back," was the reply; where Booth saw an arrow extending under the "lazy-back" of the seat. Taking hold of it, Booth gave a pull, but Hallowell squirmed so that he desisted. "Pull it out!" cried the plucky driver. Booth thereupon took hold of it again, and giving a jerk or two, out it came. He was thoroughly frightened as he saw it leave the lieutenant's body; it seemed to have entered at least six inches, and the wound appeared to be a dangerous one. Hallowell, however, did not cease for a moment belabouring the mules, and his yells rang out as clear and defiant as before.

After extracting the arrow from Hallowell's back, Booth turned again to the opening in the rear of the wagon to see what new tricks the devils were up to, when Hallowell again called out, "Off to the left, Cap, quick!"

Rushing to the front as soon as possible, Booth saw one of the savages in the very act of shooting at Hallowell from the left side of the wagon, not ten feet away. The last revolver was empty, but something had to be done at once; so, levelling the weapon at him, Booth shouted "Bang! you son-of-a-gun!" Down the Indian ducked his head; rap, rap, went his knees against his pony's sides, and away he flew over the prairie!

Back to his old place in the rear tumbled Booth, to load his revolver. The cartridges they used in the army in those days were the old-fashioned kind made of paper. Biting off one end, he endeavoured to pour the powder into the chamber of the pistol; but as the wagon was tumbling from side to side, and jumping up and down, as it fairly flew over the rough Trail, more fell into the bottom of the wagon than into the revolver. Just as he was inserting a ball, Hallowell yelled, "To the left, Cap, quick!"

Over the seat Booth piled once more, and there was another Indian with his bow and arrow all ready to pinion the brave lieutenant. Pointing his revolver at him, Booth yelled as he had at the other, but this savage had evidently noticed the first failure, and concluded there were no more loads left; so, instead of taking a hasty departure, he grinned demoniacally and endeavoured to fix the arrow in his bow. Booth rose up in the wagon, and grasping hold of one of its bows with his left hand, seized the revolver by the muzzle, and with all the force he could muster hurled it at the impudent brute. It was a Remington, its barrel octagon-shaped, with sharp corners, and when it was thrown, it turned in the air, and striking the Indian muzzle-first on the ribs, cut a long gash.

"Ugh!" he grunted, as, dropping his bow and spear, he flung himself over the side of his pony, and away he went across the prairie.

Only one revolver remaining now, and that empty, with the savages still howling around the apparently doomed men like so many demons! Booth fell over the seat, as was his usual fate whenever he attempted to get to the back of the wagon, picked up the empty revolver, and tried to load it; but before he could bite the end of a cartridge, Hallowell yelled, "Cap, I'm hit again!"

"Where this time?" inquired Booth, anxiously. "In the hand," replied Hallowell; and, looking around, Booth noticed that although his right arm was still thrashing at the now lagging mules with as much energy as ever, through the fleshy part of the thumb was an arrow, which was flopping up and down as he raised and lowered his hand in ceaseless efforts to keep up the speed of the almost exhausted animals.

"Let me pull it out," said Booth, as he came forward to do so.

"No, never mind," replied Hallowell; "can't stop! can't stop!" and up and down went the arm, and flip, flap, went the arrow with it, until finally it tore through the flesh and fell to the ground.

Along they bowled, the Indians yelling, and the occupants of the little wagon defiantly answering them, while Booth continued to struggle desperately with that empty pistol, in his vain efforts to load it. In another moment Hallowell shouted, "Booth, they are trying to crowd the mules into the sunflowers!"

Alongside of the Trail huge sunflowers had grown the previous summer, and now their dry stalks stood as thick as a cane-brake; if the wagon once got among them, it would be impossible for the mules to keep up their gallop. The savages seemed to realize this; for one huge old fellow kept riding alongside the off mule, throwing his spear at him and then jerking it back with the thong, one end of which was fastened to his wrist. The near mule was constantly pushed further and further from the Trail by his mate, which was jumping frantically, scared out of his senses by the Indian.

At this perilous juncture, Booth stepped out on the foot-board of the wagon, and, holding on by a bow, commenced to kick the frightened mule vigorously, while Hallowell pulled on one line, whipping and yelling at the same time; so together they succeeded in forcing the animals back into the Trail.

The Indians kept close to the mules in their efforts to force them into the sunflowers, and Booth made several attempts to scare the old fellow that was nearest by pointing his empty revolver at him, but he would not scare; so in his desperation Booth threw it at him. He missed the old brute, but hit his pony just behind its rider's leg, which started the animal into a sort of a stampede; his ugly master could not control him, and thus the immediate peril from the persistent cuss was delayed.

Now the pair were absolutely without firearms of any kind, with nothing left except their sabres and valises, and the savages came closer and closer. In turn the two swords were thrown at them as they came almost within striking distance; then followed the scabbards, as the howling fiends surrounded the wagon and attempted to spear the mules. Fortunately their arrows were exhausted.

The cantonment on the Walnut was still a mile and a half away, and there was nothing for our luckless travellers to do but whip and kick, both of which they did most vigorously. Hallowell sat as immovable as the Sphinx, excepting his right arm, which from the moment they had started on the back trail had not once ceased its incessant motion.

Happening to cast his eyes back on the Trail, Booth saw to his dismay twelve or fifteen of the savages coming up on the run with fresh energy, their spears poised ready for action, and he felt that something must be done very speedily to divert them; for if these added their number to those already surrounding the wagon, the chances were they would succeed in forcing the mules into the sunflowers, and his scalp and Hallowell's would dangle at the belt of the leader.

Glancing around in the bottom of the wagon for some kind of weapon, his eye fell on the two valises containing the dress-suits. He snatched up his own, and threw it out while the pursuers were yet five or six rods in the rear. The Indians noticed this new trick with a great yell of satisfaction, and the moment they arrived at the spot where the valise lay, all dismounted; one of them, seizing it by the two handles, pulled with all his strength to open it, and when he failed, another drew a long knife from under his blanket and ripped it apart. He then put his hand in, pulling out a sash, which he began to wind around his head, like a negress with a bandanna, letting the tassels hang down his back. While he was thus amusing himself, one of the others had taken out a dress-coat, a third a pair of drawers, and still another a shirt, which they proceeded to put on, meanwhile dancing around and howling.

Booth told Hallowell of the sacrifice of the valise, and said, "I'm going to throw out yours." "All right," replied Hallowell; "all we want is time." So out it went on the Trail, and shared the same fate as the other.

The lull in hostilities caused by their outstripping their pursuers gave the almost despairing men time to talk over their situation. Hallowell said he did not propose to be captured and then butchered or burned at the pleasure of the Indians. He said to Booth: "If they kill one of the mules, and so stop us, let's kick, strike, throw dirt or anything, and compel them to kill us on the spot." So it was agreed, if the worst came to the worst, to stand back to back and fight.

During this discussion the arm of Hallowell still plied the effective lash, and they drew perceptibly nearer the camp, and as they caught the first glimpse of its tents and dugouts, hope sprang up within them. The mules were panting like a hound after a deer; wherever the harness touched them, it was white with lather, and it was evident they could keep on their feet but a short time longer. Would they hold out until the bridge was reached? The whipping and the kicking had but little effect on them now. They still continued their gallop, but it was slower and more laboured than before.

The Indians who had torn open the valises had not returned to the chase, and although there were still a sufficient number of the fiends pursuing to make it interesting, they did not succeed in spearing the mules, as at every attempt the plucky animals would jump sideways or forward and evade the impending blow.

The little log bridge was reached; the savages had all retreated, but the valorous Hallowell kept the mules at their fastest pace. The bridge was constructed of half-round logs, and of course was extremely rough; the wagon bounded up and down enough to shake the teeth out of one's head as the little animals went flying over it. Booth called out to Hallowell, "No need to drive so fast now, the Indians have all left us"; but he replied, "I ain't going to stop until I get across"; and down came the whip, on sped the mules, not breaking their short gallop until they were pulled up in front of Captain Conkey's quarters.

The rattling of the wagon on the bridge was the first intimation the garrison had of its return.

The officers came running out of their tents, the enlisted men poured out of their dugouts like a lot of ants, and Booth and Hallowell were surrounded by their friends in a moment. Captain Conkey ordered his bugler to sound "Boots and Saddles," and in less than ten minutes ninety troopers were mounted, and with the captain at their head started after the Indians.

When Hallowell tried to rise from his seat so as to get out every effort only resulted in his falling back. Some one stepped around to the other side to assist him, when it was discovered that the skirt of his overcoat had worked outside of the wagon-sheet and hung over the edge, and that three or four of the arrows fired at him by the savages had struck the side of the wagon, and, passing through the flap of his coat, had pinned him down. Booth pulled the arrows out and helped him up; he was pretty stiff from sitting in his cramped position so long, and his right arm dropped by his side as if paralysed.

Booth stood looking on while his comrade's wounds were being dressed, when the adjutant asked him: "What makes you shrug your shoulder so?" He answered, "I don't know; something makes it smart." The officer looked at him and said, "Well, I don't wonder; I should think it would smart; here's an arrow-head sticking into you," and he tried to pull it out, but it would not come. Captain Goldsborough then attempted it, but was not any more successful. The doctor then told them to let it alone, and he would attend to Booth after he had done with Hallowell. When he examined Booth's shoulder, he found that the arrow-head had struck the thick portion of the shoulder-blade, and had made two complete turns, wrapping itself around the muscles, which had to be cut apart before the sharp point could be withdrawn.

Booth was not seriously hurt. Hallowell, however, had received two severe wounds; the arrow that had lodged in his back had penetrated almost to his kidneys, and the wound in his thumb was very painful, not so much from the simple impact of the arrow as from the tearing away of the muscle by the shaft while he was whipping his mules; his right arm, too, was swollen terribly, and so stiff from the incessant use of it during the drive that for more than a month he required assistance in dressing and undressing.

The mules who had saved their lives were of small account after their memorable trip; they remained stiff and sore from the rough road and their continued forced speed. Booth and Hallowell went out to look at them the next morning, as they hobbled around the corral, and from the bottom of their hearts wished them well.

Captain Conkey's command returned to the cantonment about midnight. But one Indian had been seen, and he was south of the Arkansas in the sand hills.

The next morning a scouting-party of forty men, under command of a sergeant, started out to scour the country toward Cow Creek, northeast from the Walnut.

As I have stated, the troopers stationed at the cantonment on the Walnut were mostly recruits. Now the cavalry recruit of the old regular army on the frontier, thirty or forty years ago, mounted on a great big American horse and sent out with well-trained comrades on a scout after the hostile savages of the plains, was the most helpless individual imaginable. Coming fresh from some large city probably, as soon as he arrived at his station he was placed on the back of an animal of whose habits he knew as little as he did of the differential calculus; loaded down with a carbine, the muzzle of which he could hardly distinguish from the breech; a sabre buckled around his waist; a couple of enormous pistols stuck in his holsters; his blankets strapped to the cantle of his saddle, and, to complete the hopelessness of his condition in a possible encounter with a savage enemy who was ever on the alert, he was often handicapped by a camp-kettle or two, a frying-pan, and ten days' rations. No wonder this doughty representative of Uncle Sam's power was an easy prey for "Poor Lo," who, when he caught the unfortunate soldier away from his command and started after him, must have laughed at the ridiculous appearance of his enemy, with both hands glued to the pommel of his saddle, his hair on end, his sabre flying and striking his horse at every jump as the animal tore down the trail toward camp, while the Indian, rapidly gaining, in a few minutes had the scalp of the hapless rider dangling at his belt, and another of the "boys in blue" had joined the majority.

The scouting-party had proceeded about four or five miles, when one of the corporals asked permission for himself and a recruit to go over to the Upper Walnut to find out whether they could discover any signs of Indians.

While they were carelessly riding along the big curve which the northern branch of the Walnut makes at that point, there suddenly sprang from their ambush in the timber on the margin of the stream about three hundred Indians, whooping and yelling. The two troopers of course, immediately whirled their horses and started down the creek toward the camp, hotly pursued by the howling savages.

The corporal was an excellent rider; a well-trained and disciplined soldier, having seen much service on the plains. He led in the flight, closely followed by the unfortunate recruit, who had been enlisted but a short time. Not more than an eighth of a mile had been covered, when the corporal heard his companion exclaim,--

"Don't leave me! Don't leave me!"

Looking back, the corporal saw that the poor recruit was losing ground rapidly; his horse was rearing and plunging, making very little headway, while his rider was jerking and pulling on the bit, a curb of the severest kind. Perceiving the strait his comrade was in, the corporal reined up for a moment and called out,--

"Let him go! Let him go! Don't jerk on the bit so!"

The Indians were gaining ground rapidly, and in another moment the corporal heard the recruit again cry out,--

"Oh! Don't--"

Realizing that it would be fatal to delay, and that he could be of no assistance to his companion, already killed and scalped, he leaned forward on his horse, and sinking his spurs deep in the animal's flanks fairly flew down the valley, with the three hundred savages close in his wake.

The officers at the camp were sitting in their tents when the sentinel on post No. 1 fired his piece, upon which all rushed out to learn the cause of the alarm; for there was no random shooting in those days allowed around camp or in garrison. Looking up the valley of the Walnut, they could see the lucky corporal, with his long hair streaming in the wind, and his heels rapping his horse's sides, as he dashed over the brown sod of the winter prairie.

The corporal now slackened his pace, rode up to the commanding officer's tent, reported the affair, and then was allowed to go to his own quarters for the rest he so much needed.

Captain Conkey immediately ordered a mounted squad, accompanied by an ambulance, to go up the creek to recover the body of the unfortunate recruit. The party were absent a little over an hour, and brought back with them the remains of the dead soldier. He had been shot with an arrow, the point of which was still sticking out through his breast-bone. His scalp had been torn completely off, and the lapels of his coat and the legs of his trousers carried away by the savages. He was buried the next morning with military honours, in the little graveyard on the bank of the Walnut, where his body still rests in the dooryard of the ranch.

CHAPTER XXIII.

HANCOCK'S EXPEDITION.

In the spring of 1867, General Hancock, who then commanded the military division of the Missouri, with headquarters at Fort Leavenworth, Kansas, organized an expedition against the Indians of the great plains, which he led in person. With him was General Custer, second ranking officer, from whom I quote the story of the march and some of the incidents of the raid.

General Hancock, with the artillery and six companies of infantry, arrived at Fort Riley, Kansas, the last week in March, where he was joined by four companies of the Seventh Cavalry, commanded by the intrepid Custer.

From Fort Riley the expedition marched to Fort Harker, seventy-two miles farther west, on the Smoky Hill, where the force was increased by the addition of two more troops of cavalry. Remaining there only long enough to replenish their commissary supplies, the march was directed to Fort Larned on the Old Santa Fe Trail. On the 7th of April the command reached the latter post, accompanied by the agent of the Comanches and Kiowas; at the fort the agent of the Cheyennes, Arapahoes, and Apaches was waiting for the arrival of the general. The agent of the three last-mentioned tribes had already sent runners to the head chiefs, inviting them to a grand council which was to assemble near the fort on the 10th of the month, and he requested General Hancock to remain at the fort with his command until that date.

On the 9th of April a terrible snow-storm came on while the troops were encamped waiting for the head men of the various tribes to arrive. Custer says:

It was our good fortune to be in camp rather than on the march; had it been otherwise, we could not well have escaped without loss of life. The cavalry horses suffered severely, and were only preserved by doubling their rations of oats, while to prevent their being frozen during the intensely cold night which followed, the guards were instructed to pass along the picket lines with a whip, and keep the horses moving constantly. The snow was eight inches deep. The council, which was to take place the next day, had to be postponed until the return of good weather. Now began the display of a kind of diplomacy for which the Indian is peculiar. The Cheyennes and a band of Sioux were encamped on Pawnee Fork, about thirty miles above Fort Larned. They neither desired to move nearer to us or have us approach nearer to them. On the morning of the 11th, they sent us word that they had started to visit us, but, discovering a large herd of buffalo near their camp, they had stopped to procure a supply of meat. This message was not received with much confidence, nor was a buffalo hunt deemed of sufficient importance to justify the Indians in breaking their engagement. General Hancock decided, however, to delay another day, when, if the Indians still failed to come in, he would move his command to the vicinity of their village and hold the conference there.

Orders were issued on the evening of the 12th for the march to be resumed on the following day. Late in the evening two chiefs of the "Dog-Soldiers," a band composed of the most warlike and troublesome Indians on the plains, chiefly made up of Cheyennes, visited our camp. They were accompanied by a dozen warriors, and expressed a desire to hold a conference with General Hancock, to which he assented. A large council-fire was built in front of the general's tent, and all the officers of his command assembled there. A tent had been erected for the accommodation of the chiefs a short distance from the general's. Before they could feel equal to the occasion, and in order to obtain time to collect their thoughts, they desired that supper might be prepared for them, which was done. When finally ready, they advanced from their tent to the council-fire in single file, accompanied by their agent and an interpreter. Arrived at the fire, another brief delay ensued. No matter how pressing or momentous the occasion, an Indian invariably declines to engage in a council until he has filled his pipe and gone through with the important ceremony of a smoke. This attended to, the chiefs announced that they were ready "to talk." They were then introduced to the principal officers of the group, and seemed much struck with the

flashy uniforms of the few artillery officers, who were
present in all the glory of red horsehair plumes,
aiguillettes, etc. The chiefs seemed puzzled to determine
whether these insignia designated chieftains or medicine men.
General Hancock began the conference by a speech, in which
he explained to the Indians his purpose in coming to see
them, and what he expected of them in the future.
He particularly informed them that he was not there to make
war, but to promote peace. Then, expressing his regrets
that more of the chiefs had not visited him, he announced
his intention of proceeding on the morrow with his command
to the vicinity of their village, and there holding a
council with all the chiefs. Tall Bull, a fine, warlike-looking
chieftain, replied to General Hancock, but his speech
contained nothing important, being made up of allusions to
the growing scarcity of the buffalo, his love for the white
man, and the usual hint that a donation in the way of
refreshments would be highly acceptable; he added that he
would have nothing new to say at the village.

Rightly concluding that the Indians did not intend to come
to our camp, as they had at first agreed to, it was decided
to move nearer their village. On the morning following the
conference our entire force, therefore, marched from
Fort Larned up Pawnee Fork in the direction of the main
village, encamping the first night about twenty-one miles
from Larned. Several parties of Indians were seen in our
advance during the day, evidently watching our movements,
while a heavy smoke, seen to rise in the direction of the
Indian village, indicated that something more than usual
was going on. The smoke, we afterward learned, arose from
burning grass. The Indians, thinking to prevent us from
encamping in their vicinity, had set fire to and burned all
the grass for miles in the direction from which they
expected us. Before we arrived at our camping-ground,
we were met by several chiefs and warriors belonging to the
Cheyennes and Sioux. Among the chiefs were Pawnee Killer,

of the Sioux, and White Horse, of the Cheyennes. It was
arranged that these chiefs should accept our hospitality
and remain with us during the night, and in the morning all
the chiefs of the two tribes then in the village were to
come to General Hancock's head-quarters and hold a council.
On the morning of the 14th, Pawnee Killer left our camp at
an early hour, as he said for the purpose of going to the
village to bring in the other chiefs to the council.
Nine o'clock had been agreed upon as the time at which the
council should assemble. The hour came, but the chiefs
did not. Now an Indian council is not only often an
important, but always an interesting, occasion. At this
juncture, Bull Bear, an influential chief among the
Cheyennes, came in and reported that the chiefs were on
their way to our camp, but would not be able to reach it
for some time. This was a mere artifice to secure delay.
General Hancock informed Bull Bear that, as the chiefs
could not arrive for some time, he would move his forces
up the stream nearer the village, and the council could be
held at our camp that night. To this proposition Bull Bear
gave his consent.

At 11 A.M. we resumed the march, and had proceeded but a few
miles when we witnessed one of the finest and most imposing
military displays, according to the Indian art of war,
which it has been my lot to behold. It was nothing more
nor less than an Indian line of battle drawn directly
across our line of march, as if to say, "Thus far and no
further." Most of the Indians were mounted; all were
bedecked in their brightest colours, their heads crowned
with the brilliant war-bonnet, their lances bearing the
crimson pennant, bows strung, and quivers full of barbed
arrows. In addition to these weapons, which, with the
hunting-knife and tomahawk, are considered as forming the
armament of the warrior, each one was supplied with either
a breech-loading rifle or revolver, sometimes with both--
the latter obtained through the wise forethought and strong

love of fair play which prevails in the Indian department,
which, seeing that its wards are determined to fight,
is equally determined that there shall be no advantage taken,
but that the two sides shall be armed alike; proving, too,
in this manner, the wonderful liberality of our government,
which is not only able to furnish its soldiers with the
latest style of breech-loaders to defend it and themselves,
but is equally able and willing to give the same pattern
of arms to the common foe. The only difference is, that if
the soldier loses his weapon, he is charged double price
for it, while to avoid making any such charge against the
Indian, his weapons are given him without conditions attached.

In the line of battle before us there were several hundred
Indians, while further to the rear and at different
distances were other organized bodies, acting apparently
as reserves. Still further behind were small detachments
who seemed to perform the duty of couriers, and were held
in readiness to convey messages to the village. The ground
beyond was favourable for an extended view, and as far as
the eye could reach, small groups of individuals could be
seen in the direction of the village; these were evidently
parties of observation, whose sole object was to learn the
result of our meeting with the main body and hasten with
the news to the village.

For a few moments appearances seemed to foreshadow anything
but a peaceable issue. The infantry was in the advance,
followed closely by the artillery, while my command,
the cavalry, was marching on the flank. General Hancock,
who was riding with his staff at the head of the column,
coming suddenly in view of the wild, fantastic battle array,
which extended far to our right and left, and was not more
than half a mile in our front, hastily sent orders to the
infantry, artillery, and cavalry to form in line of battle,
evidently determined that, if war was intended, we should be
prepared. The cavalry being the last to form on the right,

came into line on a gallop, and without waiting to align
the ranks carefully, the command was given to "Draw sabre."
As the bright blades flashed from their scabbards into the
morning sunlight, and the infantry brought their muskets
to a carry, a contrast was presented which, to a military
eye, could but be striking. Here in battle array, facing
each other, were the representatives of civilized and
barbarous warfare. The one, with few modifications, stood
clothed in the same rude style of dress, bearing the same
patterned shield and weapon that his ancestors had borne
centuries before; the other confronted him in the dress
and supplied with the implements of war which an advanced
stage of civilization had pronounced the most perfect.
Was the comparative superiority of these two classes to be
subjected to the mere test of war here? All was eager
anxiety and expectation. Neither side seemed to comprehend
the object or intentions of the other; each was waiting
for the other to deliver the first blow. A more beautiful
battle-ground could not have been chosen. Not a bush or
even the slightest irregularity of ground intervened between
the two lines, which now stood frowning and facing each other.
Chiefs could be seen riding along the line, as if directing
and exhorting their braves to deeds of heroism.

After a few moments of painful suspense, General Hancock,
accompanied by General A. J. Smith and other officers,
rode forward, and through an interpreter invited the chiefs
to meet us midway for the purpose of an interview.
In response to this invitation, Roman Nose, bearing a white
flag, accompanied by Bull Bear, White Horse, Gray Beard,
and Medicine Wolf, on the part of the Cheyennes, and Pawnee
Killer, Bad Wound, Tall-Bear-That-Walks-under-the-Ground,
Left Hand, Little Bear, and Little Bull, on the part of the
Sioux, rode forward to the middle of the open space between
the two lines. Here we shook hands with all the chiefs,
most of them exhibiting unmistakable signs of gratification
at this apparently peaceful termination of our rencounter.

General Hancock very naturally inquired the object of the hostile attitude displayed before us, saying to the chiefs that if war was their object, we were ready then and there to participate. Their immediate answer was that they did not desire war, but were peacefully disposed. They were then told that we would continue our march toward the village, and encamp near it, but would establish such regulations that none of the soldiers would be permitted to approach or disturb them. An arrangement was then effected by which the chiefs were to assemble at General Hancock's headquarters as soon as our camp was pitched. The interview then terminated, and the Indians moved off in the direction of their village, we following leisurely in the rear.

A march of a few miles brought us in sight of the village, which was situated in a beautiful grove on the bank of the stream up which we had been marching. It consisted of upwards of three hundred lodges, a small fraction over half belonging to the Cheyennes, the remainder to the Sioux. Like all Indian encampments, the ground chosen was a most romantic spot, and at the same time fulfilled in every respect the requirements of a good camping-ground; wood, water, and grass were abundant. The village was placed on a wide, level plateau, while on the north and west, at a short distance off, rose high bluffs, which admirably served as a shelter against the cold winds which at that season of the year prevail from those directions. Our tents were pitched within a mile of the village. Guards were placed between to prevent intrusion upon our part. We had scarcely pitched our tents when Roman Nose, Bull Bear, Gray Beard, and Medicine Wolf, all prominent chiefs of the Cheyenne nation, came into camp with the information that upon our approach their women and children had all fled from the village, alarmed by the presence of so many soldiers, and imagining a second Chivington massacre to be intended. General Hancock insisted that they should all return,

promising protection and good treatment to all; that if
the camp was abandoned, he would hold it responsible.
The chiefs then stated their belief in their ability to
recall the fugitives, could they be furnished with horses
to overtake them. This was accordingly done, and two of
them set out mounted on two of our horses. An agreement
was also entered into at the same time, that one of our
interpreters, Ed Gurrier, a half-breed Cheyenne, who was in
the employ of the government, should remain in the village
and report every two hours as to whether any Indians were
leaving there. This was about seven o'clock in the evening.
At half-past nine the half-breed returned to head-quarters
with the intelligence that all the chiefs and warriors were
saddling up to leave, under circumstances showing that they
had no intention of returning, such as packing up every
article that could be carried with them, and cutting and
destroying their lodges--this last being done to obtain
small pieces for temporary shelter.

I had retired to my tent, which was some few hundred yards
from that of General Hancock, when a messenger from the
latter awakened me with the information that the general
desired my presence in his tent. He briefly stated the
situation of affairs, and directed me to mount my command
as quickly and as silently as possible, surround the Indian
village, and prevent the departure of its inhabitants.
Easily said, but not so easily done. Under ordinary
circumstances, silence not being necessary, I could have
returned to my camp, and by a few blasts from the trumpet,
placed every soldier on his saddle almost as quickly as it
has taken time to write this short sentence. No bugle calls
must be sounded; we were to adopt some of the stealth of the
Indians--how successfully remained to be seen. By this time
every soldier and officer was in his tent sound asleep.
First going to the tent of the adjutant and arousing him,
I procured an experienced assistant in my labours. Next the
captains of companies were awakened and orders imparted

to them. They in turn transmitted the order to the first
sergeant, who similarly aroused the men. It has often
surprised me to observe the alacrity with which disciplined
soldiers, experienced in campaigning, will hasten to prepare
themselves for the march in an emergency like this.
No questions are asked, no time is wasted. A soldier's
toilet, on an Indian campaign, is a simple affair, and
requires little time for arranging. His clothes are
gathered up hurriedly, no matter how, so long as he retains
possession of them. The first object is to get his horse
saddled and bridled, and until this is done his own dress
is a matter of secondary importance, and one button or hook
must do the duty of half a dozen. When his horse is ready
for the mount, the rider will be seen completing his own
equipment; stray buttons will receive attention, arms will
be overhauled, spurs restrapped; then, if there still remain
a few spare moments, the homely black pipe is filled and
lighted, and the soldier's preparation is complete.

The night was all that could be desired for the success of
our enterprise. The air was mild and pleasant; the moon,
although nearly full, kept almost constantly behind the
clouds, as if to screen us in our hazardous undertaking.
I say hazardous, because none of us imagined for one moment
that if the Indians discovered us in our attempt to surround
them and their village, we should escape without a fight--
a fight, too, in which the Indians, sheltered behind the
trunks of the stately forest trees under which their lodges
were pitched, would possess all the advantage. General
Hancock, anticipating that the Indians would discover our
approach, and that a fight would ensue, ordered the
artillery and infantry under arms, to await the result of
our moonlight adventure. My command was soon in the saddle,
and silently making its way toward the village.
Instructions had been given forbidding all conversation
except in a whisper. Sabres were disposed of to prevent
clanging. Taking a camp-fire which we could see in the

village as our guiding point, we made a detour so as to place the village between ourselves and the infantry. Occasionally the moon would peep out from the clouds and enable us to catch a hasty glance at the village. Here and there under the thick foliage we could see the white, conical-shaped lodges. Were the inmates slumbering, unaware of our close proximity, or were their dusky defenders concealed, as well they might have been, along the banks of the Pawnee, quietly awaiting our approach, and prepared to greet us with their well-known war-whoop? These were questions that were probably suggested to the mind of each individual of my command. If we were discovered approaching in the stealthy, suspicious manner which characterized our movements, the hour being midnight, it would require a more confiding nature than that of the Indian to assign a friendly or peaceful motive to our conduct. The same flashes of moonlight which gave us hurried glimpses of the village enabled us to see our own column of horsemen stretching its silent length far into the dim darkness, and winding its course, like some huge anaconda about to envelop its victim.

The method by which it was determined to establish a cordon of armed troopers about the fated village, was to direct the march in a circle, with the village in the centre, the commanding officer of each rear troop halting his command at the proper point, and deploying his men similarly to a line of skirmishers--the entire circle, when thus formed, facing toward the village, and, distant from it perhaps a few hundred yards. No sooner was our line completely formed than the moon, as if deeming darkness no longer essential to our success, appeared from behind her screen and lighted up the entire scene. And beautiful it was! The great circle of troops, each individual of which sat on his steed silent as a statue, the dense foliage of the cotton trees sheltering the bleached, skin-clad lodges of the red men, the little stream in the midst murmuring undisturbedly in its channel, all combined to produce an artistic effect, as striking as it was interesting. But we were not there to study artistic effects. The next step was to determine whether we had captured an inhabited village, involving almost necessarily a severe conflict with its savage occupants, or whether the red man had again proven too wily and crafty for his more civilized brothers.

Directing the entire line of troopers to remain mounted with carbines held at the "Advance," I dismounted, and taking with me Gurrier, the half-breed, Dr. Coates, one of our medical staff, and Lieutenant Moylan, the adjutant, we proceeded on our hands and knees toward the village. The prevailing opinion was that the Indians were still asleep. I desired to approach near enough to the lodges to enable the half-breed to hail the village in the Indian tongue, and if possible establish friendly relations at once. It became a question of prudence with us, which we discussed in whispers as we proceeded on our "Tramp, tramp, tramp, the boys are creeping," how far from our horses and how near to the village we dared to go. If so few of us were discovered entering the village in this questionable manner, it was more than probable that, like the returners of stolen property, we should be suitably rewarded and no questions asked. The opinion of Gurrier, the half-breed, was eagerly sought for and generally deferred to. His wife, a full-blooded Cheyenne, was a resident of the village. This with him was an additional reason for wishing a peaceful termination to our efforts. When we had passed over two-thirds of the distance between our horses and the village, it was thought best to make our presence known. Thus far not a sound had been heard to disturb the stillness of the night. Gurrier called out at the top of his voice in the Cheyenne tongue. The only response came from the throats of a score or more of Indian dogs which set up a fierce barking. At the same time one or two of our party asserted that they saw figure moving beneath the trees.

Gurrier repeated his summons, but with no better results
than before.

A hurried consultation ensued. The presence of so many dogs
in the village was regarded by the half-breed as almost
positive assurance that the Indians were still there.
Yet it was difficult to account for their silence. Gurrier
in a loud tone repeated who he was, and that our mission was
friendly. Still no answer. He then gave it as his opinion
that the Indians were on the alert, and were probably
waiting in the shadow of the trees for us to approach nearer,
when they would pounce upon us. This comforting opinion
induced another conference. We must ascertain the truth of
the matter; our party could do this as well as a larger
number, and to go back and send another party in our stead
could not be thought of.

Forward! was the verdict. Each one grasped his revolver,
resolved to do his best, whether it was in running or
fighting. I think most of us would have preferred to take
our own chances at running. We had approached near enough
to see that some of the lodges were detached some distance
from the main encampment. Selecting the nearest of these,
we directed our advance on it. While all of us were full
of the spirit of adventure, and were further encouraged
with the idea that we were in the discharge of our duty,
there was scarcely one of us who would not have felt more
comfortable if we could have got back to our horses without
loss of pride. Yet nothing, under the circumstances, but
a positive order would have induced any one to withdraw.

Cautiously approaching, on all fours, to within a few yards
of the nearest lodge, occasionally halting and listening to
discover whether the village was deserted or not, we finally
decided that the Indians had fled before the arrival of the
cavalry, and that none but empty lodges were before us.
This conclusion somewhat emboldened as well as accelerated

311

our progress. Arriving at the first lodge, one of our party raised the curtain or mat which served as a door, and the doctor and myself entered. The interior of the lodge was dimly lighted by the dying embers of a small fire built in the centre. All around us were to be seen the usual adornments and articles which constitute the household effects of an Indian family. Buffalo-robes were spread like carpets over the floor; head-mats, used to recline on, were arranged as if for the comfort of their owners; parfleches, a sort of Indian band-box, with their contents apparently undisturbed, were carefully stowed away under the edges or borders of the lodge. These, with the door-mats, paint-bags, rawhide ropes, and other articles of Indian equipment, were left as if the owners had only absented themselves for a brief period. To complete the picture of an Indian lodge, over the fire hung a camp-kettle, in which, by means of the dim light of the fire, we could see what had been intended for the supper of the late occupants of the lodge.

The doctor, ever on the alert to discover additional items of knowledge, whether pertaining to history or science, snuffed the savoury odours which arose from the dark recesses of the mysterious kettle. Casting about the lodge for some instrument to aid him in his pursuit of knowledge, he found a horn spoon, with which he began his investigation of the contents, finally succeeding in getting possession of a fragment which might have been the half of a duck or rabbit, judging from its size merely. "Ah!" said the doctor, in his most complacent manner, "here is the opportunity I have long been waiting for. I have often desired to test the Indian mode of cooking. What do you suppose this is?" holding up the dripping morsel. Unable to obtain the desired information, the doctor, whose naturally good appetite had been sensibly sharpened by his recent exercise, set to with a will and ate heartily of the mysterious contents of the kettle. He was only satisfied on one point, that it was delicious--a dish fit for a king. Just then Gurrier, the half-breed, entered the lodge. He could solve

the mystery, having spent years among the Indians. To him
the doctor appealed for information. Fishing out a huge
piece, and attacking it with the voracity of a hungry wolf,
he was not long in determining what the doctor had supped
heartily upon. His first words settled the mystery: "Why,
this is dog." I will not attempt to repeat the few but
emphatic words uttered by the heartily disgusted member of
the medical fraternity as he rushed from the lodge.

Other members of our small party had entered other lodges,
only to find them, like the first, deserted. But little of
the furniture belonging to the lodges had been taken,
showing how urgent and hasty had been the flight of the
owners. To aid in the examination of the village,
reinforcements were added to our party, and an exploration
of each lodge was determined upon. At the same time a
messenger was despatched to General Hancock, informing him
of the flight of the Indians. Some of the lodges were
closed by having brush or timber piled up against the
entrance, as if to preserve the contents. Others had huge
pieces cut from their sides, these pieces evidently being
carried away to furnish temporary shelter for the fugitives.
In most of the lodges the fires were still burning. I had
entered several without discovering anything important.
Finally, in company with the doctor, I arrived at one the
interior of which was quite dark, the fire having almost
died out. Procuring a lighted fagot, I prepared to explore it,
as I had done the others; but no sooner had I entered the
lodge than my fagot failed me, leaving me in total darkness.
Handing it to the doctor to be relighted, I began to feel
my way about the interior of the lodge. I had almost made
the circuit when my hand came in contact with a human foot;
at the same time a voice unmistakably Indian, and which
evidently came from the owner of the foot, convinced me that
I was not alone. My first impressions were that in their
hasty flight the Indians had gone off, leaving this one
asleep. My next, very naturally, related to myself.

I would gladly have placed myself on the outside of the lodge, and there matured plans for interviewing its occupant; but unfortunately to reach the entrance of the lodge, I must either pass over or around the owner of the before-mentioned foot and voice. Could I have been convinced that among its other possessions there was neither tomahawk nor scalping-knife, pistol nor war-club, or any similar article of the noble red-man's toilet, I would have risked an attempt to escape through the low narrow opening of the lodge; but who ever saw an Indian without one or all of these interesting trinkets? Had I made the attempt, I should have expected to encounter either the keen edge of the scalping-knife or the blow of the tomahawk, and to have engaged in a questionable struggle for life. This would not do. I crouched in silence for a few moments, hoping the doctor would return with the lighted fagot. I need not say that each succeeding moment spent in the darkness of that lodge seemed an age. I could hear a slight movement on the part of my unknown neighbour, which did not add to my comfort. Why does not the doctor return? At last I discovered the approach of a light on the outside. When it neared the entrance, I called the doctor and informed him that an Indian was in the lodge, and that he had better have his weapons ready for a conflict. I had, upon discovering the foot, drawn my hunting-knife from its scabbard, and now stood waiting the denouement. With his lighted fagot in one hand and cocked revolver in the other, the doctor cautiously entered the lodge. And there directly between us, wrapped in a buffalo-robe, lay the cause of my anxiety--a little Indian girl, probably ten years old; not a full-blood, but a half-breed. She was terribly frightened at finding herself in our hands, with none of her people near. Other parties in exploring the deserted village found an old, decrepit Indian of the Sioux tribe, who had also been deserted, owing to his infirmities and inability to travel with the tribe. Nothing was gleaned from our search of the village which might indicate the

direction of the flight. General Hancock, on learning the
situation of affairs, despatched some companies of infantry
with orders to replace the cavalry and protect the village
and its contents from disturbance until its final disposition
could be determined upon, and it was decided that with eight
troops of cavalry I should start in pursuit of the Indians
at early dawn on the following morning.

The Indians, after leaving their village, went up on the
Smoky Hill, and committed the most horrible depredations
upon the scattered settlers in that region. Upon this news,
General Hancock issued the following order:--

"As a punishment of the bad faith practised by the Cheyennes
and Sioux who occupied the Indian village at this place, and
as a chastisement for murders and depredations committed
since the arrival of the command at this point, by the
people of these tribes, the village recently occupied by
them, which is now in our hands, will be utterly destroyed."

The Cheyennes, Arapahoes, and Apaches had been united under
one agency; the Kiowas and Comanches under another.
As General Hancock's expedition had reference to all these
tribes, he had invited both the agents to accompany him
into the Indian country and be present at all interviews
with the representatives of these tribes, for the purpose,
as the invitation stated, of showing the Indians "that the
officers of the government are acting in harmony."

In conversation with the general the agents admitted that
Indians had been guilty of all the outrages charged against
them, but each asserted the innocence of the particular
tribes under his charge, and endeavoured to lay their crimes
at the door of their neighbours.

Here was positive evidence from the agents themselves that
the Indians against whom we were operating were deserving
of severe punishment. The only conflicting portion of the

testimony was as to which tribe was most guilty. Subsequent
events proved, however, that all of the five tribes named,
as well as the Sioux, had combined for a general war
throughout the plains and along our frontier. Such a war
had been threatened to our post commanders along the
Arkansas on many occasions during the winter. The movement
of the Sioux and Cheyennes toward the north indicated that
the principal theatre of military operations during the
summer would be between the Smoky Hill and Platte rivers.
General Hancock accordingly assembled the principal chiefs
of the Kiowas and Arapahoes in council at Fort Dodge,
hoping to induce them to remain at peace and observe their
treaty obligations.

The most prominent chiefs in council were Satanta, Lone Wolf,
and Kicking Bird of the Kiowas, and Little Raven and Yellow
Bear of the Arapahoes. During the council extravagant
promises of future good behaviour were made by these chiefs.
So effective and convincing was the oratorical effort of
Satanta, that at the termination of his address, the
department commander and his staff presented him with the
uniform coat, sash, and hat of a major-general. In return
for this compliment, Satanta, within a few weeks, attacked
the post at which the council was held, arrayed in his
new uniform.

In the spring of 1878, the Indians commenced a series of depredations along the
Santa Fe Trail and against the scattered settlers of the frontier, that were unparalleled
in their barbarity. General Alfred Sully, a noted Indian fighter, who commanded
the district of the Upper Arkansas, early concentrated a portion of the Seventh
and Tenth Cavalry and Third Infantry along the line of the Old Santa Fe Trail, and
kept out small expeditions of scouting parties to protect the overland coaches and
freight caravans; but the troops effected very little in stopping the devilish acts of
the Indians, who were now fully determined to carry out their threats of a general
war, which culminated in the winter expedition of General Sheridan, who completely
subdued them, and forced all the tribes on reservations; since which time there has
never been any trouble with the plains Indians worthy of mention.[69]

General Sully, about the 1st of September, with eight companies of the Seventh Cavalry and five companies of infantry, left Fort Dodge, on the Arkansas, on a hurried expedition against the Kiowas, Arapahoes, and Cheyennes. The command marched in a general southeasterly direction, and reached the sand hills of the Beaver and Wolf rivers, by a circuitous route, on the fifth day. When nearly through that barren region, they were attacked by a force of eight hundred of the allied tribes under the leadership of the famous Kiowa chief, Satanta. A running fight was kept up with the savages on the first day, in which two of the cavalry were killed and one wounded.

That night the savages came close enough to camp to fire into it (an unusual proceeding in Indian warfare, as they rarely molest troops during the night), I now quote from Custer again:

The next day General Sully directed his march down the
valley of the Beaver; but just as his troops were breaking
camp, the long wagon-train having already "pulled out," and
the rear guard of the command having barely got into their
saddles, a party of between two and three hundred warriors,
who had evidently in some inexplicable manner contrived to
conceal themselves until the proper moment, dashed into the
deserted camp within a few yards of the rear of the troops,
and succeeded in cutting off a few led horses and two of
the cavalrymen who, as is often the case, had lingered a
moment behind the column.

Fortunately, the acting adjutant of the cavalry, Brevet
Captain A. E. Smith, was riding at the rear of the column
and witnessed the attack of the Indians. Captain Hamilton,[70]
of the Seventh Cavalry, was also present in command of the
rear guard. Wheeling to the rightabout, he at once prepared
to charge the Indians and attempt the rescue of the two
troopers who were being carried off before his very eyes.
At the same time, Captain Smith, as representative of the
commanding officer of the cavalry, promptly took the
responsibility of directing a squadron of the cavalry to
wheel out of column and advance in support of Captain
Hamilton's guard. With this hastily formed detachment,
the Indians, still within pistol-range, but moving off with

317

their prisoners, were gallantly charged and so closely
pressed that they were forced to relinquish one of their
prisoners, but not before shooting him through the body and
leaving him on the ground, as they supposed, mortally wounded.
The troops continued to charge the retreating Indians,
upon whom they were gaining, determined, if possible,
to effect the rescue of their remaining comrade. They were
advancing down one slope while the Indians, just across
a ravine, were endeavouring to escape with their prisoner
up the opposite ascent, when a peremptory order reached the
officers commanding the pursuing force to withdraw their men
and reform the column at once. The terrible fate awaiting
the unfortunate trooper carried off by the Indians spread
a deep gloom throughout the command. All were too familiar
with the horrid customs of the savages to hope for a moment
that the captive would be reserved for aught but a slow,
lingering death, from tortures the most horrible and painful
which blood-thirsty minds could suggest. Such was the truth
in his case, as we learned afterwards when peace (?) was
established with the tribes then engaged in war.

The expedition proceeded down the valley of the Beaver,
the Indians contesting every step of the way. In the
afternoon, about three o'clock, the troops arrived at
a ridge of sand hills a few miles southeast of the
presentsite of Camp Supply, where quite a determined
engagement took place between the command and the three
tribes, Cheyennes, Arapahoes, and Kiowas, the Indians
being the assailants. The Indians seemed to have reserved
their strongest efforts until the troops and train had
advanced well into the sand hills, when a most obstinate
resistance--and well conducted, too--was offered the
farther advance of the troops. It was evident that the
troops were probably nearing the Indian villages, and that
this opposition to further advance was to save them. The
character of the country immediately about the troops was
not favourable to the operations of cavalry; the surface

of the rolling plain was cut up by irregular and closely
located sand hills, too steep and sandy to allow cavalry
to move with freedom, yet capable of being easily cleared
of savages by troops fighting on foot. The Indians took
post on the hilltops and began a harassing fire on the
troops and train. Captain Yates, with a single troop of
cavalry, was ordered forward to drive them away. This was
a proceeding which did not seem to meet with favour from
the savages. Captain Yates could drive them wherever he
encountered them, but they appeared in increased numbers
at some other threatened point. After contending in this
non-effective manner for a couple of hours, the impression
arose in the minds of some that the train could not be
conducted through the sand hills in the face of the strong
opposition offered by the Indians. The order was issued
to turn about and withdraw. The order was executed, and
the troop and train, followed by the exultant Indians,
retired a few miles to the Beaver, and encamped for the
night on the ground afterward known as Camp Supply.

Captain Yates had caused to be brought off the field, when
his troop was ordered to retire, the body of one of his men,
who had been slain in the fight. As the troops were to
continue their backward march next day, and it was impossible
to transport the dead body further, Captain Yates ordered
preparations made for interring it in camp that night.
Knowing that the Indians would thoroughly search the deserted
camp-ground almost before the troops should get out of sight,
and would be quick, with their watchful eyes, to detect a
grave, and, if successful in discovering it, would unearth
the body in order to get the scalp, directions were given
to prepare the grave after nightfall; and the spot selected
would have baffled any one but an Indian. The grave was
dug under the picket line to which the seventy or eighty
horses of the troop would be tethered during the night,
so that their constant tramping and pawing should completely
cover up and obliterate all traces. The following morning,

319

even those who had performed the sad rites of burial to
their fallen comrade could scarcely have indicated the exact
location of the grave. Yet when we returned to that point
a few weeks later, it was discovered that the wily savages
had found the place, unearthed the body, and removed the
scalp of their victim on the day following the interment.[71]

After leaving the camp at Supply, the Indians gradually increased their force,
until they mustered about two thousand warriors. For four days and nights they
hovered around the command, and by the time it reached Mulberry Creek there
were not one thousand rounds of ammunition left in the whole force of troopers
and infantrymen. At the creek, the incessant charges of the now infuriated savages
compelled the troops to use this small amount held in reserve, and they found
themselves almost at the mercy of the Indians. But before they were absolutely
defenceless, Colonel Keogh had sent a trusty messenger in the night to Fort Dodge
for a supply of cartridges to meet the command at the creek, which fortunately
arrived there in time to save that spot from being a veritable "last ditch."

The savages, in the little but exciting encounter at the creek before the
ammunition arrived, would ride up boldly toward the squadrons of cavalry, discharge
the shots from their revolvers, and then, in their rage, throw them at the skirmishers
on the flanks of the supply-train, while the latter, nearly out of ammunition, were
compelled to sit quietly in their saddles, idle spectators of the extraordinary scene.
[72]

Many of the Indians were killed on their ponies, however, by those who were
fortunate enough to have a few cartridges left; but none were captured, as the
savages had taken their usual precaution to tie themselves to their animals, and as
soon as dead were dragged away by them.

CHAPTER XXIV.

INVASION OF THE RAILROAD.

The tourist who to-day, in a palace car, surrounded by all the conveniences of our American railway service, commences his tour of the prairies at the Missouri River, enters classic ground the moment the train leaves the muddy flood of that stream on its swift flight toward the golden shores of the Pacific.

He finds a large city at the very portals of the once far West, with all the bustle and energy which is so characteristic of American enterprise.

Gradually, as he is whirled along the iron trail, the woods lessen; he catches views of beautiful intervales; a bright little stream flashes and foams in the sunlight as the trees grow fewer, and soon he emerges on the broad sea of prairie, shut in only by the great circle of the heavens.

Dotting this motionless ocean everywhere, like whitened sails, are quiet homes, real argosies ventured by the sturdy and industrious people who have fought their way through almost insurmountable difficulties to the tranquillity which now surrounds them.

A few miles west of Topeka, the capital of Kansas, when the train reaches the little hamlet of Wakarusa, the track of the railroad commences to follow the route of the Old Santa Fe Trail. At that point, too, the Oregon Trail branches off for the heavily timbered regions of the Columbia. Now begins the classic ground of the once famous highway to New Mexico; nearly every stream, hill, and wooded dell has its story of adventure in those days when the railroad was regarded as an impossibility, and the region beyond the Missouri as a veritable desert.

After some hours' rapid travelling, if our tourist happens to be a passenger on the "California Limited," the swift train that annihilates distance, he will pass by towns, hamlets, and immense cattle ranches, stopping only at county-seats, and enter the justly famous Arkansas valley at the city of Hutchinson. The Old Trail now passes a few miles north of this busy place, which is noted for its extensive salt works, nor does the railroad again meet with it until the site of old Fort Zarah is reached, forty-seven miles west of Hutchinson, though it runs nearly parallel to the once great highway at varying distances for the whole detour.

The ruins of the once important military post may be seen from the car-windows on the right, as the train crosses the iron bridge spanning the Walnut, and here the Old Trail exactly coincides with the railroad, the track of the latter running immediately on the old highway.

Three miles westward from the classic little Walnut the Old Trail ran through what is now the Court House Square of the town of Great Bend; it may be seen from the station, and on that very spot occurred the terrible fight of Captains Booth and Hallowell in 1864.

Thirteen miles further mountainward, on the right of the railroad, not far from the track, stands all that remains of the once dreaded Pawnee Rock. It lies just beyond the limits of the little hamlet bearing its name. It would not be recognized by any of the old plainsmen were they to come out of their isolated graves; for it is only a disintegrated, low mass of sandstone now, utilized for the base purposes of a corral, in which the village herd of milch cows lie down at night and chew their cuds, such peaceful transformation has that great civilizer, the locomotive, wrought in less than two decades.

Another five or six miles, and the train crosses Ash Creek, which, too, was once one of the favourite haunts of the Pawnee and Comanche on their predatory excursions, in the days when the mules and horses of passing freight caravans excited their cupidity. A short whirl again, and the town of Larned, lying peacefully on the Arkansas and Pawnee Fork, is reached. Immediately opposite the centre of the street through which the railroad runs, and which was also the course of the Old Trail, lying in the Arkansas River, close to its northern bank, is a small thickly-wooded island, now reached by a bridge, that is famous as the battle-ground of a terrible conflict thirty years ago, between the Pawnees and Cheyennes, hereditary enemies, in which the latter tribe was cruelly defeated.

The railroad bridge crosses Pawnee Fork at the precise spot where the Old Trail did. This locality has been the scene of some of the bloodiest encounters between the various tribes of savages themselves, and between them and the freight caravans, the overland coaches, and every other kind of outfit that formerly attempted the passage of the now peaceful stream. In fact, the whole region from Walnut Creek to the mouth of the Pawnee, which includes in its area Ash Creek and Pawnee Rock, seemed to be the greatest resort for the Indians, who hovered about the Santa Fe Trail for the sole purpose of robbery and murder; it was a very lucky caravan or coach, indeed, that passed through that portion of the route without being attacked.

All the once dangerous points of the Old Trail having been successfully passed-- Cow Creek, Big and Little Coon, and Ash Creek, Fort Dodge, Fort Aubrey,[73] and Point of Rocks--the tourist arrives at last at the foot-hills. At La Junta the railroad separates into two branches; one going to Denver, the other on to New Mexico. Here, a relatively short distance to the northwest, on the right of the train, may be seen the ruins of Bent's Fort, the tourist having already passed the site of the once famous Big

Timbers, a favourite winter camping-ground of the Cheyennes and Arapahoes; but everywhere around him there reigns such perfect quiet and pastoral beauty, he might imagine that the peaceful landscape upon which he looks had never been a bloody arena.

I suggest to the lover of nature that he should cross the Raton Range in the early morning, or late in the afternoon; for then the magnificent scenery of the Trail over the high divide into New Mexico assumes its most beautiful aspect.

In approaching the range from the Old Trail, or now from the railroad, their snow-clad peaks may be seen at a distance of sixty miles. In the era of caravans and pack-trains, for hour after hour, as they moved slowly toward the goal of their ambition, the summit of the fearful pathway on the divide, the huge forms of the mountains seemed to recede, and yet ascend higher. On the next day's journey their outlines appeared more irregular and ragged. Drawing still nearer, their base presented a long, dark strip stretching throughout their whole course, ever widening until it seemed like a fathomless gulf, separating the world of reality from the realms of imagination beyond.

Another weary twenty miles of dusty travel, and the black void slowly dissolved, and out of the shadows lines of broken, sterile, ferruginous buttes and detached masses of rocks, whose soilless surface refuses sustenance, save to a few scattered, stunted pines and lifeless mosses, emerged to view.

The progress of the weary-footed mules or oxen was now through ravines and around rocks; up narrow paths which the melting snows have washed out; sometimes between beetling cliffs, often to their very edge, where hundreds of feet below the Trail the tall trees seemed diminished into shrubs. Then again the road led over an immense broad terrace, for thousands of yards around, with a bright lake gleaming in the refracted light, and brilliant Alpine plants waving their beautiful flowers on its margin. Still the coveted summit appeared so far off as to be beyond the range of vision, and it seemed as if, instead of ascending, the entire mass underneath had been receding, like the mountains of ice over which Arctic explorers attempt to reach the pole. Now the tortuous Trail passed through snow-wreaths which the winds had eddied into indentations; then over bright, glassy surfaces of ice and fragments of rocks, until the pinnacle was reached. Nearer, along the broad successive terraces of the opposite mountains, the evergreen pine, the cedar, with its stiff, angular branches, and the cottonwood, with its varied curves and bright colours, were crowded into bunches or strung into zigzag lines, interspersed with shrubs and mountain plants, among which the flaming cactus was conspicuous. To the right and left, the bare cones of the barren peaks rose in multitude, with their calm, awful forms shrouded in snow, and their dark shadows reflected far into the valleys, like spectres from a chaotic world.

In going through the Raton Pass, the Old Santa Fe Trail meandered up a steep valley, enclosed on either side by abrupt hills covered with pine and masses of gray rock. The road ran along the points of varying elevations, now in the stony bed of Raton Creek, which it crossed fifty-three times, the sparkling, flitting waters of the bubbling stream leaping and foaming against the animals' feet as they hauled the great wagons of the freight caravans over the tortuous passage. The creek often rushed rapidly under large flat stones, lost to sight for a moment, then reappearing with a fresh impetus and dashing over its flinty, uneven bed until it mingled with the pure waters of Le Purgatoire.

Still ascending, the scenery assumed a bolder, rougher cast; then sudden turns gave you hurried glimpses of the great valley below. A gentle dell sloped to the summit of the pass on the west, then, rising on the east by a succession of terraces, the bald, bare cliff was reached, overlooking the whole region for many miles, and this is Raton Peak.[74]

The extreme top of this famous peak was only reached after more than an hour's arduous struggle. On the lofty plateau the caravans and pack-trains rested their tired animals. Here, too, the lonely trapper, when crossing the range in quest of beaver, often chose this lofty spot on which to kindle his little fire and broil juicy steaks of the black-tail deer, the finest venison in the world; but before he indulged in the savoury morsels, if he was in the least superstitious or devout, or inspired by the sublime scene around him, he lighted his pipe, and after saluting the elevated ridge on which he sat by the first whiff of the fragrant kinnikinick, Indian-fashion, he in turn offered homage in the same manner to the sky above him, the earth beneath, and to the cardinal points of the compass, and was then prepared to eat his solitary meal in a spirit of thankfulness.

Far below this magnificent vantage-ground lies the valley of the Rio Las Animas Perdidas. On the other verge of the great depression rise the peerless, everlastingly snow-wreathed Spanish Peaks,[75] whose giant summits are grim sentinels that for untold ages have witnessed hundreds of sanguinary conflicts between the wily nomads of the vast plains watered by the silent Arkansas.

All around you snow-clad mountains lift their serrated crowns above the horizon, dim, white, and indistinct, like icebergs seen at sea by moonlight; others, nearer, more rugged, naked of verdure, and irregular in contour, seem to lose their lofty summits in the intense blue of the sky.

Fisher's Peak, which is in full view from the train, was named from the following circumstance: Captain Fisher was a German artillery officer commanding a battery in General Kearney's Army of the West in the conquest of New Mexico and was encamped at the base of the peak to which he involuntarily gave his name. He was intently gazing at the lofty summit wrapped in the early mist, and not being familiar with the illusory atmospheric effects of the region, he thought that to go there would be merely a pleasant promenade. So, leaving word that he would return to breakfast, he struck out at a brisk walk for the crest. That whole day, the following night, and the succeeding day, dragged their weary hours on, but no tidings of the commanding officer were received at the battery, and ill rumours were current of his death by Indians or bears, when, just as his mess were about to take their seats at the table for the evening meal, their captain put in an appearance, a very tired but a wiser man. He started to go to the peak, and he went there!

On the summit of another rock-ribbed elevation close by, the tourist will notice the shaft of an obelisk. It is over the grave of George Simpson, once a noted mountaineer in the days of the great fur companies. For a long time he made his home there, and it was his dying request that the lofty peak he loved so well while living should be his last resting-place. The peak is known as "Simpson's Rest," and is one of the notable features of the rugged landscape.

Pike's Peak, far away to the north, intensely white and silvery in the clear sky, hangs like a great dome high in the region of the clouds, a marked object, worthy to commemorate the indefatigable efforts of the early voyageur whose name it bears.

In this wonderful locality, both Pike's Peak and the snowy range over two hundred miles from our point of observation really seem to the uninitiated as if a brisk walk of an hour or two would enable one to reach them, so deceptive is the atmosphere of these elevated regions.

About two miles from the crest of the range, yet over seven thousand feet above the sea-level, in a pretty little depression about as large as a medium-sized corn-field in the Eastern States, Uncle Dick Wooton lived, and here, too, was his toll-gate. The veteran mountaineer erected a substantial house of adobe, after the style of one of the old-time Southern plantation residences, a memory, perhaps, of his youth, when he raised tobacco in his father's fields in Kentucky.[76]

The most charming hour in which to be on the crest of Raton Range is in the afternoon, when the weather is clear and calm. As the night comes on apace in the distant valley beneath, the evening shadows drop down, pencilled with broad bands of rosy light as they creep slowly across the beautiful landscape, while the rugged vista below is enveloped in a diffused haze like that which marks the season of the Indian summer in the lower great plains. Above, the sky curves toward the relatively restricted horizon, with not a cloud to dim its intense blue, nowhere so beautiful as in these lofty altitudes.

The sun, however, does not always shine resplendently; there are times when the most terrific storms of wind, hail, and rain change the entire aspect of the scene. Fortunately, these violent bursts never last long; they vanish as rapidly as they come, leaving in their wake the most phenomenally beautiful rainbows, whose trailing splendours which they owe to the dry and rare air of the region, and its high refractory power, are gorgeous in the extreme.

In 1872 the Atchison, Topeka, and Santa Fe Railroad entered the valley of the Upper Arkansas. Twenty-four years ago, on a delicious October afternoon, I stood on the absolutely level plateau at the mouth of Pawnee Fork where that historic creek debouches into the great river. The remembrance of that view will never pass from my memory, for it showed a curious temporary blending of two distinct civilizations. One, the new, marking the course of empire in its restless march westward; the other, that of the aboriginal, which, like a dissolving view, was soon to fade away and be forgotten.

The box-elders and cottonwoods thinly covering the creek-bottom were gradually donning their autumn dress of russet, and the mirage had already commenced its fantastic play with the landscape. On the sides and crests of the sparsely grassed sand hills south of the Arkansas a few buffaloes were grazing in company with hundreds of Texas cattle, while in the broad valley beneath, small flocks of graceful antelope were lying down, quietly ruminating their midday meal.

In the distance, far eastwardly, a train of cars could be seen approaching; as far as the eye could reach, on either side of the track, the virgin sod had been turned to the sun; the "empire of the plough" was established, and the march of immigration in its hunger for the horizon had begun.

Half a mile away from the bridge spanning the Fork, under the grateful shade of the largest trees, about twenty skin lodges were irregularly grouped; on the brown sod of the sun-cured grass a herd of a hundred ponies were lazily feeding, while a troop of dusky little children were chasing the yellow butterflies from the dried and withered sunflower stalks which once so conspicuously marked the well-worn highway to the mountains. These Indians, the remnant of a tribe powerful in the years of savage sovereignty, were on their way, in charge of their agent, to their new homes, on the reservation just allotted to them by the government, a hundred miles south of the Arkansas.

Their primitive lodges contrasted strangely with the peaceful little sod-houses, dugouts, and white cottages of the incoming settlers on the public lands, with the villages struggling into existence, and above all with the rapidly moving cars; unmistakable evidences that the new civilization was soon to sweep the red men before it like chaff before the wind.

Farther to the west, a caravan of white-covered wagons loaded with supplies for some remote military post, the last that would ever travel the Old Trail, was slowly crawling toward the setting sun. I watched it until only a cloud of dust marked its place low down on the horizon, and it was soon lost sight of in the purple mist that was rapidly overspreading the far-reaching prairie.

It was the beginning of the end; on the 9th of February, 1880, the first train over the Atchison, Topeka, and Santa Fe Railroad arrived at Santa Fe and the Old Trail as a route of commerce was closed forever. The once great highway is now only a picture in the memory of the few who have travelled its weary course, following the windings of the silent Arkansas, on to the portals that guard the rugged pathway leading to the shores of the blue Pacific.

FOOTNOTES.

[1] The whole country watered by the Mississippi and Missouri was called Florida at that time.

[2] The celebrated Jesuit, author of *The History of New France, Journals of a Voyage to North America, Letters to the Duchess*, etc.

[3] Otoes.

[4] Iowas.

[5] Boulevard, Promenade.

[6] Notes of a Military Reconnoissance from Fort Leavenworth, in Missouri, to San Diego, in California, including parts of the Arkansas, Del Norte, and Gila Rivers. Brevet Major W. H. Emory, Corps of Topographical Engineers, United States Army, 1846.

[7] Hon. W. F. Arny, in his Centennial Celebration Address at Santa Fe, July 4, 1876.

[8] Edwards, *Conquest of New Mexico*.

[9] I think this is Bancroft's idea.

[10] *Historical Sketches of New Mexico*, L. Bradford Prince, late Chief Justice of New Mexico, 1883.

[11] D. H. Coyner, 1847.

[12] He was travelling parallel to the Old Santa Fe Trail all the time, but did not know it until he was overtaken by a band of Kaw Indians.

[13] McKnight was murdered south of the Arkansas by the Comanches in the winter of 1822.

[14] Chouteau's Island.

[15] *Hennepin's Journal.*

[16] The line between the United States and Mexico (or New Spain, as it was called) was defined by a treaty negotiated in 1819, between the Chevalier de Onis, then Spanish minister at Washington, and John Quincy Adams, Secretary of State. According to its provisions, the boundary between Mexico and Louisiana, which had been added to the Union, commenced with the river Sabine at its entrance into the Gulf of Mexico, at about the twenty-ninth degree of north latitude and the ninety-fourth degree of longitude, west from Greenwich, and followed it as far as its junction with the Red River of Natchitoches, which then served to mark the frontier up to the one hundredth degree of west longitude, where the line ran directly north to the Arkansas, which it followed to its source at the forty-second degree of north latitude, whence another straight line was drawn up the same parallel to the Pacific coast.

[17] This tribe kept up its reputation under the dreaded Satanta, until 1868--a period of forty years--when it was whipped into submission by the gallant Custer. Satanta was its war chief, one of the most cruel savages the great plains ever produced. He died a few years ago in the state prison of Texas.

[18] McNess Creek is on the old Cimarron Trail to Santa Fe, a little east of a line drawn south from Bent's Fort.

[19] Mr. Bryant, of Kansas, who died a few years ago, was one of the pioneers in the trade with Santa Fe. Previous to his decease he wrote for a Kansas newspaper a narrative of his first trip across the great plains; an interesting monograph of hardship and suffering. For the use of this document I am indebted to Hon. Sol. Miller, the editor of the journal in which it originally appeared. I have also used very extensively the notes of Mr. William Y. Hitt, one of the Bryant party, whose son kindly placed them at my disposal, and copied liberally from the official report of Major Bennett Riley-- afterward the celebrated general of Mexican War fame, and for whom the Cavalry Depot in Kansas is named; as also from the journal of Captain Philip St. George Cooke, who accompanied Major Riley on

his expedition.

[20] Chouteau's Island, at the mouth of Sand Creek.

[21] Valley of the Upper Arkansas.

[22] About three miles east of the town of Great Bend, Barton County, Kansas.

[23] The Old Santa Fe Trail crosses the creek some miles north of Hutchinson, and coincides with the track again at the mouth of Walnut Creek, three miles east of Great Bend.

[24] There are many conflicting accounts in regard to the sum Don Antonio carried with him on that unfortunate trip. Some authorities put it as high as sixty thousand; I have taken a mean of the various sums, and as this method will suffice in mathematics, perhaps we can approximate the truth in this instance.

[25] General Emory of the Union army during the Civil War. He made an official report of the country through which the Army of the West passed, accompanied by maps, and his *Reconnoissance in New Mexico and California*, published by the government in 1848, is the first authentic record of the region, considered topographically and geologically.

[26] *Doniphan's Expedition, containing an account of the Conquest of New Mexico*, etc. John T. Hughes, A.B., of the First Regiment of Missouri Cavalry. 1850.

[27] Deep Gorge.

[28] Colonel Leavenworth, for whom Fort Leavenworth is named, and who built several army posts in the far West.

[29] Colonel A. G. Boone, a grandson of the immortal Daniel, was one of the grandest old mountaineers I ever knew. He was as loyal as anybody, but honest in his dealings with the Indians, and that was often a fault in the eyes of those at Washington who controlled

these agents. Kit Carson was of the same honest class as Boone, and he, too, was removed for the same cause.

[30] A narrow defile on the Trail, about ninety miles east of Fort Union. It is called the "canyon of the Canadian, or Red, River," and is situated between high walls of earth and rock. It was once a very dangerous spot on account of the ease and rapidity with which the savages could ambush themselves.

[31] Carson, Wooton, and all other expert mountaineers, when following a trail, could always tell just what time had elapsed since it was made. This may seem strange to the uninitiated, but it was part of their necessary education. They could tell what kind of a track it was, which way the person or animal had walked, and even the tribe to which the savage belonged, either by the shape of the moccasin or the arrows which were occasionally dropped.

[32] Lieutenant Bell belonged to the Second Dragoons. He was conspicuous in extraordinary marches and in action, and also an accomplished horseman and shot, once running and killing five buffalo in a quarter of a mile. He died early in 1861, and his death was a great loss to the service.

[33] Known to this day as "The Cheyenne Bottoms."

[34] Lone Wolf was really the head chief of the Kiowas.

[35] The battle lasted three days.

[36] Kicking Bird was ever afterward so regarded by the authorities of the Indian department.

[37] Lorenzo Thomas, adjutant-general of the United States army.

[38] Kendall's *Santa Fe Expedition* may be found in all the large libraries.

[39] A summer-house, bower, or arbour.

[40] Frank Hall, Chicago, 1885.

[41] The greater portion of this chapter I originally wrote for *Harper's Weekly*. By the kind permission of the publishers, I am permitted to use it here.

[42] These statistics I have carefully gathered from the freight departments of the railroads, which kept a record of all the bones that were shipped, and from the purchasers of the carbon works, who paid out the money at various points. Some of the bones, however, may have been on the ground for a longer time, as decay is very slow in the dry air of the plains.

[43] La Jeunesse was one of the bravest of the old French Canadian trappers. He was a warm friend of Kit Carson and was killed by the Indians in the following manner. They were camping one night in the mountains; Kit, La Jeunesse, and others had wrapped themselves up in their blankets near the fire, and were sleeping soundly; Fremont sat up until after midnight reading letters he had received from the United States, after finishing which, he, too, turned in and fell asleep. Everything was quiet for a while, when Kit was awakened by a noise that sounded like the stroke of an axe. Rising cautiously, he discovered Indians in the camp; he gave the alarm at once, but two of his companions were dead. One of them was La Jeunesse, and the noise he had heard was the tomahawk as it buried itself in the brave fellow's head.

[44] This black is made from a species of plumbago found on the hills of the region.

[45] The Pawnees and Cheyennes were hereditary enemies, and they frequently met in sanguinary conflict.

[46] A French term Anglicised, as were many other foreign words by the trappers in the mountains. Its literal meaning is, arrow fender, for from it the plains Indians construct their shields; it is buffalo-hide prepared in a certain manner.

[47] Boiling Spring River.

[48] For some reason the Senate refused to confirm the appointment, and he had consequently no connection with the regular army.

[49] Point of Rocks is six hundred and forty seven miles from Independence, and was always a favourite place of resort for the Indians of the great plains; consequently it was one of the most dangerous camping-spots for the freight caravans on the Trail. It comprises a series of continuous hills, which project far out on the prairie in bold relief. They end abruptly in a mass of rocks, out of which gushes a cold, refreshing spring, which is, of course, the main attraction of the place. The Trail winds about near this point, and many encounters with the various tribes have occurred there.

[50] "Little Mountain."

[51] General Gatlin was a North Carolinian, and seceded with his State at the breaking out of the Rebellion, but refused to leave his native heath to fight, so indelibly was he impressed with the theory of State rights. He was willing to defend the soil of North Carolina, but declined to step across its boundary to repel invasion in other States.

[52] The name of "Crow," as applied to the once powerful nation of mountain Indians, is a misnomer, the fault of some early interpreter. The proper appellation is "Sparrowhawks," but they are officially recognized as "Crows."

[53] Kit Carson, ten years before, when on his first journey, met with the same adventure while on post at Pawnee Rock.

[54] The fusee was a fire-lock musket with an immense bore, from which either slugs or balls could be shot, although not with any great degree of accuracy.

[55] The Indians always knew when the caravans were to pass certain points on the Trail, by their runners or spies probably.

[56] It was one of the rigid laws of Indian hospitality always to respect the person of any one who voluntarily entered their camps or temporary halting-places. As long as the stranger, red or white, remained with them, he enjoyed perfect immunity from harm; but after he had left, although he had progressed but half a mile, it was just as honourable to follow and kill him.

[57] In their own fights with their enemies one or two of the defeated party are always spared, and sent back to their tribe to carry the news of the slaughter.

[58] The story of the way in which this name became corrupted into "Picketwire," by which it is generally known in New Mexico, is this: When Spain owned all Mexico and Florida, as the vast region of the Mississippi valley was called, long before the United States had an existence as a separate government, the commanding officer at Santa Fe received an order to open communication with the country of Florida. For this purpose an infantry regiment was selected. It left Santa Fe rather late in the season, and wintered at a point on the Old Trail now known as Trinidad. In the spring, the colonel, leaving all camp-followers behind him, both men and women, marched down the stream, which flows for many miles through a magnificent canyon. Not one of the regiment returned or was ever heard of. When all hope had departed from the wives, children, and friends left behind at Trinidad, information was sent to Santa Fe, and a wail went up through the land. The priests and people then called this stream "El Rio de las Animas Perditas" ("The river of lost souls"). Years after, when the Spanish power was weakened, and French trappers came into the country under the auspices of the great fur companies, they adopted a more concise name; they called the river "Le Purgatoire." Then came the Great American Bull-Whacker. Utterly unable to twist his tongue into any such Frenchified expression, he called the stream with its sad story "Picketwire," and by that name it is known to all frontiersmen, trappers, and the settlers along its banks.

[59] The ranch is now in charge of Mr. Harry Whigham, an English gentleman, who keeps up the old hospitality of the famous place.

[60] "River of Souls." The stream is also called Le Purgatoire, corrupted by the Americans into Picketwire.

[61] Pawnee Rock is no longer conspicuous. Its material has been torn away by both the railroad and the settlers in the vicinity, to build foundations for water-tanks, in the one instance, and for the construction of their houses, barns, and sheds, in the other. Nothing remains of the once famous landmark; its site is occupied as a cattle corral by the owner of the claim in which it is included.

[62] The crossing of the Old Santa Fe Trail at Pawnee Fork is now within the corporate limits of the pretty little town of Larned, the county-seat of Pawnee County. The tourist from his car-window may look right down upon one of the worst places for Indians that there was in those days of the commerce of the prairies, as the road crosses the stream at the exact spot where the Trail crossed it.

[63] This was a favourite expression of his whenever he referred to any trouble with the Indians.

[64] Indians will risk the lives of a dozen of their best warriors to prevent the body of any one of their number from falling into the white man's possession. The reason for this is the belief, which prevails among all tribes, that if a warrior loses his scalp he forfeits his hope of ever reaching the happy hunting-ground.

[65] It was in this fight that the infamous Charles Bent received his death-wound.

[66] The Atchison, Topeka, and Santa Fe Railroad track runs very close to the mound, and there is a station named for the great mesa.

[67] The venerable Colonel A. S. Johnson, of Topeka, Kansas, the first white child born on the great State's soil, who related to me this adventure of Hatcher's, knew him well. He says that he was a small man, full of muscle, and as fearless as can be conceived.

[68] The place where they turned is about a hundred yards east of

the Court House Square, in the present town of Great Bend; it may be seen from the cars.

[69] See Sheridan's *Memoirs*, Custer's *Life on the Plains*, and Buffalo Bill's book, in which all the stirring events of that campaign--nearly every fight of which was north or far south of the Santa Fe Trail--are graphically told.

[70] A grandson of Alexander Hamilton; killed at the battle of the Washita, in the charge on Black Kettle's camp under Custer.

[71] This ends Custer's narrative. The following fight, which occurred a few days afterward, at the mouth of Mulberry Creek, twelve miles below Fort Dodge, and within a stone's throw of the Old Trail, was related to me personally by Colonel Keogh, who was killed at the Rosebud, in Custer's disastrous battle with Sitting Bull. We were both attached to General Sully's staff.

[72] It was in this fight that Colonel Keogh's celebrated horse Comanche received his first wound. It will be remembered that Comanche and a Crow Indian were the only survivors of that unequal contest in the valley of the Big Horn, commonly called the battle of the Rosebud, where Custer and his command was massacred.

[73] Now Kendall, a little village in Hamilton County, Kansas.

[74] Raton is the name given by the early Spaniards to this range, meaning both mouse and squirrel. It had its origin either in the fact that one of its several peaks bore a fanciful resemblance to a squirrel, or because of the immense numbers of that little rodent always to be found in its pine forests.

[75] In the beautiful language of the country's early conquerors, "Las Cumbres Espanolas," or "Las dos Hermanas" (The Two Sisters), and in the Ute tongue, "Wahtoya" (The Twins).

[76] The house was destroyed by fire two or three years ago.

Lightning Source UK Ltd.
Milton Keynes UK
UKOW030030290513

211391UK00013B/870/P